MAXIMUM ENTROPY ECONOMETRICS

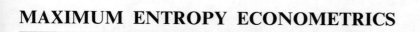

SERIES IN FINANCIAL ECONOMICS AND QUANTITATIVE ANALYSIS

The Economics of Pensions and Variable Retirement Schemes
Oliver Fabel

Applied General Equilibrium Modelling:
Imperfect Competition and European Integration
Dirk Willenbockel

Housing, Financial Markets and the Wider Economy
David Miles

Maximum Entropy Econometrics: Robust Estimation with Limited Data
Amos Golan, George Judge and Douglas Miller

Quantitative Financial Economics: Stocks, Bonds and Foreign Exchange
Keith Cuthbertson

Further titles in preparation
Proposals will be welcomed by the Series Editor

MAXIMUM ENTROPY ECONOMETRICS: ROBUST ESTIMATION WITH LIMITED DATA

Amos Golan
University of California, Berkeley

George Judge
University of California, Berkeley

Douglas Miller
Iowa State University

JOHN WILEY & SONS

Chichester • New York • Brisbane • Toronto • Singapore

National 01243 779777
International (+44) 1243 779777

Other Wiley Editorial Offices

John Wiley & Sons, Inc., 605 Third Avenue,
New York, NY 10158-0012, USA

Jacaranda Wiley Ltd, 33 Park Road, Milton,
Queensland 4064, Australia

John Wiley & Sons (Canada) Ltd, 22 Worcester Road,
Rexdale, Ontario M9W 1L1, Canada

John Wiley & Sons (SEA) (Asia) Pte Ltd, 2 Clementi Loop #02-01,
Jin Xing Distripark, Singapore 0512

Library of Congress Cataloging-in-Publication Data

Golan, Amos.
Maximum entropy econometrics : robust estimation with limited data / Amos Golan, George Judge and Douglas Miller.
p. cm. — (Series in financial economics and quantitative analysis)
Includes bibliographical references and index.
ISBN 0-471-95311-3 (cloth : alk. paper)
1. Econometrics. 2. Maximum entropy method. 3. Estimation theory. I. Golan, Amos. II. Miller, Douglas. III. Title.
IV. Series.
HB139.J795 1996
330′.01′5195—dc20 95–41281
CIP

British Library Cataloguing in Publication Data

A catalogue record for this book is available from the British Library

ISBN 0-471-95311-3

Typeset in 10/12pt Times by Keyword Publishing Services Ltd
Printed and bound in Great Britain by Biddles Ltd, Guildford, Surrey
This book is printed on acid-free paper responsibly manufactured from sustainable forestation, for which at least two trees are planted for each one used for paper production.

To

Elise
William Judge
Jennifer Miller

Contents

Series preface

This series aims to publish books which give authoritative accounts of major new topics in financial economics and general quantitative analysis. The coverage of the series includes both macro- and microeconomics, and its aim is to be of interest to practitioners and policy makers as well as the wider academic community.

The development of new techniques and ideas in econometrics has been rapid in recent years and these developments are now being applied to a wide range of areas and markets. Our hope is that this series will provide a rapid and effective means of communicating these ideas to a wide international audience and that in turn this will contribute to the growth of knowledge, the exchange of scientific information and techniques and the development of cooperation in the field of economics.

This book makes an important contribution in the field of econometric theory which opens a range of new and exciting techniques to the applied researcher and practitioner. We are often faced with the problem of small samples or non-standard error distributions. A range of new methods are presented here which should increase the efficiency of information recovery with financial and economic data and produce more robust estimation strategies.

Stephen Hall
London Business School, UK

Authors' preface

In the theory and practice of econometrics the model, the method and the data are all interdependent links in information recovery and inference. Seldom, however, are the economic and statistical models correctly specified, the data complete or capable of being replicated, the estimation rules 'optimal' and the inferences free of distortion. Faced with this set of challenging problems, in this book we specify and demonstrate a new basis for learning from economic and statistical models that *may* be non-regular in the sense that they are ill-posed or underdetermined and the data are partial-incomplete. Traditionally, when certain regularity conditions are fulfilled, the sampling theory and Bayesian (likelihood-based methods) have provided a basis for parametric estimation and hypothesis testing. For example, the likelihood-based sampling theory method with its elegant asymptotic theory is applicable when, in the neighborhood of the true unknown parameter vector $\boldsymbol{\beta}$, the log-likelihood is closely approximated in probability by a concave function whose maximum converges to $\boldsymbol{\beta}$ as the sample size increases.

Unfortunately, in econometrics, non-regular estimation problems may be the rule rather than the exception. Therefore, with the objectives of extending the range of viable econometric-statistical models and improving the efficiency of sample and non-sample information recovery, we make use of the entropy metric and the maximum entropy formalism. The entropy measure was first proposed by Boltzman in the 1870s to measure the information in a distribution that defines the thermodynamic state of a physical system. This same measure was later developed and proposed in 1948 by Shannon to measure the uncertainty in the mind of someone receiving a message that contains noise. Later, in 1957 Jaynes made use of Shannon's entropy metric to specify a maximum entropy principle that formed a basis for estimation and inference of pure inverse problems that were not tractable using traditional procedures of mathematical inversion. In this monograph we extend Jaynes maximum entropy formulation to include inverse problems with noise and use this generalized maximum entropy formulation as a basis for estimation and inference in a range of econometric-statistical models. In many cases, traditional estimators are special cases of the entropy based information processing rules that we develop.

This is not a book concerned with the philosophical issues underlying entropy. Also, although we propose and use certain information measures, this is not a book about information theory. This is a book that is concerned with developing entropy based formulations that permit us to cope with estimation and inference in a range of statistical models that are basic to economic analysis. Often inconvenient economic data generation processes get in the way of assumptions we need to make in order to use traditional procedures. Consequently, we are concerned with developing econometric procedures that are robust in the sense that you are freed from making assumptions that you do not want to make and that you have to make if you use traditional sampling theoretic and Bayes methods.

Many persons have contributed to the words and symbols contained in this book. Ed Jaynes early on sent us a complete set of his writing in the maximum entropy (ME) area and encouraged us to have a go at ME since he felt that 'in economics a truly well posed problem is virtually unknown'. T. C. Lee was instrumental in some of our earlier work as it related to finite stationary Markov models. Sherman Robinson introduced us to GAMS and worked with us on the analysis of sectoral data. Our great Giannini colleagues Jeffrey Perloff worked with us on the discrete choice and other latent variable problems, and Larry Karp worked with us on dynamic and inverse control problems. David Blackwell and Rudy Beran generously offered technical help and encouragement. William Griffiths, Carter Hill, Mary Ellen Bock and Arnold Zellner gave their usual generous help and contributed by listening to our ideas, reading our papers and offering constructive comments. Our colleague at the word processor, Dana Keil, helped us through many versions of each problem formulation and at each stage gave us a superb copy to mark up. In the final stage of the manuscript preparation, Mary Graham and Joel Adlen gave generously of their time and expertise to make sure a 'perfect' copy went to the publisher. To these individuals and to many others, we want to say a *very* appreciative thanks.

For the authors this has been a joint research venture and the order of the names that appears on the cover has little significance.

Amos Golan
George Judge
Douglas Miller

CHAPTER 1

Introduction

1.1 THE PROBLEM SETTING

In this book we focus on the problem of recovering and processing information when the underlying sampling model is incompletely or incorrectly known and the data are limited, partial or incomplete. Furthermore, given the non-experimental model building and data generation restrictions of economics (in particular) and in the social sciences (in general), many of the economic-statistical models that form the basis for conventional estimation and inference are ill-posed or underdetermined. Within this context, for a wide range of problems normally found in applied mathematics and econometric practice, we develop and demonstrate a non-linear inversion procedure that provides a basis for information recovery and for making conservative inferences about an unknown *and unobservable* number, vector or function. This new information processing rule is, in many situations, a generalization of the more traditional estimation rules.

Given non-experimental data generation processes in economics and finance, and the corresponding data available for applied econometric analyses, we face the problem of how to make predictions for the population, or how to construct an image of it, using the information at hand. Unfortunately, in many cases, the models that economists use for analysis and choice purposes contain unknowns that are unobserved and indeed are not accessible to direct measurement. For example, we can observe, on an individual, household or some other aggregate basis, data on income and consumption, but we cannot observe the corresponding 'marginal propensity to consume' parameter that we desire. Alternatively, we can observe inputs and outputs but we cannot observe the corresponding marginal products or the elasticity of production coefficients. Consequently, in order to recover the unknown parameters, representing the economic system of interest, we are faced with an inverse problem that may be formalized in the following way. We observe the outcome of an economic variable or variables $\mathbf{y}$. However, our interest centers on an unknown and unobservable $\boldsymbol{\beta}$ which may be a number, a vector or a function. Since we cannot measure $\boldsymbol{\beta}$ directly, in order to recover it we must use indirect measurements on the observables. In this context consider the following finite, discrete, linear inverse problem

$$\mathbf{y} = X\boldsymbol{\beta} \tag{1.1.1}$$

where $\mathbf{y} = (y_1, y_2, \ldots, y_T)'$ is a T-dimensional vector of observations (data), $\boldsymbol{\beta}$ is an unobservable K dimensional vector of unknowns and X is a known $(T \times K)$ linear operator. Cases where the external data $\mathbf{y}$ are specified without noise, in terms of aggregates or moments, and $\boldsymbol{\beta}$ is unobservable, are called pure inverse problems.

Given (1.1.1) we are interested in using the observables to recover the unknown and unobservable vector $\boldsymbol{\beta}$ that represents information about the population or image of interest. In many cases, however, bad experimental or non-experimental design means the linear operator X is non-invertible and X^{-1} does not exist as a bounded operator, or the number of unknowns maybe larger than the number of data points. If we do not have sufficient information to recover $\boldsymbol{\beta}$ using the traditional procedures of mathematical inversion, we must consider the entire class of feasible solutions containing $(K - T)$ arbitrary parameters. Using traditional procedures, if the problem is ill-posed, we have no basis for picking out of the feasible set of solutions a particular solution vector for $\boldsymbol{\beta}$. This implies that there is no basis for reflecting the informational content of the data.

As a second problem, consider a class of finite, discrete stochastic linear additive inverse problems and assume we observe a T-dimensional vector $\mathbf{y}$ of noisy indirect observations. However, our interest centers on an unknown and unobservable K-dimensional parameter vector $\boldsymbol{\beta}$. Since $\boldsymbol{\beta}$ cannot be measured directly, to recover it we use indirect measurements on the noisy observables

$$\mathbf{y} = X\boldsymbol{\beta} + \mathbf{e} \tag{1.1.2}$$

where X is a $(T \times K)$ known linear operator, and $\mathbf{e}$ is a T-dimensional noise vector with a finite scale parameter. Thus, we know X and observe $\mathbf{y}$ and wish to determine the unknown and unobservable parameter vector $\boldsymbol{\beta}$. Again, the problem is defined as an inverse problem since we must recover $\boldsymbol{\beta}$ based only on indirect partial, sparse or incomplete information. The problem is ill-posed if there is not enough information contained in X and the noisy data $\mathbf{y}$ to permit the recovery of the desired K-dimensional $\boldsymbol{\beta}$ parameter vector by traditional estimation methods, or in general, when an unknown function has to be inferred from insufficient information that specifies only a feasible set of functions. The ill-posed aspect may arise because

- non-stationarity or other model specification reasons may cause the number of unknown parameters to exceed the number of data points
- the data are mutually inconsistent

- the experiment may be badly designed, or the non-experimentally generated data, causes the columns of the design matrix X, to be linearly dependent or nearly so.

In these situations, if traditional estimation procedures are used,

- there may be arbitrary parameters
- the solution may be undefined, and/or
- the estimates can be highly unstable giving rise to high variance or low precision for the recovered parameters.

Unfortunately, because of limited, partial data or insufficient information, many econometric problems fall in the ill-posed, underdetermined category. *Convenient assumptions*, representing information we do not possess, are typically used to convert ill-posed problems into seemingly well-posed statistical models that can be analyzed with the familiar classical or Bayesian tools. However, this approach often leads to erroneous interpretations and treatments. In fact, in applied mathematics, statistics and econometrics, ill-posed inverse problems may be the rule rather than the exception. Consequently, it is necessary to consider the best way to proceed in analyzing these logically indeterminate situations.

Given this setting, in the context of economics, finance, and the social science, we specify a range of ill-posed, underdetermined pure and noise inverse problems and suggest, in each case, solution procedures for recovering the unknowns along with corresponding measures for gauging the sharpness of the inference. The emphasis here is on recovering *whatever information* there is in the data, and only indirectly on devising a way to get a unique solution. The estimation and inference procedures developed and demonstrated here are non-traditional in nature and the focus is on developing methods of emerging importance in analyzing real-world problems.

1.2 ORGANIZATION OF THE BOOK

In Chapter 2 we introduce the entropy measure and the maximum entropy formalism for solving pure ill-posed problems. After a brief review, we present a simple problem to demonstrate the classical maximum entropy formalism. This formalism is used when:

- the data are in the form of averages or aggregates where, as a result, probabilities must be used to represent partial information about individual outcomes
- we know something but we don't know everything
- we don't want to tell any more or any less than we know.

The remainder of the book is divided into six parts.

Part I introduces the concept of a pure inverse problem and develops the maximum entropy and cross-entropy formalisms as a basis for information recovery for both well- and ill-posed or underdetermined problems. Maximum entropy formulations and solutions are demonstrated for:

- recovering the size distribution of firms
- recovering estimates of the elements of a matrix of expenditures, trade, and/or income flows from multisectoral data
- recovering estimates of the transition probabilities for a stationary Markov process from aggregate proportion data.

In Part II the concept of a finite discrete linear inverse problem with noise is introduced. The statistical model is reparameterized so that it conforms to the maximum entropy (ME) format in which the unknown parameters have the properties of probabilities, and the generalized maximum entropy (GME) and generalized cross-entropy (GCE) formulations are developed as a basis for information recovery. Within the context of GME and GCE data analysis, the inverse problem with noise is solved under a dual criterion function. The resulting inferences are based only on the information in the data, or in the empirical moments. Large and small sample analytical properties of the GME-GCE estimators are demonstrated and a comparison with traditional estimators is given.

In Part III the GME and GCE formulations developed in Part II, are used as a basis for information recovery, estimation and inference when the design matrix X in (1.1.2) is ill-conditioned (collinear) and/or when the error process $\mathbf{e}$ in (1.1.2) is autocorrelated and/or heteroskedastic. In the last chapter of Part III the problem of choosing the correct subset model from a set of K variables, some of which may be extraneous, is investigated. A new model selection criterion is proposed and an information measure is suggested for discriminating between the true and extraneous variables. A basis for expressing model uncertainty as it relates to two or more possible model specification errors is developed and demonstrated.

In Part IV, building on the results in Part III, we first consider GME and GCE formulations of the sets of regression equations problem first raised by Zellner under the name of seemingly unrelated regressions (SUR). In contrast to the two-stage estimation procedures traditionally proposed, the unknown elements of the error covariance matrix Σ are estimated along with the unknown β_k's in the GME-GCE formulations. The SUR statistical model is then generalized to accommodate an instantaneous feedback mechanism between some of the variables, and a GME formulation is proposed and demonstrated for a single equation in a simultaneous system of equations and for the entire system of equations. The performance of the GME and general method of moments (GMM) is evaluated and contrasted.

In Part V we consider estimation problems based on dynamic discrete time models where the statistical model involves at least two sets of equations. The first problem involves noisy state observations, where the state equation and the observation equation are linear or non-linear. The objective is to estimate the unknown parameters of the state and observation equations and the unknown values of the state variable. Next we consider the problem of estimating the parameters of the objective function and of the state equation in a linear-quadratic control problem. In each case, given time series observations, we suggest a non-linear inversion procedure that permits the unknown underlying parameters to be estimated simultaneously. Examples are presented to suggest the operational nature of the results.

In Part VI a new approach based on the GME principle is proposed for recovering estimates of unknown parameters in multinomial discrete choice problems. In developing traditional solutions in multinomial problems, strong assumptions are needed to ensure that the moment conditions hold. Given the uncertainty about the appropriate statistical model that normally holds in practice, we work with a general exponential family formulation and a dual criterion function and demonstrate an estimator that is consistent and converges faster than traditional estimators in finite samples. In addition to the analytical results, sampling experiments are presented. Finally, attention is directed to recovering information from linear statistical models where the dependent variable is censored or ordered. The GME approach avoids some of the strong parametric assumptions required with traditional procedures and performs well over a range of non-Gaussian error distributions and ill-posed and well-posed problems. Analytical and illustrative sampling results are presented.

In Part VII (Chapter 17) non-linear solution algorithms and programming issues (including examples) are discussed and the availability of computer software packages for ME, GME and GCE is noted.

In Part VIII we assess the implications of the ME, GME and GCE formulations for recovering information and developing information processing rules, when faced with partial or incomplete data and possibly incorrect and ill-posed economic-statistical models.

CHAPTER 2

The classical maximum entropy formalism: a review

2.1 THE PROBLEM

In developing effective information processing rules we are restricted, in many cases, by the fact that the underlying sampling model is incomplete or incorrectly specified. Further, the passively generated data that are normally available in practice are limited, partial, aggregated and incomplete. Under these constraints, achieving a tractable economic-statistical model may not be possible, and conventional inference methods may fail to determine a unique solution. When this occurs, we define the problem as ill-posed, underdetermined or logically indeterminate. As Jaynes (1984, p. 151) has noted, when ill-posed problems arise, creative assumptions or prior information are used to induce a well-posed problem that is amenable to solution by one of the formulations in the traditional econometric tool chest. While this route of working with well-posed mathematical and statistical models has been essential in the discovery of new knowledge, it may lead to erroneous interpretations and conclusions. Because we must, by necessity, cope with partial-incomplete information and ill-posed inverse problems, it is important to seek a basis for reasoning in logically indeterminate situations. Although, in a traditional sense we do not know everything we should know about a situation, we would like the principle or formalism we are using to give us the 'best' conclusions possible based on the data at hand. In seeking such a principle or formalism two requirements appear essential:

- you know something but you do not know everything or perhaps not enough to proceed in a traditional way
- you do not want to claim any more or any less than you know.

Building on these guidelines, in the next section we present the solution that Jaynes proposed for this problem.

2.2 FORMULATION OF THE MAXIMUM ENTROPY PRINCIPLE

Suppose in the context of Chapter 1 we consider the finite, discrete, linear version of the pure inverse problem

$$\mathbf{y} = X\boldsymbol{\beta} = X\mathbf{p} \tag{2.2.1}$$

where, given data (observations) in the form of a T-dimensional vector $\mathbf{y}$, and the linear operator X is a $(T \times (K > T))$ non-invertible matrix, we wish to determine the unknown and unobservable frequencies $\mathbf{p} = (p_1, p_2, \ldots, p_K)'$ that represent the data generating process. Thus, out of all the probability distributions that satisfy (2.2.1) and fulfill the conditions $\sum_{k=1}^{K} p_k = 1$ and $p_k \geq 0$, we are asked to recover, assign or choose unambiguous probabilities p_k. Given this specification, the information contained in (2.2.1) does not appear adequate to determine the unknown probabilities $\mathbf{p}$. That is, because the number of data points are less than the number of unknowns, in its present form the problem appears underdetermined, and the basis for assigning a probability is, at this point, unresolved.

Faced with this limited information, if we wish to make an inference we must choose some estimate

$$\hat{\mathbf{p}} = A\mathbf{y} \tag{2.2.2}$$

from the data, where A is the unknown operator to be chosen. But how do we go about choosing A, or, in other words, *what criterion do we use for determining* A? If in this choice we make use of the rules of logic, then the A that is chosen must yield a $\hat{\mathbf{p}}$ in the class of possible $\{\mathbf{p}\}$ that satisfies

$$\mathbf{y} = X\hat{\mathbf{p}} \Rightarrow XA\mathbf{y} = XAX\mathbf{p} \tag{2.2.3}$$

This means, given (2.2.3), that

$$XAX = X \tag{2.2.4}$$

and, therefore, A is a generalized inverse (Kalman, 1960). This restriction is helpful in that it permits us to identify *the class of solutions* within which the true $\mathbf{p}$ must lie. Unfortunately, it gives us no basis for making a choice of A or $\hat{\mathbf{p}}$ within this class, since $\hat{\mathbf{p}}$ cannot be distinguished from the true $\mathbf{p}$. In fact, there are an infinite number of linear and non-linear operators A that satisfy (2.2.1) and yield estimates $\hat{\mathbf{p}}$ in the class of possible solutions that contain $(K - T)$ arbitrary parameters.

Given this unhappy situation, is there a way of proceeding in the face of seemingly unsolvable or underdetermined problems that results in an unambiguous solution? One piece of the puzzle was provided by Shannon, a communications engineer, who wanted some basis to measure the uncertainty in the mind of someone about to receive a noisy message. Since it is traditional to use probability as a measure of the uncertainty (state of knowledge) we have about the occurrence of a single event, Shannon (1948) used an axiomatic method to define a unique function to measure the uncertainty of a collection of events. Letting $\mathbf{x}$ be a random variable with possible outcome values x_k, $k = 1, 2, \ldots, K$ and probabilities p_k such that $\sum_k p_k = 1$, Shannon defined the *entropy* of the distribution of probabilities, $\mathbf{p} = (p_1, p_2, \ldots, p_K)'$ as the measure

$$H(\mathbf{p}) \equiv -\sum_k p_k \ln p_k \tag{2.2.5}$$

where $0 \cdot \ln(0) = 0$. The measure H, that Shannon used to measure the uncertainty of a collection of events, reaches a maximum when

$$p_1 = p_2 = \ldots = p_K = 1/K \tag{2.2.6}$$

or, in other words, when the probabilities are uniform. Using the entropy concept, which has a rich history dating back to Boltzman (in the 1870s) as well as Maxwell, Gibbs and Shannon and related work by Bernoulli, Laplace, Jeffreys and Cox, Jaynes (1957a, b) proposed making use of the entropy concept in choosing the unknown distribution of probabilities in (2.2.1). Under what Jaynes called the maximum entropy principle, one chooses the distribution for which the information (the data) is just sufficient to determine the probability assignment.

In developing this approach, let's suppose that nature or society is carrying out N trials (repetitions) of an experiment that has K possible outcomes (states). Let $N_1, N_2, \ldots, N_K$ be the number of times that each outcome occurs in the experiment of length N, where

$$\sum_k N_k = N, \qquad N_k \geq 0 \quad \text{and} \quad k = 1, 2, \ldots, K \tag{2.2.7}$$

Since there are N trials and each trial has K possible outcomes, there are K^N conceivable outcomes in the sequence of N trials. Of these, a particular set of frequencies

$$p_k = \frac{N_k}{N} \quad \text{or} \quad N_k = Np_k \qquad \text{for } k = 1, 2, \ldots, K \tag{2.2.8}$$

can be realized in a given number of ways as measured by the multiplicity factor (possible permutations). Thus, we can represent the number of ways a particular set of N_k can be realized by the multinomial coefficient

$$W = \frac{N!}{Np!\, Np_2! \ldots Np_k!} = \frac{N!}{\Pi_k N_k!} \tag{2.2.9a}$$

or the monotonic function of W

$$\ln W = \ln N! - \sum_{k=1}^{K} \ln N_k! \tag{2.2.9b}$$

Given (2.2.9), we use Stirling's approximation,

$$\ln x! \approx x \ln x - x, \qquad \text{as } 0 < x \to \infty \tag{2.2.10}$$

to approximate each component on the right-hand side of (2.2.9b). Then, for large N

$$\ln W \approx N \ln N - N - \sum_{k=1}^{K} N_k \ln N_k + \sum_{k=1}^{K} N_k \tag{2.2.11a}$$

Since $\sum_{k=1}^{K} N_k = N$, we have

$$\ln W \approx N \ln N - \sum_{k=1}^{K} N_k \ln N_k \tag{2.2.11b}$$

The ratio N_k/N represents the frequency of the occurrence of the possible K outcomes in a sequence of length N and

$$\frac{N_k}{N} \to p_k \qquad \text{as } N \to \infty.$$

Consequently, (2.2.11b) yields

$$\ln W \approx N \ln N - \sum_{k=1}^{K} Np_k \ln Np_k \tag{2.2.12a}$$

or

$$\ln W \approx N \ln N - \sum_{k=1}^{K} N_k \ln N - N \sum_{k=1}^{K} p_k \ln p_k \tag{2.2.12b}$$

or

$$\ln W \approx -N \sum_{k=1}^{K} p_k \ln p_k \tag{2.2.12c}$$

Finally,

$$N^{-1} \ln W \approx - \sum_{k=1}^{K} p_k \ln p_k = H(\mathbf{p}) \tag{2.2.13}$$

which is the Shannon entropy measure (2.2.5) where $p_k \ln p_k$ is taken to be 0 when $p_k = 0$. The entropy (2.2.5), or (2.2.13), is maximized, with maximum value $\ln K$, when $p_1 = p_2 = \ldots = p_k = 1/K$. Given (2.2.13), if we follow Jaynes

(1957a, b; 1984) and maximize this monotonic function of W subject to the limited, aggregated data (2.2.1), we obtain the set p_k(frequency distribution) that can be realized in the greatest number of ways *consistent with what we know.* Consequently, H is a measure of the amount of uncertainty in the distribution of probabilities and is numerically equal to the distribution of probabilities that maximizes the Shannon–Jaynes entropy where

$$W = e^{NH} \tag{2.2.14}$$

Thus, if asked which particular set of relative frequencies we consider the best approximation for the p_k, it seems reasonable to follow Jaynes and favor the one that could have been generated in the greatest number of ways consistent with what we know (the data). This means we choose the $\mathbf{p}$ that maximizes

$$H(\mathbf{p}) = -\sum_{k=1}^{K} p_k \ln p_k = -\mathbf{p}' \ln \mathbf{p} \tag{2.2.15}$$

subject to data *consistency* and *normalization-additivity* requirements

$$\mathbf{y} = X\mathbf{p} \tag{2.2.16}$$

and

$$\mathbf{p}'\mathbf{1} = 1 \tag{2.2.17}$$

where $\mathbf{1}$ is an $(K \times 1)$ vector of ones and $\ln \mathbf{p}$ is a $(K \times 1)$ vector. Throughout, operations on vectors are taken to be elementwise. Consequently, we have converted our problem from one of deductive mathematics to one of inference where *we seek to make the best predictions possible from the information that we have.* Through the use of the principle of maximum entropy (ME) we have a basis for using or transforming the evidence–data–empirical moments into a distribution of probabilities describing our state of knowledge. Thus, in the ME approach we take into account not only the data, but also relevant information about the multiplicity of all the different possible outcomes.

The maximum entropy formulation that is based on the work of Shannon (1948) and Jaynes (1957a, b; 1984), has been extended by Kullback (1959), Levine (1980) and many others who are identified in the collection of papers in Levine and Tribus (1979). Axiomatic arguments for the justification of the ME principle have been made by Shore and Johnson (1980), Jaynes (1984), Skilling (1989) and Csiszár (1991). An incomplete list of suggested readings in entropy and maximum entropy appears at the end of the book.

The analytical solution to the maximization problem (2.2.15)–(2.2.17) can be obtained from the Lagrangian function

$$L = -\mathbf{p}' \ln \mathbf{p} + \boldsymbol{\lambda}'(\mathbf{y} - X\mathbf{p}) + \mu(1 - \mathbf{p}'\mathbf{1}) \tag{2.2.18}$$

with optimality conditions

$$\partial L/\partial \mathbf{p} = -\ln \hat{\mathbf{p}} - \mathbf{1} - X'\hat{\boldsymbol{\lambda}} - \hat{\mu} = \mathbf{0} \tag{2.2.19}$$

$$\partial L/\partial \boldsymbol{\lambda} = \mathbf{y} - X\hat{\mathbf{p}} = \mathbf{0} \tag{2.2.20}$$

$$\partial L/\partial \mu = 1 - \hat{\mathbf{p}}'\mathbf{1} = 0 \tag{2.2.21}$$

From (2.2.19)–(2.2.21) we can solve for $\hat{\mathbf{p}}$, in terms of the $\hat{\boldsymbol{\lambda}}$ to get

$$\hat{\mathbf{p}} = \exp(-X'\hat{\boldsymbol{\lambda}})/\Omega(\hat{\boldsymbol{\lambda}}) \tag{2.2.22}$$

where

$$\Omega(\hat{\boldsymbol{\lambda}}) = \sum_k \exp(-X'\hat{\boldsymbol{\lambda}}) \tag{2.2.23}$$

is a normalization factor that converts the relative probabilities into absolute probabilities. The solution (2.2.22) establishes a unique non-linear relation between $\hat{\mathbf{p}}$ and $\mathbf{y}$ through $\hat{\boldsymbol{\lambda}}$. The ME formulation and the characteristics of the solution are discussed and developed in detail in Chapter 3.

2.2.1 MINIMUM CROSS-ENTROPY

In many situations normally found in practice we may have non-sample or pre-sample information about the unknown $\mathbf{p} = (p_1, p_2, \ldots, p_K)'$ in the form of a prior distribution of probabilities $\mathbf{q} = (q_1, q_2, \ldots, q_K)'$. That is, before making use of the data that enter as the consistency relations (2.2.16), there may be some distribution $\mathbf{q}$ that may seem reasonable as an initial hypothesis. When such prior knowledge exists, we wish to incorporate it into the ME formalism. Of course after the sample evidence is in, the prior distribution $\mathbf{q}$ may be found to be incompatible with the data-moment condition (2.2.16). Following Kullback (1959) and Good (1963), the principle of minimum cross-entropy or minimal discriminability implies one would choose, given the constraints (2.2.16) and (2.2.17), the estimate of $\mathbf{p}$ that can be discriminated from $\mathbf{q}$ with a minimum of difference. This leads to the cross-entropy between $\mathbf{p}$ and $\mathbf{q}$, that is defined as

$$\begin{aligned} I(\mathbf{p}, \mathbf{q}) &= \sum_{k=1}^{K} p_k \ln(p_k/q_k) = \sum_k p_k \ln p_k - \sum_k p_k \ln q_k \\ &= \mathbf{p}' \ln \mathbf{p} - \mathbf{p}' \ln \mathbf{q} \end{aligned} \tag{2.2.24}$$

or the difference between E[ln $\mathbf{p}$] – E[ln $\mathbf{q}$]. This criterion leads to a natural measure of the deviation of the distribution of probabilities $\mathbf{p}$ and $\mathbf{q}$. Under the principle of minimum discriminability the difference $I(\mathbf{p}, \mathbf{q})$ is minimized. Consequently, to take account of both the prior and sample information, the minimum cross-entropy solution may be obtained from the minimization problem

$$\min_{\mathbf{p}} I(\mathbf{p}, \mathbf{q}) = \sum_k p_k \ln(p_k/q_k) = \mathbf{p}' \ln \mathbf{p} - \mathbf{p}' \ln \mathbf{q} \tag{2.2.25}$$

subject to

$$\mathbf{y} = X\mathbf{p} \tag{2.2.16$'$}$$

$$\mathbf{p}'\mathbf{1} = 1 \tag{2.2.17$'$}$$

If the prior information $\mathbf{q}$ is consistent with the data, then $\tilde{\mathbf{p}} = \mathbf{q}$ and (2.2.25) has a zero solution value. This means that the data has no additional information relative to the prior. If, within a CE formulation, $\mathbf{q}$ is a uniform distribution, $q_k = 1/K$ for all K, the ME solution (2.2.22) results. Through the CE criterion and the minimization problem (2.2.25), (2.2.16) and (2.2.17), the data and prior probabilities are transformed into the estimated posterior probabilities $\tilde{\mathbf{p}}$. The CE formulation can be viewed as a shrinkage rule where the small frequencies are shrunk more than the large frequencies (see Section 3.3.2).

2.3 AN ILLUSTRATIVE EXAMPLE

To demonstrate the ME method for solving an ill-posed underdetermined problem, consider a variant of the dice problem introduced by Jaynes (1963) in his Brandeis lectures. Suppose you are given a six-sided die that can take on the values $k = 1, 2, \ldots, 6$, and you are asked to estimate the probabilities $\mathbf{p} = (p_1, p_2, \ldots, p_6)'$ for each possible outcome in the next roll of the die. The only information you are given is that the average outcome from a large number of independent rolls of the die was y. Even though the weak law of large numbers implies that the sample average will converge in probability to the true mean of the distribution, there are an infinite number of distributions supported on $\{1, 2, \ldots, 6\}$ that have a mean of y. Note that we are *not* given the observed frequency distribution of the sample, which would yield the maximum likelihood estimator for a multinomial distribution.

The problem is clearly *ill-posed* or underdetermined because there are six unknown probabilities, but we only have two pieces of information. Namely, the six probabilities must sum to 1 and the mean of the distribution of probabilities is y. Ill-posed problems may be solved by using prior or non-sample information to choose from the feasible set of solutions. For instance, suppose we expect the die to be roughly 'fair', and the observed average matches the mean of the discrete uniform distribution, $y = 3.5$. Then, many would assert that the underlying distribution is discrete uniform because the sample information matches our prior beliefs. However, if $y \neq 3.5$, the sample information suggests that the underlying distribution is not likely to be uniform. In a situation like this, we follow the ME formalism discussed in Section 2.2 and developed by Jaynes (1957a, b). Formally, we select the probabilities that maximize

$$H(\mathbf{p}) = -\sum_{k=1}^{6} p_k \ln(p_k) \tag{2.3.1}$$

subject to

$$\sum_{k=1}^{6} p_k x_k = y \tag{2.3.2}$$

$$\sum_{k=1}^{6} p_k = 1 \tag{2.3.3}$$

where $x_k = k$ for each $k = 1, \ldots, 6$.

The Lagrangian for the problem is:

$$L = -\sum_{k=1}^{6} p_k \ln(p_k) + \lambda\left(y - \sum_{k=1}^{6} p_k x_k\right) + \gamma\left(1 - \sum_{k=1}^{6} p_k\right) \tag{2.3.4}$$

If $y \in (1, 6)$, the constraint set is non-empty and compact. Given that H is strictly concave, there is a unique, interior solution to the problem. By solving the first-order conditions, the ME probability distribution places the weight

$$\hat{p}_k = \frac{\exp(-x_k\hat{\lambda})}{\sum_{k=1}^{6}\exp(-x_k\hat{\lambda})} = \frac{\exp(-x_k\hat{\lambda})}{\Omega(\hat{\lambda})} \tag{2.3.5}$$

on the kth outcome. Here, $\hat{p}_k$ is a function of $\hat{\lambda}$, the Lagrange multiplier on the moment constraint (2.3.2). The constraint (2.3.2) is the only information used and may lead us to modify, relative to an honest die, the distribution of probabilities on a space of six points. Because $\hat{p}_k$ is a function of $\hat{\lambda}$, the maximum entropy distribution does not have a closed-form solution, and we must use numerical optimization techniques to compute the probabilities.

Taking p_k to be a probability mass function indexed by $\lambda \in \mathbb{R}$, note that $p(\lambda)$ is a member of the canonical exponential family and thus the non-negativity requirement that $p_k \geq 0$, is satisfied. The mean of the distribution is

$$\sum_{k=1}^{6} p_k(\lambda) x_k = y \tag{2.3.6}$$

Table 2.3.1 The estimated maximum entropy distributions for the die problem

y	$\hat{p}_1$	$\hat{p}_2$	$\hat{p}_3$	$\hat{p}_4$	$\hat{p}_5$	$\hat{p}_6$	$H(\hat{\mathbf{p}})$
2.0	0.478	0.255	0.136	0.072	0.038	0.021	1.367
3.0	0.247	0.207	0.174	0.146	0.123	0.103	1.748
3.5	0.167	0.167	0.167	0.167	0.167	0.167	1.792
4.0	0.103	0.123	0.146	0.174	0.207	0.247	1.748
5.0	0.021	0.038	0.072	0.136	0.255	0.478	1.367

The associated information matrix is

$$I(\lambda) = \sum_{k=1}^{6} p_k(\lambda)x_k^2 - \left(\sum_{k=1}^{6} p_k(\lambda)x_k\right)^2 = \text{Var}(x) \tag{2.3.7}$$

Using a numerical optimization package such as GAMS, SHAZAM or Fortran (Agmon *et al.*, 1979), the estimated maximum entropy distributions, for various values of y, are given in Table 2.3.1. Note that, as expected, $y = 3.5$ results in a discrete uniform distribution and a maximum value of $H(\hat{\mathbf{p}})$. All the probabilities are monotone in x.

2.4 REMARKS

In this chapter we have reviewed the classical maximum entropy and minimum cross-entropy principles for solving ill-posed, underdetermined, pure inverse problems. In Part I of the monograph we consider pure inverse relations and look at these principles in detail, develop some analytic results and indicate how they may be used to formulate and solve a range of economic problems.

REFERENCES

Agmon, N., Alhassid, Y. and Levine R. D. (1979) An algorithm for finding the distribution of maximal entropy. *Journal of Computational Physics* **30**, 250–9.

Csiszár, I. (1991) Why least squares and maximum entropy? An axiomatic approach to inference for linear inverse problems. *Annals of Statistics* **19**, 2032–66.

Good, I. J. (1963) Maximum entropy for hypothesis formulation, especially for multidimensional contingency tables. *Annals of Mathematical Statistics* **34**, 911–34.

Jaynes, E. T. (1957a) Information theory and statistical mechanics *Physics Review* **106**, 620–30.

Jaynes, E. T. (1957b) Information theory and statistical mechanics II. *Physics Review* **108**, 171–90.

Jaynes, E. T. (1963) Information theory and statistical mechanics. In K. W. Ford (Ed.) *Statistical Physics*, pp. 181–218, W. A. Benjamin, New York.

Jaynes, E. T. (1984) Prior information and ambiguity in inverse problems. In D. W. McLaughlin (Ed.) *Inverse Problems*, pp. 151–66, SIAM Proceedings, American Mathematical Society, Providence, RI.

Kalman, R. E. (1960) A new approach to linear filtering and prediction problems. *Transactions of the American Society of Mechanical Engineers, Ser. D., Journal of Basic Engineering* **82**, 34–45.

Kullback, J. (1959) *Information Theory and Statistics.* John Wiley, New York.

Levine, R. D. (1980) An information theoretical approach to inversion problems. *Journal of Physics A* **13**, 91–108.

Levine, R. D. and Tribus, M. (1979) *The Maximum Entropy Formalism.* MIT Press, Cambridge, MA.

Shannon, C. E. (1948) A mathematical theory of communication. *Bell System Technical Journal* **27**, 379–423.

Shore, J. E. and Johnson, R. W. (1980) Axiomatic derivation of the principle of maximum entropy and the principle of minimum cross-entropy. *IEEE Transactions on Information Theory* **26**, 26–37.

Skilling, J. (1989) The axioms of maximum entropy. In J. Skilling (Ed.) *Maximum Entropy and Bayesian Methods in Science and Engineering*, pp. 173–87, Kluwer, Dordrecht.

PART I

Pure inverse problems

In Part I we begin the search for procedures that may be used to recover unknown economic parameters in the case of limited, partial, incomplete data. The statistical models consistent with these data are, in many cases, ill-posed or underdetermined and, unless restrictive assumptions are made, cannot be solved by using traditional methods. A wide range of problems normally found in economic practice may be modeled with the pure inverse relation $\mathbf{y} = X\mathbf{p}$. We demonstrate an efficient non-linear inversion procedure that provides conservative inferences for the unknown $\mathbf{p}$ that may be scalar, vector or function valued.

CHAPTER 3

Basic maximum entropy principle: formulation and extensions

The purpose of this chapter is to formulate a basic ill-posed, pure inverse problem in economics and to suggest, within the context of the maximum entropy (ME) and cross-entropy (CE) formalisms, analytical and empirical methods for recovering the corresponding unknown and unobservable parameters.

3.1 INTRODUCTION

Consider a sample of economic data. This sample is generated from an economic process or processes and, as such, comes from a population that is composed of a large but countable number of agents or outcomes. Based on this set of data, we wish to obtain information that would permit us to understand:

- the individual behavior
- the state of the system

Based on this understanding, we wish to be able to predict future economic behavior and, correspondingly, the future state of the system. However, consistent with the non-experimental nature of economic data, the sample of data may be limited and incomplete. In this context, the main limitations are:

- the inability to identify or establish the initial-boundary conditions, relative to the current state of system, and to identify the paths (trajectories) of the many members that comprise the population
- the economic models relating to the individual behavior of members of the population contain unknowns that are unobserved and not accessible to direct measurements

- the data consist of some aggregate measures, such as overall averages or moments representing the members of the population
- the number of unknowns is greater than the observable population data points and means the problem is underdetermined.

Each of the above limitations leads to an ill-posed or underdetermined data set which cannot be analyzed with the traditional tools unless creative assumptions are made. Having described the problem, we now proceed to describe the data and the suggested information recovery procedure.

Given this setting, which is consistent with many non-experimental economic data generation processes and the data used in many applied econometric analyses, we are faced with the general problem of using the available information at hand in order to make predictions for the population or to construct an image of it. Since our information is in the form of observable averages, moments or aggregates, we can use probabilities to represent our partial information about the individual micro outcomes. If the resulting inferences are to be useful, the probabilities and their corresponding parameters must be consistent with the observed data.

Consistent with the definition of the problem, let us represent the observed aggregate measures (data) by $\{y_1, \ldots, y_T\}$, where the population is partitioned into K components or cells, designated by the real variable $\mathbf{x}$, that can take on values $\{x_1, x_2, \ldots, x_K\}$. The corresponding problem is to recover or assign values to the unknown probabilities $\{p_1, p_2, \ldots, p_K\}$ on each of the states or categories. The assignment of the $\{p_k\}$ must be consistent with our information about $\mathbf{x}$ and $\{y_t\}$, and has to satisfy the properties of probabilities that involve non-negativity and adding-up conditions. Given that some probability distributions supported on $\mathbf{x}$ and consistent with $\{y_t\}$ lead to better predictions than others, the researcher still faces questions regarding the appropriate criterion and inversion algorithms for recovering $\mathbf{p}$.

The true population probabilities are unobserved and unobservable. Likewise, the models that economists use for analysis and decision purposes may contain unknowns that are unobserved and indeed not accessible to direct measurement. For example, we can observe, on an individual, household or other aggregate basis, data on income and consumption, but we cannot observe the corresponding marginal propensity to consume. Alternatively, we can observe inputs and outputs, but we cannot observe the corresponding marginal product or elasticity of production coefficient.

Within this context, in order to recover the unknown probabilities and other unknown economic parameters, we visualize an inverse problem that may be formalized as follows. Given observed outcome data $\mathbf{y}$, our interest centers on an unobservable unknown $\mathbf{p}$ which may be a scalar, a vector or a function. Since we cannot measure $\mathbf{p}$ directly, we must recover information about $\mathbf{p}$ from the indirect observable measurements.

Working toward a rational basis for handling ill-posed inverse problems in economics, consider the following finite, discrete, linear, pure inverse problem

$$\mathbf{y} = X\mathbf{p} \tag{3.1.1}$$

where $\mathbf{y} = (y_1, y_2, \ldots, y_T)'$ is a T-dimensional vector of observations (data), $\mathbf{p} = (p_1, p_2, \ldots, p_K)'$ is a K-dimensional vector of unknowns and the linear operator X is a known $(T \times K)$ matrix. Given (3.1.1) we would like to be able to use observables to recover the unknown and unobservable vector $\mathbf{p}$ that represents information about the parameters of interest. However, if because of bad design or if the number of unknowns, K, is larger than the number of data points, T, the linear operator, X, may be non-invertible so that X^{-1} does not exist as a bounded operator. As noted in Chapter 2, if we attempt to recover $\mathbf{p}$ using the traditional procedures of mathematical inversion, we must consider the entire class of feasible solutions that contains $(K - T)$ arbitrary parameters. Thus, using traditional procedures, the problem is ill-posed and we have no basis for picking a particular solution vector for $\mathbf{p}$ from the feasible set.

In economics there are many admissible models that *a priori* do not contradict observed behavior outcomes. If the data points are limited, ill-posed or underdetermined problems may be the rule rather than the exception. Consequently, in the next section, we consider the best means for recovering information about $\mathbf{p}$ in this traditionally indeterminate situation.

3.2 THE MAXIMUM ENTROPY (ME) FORMALISM: FORMULATION, SOLUTION AND INTERPRETATION

Working toward a criterion for recovering $\mathbf{p}$ in the pure inverse relation $\mathbf{y} = X\mathbf{p}$, we (in the context of Chapter 2) follow Shannon (1948), Jaynes (1957a, b) and Levine (1980) and use the entropy measure

$$H(\mathbf{p}) = -\sum_{k=1}^{K} p_k \ln p_k = -\mathbf{p}' \ln \mathbf{p} \tag{3.2.1}$$

where $p_k \ln p_k = 0$ for $p_k = 0$ and $H(p)$ reaches a maximum when $p_1 = p_2 = \cdots = p_k = 1/K$. Given the entropy metric (3.2.1), in terms of an ill-posed inverse problem $\mathbf{y} = X\mathbf{p}$, if we are asked which particular set of relative frequencies we consider most likely, it seems reasonable to favor the one that *could have been generated in the greatest number of ways consistent with what we know*. That is, by the multiplicity factor (2.2.9b), entropy represents a measure of the uncertainty associated with a distribution of the probabilities and provides one rationale for assigning probabilities consistent with the information (data) in the inverse problem $\mathbf{y} = X\mathbf{p}$. Because we do not want to tell more than we know, we choose the $\mathbf{p}$ that is closest to the uniform distribution and yet consistent with the data. In other words, we want to choose the $\mathbf{p}$ that maximizes the missing information. In terms of the pure inverse problem (3.1.2), this implies that we choose the distribution of probabilities that maximizes (3.2.1) subject to moment-consistency conditions

$$\mathbf{y} = X\mathbf{p} \tag{3.2.2}$$

and additivity (normalization) requirements

$$\mathbf{p}'\mathbf{1} = 1 \tag{3.2.3}$$

where $\mathbf{1}$ is a $(K \times 1)$ vector of ones and $\ln \mathbf{p}$ is a $(K \times 1)$ vector with elements $\ln p_k$. Thus, following the Jaynes maximum entropy formalism, the problem is converted from one of deductive mathematics to one of inference involving an optimization procedure. Through the principle of maximum entropy (ME), there is a basis for using, or transforming, the information in the data into a probability distribution that reflects our uncertainty about individual economic outcomes. In the ME approach, we take into account not only the data $\mathbf{y} = X\mathbf{p}$, which requires the solution to hold at each data point, $t = 1, 2, \ldots, T$, but also relevant information about the multiplicity of the possible outcomes. In turn, this local consistency implies global consistency for a set of recovered parameters. A detailed formulation and solution of the general problem is discussed next.

In general, the information in the constraint set (the data) may be represented by T functions $\{f_1(x), f_2(x), \ldots, f_T(x)\}$. Under the ME formalism, the problem of recovering $\mathbf{p}$ can be stated as

$$\max_{\mathbf{p}} H(\mathbf{p}) = -\sum_{k=1}^{K} p_k \ln p_k \tag{3.2.4}$$

subject to moment-consistency constraints

$$\sum_{k=1}^{K} p_k f_t(x_k) = y_t, \qquad 1 \leq t \leq T \tag{3.2.5}$$

and the adding up-normalization constraint

$$\sum_{k=1}^{K} p_k = 1 \tag{3.2.6}$$

where $\{y_1, y_2, \ldots, y_T\}$ is an observed set of data (e.g. averages or aggregates) that are consistent with the distribution of probabilities $\{p_1, p_2, \ldots, p_K\}$. Note that the problem is ill-posed or underdetermined if $T < K$.

To recover the probability vector $\mathbf{p}$, one can form the Lagrangian function

$$L = -\sum_{k=1}^{T} p_k \ln p_k + \sum_{t=1}^{T} \lambda_t \left[y_t - \sum_{k=1}^{K} p_k f_t(x_k) \right] + \mu\left(1 - \sum_{k=1}^{K} p_k\right) \tag{3.2.7}$$

with the first-order conditions

$$\frac{\partial L}{\partial p_k} = -\ln \hat{p}_k - 1 - \sum_{t=1}^{T} \hat{\lambda}_t f_t(x_t) - \hat{\mu} = 0, \qquad k = 1, 2, \ldots, K \tag{3.2.8}$$

$$\frac{\partial L}{\partial \lambda_t} = y_t - \sum_{k=1}^{K} \hat{p}_k f_t(x_k) = 0, \qquad t = 1, 2, \ldots, T \tag{3.2.9}$$

$$\frac{\partial L}{\partial \mu} = 1 - \sum_{k=1}^{K} \hat{p}_k = 0 \tag{3.2.10}$$

The solution to this sytem of $K + T + 1$ equations and parameters yields

$$\hat{p}_k = \exp\left(- \sum_{t=1}^{T} \hat{\lambda}_t f_t(x_k) - 1 - \hat{\mu} \right), \qquad k = 1, 2, \ldots, K \tag{3.2.8a}$$

$$\sum_{k=1}^{K} \exp\left(- \sum_{t=1}^{T} \hat{\lambda}_t f_t(x_k) - 1 - \hat{\mu} \right) f_t(x_k) = y_t, \qquad t = 1, 2, \ldots, T \tag{3.2.9a}$$

$$\sum_{k=1}^{K} \exp\left(- \sum_{t=1}^{T} \hat{\lambda}_t f_t(x_k) - 1 - \hat{\mu} \right) = 1 \tag{3.2.10a}$$

The formal solution is

$$\hat{p}_k = \frac{1}{\Omega(\hat{\lambda}_1, \hat{\lambda}_2, \ldots, \hat{\lambda}_T)} \exp\left[- \sum_{t=1}^{T} \hat{\lambda}_t f_t(x_t) \right] \tag{3.2.11}$$

where

$$\Omega(\hat{\lambda}) = \sum_{k=1}^{K} \exp\left[- \sum_{t=1}^{T} \hat{\lambda}_t f_t(x_k) \right] \tag{3.2.12}$$

is a normalization factor. The factor Ω converts the relative probabilities to absolute probabilities and is known in the literature as the *partition function.* The $\{\hat{\lambda}_t\}$ are Lagrange multipliers on the constraints (3.2.5) and are determined by the T simultaneous equations

$$y_t = \left(\frac{\partial}{\partial \lambda_t} \right) \ln \Omega, \qquad 1 \leq t \leq T \tag{3.2.13}$$

The value of the entropy measure H is then a function of the given data:

$$H = \ln \Omega(\hat{\lambda}) + \sum_t \hat{\lambda}_t y_t \tag{3.2.14}$$

In this characterization of the ME formalism, which is designed to solve pure ill-posed problems, it should be noted that all possible states are assumed equally likely and no prior assumptions or constraints are imposed on the information (data) set. That is, we seek a distribution of probabilities $\mathbf{p}$ that only describes what we know. Maximizing the entropy subject to no data constraints (without (3.2.5)) yields a uniform distribution. The constraints (information) restrict the initial 'missing information,' and *the ME formalism seeks a solution that maximizes the missing information.* As formulated in (3.2.4)–(3.2.6), the traditional ME formalism is a non-linear inversion procedure for solving inverse problems where the object to be recovered is known to be positive. By letting the discrete variate $K \to \infty$, a continuous probability distribution formulation of the entropy formalism can be formulated. This is developed in Appendix 3.A.

3.2.1 UNIQUENESS OF THE PRIMAL ME SOLUTION

Given the Lagrangian (3.2.7), and the corresponding first-order conditions (3.2.8)–(3.2.10), an element of the Hessian is

$$\frac{\partial^2 L}{\partial p_k^2} = -\frac{\mathbf{1}' \exp(\mathbf{f}(\mathbf{x}_k)'\boldsymbol{\lambda})}{\exp(\mathbf{f}(\mathbf{x}_k)'\boldsymbol{\lambda})} = -\frac{1}{p_k} \quad \text{for the diagonal elements}$$

and

$$\frac{\partial^2 L}{\partial p_k \partial p_j} = 0 \quad \text{for the off-diagonal elements.}$$

The resulting Hessian is

$$H = \begin{bmatrix} -\frac{1}{p_1} & & & 0 \\ & -\frac{1}{p_2} & & \\ & & \ddots & \\ 0 & & & -\frac{1}{p_K} \end{bmatrix} \qquad (3.2.15)$$

which is negative definite for $p_k > 0$ and thus satisfies the sufficient conditions for a unique global maximum.

The solution $\hat{\mathbf{p}}$ satisfies the adding up constraints (3.2.6) and the $\hat{p}_k$'s are strictly positive. However, the ME solution depends on the Lagrange multipliers, $\hat{\boldsymbol{\lambda}}$. The only remaining information in the first-order conditions is the set of moment-consistency constraints (3.2.5), which are not a function of $\boldsymbol{\lambda}$. Hence, there is no closed-form solution for the ME formulation, and the solution must be found numerically. Nonetheless, it is possible to formulate a dual-ME approach in order to investigate the properties of the ME formalism within the extremum or M-estimation framework developed by Huber (1981) and to increase computational efficiency.

3.2.2 THE UNCONSTRAINED DUAL PROBLEM

An unconstrained dual form of the ME problem (3.2.4)–(3.3.6) initially was formulated by Agmon *et al.* (1979), and generalized by Miller (1994) and Golan *et al.* (1996). To simplify the presentation, and without loss of generality, we work with the discrete linear model $\mathbf{y} = X\mathbf{p}$ instead of the general case $\mathbf{y} = f(X)\mathbf{p}$. Building on the Lagrangian (3.2.7) and the solution (3.2.11), the dual objective, as a function of the Lagrange multipliers, $\boldsymbol{\lambda}$, is

$$\begin{aligned} L(\boldsymbol{\lambda}) &= -\mathbf{p}' \ln \mathbf{p}(\boldsymbol{\lambda}) + \boldsymbol{\lambda}'[\mathbf{y} - X\mathbf{p}(\boldsymbol{\lambda})] \\ &= -\mathbf{p}(\boldsymbol{\lambda})'[-X'\boldsymbol{\lambda} - \ln(\Omega(\boldsymbol{\lambda}))] + [\mathbf{y}' - \mathbf{p}(\boldsymbol{\lambda})'X']\boldsymbol{\lambda} \\ &= \mathbf{y}'\boldsymbol{\lambda} + \mathbf{p}(\boldsymbol{\lambda})' \ln(\Omega(\boldsymbol{\lambda})) - \mathbf{p}(\boldsymbol{\lambda})'X'\boldsymbol{\lambda} + \mathbf{p}(\boldsymbol{\lambda})'X'\boldsymbol{\lambda} \\ &= \mathbf{y}'\boldsymbol{\lambda} + \ln(\Omega(\boldsymbol{\lambda})) \equiv M(\boldsymbol{\lambda}) \end{aligned} \tag{3.2.16}$$

where the optimal $\mathbf{p}(\boldsymbol{\lambda})$ satisfies the adding up constraints and $M(\boldsymbol{\lambda})$ is strictly convex in $\boldsymbol{\lambda}$. This unconstrained dual function is just (3.2.14), where $\hat{\boldsymbol{\lambda}}$ is substituted for $\boldsymbol{\lambda}$. Further, the gradient ∇_λ of $M(\boldsymbol{\lambda})$ is just the set of moment-consistency conditions (3.2.5)

$$\nabla_\lambda M(\boldsymbol{\lambda}) = \mathbf{y} - X\mathbf{p} \tag{3.2.17}$$

Minimizing $M(\boldsymbol{\lambda})$ with respect to $\boldsymbol{\lambda}$ yields $\hat{\boldsymbol{\lambda}}$, which in turn yield $\hat{\mathbf{p}}$. The minimal value of the dual objective function, also known as the potential function (Agmon *et al.*, 1979), is the *upper bound* for the entropy of the distribution $\mathbf{p}$, that is consistent with the data constraints (3.2.5). Thus, the value $\min[M(\boldsymbol{\lambda})]$ equals the value $\max[H(\mathbf{p})]$. See, for example. Alhassid *et al.* (1978).

Finally, within the maximum likelihood (ML) approach, the dual unconstrained function $M(\boldsymbol{\lambda})$ can be interpreted as a log-likelihood function involving both the moments of the data and the exponential distribution of the unknowns. A further discussion and comparison with the ML is given in Chapters 6 and 15.

3.2.3 THE INFORMATION COVARIANCE MATRIX

As noted in Chapter 2, we can view $p(\boldsymbol{\lambda})$ as an exponential family parameterized by $\boldsymbol{\lambda}$. Accordingly, the dual objective function, $M(\boldsymbol{\lambda})$, is the *negative expected log likelihood function* for $\boldsymbol{\lambda}$. By introducing the expectation and differentiation operators, we can see that the Hessian matrix of $M(\boldsymbol{\lambda})$ is simply the information matrix for $\boldsymbol{\lambda}$.

The Hessian matrix $\nabla_{\lambda\lambda'}$, of the dual objective $\mathbf{M}(\boldsymbol{\lambda})$ (3.2.16) is

$$\nabla_{\lambda\lambda'} M(\boldsymbol{\lambda}) = -X\nabla_{\lambda'}\mathbf{p}(\boldsymbol{\lambda}) \tag{3.2.18}$$

Noting the tth equation in $\nabla_\lambda M(\boldsymbol{\lambda})$ is

$$y_t - \sum_k x_{kt} p_k \tag{3.2.19}$$

an element of the diagonal of the $(T \times T)$ Hessian is

$$\begin{aligned}\frac{\partial^2 M}{\partial \lambda_t^2} = I(\lambda_t) &= -\sum_k x_{tk} \frac{\partial \hat{p}_k}{\partial \lambda_t} = \sum_k x_{tk}\left(x_{tk}\hat{p}_k - \hat{p}_k \sum_k x_{tk}\hat{p}_k\right) \\ &= \sum_k x_{tk}^2 \hat{p}_k - \left(\sum_k x_{tk}\hat{p}_k\right)^2 \equiv \mathrm{Var}(x_t)\end{aligned} \tag{3.2.20}$$

and an off-diagonal element is

$$\begin{aligned}\frac{\partial^2 M}{\partial \lambda_t \partial \lambda_r} = I(\lambda_t, \lambda_r) &= -\sum_k x_{tk} \frac{\partial \hat{p}_k}{\partial \lambda_r} = \sum_k x_{tk}\left(x_{rk}\hat{p}_k - \hat{p}_k \sum_k x_{rk}\hat{p}_k\right) \\ &= \sum_k x_{tk}x_{rk}\hat{p}_k - \left(\sum_k x_{tk}\hat{p}_k\right)\left(\sum_k x_{rk}\hat{p}_k\right) \equiv \mathrm{Cov}(x_t, x_r)\end{aligned} \tag{3.2.21}$$

Finally, rearranging the $(T \times T)$ Hessian, we get

$$\frac{\partial^2 M}{\partial \lambda_t \partial \lambda_r} = I(\boldsymbol{\lambda}) \tag{3.2.22}$$

which is the information matrix for $\boldsymbol{\lambda}$. In this case, however, $I(\boldsymbol{\lambda})$ is just the variance–covariance matrix of the random variable $\mathbf{x}$ implied by $\hat{\mathbf{p}}$. As $\mathbf{p}$ is strictly positive and the variance–covariance matrix is positive definite, the Hessian is positive definite assuring a unique global solution for $\boldsymbol{\lambda}$. An alternative approach to developing the variance–covariance matrix is given in Appendix 3.C. Finally, we note that, even though the information recovery formalism used here is known as the 'pure' ME, there is inherent noise in the system. However, this noise is assumed to be 'washed out' during the aggregation (or averaging) process. In Chapter 6, we analyze systems where the noise is a component of the inverse relation.

3.2.4 INTERPRETATION OF THE LAGRANGE MULTIPLIERS

Similar to all optimization problems, the Lagrange multipliers reflect the change in the objective value as a result of a marginal change in the constraint set. That is, the Lagrange multipliers are just the partial derivatives of $\max\{H\}$ with respect to y_t, and as such are marginal entropies. However, for the ME formulation, the Lagrange multipliers have more meaningful economic-statistical interpretation that changes from problem to problem, but can be summarized as follows: for the primal ME problem, the $\boldsymbol{\lambda}$'s reflect the more traditional notion of the 'relative contribution' of each data point-constraint to the optimal objective value. Consequently the λ's reflect the information content of each constraint. For example, $\lambda_t = 0$ implies the tth constraint is redundant and has no informational value and, as such, does not reduce the maximum entropy level or the level of uncertainty.

In the dual approach, we view the λ's as the unknown parameters to be determined for the ME distribution of probabilities, where the unknown p_k's are determined directly from the λ's. Further, the dual unconstrained functions $M(\lambda)$ is, given the data, just the potential function of the system analyzed. For a discussion within an economic framework, see Golan (1994). In many economic-statistical models these λ's are the parameters of interest. For example, in the multinomial choice problem developed in Chapter 15, interest centers on the unknown λ's for the ME distribution. Alternatively, in Chapter 4 when estimating the size distribution of firms the Lagrange parameters are used to determine the scale properties of the industry. A discussion and interpretation of the Lagrange multipliers, for different economic-statistical models, is given throughout the monograph.

3.2.5 NORMALIZED ENTROPY

To measure the information content in a system, and to measure the importance of the contribution of each piece of data or constraint ($t = 1, 2, \ldots, T$) in reducing uncertainty, we define the normalized-entropy measure (Golan, 1988, 1994; Soofi, 1992, 1994). In the ME formulation, the maximum level of entropy-uncertainty results when the information-moment constraints (3.2.5) are not enforced and the distribution of probabilities over the K states is uniform. As we add each piece of effective data, a departure from the uniform distribution results and implies a reduction of uncertainty. The proportion of the remaining total uncertainty is measured by the normalized entropy

$$S(\hat{\mathbf{p}}) = \left(-\sum_k \hat{p}_k \ln \hat{p}_k \right) \Big/ \ln(K) \tag{3.2.23}$$

where $S(\hat{\mathbf{p}}) \in [0, 1]$ and where $\ln(K)$ represents maximum uncertainty (the entropy level of the uniform distribution with K outcomes). A value $S(\hat{\mathbf{p}}) = \mathbf{0}$ implies no uncertainty (i.e. $p_k = 1$ for some k and $p_j = 0$ for all $j \neq k$). Alternatively, an $S(\hat{\mathbf{p}}) = 1$ implies perfect uncertainty (i.e. $p_k = 1/K$ for all $k = 1, 2, \ldots, K$). An analog measure $1 - S(\hat{\mathbf{p}})$, called the *information index*, serves to measure the reduction in uncertainty (Soofi, 1992).

Because $S(\hat{\mathbf{p}})$ is a relative measure of uncertainty, it can be used to compare different cases or scenarios. For example, we can add, or delete, a data point (or constraint) and compare $S(T)$ with $S(T-1)$. If $S(T) = S(T-1)$, we conclude that there is no additional information embodied in the data-constraint. However, if $S(T) < S(T-1)$, this additional piece of information gives us a better, more informed, set of recovered probabilities and reduces the uncertainty about the unknown, recovered parameters. More formally, let $\hat{\mathbf{p}}_0(\mathbf{x})$ be the ME distribution for the T constraints, and $\hat{\mathbf{p}}_1(\mathbf{x})$ be the ME distribution for the $T-1$ constraints. Levine (1980) shows that

$$0 \leqq \sum_k \hat{p}_{0k} \ln(\hat{p}_{0k}/\hat{p}_{1k}) = H(\hat{\mathbf{p}}_1) - H(\hat{\mathbf{p}}_0) \tag{3.2.24}$$

where he uses both Gibb's inequality and the argument that, by the definition of the problem, $\hat{\mathbf{p}}_0$ is consistent with all the first $T-1$ constraints used to characterize $\hat{\mathbf{p}}_1$. The equality part of (3.2.24) holds if and only if $\hat{\mathbf{p}}_0 = \hat{\mathbf{p}}_1$. Thus, if more constraints are added, the ME distribution remains unchanged or the distribution is changed in such a direction that the value of its entropy *decreases*. Finally, (3.2.24) implies that $S(\hat{\mathbf{p}}_1) \geqq S(\hat{\mathbf{p}}_0)$.

Building on this information measure we develop similar measures for each specific problem throughout the monograph. However, it should be remembered that, within the classical ME principle discussed in this chapter, each data point (constraint) reflects the first moments of an additional variable such as an input, output or income. As such, this is somewhat different than in the more traditional way of describing a data set where each data point corresponds to an observation as a function of all the variables of the system. Given the above example and the current interpretation, adding a constraint is like adding a covariate in the more traditional set-up. When generalizing the model (Chapters 5–16), we generalize the above information measures accordingly.

3.2.6 THE MAXIMUM NORMALIZED ENTROPY: MINIMUM VARIANCE RELATION

Having developed the normalized entropy measure as well as the variance–covariance matrix for $\boldsymbol{\lambda}$, we now show that, for a given data set $\mathbf{y}$ and X, there exists a unique relationship between $S(\hat{\mathbf{p}})$ and $I(\hat{\boldsymbol{\lambda}})$. In particular, we will show that max $S(\hat{\mathbf{p}})$ implies $\min\{\sum_t \mathrm{Var}(\hat{\lambda}_t)\}$, where $\mathrm{Var}(\boldsymbol{\lambda}) = I^{-1}(\boldsymbol{\lambda})$ by Conventional Approximation.

The logic for this statement is

- $S(\hat{\mathbf{p}})$ is a continuous function on $[0, 1]$ with $S(\hat{\mathbf{p}}) = \mathbf{0}$ for the degenerate case of $p_k = 1$, for some k and $p_j = 0$ for all $j \neq k$, and $S(\hat{\mathbf{p}}) = 1$ for the uniform ($p_k = 1/K$ for all $k = 1, 2, \ldots, K$) distribution of probabilities.
- The sum of the diagonal elements of $I(\boldsymbol{\lambda})$, (3.2.22), is also a continuous function on $[0, \max\{\sum_t I(\lambda_t)\}]$ with zero for the degenerate case of $p_k = 1$, for some k, and $p_j = 0$ for all $j \neq k$. The max$(\cdot)$ is associated with the uniform probability distribution ($p_k = 1/K$ for all $k = 1, 2, \ldots, K$).
- As both functions are continuous in $\mathbf{p}$, it follows that max $S(\hat{\mathbf{p}})$ is associated with the $\max\{\sum_t \mathrm{I}(\lambda_t)\}$, which is just $\min\{\sum_t \mathrm{Var}(\hat{\lambda}_t)\}$. In other words,

maximizing the entropy (or the normalized entropy measure) subject to the data is equivalent to maximizing the variance of the unknown distribution of probabilities, which is just minimizing the variances of the unknown λ_t's while forcing the constraints (data) to hold. This proposition is generalized in Chapters 7 and 15 to accommodate the different statistical models analyzed.

3.3 THE CROSS-ENTROPY (CE) FORMALISM

In addition to the data, now suppose some form of conceptual knowledge exists and relates to the properties of the system. As in Section 2.2.1, suppose this information can be expressed in the form of a probability vector $\mathbf{q}$. In constrast to the ME pure inverse problem framework, the objective may be reformulated to minimize the entropy distance between the data in the form of $\mathbf{p}$ and the prior $\mathbf{q}$. That is, the underlying principle is that of probabilistic distance or divergence. Following Good (1963), one minimizes the cross-entropy (Gokhale and Kullback, 1978; Levine, 1980; Shore and Johnson, 1980; Csiszár, 1991) between the probabilities that are consistent with the information in the data and the prior information $\mathbf{q}$. The object is to find, out of all the distributions of probabilities satisfying the constraints, the one closest to $\mathbf{q}$. When a non-informative (uniform) distribution is used for $\mathbf{q}$, the ME solution results.

Making use of the ME metric and following the development in Chapter 2, this means

$$\min_{\mathrm{p}} I(p, q) = \sum_{k=1}^{K} p_k \ln(p_k/q_k) = \sum_{k=1}^{K} p_k \ln p_k - \sum_{k=1}^{K} p_k \ln q_k \qquad (3.3.1)$$

subject to (3.2.5) and (3.2.6). As before, the probability vector $\mathbf{p}$ may be recovered by forming the Lagrangian function

$$L = \sum_{k=1}^{K} p_k \ln(p_k/q_k) + \sum_{t=1}^{T} \lambda_t\left[y_t - \sum_{k=1}^{K} p_k f_t(x_k)\right] + \mu\left(1 - \sum_{k=1}^{K} p_k\right) \qquad (3.3.2)$$

with the optimal conditions $\partial L/\partial(\cdot) = 0$. Solving this system of $T + K + 1$ equations and parameters yields $\tilde{\mathbf{p}}$, $\tilde{\boldsymbol{\lambda}}$ and $\tilde{\mu}$. The formal solution, within the traditional ME framework, that combines the information from the data and the prior is

$$\tilde{p}_k = \frac{q_k}{\Omega(\tilde{\lambda}_1, \tilde{\lambda}_2, \ldots, \tilde{\lambda}_T)} \exp\left[\sum_{t=1}^{T} \tilde{\lambda}_t f_t(x_k)\right], \qquad k = 1, 2, \ldots, K \qquad (3.3.3)$$

where

$$\Omega(\tilde{\boldsymbol{\lambda}}) = \sum_{k=1}^{K} q_k \exp\left[\sum_{t=1}^{T} \tilde{\lambda}_t f_t(x_k)\right] \qquad (3.3.4)$$

is the partition function. Finally, as in Section 3.2, we note that the cross-entropy $I(\mathbf{p}, \mathbf{q})$ is a function of the information contained in both the data and the prior. In Appendix 3.B, the similarities of the CE and Bayes approaches to learning from a sample of data are discussed.

Finally, the normalized entropy $S(\hat{\mathbf{p}})$, developed for the uniform prior (ME case), is generalized to

$$S(\tilde{\mathbf{p}}) = \left(-\sum_k \tilde{\mathbf{p}}_k \ln \tilde{\mathbf{p}}_k\right) \Big/ \left(-\sum_k q_k \ln q_k\right) \tag{3.3.5}$$

for $\mathbf{q} \ll 0$. For uniform q_k (3.3.5) is equivalent to (3.2.23).

3.3.1 THE UNCONSTRAINED CE DUAL

Similar to the unconstrained dual ME objective developed in (3.2.16), the dual CE objective is

$$\begin{aligned} L(\boldsymbol{\lambda}) &= \sum_k p_k \ln(p_k/q_k) + \sum_t \lambda_t \left[y_t - \sum_k p_k x_{tk} \right] \\ &= \sum_k p_k(\boldsymbol{\lambda}) \left[\sum_t \lambda_t x_{tk} - \ln(\Omega(\boldsymbol{\lambda})) \right] + \sum_t \lambda_t \left[y_t - \sum_k p_k x_{tk} \right] \\ &= \sum_t \lambda_t y_t - \ln(\Omega(\boldsymbol{\lambda})) \equiv M(\boldsymbol{\lambda}) \end{aligned} \tag{3.3.6}$$

where, again, the adding up constraints are taken into account in $\mathbf{p}(\boldsymbol{\lambda})$, and the gradient of $M(\boldsymbol{\lambda})$ with respect to $\boldsymbol{\lambda}$ is just the moment-consistency relations. The q_k priors are taken into account in the normalization factor Ω as derived in (3.3.4).

Proceeding as in Sections (3.2.2)–(3.2.3), the maximization of the dual CE problem yields a negative definite Hessian, which assures a unique global solution for the $\hat{\boldsymbol{\lambda}}_t$'s. The variance–covariance matrix is similar to the one developed in (3.2.20)–(3.2.21) where the recovered CE probabilities, $\tilde{\mathbf{p}}$, substitute for the ME probabilities, $\hat{\mathbf{p}}$.

3.3.2 CE AS A SHRINKAGE RULE

Using an approximation for the CE objective (3.3.1) we show that, like the Stein family of estimators, the CE formulation results in a form of a shrinkage estimator. The following approximation is an extension of the work of Denzau *et al.* (1989).

Proposition 3.3.1

$$I(\mathbf{p}, \mathbf{q}) = \sum_k p_k \ln(p_k/q_k) \approx \sum_k \frac{1}{q_k}(p_k - q_k)^2 \qquad \text{for } q_k > 0 \qquad (3.3.7)$$

Proof.

(i) Since $\ln(1 + x) = x - \frac{1}{2}x^2 + \frac{1}{3}x^3 - \frac{1}{4}x^4 + \ldots \forall x \in (-1, 1]$, then $\ln(y) = (y - 1) - \frac{1}{2}(y - 1)^2 + \frac{1}{3}(y - 1)^3 - R$ where $R = \frac{1}{4}(y - 1)^4 + \ldots \forall y \in (0, 2]$ is the remainder. In general $\ln(x) \approx (x - 1) - \frac{1}{2}(x - 1)^2 + \ldots$.

(ii) If $p_k \approx q_k$, then $\ln(p_k/q_k) \approx (p_k/q_k) - 1$. Thus,

$$\sum_k p_k \ln\left(\frac{p_k}{q_k}\right) \approx \sum_k p_k\left(\frac{p_k}{q_k} - 1\right) = \sum_k \left(\frac{p_k^2}{q_k} - p_k\right) = \sum_k \frac{1}{q_k}(p_k^2 - p_k q_k) \qquad (3.3.8)$$

Since $\sum_k q_k = \sum_k p_k = 1$ we rewrite (3.3.8) as

$$\begin{aligned}
\sum_k \frac{1}{q_k}(p_k^2 - p_k q_k) + 1 - 1 &= \sum_k \frac{1}{q_k}(p_k^2 - p_k q_k) + \sum_k q_k - \sum_k p_k \\
&= \sum_k \frac{1}{q_k}(p_k^2 - p_k q_k) + \sum_k \frac{1}{q_k}(q_k)^2 - \sum_k \frac{1}{q_k}(p_k q_k) \\
&= \sum_k \frac{1}{q_k}(p_k^2 - 2p_k q_k + q_k^2) \\
&= \sum_k \frac{1}{q_k}(p_k - q_k)^2 \qquad (3.3.9)
\end{aligned}$$

□

Thus, like the new Stein estimator (Stein, 1981), we effectively shrink small frequencies more than large frequencies under the CE criterion. That is, the smaller the prior q_k, the larger the weight associated with that element in the objective function (3.3.7). As a result, the corresponding p_k is shrunk 'faster' toward zero. Note that as $p_k \to q_k$, $R \to 0$.

Applying the same approximation to the ME objective (3.2.4), where $q_k = 1/K$ for all $k = 1, 2, \ldots, K$, yields

$$\begin{aligned}
\sum_k p_k \ln\left(\frac{p_k}{q_k}\right) &= \sum_k p_k \ln(K p_k) = \sum_k p_k \ln p_k + \ln(K) \\
&\approx \sum_k \mathrm{K}\left(p_k - \frac{1}{K}\right)^2 \qquad (3.3.10)
\end{aligned}$$

Again, for $p_k = 1/K$, $R = 0$.

3.4 THE ME–CE DISTRIBUTION

The ME distribution of probabilities, resulting from the optimization framework discussed in Sections 3.2 and 3.3, may be related to a broad family of probability distributions with mass functions

$$p_{\lambda}(\mathbf{x}, q) = \frac{q(\mathbf{x})\exp(\mathbf{x}_t, \boldsymbol{\lambda})}{\Omega(\boldsymbol{\lambda})} \tag{3.4.1}$$

where $p_{\lambda}(\mathbf{x}, q)$ is a generalized version of the Maxwell–Boltzman distribution (Rao, 1973; p. 173), which is a member of the canonical exponential family

$$p(\mathbf{x}, \boldsymbol{\theta}) = h(\mathbf{x})\cdot\exp[\boldsymbol{\theta}E(\mathbf{x}) - c(\boldsymbol{\theta})] \tag{3.4.2}$$

where $h(\mathbf{x}) = q(\mathbf{x})$, $\boldsymbol{\theta} = \boldsymbol{\lambda}$, $t(\mathbf{x}) = \mathbf{x}$ and $c(\boldsymbol{\theta}) = \log[\Omega(\boldsymbol{\lambda})]$. The natural parameter space is $\Lambda = \mathbb{R}^T$, and the canonical family is full rank if none of the constraints are trivial. For a discussion of the general exponential family of distributions including the normal, multinomial and Poisson distributions among others, see Brown (1986).

The ME distribution $p_{\lambda}(\mathbf{x}, q)$, is a particular member of the Maxwell–Boltzman family, and the properties of the canonical exponential family may be used to calculate the ME solution. In particular, the information matrix of $p_{\lambda}(\mathbf{x}, q)$ is

$$I(\hat{\boldsymbol{\lambda}}) = -\mathrm{E}_{\lambda}[p''_{\hat{\lambda}}(\mathbf{x}, q)] = \mathrm{Var}_{\hat{\lambda}}(\mathbf{x}_t) \tag{3.4.3}$$

which is strictly positive for an interior solution. Given that the moments of $p_{\hat{\lambda}}(\mathbf{x}, q)$ match the observed moments up to order t, the moment generating function

$$K(\mathbf{s}) = \exp[c(\boldsymbol{\theta} + \mathbf{s}) - c(\boldsymbol{\theta})] = \frac{\Omega(\hat{\boldsymbol{\lambda}} + \mathbf{s})}{\Omega(\hat{\boldsymbol{\lambda}})} \tag{3.4.4}$$

given by Bickel and Docksum (1977, Theorem 2.3.2) may be viewed as the *empirical* moment generating function.

3.4.1 DISCRETE RANDOM VARIABLES

For a discrete random variable $x = 0, 1, \ldots, \infty$, the ME distribution with mean y is derived by maximizing

$$H(\mathbf{p}) = \sum_{x=0}^{\infty} p(x) \ln p(x) \tag{3.4.5}$$

subject to

$$\sum_{x=0}^{\infty} xp(x) = y \tag{3.4.6}$$

$$\sum_{x=0}^{\infty} p(x) = 1 \tag{3.4.7}$$

If $\hat{\lambda} > 0$, Berger (1985, p. 92) notes that the solution to this problem is the geometric distribution

$$p(x) = [1 - \exp(-\hat{\lambda})]\exp(-\hat{\lambda}x) \tag{3.4.8}$$

with parameter $\theta = 1 - \exp(-\hat{\lambda})$. As with the Maxwell–Boltzmann distribution, any admissible value of lambda provides a member of the geometric family. The ME distribution is a special case in which $\lambda = \ln(y + 1)$.

Golan (1988, 1994) provides an interesting extension of the result to cases in which the support of the random variable is $x = 0, \varepsilon, 2\varepsilon, \ldots, \infty$ for some $\varepsilon > 0$ and the constraints are linear. In this case the ME distribution may be written as

$$p(x) = (1 - Q)Q^x \tag{3.4.9}$$

where $Q = \exp(-\lambda\varepsilon)$. The mean of the distribution is

$$\begin{aligned} b(\varepsilon) &= \sum_{x=0}^{\infty} xQ^x(1-Q) = (1-Q)Q\sum_{x=1}^{\infty} xQ^{x-1} \\ &= (1-Q)Q\frac{d}{dQ}(1-Q)^{-1} = (1-Q)Q(1-Q)^{-2} = \frac{Q}{1-Q} = \frac{1}{Q^{-1}-1} \end{aligned} \tag{3.4.10}$$

By substitution

$$b(\varepsilon) = \frac{1}{\exp(\lambda\varepsilon) - 1} \tag{3.4.11}$$

which is the Bose–Einstein distribution used in the physics literature. In general, $p(x)$ is the distribution of particles across energy states, and $b(\varepsilon)$ is the probability that a state of energy ε is occupied. For an economic interpretation and additional details, refer to the discussion in Golan (1988, 1994).

In the more common case where K is finite, we rewrite the normalization factor as

$$\Omega(\boldsymbol{\lambda}) = \sum_{k=0}^{K} \exp\left(-\sum_t \lambda_t x_{tk}\right) - 1 \tag{3.4.12}$$

where 1 represents the case of $k = 0$.

If we let $Q_k \equiv \exp(-\sum_t \lambda_t x_{tk})$ and $Q = \prod_k Q_k$ we get

$$\begin{aligned} \Omega(\boldsymbol{\lambda}) &= -1 + \sum_{k=1}^{K} Q^k = -1 + \frac{1 - Q^{K+1}}{1-Q} = \frac{Q - Q^{K+1}}{1-Q} \\ &= \frac{1 - Q^K}{Q^{-1} - 1} = \frac{1 - \exp\left(-K\sum_t \lambda_t x_{tk}\right)}{\exp\left(-\sum_t \lambda_t x_{tk}\right) - 1}, \qquad \text{for } |Q_k| < 1 \end{aligned} \tag{3.4.13}$$

Substituting back into p_k yields

$$p_k = \frac{1}{\left[1 - \exp\left(-K \sum_t \lambda_t x_{tk}\right)\right]\left[\exp\left(\sum_t \lambda_t x_t\right) - 1\right]^{-1}\left[\exp\left(\sum_t \lambda_t x_{tk}\right)\right]} \tag{3.4.14}$$

which is an extension of the Bose–Einstein distribution for linear constraints.

Next we discuss the characteristics of the ME distributions for a range of problems.

3.4.3 CONTINUOUS RANDOM VARIABLE

In line with Appendix 3.A, in a continuous probability density case, the entropy is defined as

$$H = -\int f(x) \ln f(x) \, dx \tag{3.4.15}$$

If we just make use of the normalization $\int f(x)\,dx = 1$, and no other restrictions are imposed, then the Lagrangian function is

$$\begin{aligned} L &= -\int f(x) \ln f(x) + \mu\left(1 - \int f(x)\,dx\right) \\ &= \mu + \int [-f(x)\ln f(x) - \mu f(x)]\,dx \end{aligned} \tag{3.4.16}$$

By using the calculus of variations, the optimal condition is the Euler equation

$$-d[f(x)\ln f(x) + \mu f(x)]/dx = 0 \tag{3.4.17}$$

or

$$(\ln \hat{f}(x) + 1 + \hat{\mu})\hat{f}(x) = 0 \tag{3.4.18}$$

and

$$\hat{f}(x) = \exp(-1 - \hat{\mu}) \tag{3.4.19}$$

Since this function is independent of x, it can take on values over the real line and $f(x)$ is an improper (diffuse) density if the restraint is ignored. However, bounding the parameter space through a constraint is one way to obtain a proper solution. Consequently, if the variable x is confined to a certain range between a and b, then $f(x) = 1/(b - a)$ is uniformly distributed with mean $(a + b)/2$ and variance $(b - a)^2/12$ where $\mu = \ln(b - a) - 1$, and the entropy value is $-\ln(b - a)$.

Alternatively, if the variable x is non-negative, from zero to infinity, and the expectation of the distribution is known to be

$$\int xf(x)\,\mathrm{d}x = a \tag{3.4.20}$$

then the Lagrangian function becomes

$$L = -\int f(x)\ln f(x)\,\mathrm{d}x + \mu\left(1 - \int f(x)\,\mathrm{d}x\right) + \lambda\left(a - \int xf(x)\,\mathrm{d}x\right) \tag{3.4.21}$$

$$= \lambda a + \mu - \int [f(x)\ln f(x) + \mu f(x) + \lambda xf(x)]\,\mathrm{d}x \tag{3.4.22}$$

where the domain of integration is from zero to infinity. Again, using the calculus of variations, the optimal condition is the Euler equation

$$-\mathrm{d}[f(x)\ln f(x) + \mu f(x) + \lambda xf(x)]/\mathrm{d}x = 0 \tag{3.4.23}$$

or

$$-(\ln \hat{f}(x) + 1 + \hat{\mu} + \hat{\lambda}x) = 0 \tag{3.4.24}$$

Solving the above equation together with the restraints for $f(x)$, we obtain

$$\hat{f}(x) = (1/a)\exp(-x/a) \tag{3.4.25}$$

which is an exponential distribution with mean a and variance a^2 and relates back to (3.4.1) and (3.4.2). The density has an entropy value of $1 + \ln(a)$.

If restrictions such as mean zero and variance σ^2 are imposed, then

$$\int xf(x)\,\mathrm{d}x = 0 \tag{3.4.26}$$

$$\int x^2 f(x)\,\mathrm{d}x = \sigma^2 \tag{3.4.27}$$

and the Lagrangian function is

$$\begin{aligned} L = &-\int f(x)\ln f(x)\,\mathrm{d}x + \mu\left(1 - \int f(x)\,\mathrm{d}x\right) \\ &+ \lambda_1\left(0 - \int xf(x)\,\mathrm{d}x\right) + \lambda_2\left(\sigma^2 - \int x^2 f(x)\,\mathrm{d}x\right) \\ = &\ \mu + \int [-f(x)\ln f(x) - \mu f(x) - \lambda_1 xf(x) - \lambda_2 x^2 f(x)]\,\mathrm{d}x \end{aligned} \tag{3.4.28}$$

Again, using the calculus of variations, the optimal condition is the Euler equation

$$-\ln \hat{f}(x) - 1 - \hat{\mu} - \hat{\lambda}_2 x - \hat{\lambda}_2 x^2 = 0 \qquad (3.4.29)$$

and the solution is

$$\hat{f}(x) = \exp(-1 - \hat{\mu} - \hat{\lambda}_1 x - \hat{\lambda}_2 x^2) + (1/2\pi\sigma^2)^{1/2} \exp(-x^2/(2\sigma^2)) \qquad (3.4.30)$$

where

$$\hat{\mu} = (1/2)\ln(2\pi\sigma^2) - 1, \qquad \hat{\lambda}_1 = 0, \hat{\lambda}_2 = 1/2\sigma^2 \qquad (3.4.31)$$

and x is a normally distributed density with mean zero and variance σ^2.

In this case, the maximum entropy value is

$$H(\hat{\mathbf{p}}) = -\int f(x)\ln f(x)\,\mathrm{d}x = \int f(x)[(1/2)\ln(2\pi\sigma^2) + x^2/(2\sigma^2)]\,\mathrm{d}x$$
$$= (1/2)\ln(2\pi\sigma^2) + (1/2) = (1/2)\ln(2\pi e\sigma^2) \qquad (3.4.32)$$

3.4.3 HIGHER MOMENT RESTRICTIONS

As a generalization of these results, Zellner and Highfield (1988) extended the formulation in Section 3.4.2 to higher moments and investigated the following ME problem:

$$\max_f H = -\int f(x)\ln f(x)\,\mathrm{d}x \qquad (3.4.33)$$

subject to

$$\int x^t f(x) = \mu_t, \qquad \text{for } t = 0, 1, \ldots, T \qquad (3.4.34)$$

when μ_t is known. Again, using the Lagrangian method produces the following maximum entropy solution:

$$\hat{f}(x) = \exp\left(\sum_n c_n x^n\right) \qquad (3.4.35)$$

with a distribution satisfying $\int x^t f(x)\,\mathrm{d}x = \mu_t$, for $t = 0, 1, \ldots, T$ where c_n's are unknown values. By changing the constraints, Zellner and Highfield (1988) derive a general class of densities.

3.5 ENTROPY OF ORDER α

For completeness we note that Schützenberger (1954) and Rényi (1961) have introduced a generalized concept of entropy. For a discrete random variable

$\mathbf{x}$ with probability distribution $\mathbf{p}$, the entropy of order α is

$$H(\mathbf{p}; \alpha) = \frac{1}{1-\alpha} \ln \sum_k p_k^\alpha \tag{3.5.1}$$

for any real value α. At the limit of $\alpha \to 1$, (3.5.1) reduces to the Shannon's entropy

$$H(p; \alpha = 1) = -\sum_k p_k \ln p_k.$$

The α-entropy is used for analysis of time series data and is related to the correlation function and information dimensions which are used to distinguish chaotic data from 'random' data. See, for example, Pompe (1994). In this monograph we only make use of the $\alpha = 1$ entropy measure.

3.6 REMARKS

The focus of this chapter has been on developing an analytical basis and corresponding empirical solution for basic ill-posed, pure inverse problems in economics. In particular we note that:

- The maximum entropy formalism is traditionally used, in the case of ill-posed, underdetermined pure inverse problems, to recover probability distributions that are consistent with the data and adding up constraints.
- The adding up constraints act as a consistency check on the entropy measure, and under the general entropy formulations, provide a basis for evaluating the informational content of each additional constraint.
- The entropy and cross-entropy procedures are, like Bayes' rule, efficient information processing rules.
- There are significant similarities between the entropy solutions and the posterior resulting from Bayes' rule.
- In the cross-entropy formulations the discrete prior probability densities appear in the objective function and not in the constraints.
- The ME approach is based on information theory and, as such, yields an information measure we have defined as the normalized entropy.
- There is a unique relationship between the variances and the normalized entropy measure.
- The ME solution may be related to a broad family of probability distributions.
- The ME approach permits many traditional problems to be expressed in more natural form or offers a solution or new solutions to previously infeasible problems.

- A dual-unconstained ME formulation is presented that leads to an information matrix and a corresponding variance–covariance matrix.

In general, the ME and CE procedures provide a basis for recovering information and making inferences in the case of ill-posed inverse problems where only limited (aggregated), non-experimental economic data are available. Efficient algorithms, which make use of the dual-unconstrained formulation, exist (see Chapter 17) for solving the resulting non-linear optimization problems.

REFERENCES

Agmon, N., Alhassid, Y. and Levine, R. D. (1979) An algorithm for finding the distribution of maximal entropy. *Journal of Computational Physics* **30,** 250–59.

Alhassid, Y., Agmon, N. and Levine, R. D. (1978) An upper bound for the entropy and its applications to the maximal entropy problem. *Chemical Physics Letters* **53,** 22–6.

Berger, J. O. (1985) *Statistical Decision Theory and Bayesian Analysis*, 2nd edn. Springer-Verlag, New York.

Bickel, P. J. and Docksum, K. A. (1977) *Mathematical Statistics.* Holden-Day, Oakland, CA.

Brown, L. D. (1986) *Fundamentals of Statistical Exponential Families.* Institute of Mathematical Statistics, Hayward, CA.

Csiszár, I. (1991) Why least squares and maximum entropy? An axiomatic approach to inference for linear inverse problems. *Annals of Statistics* **19,** 2032–66.

Denzau, A. T., Gibbons, P. C. and Greenberg, E. (1989) Bayesian estimation of proportions with a cross-entropy prior. *Communications in Statistics–Theory And Methods* **18,** 1843–61.

Gokhale, D. V. and Kullback, S. (1978) *The Information in Contingency Tables.* Marcel Dekker, New York.

Golan, A. (1988) *A Discrete Stochastic Model of Economic Production and a Model of Fluctuations in Production – Theory and Empirical Evidence.* Ph.D. Thesis, University of California, Berkeley.

Golan, A. (1994) A multi-variable stochastic theory of size distribution of firms with empirical evidence. *Advances in Econometrics* **10,** 1–46.

Golan, A., Judge, G. and Perloff, J. (1996) Recovering information from multinomial response data. *Journal of the American Statistical Association* **91**.

Good, I. J. (1963) Maximum entropy for hypothesis formulation, especially for multidimensional contingency tables. *Annals of Mathematical Statistics* **34,** 911–34.

Huber, P. (1981) *Robust Statistics* John Wiley, New York.

Jaynes, E. T. (1957a) Information theory and statistical mechanics. *Physics Review* **106,** 620–30.

Jaynes, E. T. (1957b) Information theory and statistical mechanics II. *Physics Review* **108,** 171–90.

Kapur, J. N. and Kesavan, H. K. (1993) *Entropy Optimization Principles with Applications* Academic Press, New York.

Lee, T. C. and Judge, G. G. (1996) Entropy and cross entropy procedures for estimating transition probabilities from aggregate data. In: Bayesian Conference in Statistics and Econometrics: Essays in Honor of Arnold Zellner. John Wiley, New York.

Lehmann, E. (1983) *Theory of Point Estimation.* John Wiley, New York.

Levine, R. D. (1980) An information theoretical approach to inversion problems. *Journal of Physics A* **13,** 91–108.

Miller, D. J. (1994) *Entropy and Information Recovery in Linear Economic Models.* Ph.D. Thesis, University of California, Berkeley.

Pompe, B. (1994) On some entropy methods in data analysis. *Chaos, Solitons and Fractals* **4,** 83–96.

Rao, C. R. (1973) Linear Statistical Inference and its Application, Wiley, N.Y.

Rényi, A. (1961) On measures of entropy and information. *Proceedings of Fourth Berkeley Symposium on Mathematics, Statistics and Probability, 1960,* Vol. I, p. 547.

Schützenberger, M. P. (1954) *Contribution aux applications statistiques de la théorie de l'information.* Publication of the Institute of Statistics, University of Paris.

Shannon, C. E. (1948) A mathematical theory of communication. *Bell System Technical Journal* **27,** 379–423.

Shore, J. E. and Johnson, R. W. (1980) Axiomatic derivation of the principle of maximum entropy and the principle of minimum cross-entropy. *IEEE Transactions on Information Theory* **26,** 26–37.

Soofi, E. S. (1992) A generalizable formulation of conditional logit with diagnostics. *Journal of the American Statistical Association* **87,** 812–16.

Soofi, E. S. (1994) Capturing the intangible concept of information. *Journal of the American Statistical Association* **89,** 1243–54.

Stein, C. (1981) Estimation of the mean of a multivariate normal distribution. *Annals of Statistics* **9,** 1135–51.

Zellner, A. (1988) Optimal information processing and Bayes theorem. *American Statistician* **42,** 278–84.

Zellner, A. (1990) Bayesian methods and entropy in economics and econometrics. In W. T. Grandy and L. H. Shick (Eds.), *Maximum Entropy and Bayesian Methods,* pp. 17–31. Kluwer, Dordrecht.

Zellner, A. and Highfield, R. A. (1988) Calculation of maximum entropy distributions and approximation of marginal posterior distributions. *Journal of Econometrics* **37,** 195–209.

APPENDIX

A. THE CONTINUOUS CE CASE

If we take a countable infinite set of discrete values, let $K \to \infty$, replace $\sum_{k=1}^{K}$ by integrals, and define $p(x)$ and $q(x)$ as continuous probability distributions, we may formulate the cross-entropy problem as:

minimize

$$\int p(x)\ln(p(x)/q(x))\,\mathrm{d}x = \int p(x)\ln p(x)\,\mathrm{d}x - \int p(x)\ln q(x)\,\mathrm{d}x \qquad (3.A.1)$$

subject to

$$\int p(x)f_t(x)\;\mathrm{d}x = y_t, \qquad t = 1, 2, \ldots, T \qquad (3.A.2)$$

$$\int p(x)\,\mathrm{d}x = 1 \qquad (3.A.3)$$

Using the calculus of variations, the Lagrange equation may be expressed as

$$\begin{aligned} L(\varepsilon) = & \int [p(x) + \varepsilon\gamma(p(x))]\mathrm{l_n}[p(x) + \varepsilon\gamma(p(x))]\,\mathrm{d}x \\ & - \int [p(x) + \varepsilon\gamma(p(x))]\mathrm{l_n}(q(x))\,\mathrm{d}x \\ & + \sum_{t=1}^{T} \lambda_t\left[y_t - \int [p(x) + \varepsilon\gamma(p(x))]f_t(x)\,\mathrm{d}x\right] \\ & + \mu\left[1 - \int [p(x) + \varepsilon\gamma(p(x))]\,\mathrm{d}x\right] \end{aligned} \qquad (3.A.4)$$

where ε is a small quantity and $\gamma p(x)$ is an arbitrary continuous function with a zero value at the endpoints (boundary) of integration and with a finite variance. Differentiating $L(\varepsilon)$ with respect to ε, evaluating the derivative at $\varepsilon = 0$ and carrying through the same steps as with the discrete case, the p.d.f. $p(x)$ becomes

$$\hat{p}(x) = \frac{1}{\Omega}\,q(x)\exp\left[\sum_{t=1}^{T} \hat{\lambda}_t f_t(x)\right] \qquad (3.A.5)$$

where the partition function for the continuous case is defined as

$$\Omega(\hat{\lambda}_1, \hat{\lambda}_2, \ldots, \hat{\lambda}_T) = \int q(x)\exp\left[\sum_{t=1}^{T} \hat{\lambda}_t f_t(x)\right]\mathrm{d}x \qquad (3.A.6)$$

The basic difference between the continuous and the discrete optimizations is in the partition function Ω. Also, within the ill-posed framework developed in this chapter, the number of constraints is always finite. As some have noted (Berger, 1985, p. 92 for example), there may be a problem in developing a natural definition of entropy in the continuous case.

B. EFFICIENT INFORMATION PROCESSING RULES

Using the informational measure embodied in the entropy formalism (Shannon, 1948; Jaynes, 1957a, b), it is possible to compare the information content of the data to that of the prior and to that of the posterior $\hat{p}(x)$. In terms of two p.d.f.'s, the one with a higher entropy level H is the one with the *lower* informational content and the p.d.f. closest to the uniform distribution. Under this interpretation of the entropy measure, and following Zellner (1988, 1990), an efficient processing rule of the information contained in the data and the prior has an information content of the outcome, say $\hat{p}(x)$, at least as large as that of the prior. Thus, if we minimize the distance between the information levels of the prior and the data, we search all consistent possibilities for the (posterior) p.d.f. that is consistent with the data and has an information level closest to the prior p.d.f.'s information level. Under this definition, the cross-entropy (or maximum entropy) rule discussed in Section 3.2 is an efficient information processing rule.

In all cases the cross-entropy measure, $I(\mathbf{p}, \mathbf{q})$, is *non-negative*. When $I(\mathbf{p}, \mathbf{q})$ is strictly non-negative, the information content of the posterior (post data) p.d.f. $\hat{p}(x)$ is *larger* than the information level embodied in the prior. When $I(\mathbf{p}, \mathbf{q}) = 0$ the prior and the data are fully consistent (no 'new information' is added by the data). Alternatively, since $I(\mathbf{p}, \mathbf{q})$ is always non-negative, the use of an uninformative prior (for example, a uniform prior) in the CE formulation, reduces to the ME result and thus implies the p.d.f. $\hat{p}(x)$ is based only on the data.

Since the CE method can be approached as a limiting form of Bayes' theorem, following Lee and Judge (1995), we use the CE formulation to note the close connection between the two efficient information processing rules. Following Zellner (1988) in Bayes' rule, given initial information I, there are two inputs and two outputs. The two inputs are $\pi(\theta|I)$, the prior density for the parameter θ, and the data density $f(y|\theta, I)$. The two outputs are the post data-posterior density $g(\theta|y, I)$ and $h(y|I)$ the marginal density for y. In terms of these pieces, Bayes' rule to transform prior and sample information into posterior information is

$$g(\theta|y, I) = \frac{\pi(\theta|I) f(y|\theta, I)}{h(y|I)} \tag{3.A.7}$$

Contrasting (3.A.7) and (3.A.5) or (3.3.3), we note in (3.A.5) or (3.3.3) that $\hat{p}(x)$

or $\hat{p}$ corresponds to the posterior $g(\theta|y, I)$, that $q(x)$ or q corresponds to the prior $\pi(\theta|I)$, $\exp[\sum_t \lambda_t f_t(x_t)]$ corresponds to the data density $f(y|\theta, I)$ and the normalization factor Ω corresponds to the marginal density $h(y|I)$, that serves to convert the relative probabilities into absolute ones. Furthermore, the ME formulation of Section 2 can be defined as a CE formulation with a uniform or uninformed prior. Thus, equation (3.2.11) is also consistent with Bayes' rule.

C. ALTERNATIVE DERIVATIONS OF THE VARIANCE–COVARIANCE MATRIX

In this appendix, in order to be consistent with the literature, we derive the variance–covariance matrix for the ME (or CE) distribution in two alternative ways.

The first derivation is directly related to the primal ME (or CE) formulation (3.2.4)–(3.2.6). Building on the Hessian (3.2.15) we proceed to construct the analog-information matrix by summing over $k = 1, 2, \ldots, K$ and rearranging the Hessian such that

$$I(\hat{\mathbf{p}}) = -\mathrm{E}(H(\hat{\mathbf{p}})) = \sum_{k=1}^{K} \frac{1}{\mathbf{p}_k} \mathbf{1}\mathbf{1}' \tag{3.A.8}$$

where $\mathbf{1}'$ is a K-dimensional unit vector, and $I(\hat{\mathbf{p}})$ is an analog-information matrix for the unknown p_k's. To convert the information matrix $I(\hat{\mathbf{p}})$ to the more traditional $\boldsymbol{\lambda}$ space, $I(\hat{\boldsymbol{\lambda}})$, we use Taylor series approximation, or a generalization of the following correspondence theorem from Lehmann (1983, p. 118):

$$\left(\frac{\partial \hat{\mathbf{p}}}{\partial \hat{\boldsymbol{\lambda}}}\right) I(\hat{\mathbf{p}}) \left(\frac{\partial \hat{\mathbf{p}}}{\partial \hat{\boldsymbol{\lambda}}}\right)' = I(\hat{\boldsymbol{\lambda}}) \tag{3.A.9}$$

to obtain the information matrix of the unknown $\hat{\lambda}_t$'s.

An element of the matrix (3.A.9) is

$$\begin{aligned}
\sum_k \frac{1}{\hat{p}_k}\left(\frac{\partial \hat{p}_k}{\partial \hat{\lambda}_t}\right)^2 &= \sum_k \frac{1}{\hat{p}_k}\left[\hat{p}_k x_{tk} - \hat{p}_k \sum_k \hat{p}_k x_{tk}\right]^2 \\
&= \sum_k \frac{1}{\hat{p}_k}\left[\hat{p}_k^2 x_{tk}^2 - 2\hat{p}_k^2 x_{tk} \sum_k \hat{p}_k x_{tk} + \hat{p}_k^2\left(\sum_k \hat{p}_k x_{tk}\right)^2\right] \\
&= \sum_k \hat{p}_k x_{tk}^2 - 2\left(\sum_k \hat{p}_k x_{tk}\right)^2 + \sum_k \hat{p}_k\left(\sum_k \hat{p}_k x_{tk}\right)^2 \\
&= \sum_k \hat{p}_k x_{tk}^2 - \left(\sum_k \hat{p}_k x_{tk}\right)^2 \equiv \mathrm{Var}(x_t) = I(\lambda_t)
\end{aligned} \tag{3.A.10}$$

Arranging (3.A.10) in matrix form yields the variance–covariance (3.2.22) for the random variables, which is the information matrix for the unknown λ_t's.

A different approach, discussed in detail in Kapur and Kesavan (1993), is to develop the variance–covariance matrix of the x's by investigating the convexity of $\Omega(\boldsymbol{\lambda})$ with respect to $\lambda_1, \lambda_2, \ldots, \lambda_T$. Rewriting (3.2.12) as

$$\exp(\lambda_0) \equiv \Omega(\boldsymbol{\lambda}) = \sum_{k=1}^{K} \left[-\sum_{t=1}^{T} \hat{\lambda}_t f_t(\mathbf{x}_i) \right] \tag{3.A.11}$$

and differentiating (3.A.11) twice with respect to λ_t yields

$$\frac{\partial^2 \lambda_0}{\partial^2 \lambda_t^2} = \mathrm{E}[f_t^2(X)] - \{\mathrm{E}[f_t(X)]\}^2 = \mathrm{Var}[f_t(X)] \tag{3.A.12}$$

Similarly, differentiating twice with respect to λ_t and λ_r, for some $r \neq t$, yields

$$\frac{\partial^2 \lambda_0}{\partial \lambda_t \partial \lambda_r} = \mathrm{E}[f_r(X) f_t(X)] - \mathrm{E}[f_t(X)]\mathrm{E}[f_t(X)] = \mathrm{Cov}[f_n(X), f_t(X)] \tag{3.A.13}$$

Arranging these results in a matrix form yields

$$H(\boldsymbol{\lambda}) = \begin{bmatrix} \dfrac{\partial^2 \lambda_0}{\partial \lambda_1^2} & & \cdots & \\ & \dfrac{\partial^2 \lambda_0}{\partial \lambda_2^2} & \cdots & \\ \vdots & \vdots & \ddots & \\ & & & \dfrac{\partial^2 \lambda_0}{\partial \lambda_T^2} \end{bmatrix}$$

$$= \begin{bmatrix} \mathrm{Var}(f_1(X)) & \mathrm{Cov}(f_1(X), f_2(X)) & \cdots & \mathrm{Cov}(f_1(X), f_T(X)) \\ & \mathrm{Var}(f_2(X)) & \cdots & \\ \vdots & \vdots & \ddots & \\ \mathrm{Cov}(f_1(X), f_T(X)) & & & \mathrm{Var}(f_T(X)) \end{bmatrix}$$

$$\equiv \mathrm{Var}[f(x)] \tag{3.A.14}$$

which, again, is similar to (3.2.22). Because this variance–covariance matrix is always positive definite, λ_0 is a convex function of $\lambda_1, \lambda_2, \ldots, \lambda_T$.

CHAPTER 4

Formulation and solution of pure inverse problems

In Chapter 3 we specified basic maximum entropy (ME) and cross-entropy (CE) formulations and solutions for pure inverse problems. In this chapter we build on the results of Chapter 3, and use three ill-posed economic problems involving aggregated data to demonstrate the applicability and inferential reach of the ME and CE formulations.

4.1 AN ILL-POSED SIZE DISTRIBUTION OF FIRMS PROBLEM

Assume, within an economic context, we have incomplete data that we wish to use to recover certain characteristics of a particular industry (Golan and Judge, 1995). Suppose our interest is focused on recovering the equilibrium size distribution industry of the p_k subgroups when only limited aggregate production data are available. In particular, assume our information includes only the following:

the total number of firms in the industry, N

the number of firms in each subgroup, N_k, $k = 1, 2, \ldots, K$

the average inputs for each subgroup of firms, $f_i(x_k)$, $k = 1, 2, \ldots, K$; $i = 1, 2, \ldots, T_1$

the average outputs for each subgroup of firms, $g_j(y_k)$, $k = 1, 2, \ldots, K$; $j = 1, 2, \ldots, T_2$

the average inputs over all subgroups F_i, $i = 1, 2, \ldots, T_1$

the average outputs over all subgroups G_j, $j = 1\ 2, \ldots, T_2$

From this limited and aggregated data, involving only one time period and minimal supporting assumptions, our objective is to recover information about the *equilibrium* characteristics of an industry. In particular we seek the multinomial size distribution of the industry, the long-run 'optimal' technological response coefficients and aggregate response coefficients, the long-run optimal number of firms that is consistent with the industry's equilibrium configuration, the optimal long-term input–output levels of the equilibrium configuration, and a concentration measure of the industry.

In this problem the moment-data constraints consist of specifying mean values of the $T = T_1 + T_2$ functions $\{g_1(y), g_2(y), \ldots, g_{T_2}(y), f_1(x), f_2(x), \ldots, f_{T_1}(x)\}$:

$$\sum_{k=1}^{K} p_k f_i(x_k) = F_i, \qquad 1 \le i \le T_1 \tag{4.1.1}$$

$$\sum_{k=1}^{K} p_k g_j(y_k) = G_j, \qquad 1 \le j \le T_2 \tag{4.1.2}$$

where $\{F_i\}$ and $\{G_j\}$ are numbers given in the statement of the problem (e.g. averages) and k is an index representing the number of size subgroups or types specified for the industry. This set of constraints involves T_1 input constraints and T_2 output constraints, where $(T_1 + T_2) < K$. If the industry is partitioned into K subgroups, then within the context of the ME formalism introduced in Section 3.2, we may state the problem as maximizing

$$H(\mathbf{p}) = -\sum_{k=1}^{K} p_k \ln p_k \tag{4.1.3}$$

subject to the moment constraints

$$\sum_{k=1}^{K} p_k f_i(x_k) = F_i, \qquad 1 \le i \le T_1 \tag{4.1.1$'$}$$

$$\sum_{k=1}^{K} p_k g_j(y_k) = G_j, \qquad 1 \le j \le T_2 \tag{4.1.2$'$}$$

and the adding-up constraint

$$\sum_{k=1}^{K} p_k = 1 \tag{4.1.4}$$

Following the optimization procedures of Section 3.2, this inverse problem has the formal solution:

$$\hat{p}_i = \frac{1}{\Omega(\hat{\alpha}_1, \ldots, \hat{\alpha}_{T_1}, \hat{\beta}_1, \ldots, \hat{\beta}_{T_2})} \exp\left[-\sum_i \hat{\alpha}_i f_i(x_k) - \sum_j \hat{\beta}_j g_j(y_k)\right] \tag{4.1.5}$$

where

$$\Omega(\hat{\boldsymbol{\alpha}}, \hat{\boldsymbol{\beta}}) = \sum_{k=1}^{K} \exp\left[-\sum_i \hat{\alpha}_i f_i(x_k) - \sum_j \hat{\beta}_j g_j(y_k)\right] \tag{4.1.6}$$

is the normalization factor, and $\{\alpha_i\}$ and $\{\beta_j\}$ are the Lagrange multipliers chosen to satisfy the constraints. The value of the entropy-maximum is a function of the given data:

$$S(F_1, \ldots, F_{T_1}, G_1, \ldots, G_{T_2}) = \log \Omega + \sum_i \hat{\alpha}_i F_i + \sum_j \hat{\beta}_j G_j \tag{4.1.7}$$

and (4.1.7) is just the dual unconstrained objective function for arbitrary $\boldsymbol{\alpha}$ and $\boldsymbol{\beta}$ that was discussed in Chapter 3. If this function is known, the explicit solution of (4.1.5) is $\hat{\alpha}_i = \partial S/\partial F_i$ for $1 \le i \le T_1$ and $\hat{\beta}_j = \partial S/\partial G_j$ for $1 \le j \le T_2$. Given the ME solution, one can predict $\hat{w}(x)$ by

$$\hat{w}(x) = \sum_{k=1}^{K} \hat{p}_k w(x_k) \tag{4.1.8}$$

As discussed previously, in the special case where the number of constraints $(T_1 + T_2)$ equals the number of states K, the ME method yields the unique solution commonly found by traditional inversion methods. Further, as the information $(T_1 + T_2)$ increases, the resulting ME distribution has lower entropy.

Based on the general properties of the ME size distribution, one can determine the global properties of the underlying production function of the industry (Golan, 1988, 1994; Golan and Judge, 1993b). Specifically, if the ME size distribution is concave (convex), the technology is concave (convex). If the technology has constant returns to scale, the ME size distribution is a monotone function of size (k). This result holds for both one-input, one-output industries, and for the multi-input ($i = 1, 2, \ldots, T_1$) and output ($j = 1, 2, \ldots, T_2$) industries (Golan and Zeitouni, 1993). Furthermore, the aggregate technological response coefficients may be calculated along with the long-term equilibrium levels of the different measures, such as number of firms, aggregate output and input levels. An efficient computational algorithm based on Agmon *et al.* (1979) and Miller (1994) and discussed in Chapter 17, ensures a unique global solution to this maximization problem.

4.1.1 EXAMPLE: A SINGLE INPUT–OUTPUT INDUSTRY

Given the industry problem posed in Section 4.1, consider a single input–output industry that is partitioned into 8 size (sub)groups. Artificial data reflecting the total inputs and outputs for each subgroup ($k = 1, 2, \ldots, 8$), the average total inputs $\bar{x}$ and outputs $\bar{y}$, and the number of firms in each subgroup are given in Table 4.1.1.

Within the context of Section 4.1, the problem may be formulated as

$$\max_{\mathbf{p}} H(\mathbf{p}) = -\mathbf{p}' \ln \mathbf{p} \tag{4.1.9}$$

Table 4.1.1 Input–output data for an industry

	Subgroup data									
	1	2	3	4	5	6	7	8	$\bar{x}$	$\bar{y}$
Average inputs x_k	8.16	18.78	35.44	70.30	156.57	352.2	667.23	1788.00	256.68	
Average outputs y_k	345.40	887.26	1869.79	4092.01	9130.58	20349.82	37992.10	90739.65		15777.00
Number of firms N_k	77	121	330	444	688	341	194	105	$(N = 2300)$	

subject to

$$\mathbf{p}'\mathbf{x} = \bar{x} \tag{4.1.10}$$

$$\mathbf{p}'\mathbf{y} = \bar{y} \tag{4.1.11}$$

$$p_i \geq 0 \tag{4.1.12}$$

where $\mathbf{p} = (p_1, p_2, \ldots, p_8)'$, $\mathbf{x} = [x_1/N_1, x_2/N_2, \ldots, x_8/N_8]$, $\mathbf{y} = [y_1/N_1, y_2/N_2, \ldots, y_8/N_8]$, $\bar{y} = (\sum_k y_k)/N$ and $\bar{x} = (\sum_k x_k)/N$. A solution to the problem (4.1.9)–(4.1.12), consistent with the natural logarithm of the data in Table 4.1.1, yields the probabilities (firm size distribution) presented in Table 4.1.2.

Under estimated industry equilibrium the optimal number of firms ($\hat{N}$) increased by 14%. Consistent with the optimal number of firms ($\hat{N}$), the optimal input level $\hat{\omega}(x)$ is 832 078, which is an increase of 41% and the optimal output level $\hat{\omega}(y)$ is 46 194 675, which is an increase of 27%. The equilibrium response coefficient $\hat{\omega}(x/y)$ is 0.5703. Thus, starting with limited information and the principle of maximum entropy, we have been able to obtain empirical hypotheses concerning probabilities and a range of other economic factors. Consistent with the framework developed in this section, the analysis can be extended to involve multiple inputs and outputs.

Finally, one can use the normalized entropy $S(\hat{p})$ to estimate the value of information. By adding or subtracting a single constraint and comparing normalized entropy to the base case one can observe the informational value of this constraint (see Chapters 3, 7, 10 and 15 for specific examples).

4.1.2 RECOVERING AN INDUSTRY'S DYNAMICS

Within the context of cross-entropy as discussed in Section 3.3, consider the case where more than a single period of data is available and one seeks to recover information about the dynamics of the process. Extending the industry example, suppose data for two periods are available. This increases (doubles) the constraints restricting the ME distribution, and estimates of the p_k represent the long-term stationary multivariable ME size distribution of the firms. If the industry is stationary, the estimates are based on the new p_k that are based on information from the two periods. However, in many cases the process governing the industry's dynamics is non-stationary and thus no feasible set of p_k satisfies all of the constraints. Consequently, we may not be able to solve the problem with two or more periods simultaneously within the context of our pure inverse problems. If the process is non-stationary, the question then becomes how to make use of all the data. One way is to incorporate the information for the first period in the form of a prior. For example, having estimated p_k for the initial period it may be used as the prior distribution, q_k, for the next period. The new distribution is derived from the

Table 4.1.2 Equilibrium Results

	Subgroup								
	1	2	3	4	5	6	7	8	$(\hat{N})$
Distribution of firms $\hat{p}_i$	0.022	0.040	0.075	0.133	0.165	0.191	0.210	0.165	–
$(\hat{N}_i)$	57	105	196	348	430	495	549	430	2614

second period data and the 'starting' point of the first period equilibrium vector of the $\hat{p}_k$.

Formally, building on equations (3.3.1) and (3.3.2), for any given prior distribution (taken from the previous period) $p_k^0(t-1) \equiv q_k$, $k = 1, \ldots, K$, and for T_1 input constraints and T_2 output constraints the recovered $p_k(t)$ are given by equations (3.3.3) and (3.3.4)

$$\hat{p}_k(t) = \frac{p_k^0(t-1)}{\Omega(\hat{\boldsymbol{\alpha}}, \hat{\boldsymbol{\beta}})} \exp\left[\sum_i \hat{\alpha}_i f_i(x_k) + \sum_j \hat{\beta}_j g_j(y_k)\right] \tag{4.1.13}$$

where

$$\Omega(\hat{\boldsymbol{\alpha}}, \hat{\boldsymbol{\beta}}) = \sum_{k=1}^{K} p_k^0(t-1) \exp\left[\sum_i \hat{\alpha}_i f_i(x_k) + \sum_j \hat{\beta}_j g_j(y_k)\right] \tag{4.1.14}$$

is the normalization factor. Using the outcome of a previous period as prior information, the cross-entropy method permits one to recover information about a non-stationary system. For the pure inverse case presented here, the $\{p_k\}$ represent the long-term steady state equilibrium vector that takes into account the previous period's estimated equilibrium vector. We introduce in Part IV of this book more general (linear and non-linear) formulations to capture the dynamic characteristics of a system.

4.2 AN ILL-POSED STATIONARY MARKOV INVERSE PROBLEM

The Markov process in discrete time is a probability model that has been used (see Lee *et al.* (1977) for a partial listing) as a basis for summarizing and characterizing the information in economic data in terms of transition probabilities. In many cases, longitudinal time-ordered micro data that describe individual movements from state to state are rarely available, incomplete or too expensive to obtain. Instead, a limited number of transitions for aggregate economic data that show either the number of outcomes or the corresponding proportions in each of the mutually exclusive and collectively exhaustive classes (Markov states) in each time period are often available. Given the aggregate counts, let the vector $\mathbf{x}(t)$ represent the $(K \times 1)$ vector of proportion falling in the kth Markov state in time t, and $y(t+1)$ represent the $(K \times 1)$ vector of proportions falling in each of the Markov states in time $(t+1)$, then the stationary first-order Markov process may be written as

$$\mathbf{y}'(t+1) = \mathbf{x}'(t)P \tag{4.2.1}$$

where $P = (\mathbf{p}_1 \quad \mathbf{p}_2 \quad \cdots \quad \mathbf{p}_K)$ is an unknown and unobservable $(K \times K)$

matrix of transition probabilities. If we rewrite the transition probabilities as $\mathbf{p} = (\mathbf{p}_1', \mathbf{p}_2', \ldots, \mathbf{p}_K')'$, then we may rewrite (4.2.1) as

$$\underset{(K \times 1)}{\begin{bmatrix} y_1(t+1) \\ y_2(t+1) \\ \vdots \\ y_K(t+1) \end{bmatrix}} = \underset{(K \times K^2)}{\begin{bmatrix} \mathbf{x}'(t) & & & \\ & \mathbf{x}'(t) & & \\ & & \ddots & \\ & & & \mathbf{x}'(t) \end{bmatrix}} \underset{(K^2 \times 1)}{\begin{bmatrix} \mathbf{p}_1 \\ \mathbf{p}_2 \\ \vdots \\ \mathbf{p}_K \end{bmatrix}} \tag{4.2.2a}$$

or compactly for one transition as

$$\mathbf{y}_1 = X_1 \mathbf{p} \tag{4.2.2b}$$

where $X_1 = (I_K \otimes \mathbf{x}'(t))$ and $\otimes$ denotes the Kronecker product. If we let T equal the number of data transition periods, then we may define our problem in terms of a vector of unknown transition probabilities that we wish to obtain from our data

$$\underset{(TK \times 1)}{\mathbf{y}_T} = \underset{(TK \times K^2)}{(I_K \otimes X_T)} \underset{(K^2 \times 1)}{\mathbf{p}} \tag{4.2.3}$$

If $TK < K^2$, the matrix $(I_K \otimes X_T)$ is non-invertible. Under this scenario traditional mathematical procedures yield solutions that contain $(K^2 - TK)$ arbitrary parameters.

4.2.1 THE ME SOLUTION FOR THE MARKOV PROBLEM

In order to recover the transition probabilities $\mathbf{p}$ for a K state stationary Markov problem, when using data from T transitions, we follow Lee and Judge (1996) and use the ME principle to state the problem as

$$\max_{\mathbf{p}} H(\mathbf{p}) = -\mathbf{p}' \ln \mathbf{p} = -\sum_i \sum_j p_{ij} \ln p_{ij} \tag{4.2.4}$$

subject to the first-order Markov condition

$$\underset{(TK \times K^2)}{(I_K \otimes X_T)\mathbf{p}} = \underset{(TK \times 1)}{\mathbf{y}_T} \tag{4.2.5}$$

the K transition probability row sum constraints

$$\underset{(k \times k^2)}{(\mathbf{1}' \otimes I_k)\mathbf{p}} = \underset{(k \times 1)}{\mathbf{1}} \tag{4.2.6}$$

and

$$\mathbf{p} \geq \mathbf{0} \tag{4.2.7}$$

where $\mathbf{p}$ is a $(K^2 \times 1)$ vector, $\mathbf{1}$ is a $(K \times 1)$ vector of ones, $\mathbf{y}$ is a $(TK \times 1)$ vector of state outcomes for T data transitions and X_T is a $(TK \times K^2)$ matrix of state outcomes for T transitions.

In scalar form, the corresponding Lagrangian equation is

$$\mathbf{L} = -\sum_i \sum_j p_{ij} \ln(p_{ij}) + \sum_i \sum_j \lambda_{tj}\left[y_j(t+1) - \sum_i x_i(t) p_{ij} \right] + \sum_i \mu_i \left[1 - \sum_j p_{ij} \right] \tag{4.2.8}$$

and the optimal conditions are

$$\partial \mathbf{L}/\partial p_{ij} = -\ln(\hat{p}_{ij}) - 1 - \sum_t x_i(t)\hat{\lambda}_{tj} - \hat{\mu}_i = 0 \tag{4.2.9a}$$

$$\partial \mathbf{L}/\partial \lambda_{tj} = y_j(t+1) - \sum_i x_i(t) p_{ij} = 0 \tag{4.2.9b}$$

$$\partial \mathbf{L}/\partial \mu_i = 1 - \sum_j \hat{p}_{ij} = 0 \tag{4.2.9c}$$

Following the results of Chapter 3, the normalized ME solution is

$$\hat{p}_{ij} = \frac{\exp\left(-\sum_t x_i(t)\hat{\lambda}_{tj} \right)}{\sum_n \exp\left(-\sum_t x_i(t)\hat{\lambda}_{tn} \right)} = \frac{\exp\left(-\sum_t x_i(t)\hat{\lambda}_{tj} \right)}{\Omega_i(\hat{\boldsymbol{\lambda}})} \tag{4.2.10}$$

and the dual or unconstrained objective is

$$M(\boldsymbol{\lambda}) = \sum_t \sum_j y_j(t+1)\lambda_{tj} + \sum_i \ln(\Omega_i(\boldsymbol{\lambda})) \tag{4.2.11}$$

It is important to note that T of the Lagrange multipliers (and the associated constraints) are redundant. For convenience, we will normalize these parameters by setting $\hat{\lambda}_{t1} = 0$ for each $t = 1, \ldots, T$. This implies that we can arbitrarily scale each of the probabilities by dividing the numerator and denominator by the first numerator. This provides scaled solutions of the form

$$\hat{p}_{ij} = \begin{cases} \dfrac{1}{1 + \sum_{j=2}^{K} \exp\left(-\sum_t x_i(t)(\hat{\lambda}_{tj} - \hat{\lambda}_{t1}) \right)}, & \text{for } j = 1 \\[2ex] \dfrac{\exp\left(-\sum_t x_i(t)(\hat{\lambda}_{tj} - \hat{\lambda}_{t1}) \right)}{1 + \sum_{j=2}^{K} \exp\left(-\sum_t x_i(t)(\hat{\lambda}_{tj} - \hat{\lambda}_{t1}) \right)}, & \text{otherwise} \end{cases} \tag{4.2.10a}$$

A similar normalization of the Lagrange multipliers is required for the discrete choice formulations examined in Chapter 15.

4.2.2 EXAMPLES

1. The format. Suppose we have proportion data for two transitions of the following four-state first-order Markov process

$$Y_2 = \begin{bmatrix} \begin{bmatrix} y_{11} \\ y_{12} \\ y_{13} \\ y_{14} \end{bmatrix}' \\ \begin{bmatrix} y_{21} \\ y_{22} \\ y_{23} \\ y_{24} \end{bmatrix}' \end{bmatrix} = \begin{bmatrix} x_{11} & x_{12} & x_{13} & x_{14} \\ z_{21} & x_{22} & x_{23} & x_{24} \end{bmatrix} \begin{bmatrix} p_{11} & p_{12} & p_{13} & p_{14} \\ p_{21} & p_{22} & p_{23} & p_{24} \\ p_{31} & p_{32} & p_{33} & p_{34} \\ p_{41} & p_{42} & p_{43} & p_{44} \end{bmatrix} = X_2 P \tag{4.2.12}$$

Writing this in the form of Section 4.2 where $\mathbf{p} = [\mathbf{p}'_2 \quad \mathbf{p}'_2 \quad \mathbf{p}'_3 \quad \mathbf{p}'_4]' = (p_{11}, p_{21}, \ldots, p_{34}, p_{44})'$ we may state our maximization problem as

$$\max_{\mathbf{p}} H(\mathbf{p}) = -\mathbf{p}' \ln \mathbf{p} \tag{4.2.13}$$

subject to

$$\underset{(12 \times 1)}{\begin{bmatrix} \mathbf{y}'_1 \\ \mathbf{y}'_2 \\ \mathbf{1} \end{bmatrix}} = \begin{bmatrix} y_{11} \\ y_{21} \\ y_{31} \\ y_{41} \\ y_{12} \\ y_{22} \\ y_{32} \\ y_{42} \\ \mathbf{1} \end{bmatrix} = \underset{(12 \times 16)}{\begin{bmatrix} \mathbf{x}'_{1j} & & & \\ & \mathbf{x}'_{1j} & & \\ & & \mathbf{x}'_{1j} & \\ & & & \mathbf{x}'_{1j} \\ \mathbf{x}'_{2j} & & & \\ & \mathbf{x}'_{2j} & & \\ & & \mathbf{x}'_{2j} & \\ & & & \mathbf{x}'_{2j} \\ I_4 & I_4 & I_4 & I_4 \end{bmatrix}} \underset{(16 \times 1)}{\begin{bmatrix} p_{11} \\ p_{21} \\ p_{31} \\ \vdots \\ p_{24} \\ p_{34} \\ p_{44} \end{bmatrix}} = A\mathbf{p} \tag{4.2.14}$$

where the vector $\mathbf{1}$ is of dimension 4. As before, we solve for the transition probability distribution that subject to (4.2.14) maximizes the uncertainty (maximally non-committal with respect to missing information) as measured by the Shannon entropy function (4.2.13).

The normalized entropy measure, defined in Chapter 3, for each $i = 1, 2, \ldots, K$ is

$$S(\hat{\mathbf{p}}_i) = -\sum_j \hat{p}_{ij} \ln(\hat{p}_{ij})/\ln(K) \tag{4.2.15a}$$

and the normalized entropy measure for the whole system is

$$S(\hat{\mathbf{p}}) = -\sum_i \sum_j \hat{p}_{ij} \ln(\hat{p}_{ij})/K \ln(K) \tag{4.2.15b}$$

To illustrate the procedure in the examples to follow, we use artificial data about which we know everything. Consequently, if a method behaves poorly under this scenario, we can use this as a warning against applying the method to real data.

2. Solution for Problem 1. Assume you have the following sample proportions from a four-state Markov probability model:

	1	2	3	4
T_1	0.2840	0.3960	0.2880	0.0320
T_2	0.2100	0.3404	0.3632	0.0864
T_3	0.1600	0.2905	0.3990	0.1504
T_4	0.1251	0.2492	0.4106	0.2152

Although you do not know it, these sample proportions have been generated from the following stationary Markov process:

$$P = \begin{bmatrix} 0.6 & 0.4 & 0 & 0 \\ 0.1 & 0.5 & 0.4 & 0 \\ 0 & 0.1 & 0.7 & 0.2 \\ 0 & 0 & 0.1 & 0.9 \end{bmatrix} \tag{4.2.16}$$

Suppose, within the format of Example 1, you want to use the observed sample proportions to recover estimates of the transition probabilities.

First, assume that you only use the sample proportions for one transition. In this case the ME formulation of this inverse problem is

$$\max_{\mathbf{p}} H(\mathbf{p}) = -\mathbf{p}' \ln \mathbf{p} \tag{4.2.17}$$

subject to

$$\begin{bmatrix} \mathbf{y}_1 \\ \mathbf{1} \end{bmatrix} = \underset{(8 \times 1)}{\overset{\mathbf{y}}{\begin{bmatrix} 0.284 \\ 0.396 \\ 0.288 \\ 0.032 \\ 1 \\ 1 \\ 1 \\ 1 \end{bmatrix}}} = \begin{bmatrix} \mathbf{x}'_{1j} & & & \\ & \mathbf{x}'_{1j} & & \\ & & \mathbf{x}'_{1j} & \\ & & & \mathbf{x}'_{1j} \\ I_4 & I_4 & I_4 & I_4 \end{bmatrix} \begin{bmatrix} p_{11} \\ p_{21} \\ \vdots \\ p_{34} \\ p_{44} \end{bmatrix} = A\mathbf{p} \tag{4.2.18}$$

where A in (4.2.18) is

$$\underset{(8 \times 16)}{\overset{A}{\left[\begin{array}{cccccccccccccccc} 0.2100 & 0.3404 & 0.3631 & 0.0864 & & & & & & & & & & & & \\ & & & & 0.2100 & 0.3404 & 0.3632 & 0.0864 & & & & & & & & \\ & & & & & & & & 0.2100 & 0.3404 & 0.3632 & 0.0864 & & & & \\ & & & & & & & & & & & & 0.2100 & 0.3404 & 0.3632 & 0.0864 \\ 1 & & & & 1 & & & & 1 & & & & 1 & & & \\ & 1 & & & & 1 & & & & 1 & & & & 1 & & \\ & & 1 & & & & 1 & & & & 1 & & & & 1 & \\ & & & 1 & & & & 1 & & & & 1 & & & & 1 \end{array}\right]}}$$

and $\mathbf{p}$ is of dimension (16×1).

Solving the Problem (4.2.17) and (4.2.18) yields the solution

$$\hat{P} = \begin{bmatrix} 0.2177 & 0.3336 & 0.3530 & 0.0956 \\ 0.1963 & 0.3560 & 0.3852 & 0.0625 \\ 0.2169 & 0.3345 & 0.3542 & 0.0944 \\ 0.2489 & 0.2612 & 0.2629 & 0.2269 \end{bmatrix} \tag{4.2.19}$$

with a normalized entropy measure of $S(\hat{\mathbf{p}}) = 0.936$. Since we used very little information, the estimates do not vary greatly over the four rows. Consequently, $S(\hat{\mathbf{p}})$ is close to 1, $\hat{P}$ differs greatly from the true transition matrix (P), and the squared norm of the precision error $\|\mathbf{p} - \hat{\mathbf{p}}\|^2$ is 1.161.

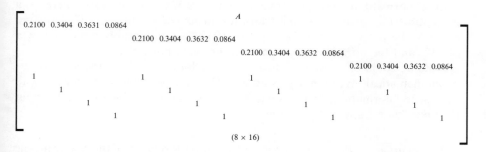

If we increase the information and use two transitions, then we have the problem (4.2.13) and (4.2.14) where x_2 and y_2 in (4.2.12) are

$$X_2 = \begin{bmatrix} 0.2840 & 0.3960 & 0.2880 & 0.0320 \\ 0.2100 & 0.3404 & 0.3632 & 0.0864 \end{bmatrix}$$

$$Y_2 = \begin{bmatrix} 0.2100 & 0.3404 & 0.3632 & 0.0864 \\ 0.1600 & 0.2905 & 0.3990 & 0.1504 \end{bmatrix}$$

The ME solution for this problem using two transitions yields

$$\hat{P} = \begin{bmatrix} 0.6011 & 0.3133 & 0.0855 & 0000 \\ 0.0991 & 0.5864 & 0.3145 & 0000 \\ 0000 & 0.0646 & 0.7354 & 0.2000 \\ 0000 & 0.0194 & 0.0800 & 0.9000 \end{bmatrix} \tag{4.2.20}$$

with a normalized entropy value of $S(\hat{\mathbf{p}}) = 0.521$. In this case there is a perceptible improvement in the transition probability estimates. The squared norm of the precision error $\|\mathbf{p} - \hat{\mathbf{p}}\|^2 = 0.0328$ is considerably improved over (4.2.19) and the normalized entropy measure is significantly lower.

Note we could not have obtained a solution for either of the above problems by mathematical inversion. By using the ME principle we have been able, with very little information, to recover a significant amount of information about the underlying transition probability system.

3. *Solution for Problem 2.* To get a feel for performance of the ME principle when the matrix contains no zero elements we use the following transition probability matrix:

$$P = \begin{bmatrix} 0.40 & 0.25 & 0.20 & 0.15 \\ 0.10 & 0.45 & 0.25 & 0.20 \\ 0.20 & 0.25 & 0.35 & 0.20 \\ 0.10 & 0.15 & 0.25 & 0.50 \end{bmatrix} \tag{4.2.21}$$

with the corresponding following sample proportions:

	1	2	3	4
T_1	0.1970	0.2845	0.2630	0.2555
T_2	0.1854	0.2814	0.2665	0.2668
T_3	0.1823	0.2796	0.2674	0.2708
T_4	0.1814	0.2788	0.2676	0.2721

Using one transition (information from T_1 and T_2), the ME approach yields the transition probability matrix

$$\hat{P} = \begin{bmatrix} 0.1986 & 0.2746 & 0.2633 & 0.2635 \\ 0.1785 & 0.2849 & 0.2681 & 0.2685 \\ 0.1833 & 0.2824 & 0.2670 & 0.2673 \\ 0.1850 & 0.2815 & 0.2665 & 0.2669 \end{bmatrix} \tag{4.2.22}$$

$$S(\hat{\mathbf{p}}) = 0.991 \qquad \|\mathbf{p} - \hat{\mathbf{p}}\|^2 = 0.1884$$

Using two transitions (T_1, T_2, T_3) yields the transition probability matrix

$$\hat{P} = \begin{bmatrix} 0.3394 & 0.3396 & 0.2108 & 0.1102 \\ 0.2069 & 0.3238 & 0.2685 & 0.2008 \\ 0.1450 & 0.2703 & 0.2875 & 0.2972 \\ 0.0843 & 0.2006 & 0.2854 & 0.4297 \end{bmatrix} \tag{4.2.23}$$

$$S(\hat{\mathbf{p}}) = 0.951 \qquad \|\mathbf{p} - \hat{\mathbf{p}}\|^2 = 0.0669$$

Using three transitions (T_1, T_2, T_3, T_4) yields the transition probability matrix

$$\hat{P} = \begin{bmatrix} 0.4016 & 0.2493 & 0.2016 & 0.1474 \\ 0.1268 & 0.4394 & 0.2756 & 0.1583 \\ 0.1445 & 0.2721 & 0.2969 & 0.2866 \\ 0.1261 & 0.1396 & 0.2750 & 0.4593 \end{bmatrix} \tag{4.2.24}$$

$$S(\hat{\mathbf{p}}) = 0.936 \qquad \|\mathbf{p} - \hat{\mathbf{p}}\|^2 = 0.0202$$

Note, the improvement in the normalized entropy and $\|\mathbf{p} - \hat{\mathbf{p}}\|^2$ measures, as the amount of information used in the *ill-posed* inverse problem is increased.

4.2.3 ENTROPY SOLUTION WITH LIMITED MICRO RESTRICTIONS

Occasionally, partial information about micro transitions or some transition probabilities may be available. For example, the aggregate number of micro units moving from one state to other states may be available, but the detailed transitions to specific other Markov states may not be known. In other words, the number of micro units remaining in the same Markov state may be available. This additional information, or any other information of this type, can be added to the restriction set within the ME formulation discussed here. In that case, we maximize the entropy (4.2.4), subject to K row sum restraints

(4.2.6), the T first-order Markov conditions (4.2.5), and the following additional J restraints from the micro transitions:

$$R\mathbf{p} = \mathbf{c} \tag{4.2.25}$$

where R is a $(J \times K^2)$ known matrix involving individual or linear combinations of $\mathbf{p}$, and $\mathbf{c}$ is a $(J \times 1)$ vector of known constants. If this additional information is combined with the other restriction set, the corresponding Lagrangian function is

$$L = -\mathbf{p} \ln \mathbf{p} + \boldsymbol{\lambda}'[\mathbf{y}_T - (I_k \otimes X_T)\mathbf{p}] + \boldsymbol{\mu}'[\mathbf{1} - (\mathbf{1}' \otimes I_K)\mathbf{p}] + \boldsymbol{\gamma}'[\mathbf{c} - R\mathbf{p}] \tag{4.2.26}$$

Solving for the first-order solution yields $K^2 + TK + K + J$ non-linear equations that can be solved to obtain, aside from the $TK + K + J$ Lagrange multipliers, the K^2 unknown stationary probabilities $\mathbf{p}$, that maximize the entropy measure.

If, in addition, we assume in this experiment that the p_{ij} for $i = j$ are known, then based on the four-state Markov process (4.2.16) and *one* transition of data, the recovered transition probability matrix is

$$\hat{P} = \begin{bmatrix} 0.6000 & 0.2318 & 0.1150 & 0.0532 \\ 0.0846 & 0.5000 & 0.3229 & 0.0925 \\ 0.0186 & 0.2610 & 0.7000 & 0.0204 \\ 0.0234 & 0.0438 & 0.0328 & 0.9000 \end{bmatrix} \tag{4.2.27}$$

With this added information, the normalized entropy measure is $S(\hat{\mathbf{p}}) = 0.610$ and the result is much closer to the underlying probability system (4.2.16). It is interesting to note that adding exact information about the diagonal elements is inferior, in terms of $\|\mathbf{p} - \hat{\mathbf{p}}\|^2$ and $S(\hat{\mathbf{p}})$ to adding a second transition as we did in obtaining (4.2.20).

4.2.4 CROSS-ENTROPY FORMULATION

With the background given in Section 3.3, the problem of estimating the stationary transition probabilities p_{ij}, can be formulated in the cross-entropy framework as

$$\min I(\mathbf{p}, \mathbf{q}) = \sum_i \sum_j p_{ij} \ln(p_{ij}/q_{ij}) \tag{4.2.28}$$

subject to

$$y_j(t+1) = \sum_i x_i(t) p_{ij} \tag{4.2.29}$$

and

$$\sum_j p_{ij} = 1 \tag{4.2.30}$$

for $i, j = 1, 2, \ldots, K$, where the prior probabilities q_{ij} are given.

As before, the Lagrangian function for the problem is

$$L = \sum_i \sum_j p_{ij} \ln p_{ij}/q_{ij} + \sum_t \sum_j \lambda_{tj} \left[y_j(t+1) - \sum_i p_{ij} x_i(t) \right] + \sum_i \mu_i \left(1 - \sum_i p_{ij} \right) \tag{4.2.31}$$

The solution yields $K^2 + 2K$ non-linear equations with the same number of unknowns. The recovered probabilities are

$$\tilde{p}_{ij} = \frac{q_{ij} \exp\left(\sum_t x_i(t) \tilde{\lambda}_{tj} \right)}{\sum_j q_{ij} \exp\left(\sum_t x_i(t) \tilde{\lambda}_{tj} \right)} \tag{4.2.32}$$

If the prior transition probabilities q_{ij} satisfy the constraints $\sum_i q_{ij} = 1$ and $y_j(t+1) = \sum_i x_i(t) q_{ij}$, then the cross-entropy (4.2.28) is minimized at $\tilde{p}_{ij} = q_{ij}$ for all i and j and the value for the cross-entropy is zero. If, on the other hand, the priors are uniform, then $\tilde{p}_{ij} = \hat{p}_{ij}$.

If the transition counts are available then one may use the maximum likelihood estimator (MLE)

$$\hat{p}_{ij} = n_{ij}(t+1)/n_i(t) \tag{4.2.33}$$

where n_{ij} is the transition counts of individuals moving from state i to state j in time $t+1$ and n_i is the number of individuals in state i in time t. If the MLE estimates (4.2.33) are used as the q_{ij}, then, because the q_{ij} are consistent with the data generation process, the cross-entropy estimator of the transition matrix is the same as the MLE.

4.3 RECOVERING INFORMATION FROM INCOMPLETE MULTISECTORAL ECONOMIC DATA

A common problem in working with regional or economy-wide equilibrium models is the need to use multisectoral economic data to estimate a matrix of expenditure, trade, and/or income flows (Hanson and Robinson, 1991; Polenske, 1993). Commonly, one starts with complete data for a particular period and seeks to estimate the matrix of flows for a later period, based only on row and column sum information. In general, the problem is to recover, from the incomplete data, a new matrix that satisfies a number of linear restrictions.

Since the unknowns outnumber the number of data points, the problem is clearly ill-posed or underdetermined.

To solve this 'matrix balancing' problem without imposing sufficient additional restrictions to make the problem solvable with traditional methods, we follow Golan *et al.* (1994), and use the entropy principle. Thus, we seek to recover the matrix of flows using only information about row and column sums, or within a cross entropy context, we use the row and column sums plus the information contained in an earlier flow matrix. To obtain a solution, we convert the problem to an ill-posed, underdetermined, pure inverse problem and apply the ME formalism presented in Chapter 3.

4.3.1 ECONOMIC FRAMEWORK

As a basis for developing estimation and inference procedures to be used with limited multisectoral economic data, consider the Leontief input–output model for an economy with K sectors, each producing a single good. The K sectors buy non-negative amounts of each other's products to use as intermediate inputs. An input–output table may include one or more rows of payments to primary factors of production (value added) and one or more columns of categories of final demand (e.g. consumption, investment and exports). A social accounting matrix (SAM) generalizes the input–output accounts, adding accounts that map from factor payments (value added) to final demand for goods. For a description of SAMs, see Pyatt and Round (1985). A simple SAM, where each entry indicates a payment by a column account to a row account, may be represented as follows:

$$A(\text{SAM}) = \begin{bmatrix} S & \mathbf{f} \\ \mathbf{v}' & 0 \end{bmatrix} \tag{4.3.1}$$

where S is a $(K \times K)$ matrix of intermediate sales, $\mathbf{f}$ is a K-dimensional vector of final demands and $\mathbf{v}$ is a K-dimensional vector of sectoral value added. A SAM is square, and corresponding column and row sums are equal.

Assume that intermediate demands are determined by a fixed coefficient matrix A, and let $\mathbf{x}$ represent sectoral sales to intermediate and final demanders. Then, we get the following standard Leontief (Miller and Blair, 1985) input–output model

$$A\mathbf{x} + \mathbf{f} = \mathbf{x} \tag{4.3.2}$$

where $S_{ij} = a_{ij}x_j$. Rearranging we may rewrite (4.3.2) as

$$\mathbf{x} - \mathbf{f} = \mathbf{y} = A\mathbf{x} \tag{4.3.3}$$

The input-output model ignores the value-added row, but a SAM model includes value-added and final demand coefficients. It is feasible to work either with the Leontief input–output model or with the SAM model. The difference is in assumptions about what column and row totals are known. In the SAM model, it is possible to introduce constraints to make it equivalent to the Leontief model by assuming known value-added and final-demand coefficients.

In practice, the a_{ij} elements of the A matrix are not known. All of the available economic information is contained in the row and column sums of the A matrix plus, perhaps, the outcome for the A matrix in a previous period. We are concerned with the problem of recovering the unknown elements of these and other sectoral (A) matrices, from limited economic data.

4.3.2 ME FORMULATION AND SOLUTION

Consider the formulation of (4.3.3)

$$\mathbf{y} = A\mathbf{x} \tag{4.3.4}$$

where $\mathbf{y}$ and $\mathbf{x}$ are K-dimensional vectors of known data and A is an unknown $(K \times K)$ matrix that must satisfy the following consistency and adding up conditions:

$$\sum_i a_{ij} = 1, \qquad \text{for all } j = 1, 2, \ldots, K \tag{4.3.5}$$

$$\sum_j a_{ij}x_j = y_i, \qquad \text{for } i = 1, 2, \ldots, K \tag{4.3.6}$$

along with the non-negativity restrictions

$$a_{ij} \geq 0, \qquad \text{for } i, j = 1, 2, \ldots, K \tag{4.3.7}$$

In (4.3.5), we assume the coefficients in each column sum to 1, which is the case in the SAM model. In an input–output model, they will sum to known numbers less than 1. Given only K observed data points on $\mathbf{y}$ and $\mathbf{x}$ and the K adding-up constraints, our objective is to recover the matrix A that contains $K(K-1)$ unknown parameters. A common method traditionally used to obtain a solution to this problem is the RAS algorithm proposed by Krutihof and discussed by Lynch (1986) and Schneider and Zenios (1990).

Given the information in (4.3.5)–(4.3.7), and using the ME principle, the problem of recovering the a_{ij} elements of the A matrix in (4.3.6) may be stated as:

maximize

$$H(\mathbf{a}) = -\sum_i \sum_j a_{ij} \ln a_{ij} \tag{4.3.8}$$

subject to

$$\sum_j a_{ij}x_j = y_i \tag{4.3.9}$$

$$\sum_i a_{ij} = 1 \tag{4.3.10}$$

where the x_j and the y_i are the observable data. Within this optimization framework, one can form the Lagrangian function

$$L = -\sum_i \sum_j a_{ij} \ln a_{ij} + \sum_i \lambda_i \left(y_i - \sum_j a_{ij} x_j \right) + \sum_j \mu_j \left(1 - \sum_i a_{ij} \right) \quad (4.3.11)$$

with optimal conditions

$$\frac{\partial L}{\partial a_{ij}} = -\ln \hat{a}_{ij} - 1 - \hat{\lambda}_i x_j - \hat{\mu}_j = 0, \qquad \text{for } i, j = 1, \ldots, K \quad (4.3.12)$$

$$\frac{\partial L}{\partial \lambda_i} = y_i - \sum_j \hat{a}_{ij} x_j = 0, \qquad j = 1, \ldots, K \quad (4.3.13)$$

$$\frac{\partial L}{\partial \mu_j} = 1 - \sum_i \hat{a}_{ij} = 0, \qquad i = 1, \ldots, K \quad (4.3.14)$$

Solving this system of $K^2 + 2K$ equations and parameters yields the solution

$$\hat{a}_{ij} = \frac{1}{\Omega_j(\hat{\lambda}_i)} \exp[-\hat{\lambda}_i x_j] \quad (4.3.15)$$

where

$$\Omega_j(\hat{\lambda}_i) = \sum_{i=1}^{K} \exp[-\hat{\lambda}_i x_j] \quad (4.3.16)$$

is a normalization factor for each j. The value of the maximum entropy measure, which is a function of the data, is

$$H = \sum_j \ln \hat{\Omega}_j + \sum_i \hat{\lambda}_i y_i \quad (4.3.17)$$

which is also the unconstrained objective for arbitrary λ. As with the Markov problem discussed in Section 4.2, the normalized entropy $S(\hat{\mathbf{p}}_j)$ can then be partitioned into $S(\hat{\mathbf{p}})$, $j = 1, 2, \ldots, K$, components that provide an uncertainty measure for each column (sector). The recovered Lagrange parameters $\hat{\lambda}_i$ reflect the sensitivity of the results to the data. The larger the absolute value of each $\hat{\lambda}_i$, the larger the effect on the recovered $\hat{a}_{ij}$. Finally, if some information such as $a_{ij} = b_{ij} = 0$ exists about one or more of the parameters, it can be added as an additional constraint of the form $a_{ij} = b_{ij}$, for some i, j, with a_{ij} and b_{ij} in $[0, 1]$.

4.3.3 A CROSS-ENTROPY FORMULATION

In many cases, a multisectoral table from a recent period may exist and provides potential information that may be used in recovering estimates of the multisectoral matrix for later periods. If such prior information, $a_{ij}^0 \equiv q_{ij}$, is deemed relevant, then the cross-entropy method (Kullback, 1959; Good, 1963) that was introduced in Chapters 2 and 3 may be employed. Formally, the cross-entropy (CE) formulation of the multisectoral problem, involving current and prior information, may be stated as:

$$\min_{\mathbf{p}} I(\mathbf{a}, \mathbf{a}^0) = \sum_i \sum_j a_{ij} \ln(a_{ij}/a_{ij}^0) = \sum_i \sum_j a_{ij} \ln(a_{ij}) - \sum_i \sum_j a_{ij} \ln(a_{ij}^0) \tag{4.3.18}$$

subject to the consistency information (row and column sums) contained in (4.3.9) and the adding up constraint (4.3.10). Under criterion (4.3.18), we minimize the entropy distance between the prior a_{ij}^0 and $\tilde{a}_{ij}$.

If the prior a_{ij}^0 is consistent with constraints (4.3.9) and (4.3.10), then the cross-entropy measure is minimized at $a_{ij} = a_{ij}^0$, for all i and j, and the value of the cross-entropy is zero. The formal cross-entropy solution is

$$\tilde{a}_{ij}(\text{CE}) = \frac{a_{ij}^0}{\Omega_j(\tilde{\lambda}_i)} \exp[\tilde{\lambda}_i x_j] \tag{4.3.19}$$

where

$$\Omega_j(\tilde{\lambda}_i) = \sum_{i=1}^{K} a_{ij}^0 \exp[\tilde{\lambda}_i x_j] \tag{4.3.20}$$

is the cross-entropy normalization factor for each j. If an uninformative prior, such as $a_{ij}^0 = \sum_i a_{ij}/K$, is used, then the cross-entropy solution reduces to the ME solution, $\hat{a}_{ij}$. Finally, the normalized entropy measures are defined exactly as (4.2.15a–4.2.15b) in the Markov problem and are normalized by the entropy of the prior distribution.

4.3.4 EXAMPLES

To indicate the reach of the ME principle in recovering the unknown parameters for sectoral matrices, we use artificial data for a four-dimensional A matrix. The sectoral data flows, the row and column totals, and the corresponding coefficient matrix for these artificial data are presented in Table 4.3.1. If the maximum entropy procedure is applied to the data presented in Table 4.3.1, the following estimated coefficient matrix results:

$$\hat{a}_{ij} = \begin{bmatrix} 0.267 & 0.265 & 0.274 & 0.315 \\ 0.270 & 0.268 & 0.279 & 0.331 \\ 0.246 & 0.246 & 0.243 & 0.221 \\ 0.218 & 0.221 & 0.204 & 0.133 \end{bmatrix} \tag{4.3.21}$$

$$S(\hat{\mathbf{p}}) = 0.9878 \qquad \text{SEM} = 0.9696$$

Table 4.3.1 Sectoral flow data and corresponding coefficient matrix

	Actual flow data				y_i	Coefficient matrix a_{ij}			
	45	0	15	80	140	0.726	0.000	0.165	0.301
	10	15	0	120	145	0.161	0.268	0.000	0.451
	7	38	65	0	110	0.113	0.678	0.714	0.000
	0	3	11	66	80	0.000	0.054	0.121	0.248
x_j	62	56	91	266	475				

The normalized entropy value $S(\hat{\mathbf{a}})$ consistent with the formulation (4.3.8)–(4.3.10) is 0.988 and the squared error measure $\|\mathbf{a} - \hat{\mathbf{a}}\|^2$ is 0.9696. Since only a small amount of information is used in this problem, the agreement between the actual coefficients a_{ij} in Table 4.3.1 and the estimated coefficients $\hat{a}_{ij}$ leave much to be desired and the average squared error is large.

To construct a synthetic prior for a cross-entropy formulation, the flow data in Table 4.3.1 were altered as follows. The flows in each row and column were multiplied by a random number generated from a normal (1, 0.1) distribution. This yielded the following coefficient matrix:

$$a_{ij}^0 = \begin{bmatrix} 0.735 & 0.000 & 0.179 & 0.254 \\ 0.156 & 0.249 & 0.000 & 0.509 \\ 0.109 & 0.699 & 0.673 & 0.000 \\ 0.000 & 0.052 & 0.149 & 0.238 \end{bmatrix} \tag{4.3.22}$$

The cross-entropy model resulted in the following estimates $\tilde{a}_{ij}$:

$$\tilde{a}_{ij} = \begin{bmatrix} 0.738 & 0.000 & 0.172 & 0.295 \\ 0.148 & 0.233 & 0.000 & 0.462 \\ 0.114 & 0.716 & 0.690 & 0.000 \\ 0.000 & 0.050 & 0.137 & 0.243 \end{bmatrix} \tag{4.3.23}$$

For this problem, the cross-entropy method resulted in low normalized entropy $S(\hat{\mathbf{p}}) = 0.609$, a squared error measure of 0.004 and $\tilde{a}_{ij}$ very close to the actual a_{ij}. Note this result occurred even though there was a considerable difference between the prior a_{ij}^0 and the actual coefficients a_{ij}. This result illustrates the potential gain of the CE over the ME approach. Finally, we note that the RAS algorithm (Schneider and Zenios, 1990) yields inferior estimates with $\|\cdot\|^2 = 0.0101$. See Golan *et al.* (1994) for further discussion, examples, discussion of the ME and CE versus RAS, and for an empirical application.

4.4 REMARKS

We have demonstrated that the entropy formalism is applicable to a range of pure inverse problems which, due to limited aggregated data, are underdetermined. These problems cannot be solved with conventional procedures. The resulting nonlinear optimization model is easy to specify and compute and *takes account of whatever prior information and data that exists.* The information recovered is based on what actually did happen, and not on creative assumptions about what might have happened but did not.

REFERENCES

Agmon, N., Alhassid, Y. and Levine, R. D. (1979) An algorithm for finding the distribution of maximal entropy. *Journal of Computational Physics* **30**, 250–59.

Golan, A. (1988) *A Discrete Stochastic Model of Economic Production and a Model of Fluctuations in Production – Theory and Empirical Evidence.* Ph.D. Thesis, University of California, Berkeley.

Golan, A. (1994) A multi-variable stochastic theory of size distribution of firms with empirical evidence. *Advances in Econometrics* **10**, 1–46.

Golan, A., Judge, G. and Robinson, S. (1994) Recovering information from incomplete or partial multisectoral economic data. *Review of Economics and Statistics* **76**, 541–9.

Golan, A. and Judge, G. G. (1995) Recovering information in the case of underdetermined problems and incomplete data. *Journal of Statistical Planning and Inference*, In press.

Golan, A., and Judge, G. G. (1993b) Recovering the parameters and forecasting in the case of ill-posed non-stationary inverse problems. Unpublished manuscript, University of California, Berkeley.

Golan, A., and Zeitouni, N. (1993) Determining the scale properties and size distribution of multi-product firms. Unpublished paper, University of Haifa, Israel.

Good, I. J. (1963) Maximum entropy for hypothesis formulation, especially for multidimensional contingency tables. *Annals of Mathematical Statistics* **34**, 911–34.

Hanson, K. A. and Robinson, S. (1991) Data, linkages and models: U.S. national income and product accounts in the framework of a social accounting matrix. *Economic Systems Research* **3**, 215–32.

Kullback, J. (1959) *Information Theory and Statistics.* John Wiley, New York.

Lee, T. C., Judge, G. G. and Zellner, A. (1977) *Estimating the Parameters of the Markov Probability Model from Aggregate Time Series Data,* (2nd edn.,). North-Holland, Amsterdam.

Lee, T. C. and Judge, M. (1996) Entropy and mass entropy for estimating transition probabilities from aggregate data. In: *Bayesian Conference in Statistics and Econometrics: Essays in Honor of Arnold Zellner*. John Wiley. New York.

Lynch, R. G. (1986) An assessment of the RAS method for updating input-output Tables. In I. Sohn (Ed.) *Readings in Input-Output Analysis*, pp. 271–284. Oxford University Press, New York.

Miller, D. J. (1994) *Entropy and Information Recovery in Linear Economic Models*. Ph.D. Thesis, University of California, Berkeley.

Miller, R. E. and Blair, P. D. (1985) *Input-Output Analysis: Foundations and Extensions*. Prentice-Hall, Englewood Cliffs, NJ.

Polenske, K. (1993) Conceptual input-output accounting and modeling framework. In R. E. Klosterman and R. K. Brail (eds.), *Spreadsheet Models for Urban and Regional Analysis*. Center for Urban Policy Research, New Brunswick, NJ.

Pyatt, G. and Round, J. (Eds.) (1985) *Social Accounting Matrices: A Basis for Planning*. World Bank, Washington, DC.

Schneider, M. H. and Zenios, S. A. (1990) A Comparative study of algorithms for matrix balancing. *Operations Research* **38**, 439–55.

CHAPTER 5

Generalized pure inverse problems

The ME and CE formulations presented in Chapter 3 seek point estimates of the unknown probabilities p_k given the moment and adding-up constraints and possibly a discrete prior q_k. Because there may be different levels of uncertainty underlying each p_k, for more general inferential purposes, point estimates and the point priors may be limiting and unrealistic. Consequently, in this chapter we generalize, following Judge *et al.* (1993), the ME–CE problem to permit a discrete probability distribution to be specified and obtained for each p_k for $k = 1, 2, \ldots, K$. Later in this chapter we will generalize the ME and CE formulations to recover unknowns that do not have the properties of probabilities and are non-stationary.

5.1 A REPARAMETERIZATION AND A GENERALIZATION

In generalizing the traditional pure ME and CE formulations, we redefine the ill-posed pure inverse problem as

$$\mathbf{y} = X\boldsymbol{\beta} \tag{5.1.1}$$

where $\mathbf{y}$ is a T-dimensional vector of observables, $\boldsymbol{\beta}$ is a $(K > T)$-dimensional vector of coordinates that reflects the unknown and unobservable coefficients, and X is a linear operator that is a known $(T \times K)$ non-invertible matrix. The objective is to recover the unknown $\boldsymbol{\beta}$ vector given information concerning $\mathbf{y}$ and X, where initially we will assume that the β_k have the properties of probabilities.

First, for each β_k, assume there exists a discrete probability distribution that is defined over the parameter space $[0, 1]$ by a set of equally distanced discrete points $\mathbf{z} = [z_1, z_2, \ldots, z_M]'$ with corresponding probabilities $\mathbf{p}_k = [p_{k1}, p_{k2}, \ldots, p_{kM}]'$ and with $M \geq 2$. Correspondingly, assume for each prior β_k^0 there exists a discrete probability distribution with prior probabilities $\mathbf{q}_k = [q_{k1}, q_{k2}, \ldots, q_{kM}]'$.

Consistent with this specification, rewrite $\boldsymbol{\beta}$ in (5.1.1) as

$$\boldsymbol{\beta} = Z\mathbf{p} \tag{5.1.2}$$

where

$$Z\mathbf{p} = \begin{bmatrix} \mathbf{z}' & & & \\ & \mathbf{z}' & & \\ & & \ddots & \\ & & & \mathbf{z}' \end{bmatrix} \begin{bmatrix} \mathbf{p}_1 \\ \mathbf{p}_2 \\ \vdots \\ \mathbf{p}_k \end{bmatrix} \tag{5.1.3}$$

$$\mathbf{z}'\mathbf{p}_k = \sum_m z_m p_{km} = \beta_k, \qquad \text{for } k = 1, 2, \ldots, K, \quad m = 1, 2, \ldots, M \tag{5.1.4}$$

$$\mathbf{z}'\mathbf{q}_k = \sum_m z_m q_{km} = \beta_k^0, \qquad \text{for } k = 1, 2, \ldots, K, \quad m = 1, 2, \ldots, M \tag{5.1.5}$$

and the reparameterized system is

$$\mathbf{y} = XZ\mathbf{p} \tag{5.1.6}$$

To avoid redundancy in presentation, we only present the CE model, which includes the ME as a special case. Given the reparameterization (5.16), the generalized CE formulation is

$$\min_{\mathbf{p}} I(\mathbf{p}, \mathbf{q}) = \sum_k \sum_m p_{km} \ln(p_{km}/q_{km}) \tag{5.1.7}$$

subject to

$$\sum_k \sum_m x_{tk} z_m p_{km} = y_t \qquad \text{for } t = 1, 2, \ldots, T, \quad m = 1, 2, \ldots, M \tag{5.1.8}$$

$$\sum_k \sum_m z_m p_{km} = 1 \tag{5.1.9}$$

$$\sum_m p_{km} = 1 \qquad \text{for all } m \tag{5.1.10}$$

Note that the definition

$$\sum_m z_m p_{km} = \beta_k \qquad \text{for all } m \tag{5.1.4'}$$

is imposed in (5.1.8) by substitution.

Following the steps of Chapters 2 and 3, the Lagrangian function is

$$L = \sum_k \sum_m p_{km} \ln(p_{km}/q_{km}) + \sum_t \lambda_t \left(y_t - \sum_k \sum_m x_{tk} z_m p_{km} \right)$$
$$+ \mu \left(1 - \sum_k \sum_m z_m p_{km} \right) + \sum_k \gamma_k \left(1 - \sum_m p_{km} \right) \tag{5.1.11}$$

with the optimal conditions

$$\frac{\partial L}{\partial p_{km}} = \ln(\tilde{p}_{km}/q_{km}) + 1 - \sum_t \tilde{\lambda}_t x_{tk} z_m - \tilde{\mu} z_m - \tilde{\gamma}_k = 0,$$

$$k = 1, 2, \ldots, K, \quad m = 1, 2, \ldots, M \tag{5.1.12}$$

$$\frac{\partial L}{\partial \lambda_t} = y_t - \sum_k \sum_m x_{tk} z_m \tilde{p}_{km} = 0, \qquad t = 1, 2, \ldots, T \tag{5.1.13}$$

$$\frac{\partial L}{\partial \mu} = 1 - \sum_k \sum_m z_m \tilde{p}_{km} = 0 \tag{5.1.14}$$

$$\frac{\partial L}{\partial \gamma_k} = 1 - \sum_m \tilde{p}_{km} = 0, \qquad k = 1, 2, \ldots, K \tag{5.1.15}$$

Solving this system of $KM + K + T + 1$ equations and parameters yields

$$\tilde{p}_{km} = q_{km} \exp\left(-1 + \sum_t \tilde{\lambda}_t x_{tk} z_m + \tilde{\mu} z_m + \tilde{\gamma}_k \right) \tag{5.1.16}$$

or alternatively,

$$\tilde{p}_{km} = \frac{q_{km}}{\Omega_k(\tilde{\lambda}_1, \tilde{\lambda}_2, \ldots, \tilde{\lambda}_T, \tilde{\mu})} \exp\left(\sum_t \tilde{\lambda}_t x_{tk} z_m + \tilde{\mu} z_m \right) \tag{5.1.17}$$

where

$$\Omega_k(\tilde{\lambda}, \tilde{\mu}) = \sum_m q_{km} \exp\left(\sum_t \tilde{\lambda}_t x_{tk} z_m + \tilde{\mu} z_m \right) \tag{5.1.18}$$

In constrast to Chapter 3, this formulation contains $K(M - 1)$ additional unknown parameters p_{km}. Finally, the $\boldsymbol{\beta}$'s are recovered from $\tilde{\mathbf{p}}$ through

$$\tilde{\boldsymbol{\beta}} = Z\tilde{\mathbf{p}} \tag{5.1.19}$$

or in scalar form

$$\tilde{\boldsymbol{\beta}}_k = \sum_m z_m \tilde{\mathbf{p}}_{km} \tag{5.1.20}$$

With an uniformative prior $q_k = 1/K$, the generalized maximum entropy solution results.

As before, the normalized entropy measure for each β_k is

$$S(\hat{\beta}_k) = -\sum_m \hat{p}_{km} \ln \hat{p}_{km}/\ln(M) \tag{5.1.21}$$

and the system's normalized entropy measure is

$$S(\hat{\boldsymbol{\beta}}) = -\sum_k \sum_m \hat{p}_{km} \ln \hat{p}_{km}/(K \ln(M)) \tag{5.1.22}$$

where corresponding normalized entropy measures can be defined, as in

Chapter 3, for the CE. Finally, as was shown in Chapter 3, all the diagonal elements of the Hessian are negative while the off-diagonal elements are zero implying the Hessian is negative definite asserting a globally unique solution.

5.2. APPLICATIONS

In this section we use artificial data and some examples to demonstrate the applicability of the generalized formulation introduced in Section 5.1. The generalized ME–CE formulations discussed in Section 5.1 can be applied to a large class of underdetermined problems in economics, the natural sciences and other social sciences. However, each problem usually has its own characteristics and information base, and thus may require refinements within the generalized pure inverse formulation.

5.2.1 A SIMPLE PURE INVERSE PROBLEM

As an example of an economic problem that may be cast as a pure inverse problem, consider the equilibrium size distribution of firms or consumers (Golan and Judge, 1992) that was discussed in Chapter 4. This type of problem is a variant of the following dice problem, discussed in Chapter 2. Assume that a die, that can take on values $1 \leq k \leq 6$, is tossed N times and we are told only that the *average* outcome number is 3.0. Given this information what probability should we assign to each outcome on the *next toss*? From a fair die, with no constraints, we would expect a uniform distribution and the average number of spots to be 3.5.

Using the empirical information that the average is 3.0, the mean value constraint may, in terms of (5.1.1), be stated as

$$\mathbf{x}'\boldsymbol{\beta} = y = 3.0 \tag{5.2.1}$$

where $\mathbf{x} = [1, 2, 3, 4, 5, 6]'$.

Since each β_k is contained in the interval [0, 1] we may reparameterize the problem by defining an M-dimensional parameter support space. If $M = 6$, then we have the natural parameter support space vector, $\mathbf{z} = [0, 0.2, 0.4, 0.6, 0.8, 1.0]'$ and corresponding unknown probabilities $\mathbf{p}_k = [p_{k1}, p_{k2}, \ldots, p_{k6}]'$ and prior probabilities (if such exist) $\mathbf{q}_k = [q_{k1}, q_{k2}, \ldots, q_{k6}]'$. Under this reparameterization we may rewrite (5.2.1) as

$$\mathbf{x}'\boldsymbol{\beta} = \mathbf{x}'Z\mathbf{p} = \mathbf{x}'\begin{bmatrix} \mathbf{z}_1' & & & \\ & \mathbf{z}_2' & & \\ & & \ddots & \\ & & & \mathbf{z}_6' \end{bmatrix}\begin{bmatrix} \mathbf{p}_1 \\ \mathbf{p}_2 \\ \vdots \\ \mathbf{p}_6 \end{bmatrix} \tag{5.2.2}$$

Table 5.2.1 Recovered probabilities $\hat{p}_{km}$, coefficients $\hat{\beta}_k$ and normalized entropies $S(\hat{\boldsymbol{\beta}}_k)$

	$m=1$	$m=2$	$m=3$	$m=4$	$m=5$	$m=6$	$\hat{\beta}_k \equiv \sum_m \hat{p}_{km} z_m$	$S(\hat{\boldsymbol{\beta}}_k)$
z_m	0	0.2	0.4	0.6	0.8	1.0		
$\hat{p}_{1m}$	0.411	0.251	0.153	0.093	0.057	0.035	0.248	0.838
$\hat{p}_{2m}$	0.468	0.255	0.139	0.076	0.041	0.022	0.207	0.775
$\hat{p}_{3m}$	0.520	0.253	0.123	0.060	0.029	0.014	0.173	0.713
$\hat{p}_{4m}$	0.569	0.247	0.107	0.047	0.020	0.009	0.145	0.653
$\hat{p}_{5m}$	0.614	0.238	0.092	0.036	0.014	0.005	0.123	0.596
$\hat{p}_{6m}$	0.655	0.227	0.079	0.272	0.009	0.003	0.104	0.544

The CE problem is identical to the problem (5.1.7)–(5.1.10) specified in Section 5.1. Using the generalized ME–CE approach of Section 5.1 yields the discrete probability distribution $\tilde{p}_{km}$ associated with each one of the $\tilde{\beta}_k$ probabilities, the vector $\tilde{\boldsymbol{\beta}}$ of estimated probabilities and the corresponding normalized entropy (uncertainty) measures. The results for this problem under an uniformative prior of $q_m = 1/M$ for all k are summarized in Table 5.2.1.

The above results demonstrate the following characteristics of the generalized framework developed in Section 5.1. First, the recovered coefficients, $\hat{\beta}_k$, under the generalized framework, with a prior $q_{km} = 1/6$ (i.e. the ME case), are all practically identical to the recovered parameters $\hat{p}_k$ of the classical ME discussed in Chapter 2. Second, the additional recovered information includes the probability distributions, and the corresponding normalized entropy measures $S(\hat{\boldsymbol{\beta}}_k)$ that reflect the distributions of the probabilities β_k, and the uncertainty (sharpness of the inference) associated with the data.

5.2.2 THE MARKOV PROBLEM

Consider again the problem of recovering from aggregate data, estimates of transition probabilities for a $(K \times K)$ transition probability matrix P for a stationary Markov problem. In Section 4.2, the classical ME and CE formulations for solving this problem were developed. As a basis for the reformulation, the problem may be restated as

$$\mathbf{y}'(t+1) = \mathbf{x}'(t)P \tag{5.2.3}$$

where P is the $(K \times K)$ unknown transition probability matrix and $\mathbf{y}$ and $\mathbf{x}$ are the aggregate proportions in each state in t and $t+1$. Moving toward a generalized ME–CE formulation, let each transition probability p_{ij} be represented by a set of discrete points, $\mathbf{z} = [z_1, z_2, \ldots, z_M]'$, with corresponding probabilities $\mathbf{p}_{ij} = [p_{1ij}, p_{2ij}, \ldots, p_{Mij}]'$. Then, we may rewrite the transition probability matrix P as

$$P = ZP_M \tag{5.2.4}$$

where

$$ZP_M = \begin{bmatrix} \mathbf{z}' & & & \\ & \mathbf{z}' & & \\ & & \ddots & \\ & & & \mathbf{z}' \end{bmatrix} \begin{bmatrix} \mathbf{p}_{11} & \mathbf{p}_{12} & \cdots & \mathbf{p}_{1K} \\ \mathbf{p}_{21} & \mathbf{p}_{22} & \cdots & \mathbf{p}_{2K} \\ \vdots & \vdots & \ddots & \vdots \\ \mathbf{p}_{K1} & \mathbf{p}_{K2} & \cdots & \mathbf{p}_{KK} \end{bmatrix} \tag{5.2.5}$$

Given the reparameterized problem and a prior probability vector $\mathbf{q}_{ij} = [q_{1ij}, q_{2ij}, \ldots, q_{Mij}]'$ the generalized cross-entropy formulation is:

minimize

$$I(\mathbf{p}, q) = \sum_i \sum_j \sum_m p_{mij} \ln(p_{mij}/q_{mij}) \tag{5.2.6}$$

subject to

$$\sum_j \sum_m z_m p_{mij} = 1, \qquad \text{for all } i \tag{5.2.7}$$

$$\sum_m p_{mij} = 1 \qquad \text{for all } i, j \tag{5.2.8}$$

$$y_j(t) = \sum_i x_i(t-1) \sum_m z_m p_{mij}(t), \qquad \text{for all } i, j \text{ and a given } t \tag{5.2.9}$$

where (5.2.9) is the first-order Markov conditions, (5.2.7) represents the adding-up conditions for each of the K states and (5.2.8) are the adding-up conditions for each p_{ij}. This optimization yields the transition probability coefficients $\tilde{p}_{ij} = \sum_m z_m \tilde{p}_{mij}$ together with a probability measure defined on each $\tilde{p}_{ij}$, and the normalized entropy (uncertainty) measures $S(\tilde{p}_{ij})$ associated with each coefficient.

Continuing the problem introduced in Section 4.2, assume you have the following aggregate proportions, given in Table 5.2.2 for a four-state Markov

Table 5.2.2 Sample proportions for a four-state Markov problem

	Aggregate proportions			
$T = 1$	0.2840	0.3960	0.2880	0.0320
$T = 2$	0.2100	0.3404	0.3632	0.0864
$T = 3$	0.1600	0.2905	0.3990	0.1504

probability model that have been generated from the following *stationary* Markov process:

$$P = \begin{bmatrix} 0.6 & 0.4 & 0 & 0 \\ 0.1 & 0.5 & 0.4 & 0 \\ 0 & 0.1 & 0.7 & 0.2 \\ 0 & 0 & 0.1 & 0.9 \end{bmatrix} \tag{5.2.10}$$

Our interest is to recover estimates of the transition probabilities while using the generalized ME method, which is similar to the generalized CE method with $q_{mij} = 1/M$ for all i and j. Let the $M = 5$ natural parameter space be $\mathbf{z} = [0, 0.25, 0.50, 0.75, 1.0]'$. If we use two transitions, involving T_1, T_2 and T_3, the generalized ME solution yields $\hat{p}_{ij}$, $\hat{p}_{mij}$ and $S(\hat{p}_{ij})$. These results, summarized in Table 5.2.3, have $S(\hat{\mathbf{p}}) = 0.521$ and $\|\hat{p}_{ij} - p_{ij}\|^2 = 0.0328$.

Although we have used a very limited set of data (two transitions) to recover sixteen transition probabilities and the large number of p_{mij}, the estimates $\hat{p}_{ij}$ are favorable, relative to the correct Markov probabilities (5.2.10). Further, a measure of the uncertainty, $S(\hat{p}_{ij})$, relative to each transition probability estimate is natural under this new formulation.

Table 5.2.3 $\hat{p}_{mij}$, $\hat{p}_{ij}$ and $S(\hat{p}_{ij})$ for the generalized ME Markov problem

	$m=1$	$m=2$	$m=3$	$m=4$	$m=5$	$\sum_m \hat{p}_{mij} z_m = \hat{p}_{ij}$	$S(\hat{p}_{ij})$
z_m	0	0.25	0.50	0.75	1.0		
$\hat{p}_{m11}$	0.126	0.156	0.192	0.236	0.290	0.602	0.974
$\hat{p}_{m21}$	0.368	0.254	0.175	0.120	0.083	0.324	0.921
$\hat{p}_{m31}$	0.770	0.177	0.041	0.009	0.002	0.074	0.432
$\hat{p}_{m41}$	1	0	0	0	0	0	0
$\hat{p}_{m12}$	0.714	0.205	0.059	0.017	0.005	0.098	0.514
$\hat{p}_{m22}$	0.143	0.167	0.195	0.228	0.266	0.577	0.985
$\hat{p}_{m32}$	0.367	0.253	0.175	0.121	0.084	0.325	0.922
$\hat{p}_{m42}$	1	0	0	0	0	0	0
$\hat{p}_{m13}$	1	0	0	0	0	0	0
$\hat{p}_{m23}$	0.786	0.168	0.036	0.008	0.002	0.068	0.408
$\hat{p}_{m33}$	0.055	0.093	0.155	0.260	0.436	0.732	0.859
$\hat{p}_{m43}$	0.531	0.256	0.124	0.060	0.029	0.200	0.755
$\hat{p}_{m14}$	0.996	0.004	0	0	0	0.001	0.017
$\hat{p}_{m24}$	0.927	0.068	0.005	0	0	0.020	0.175
$\hat{p}_{m34}$	0.758	0.184	0.045	0.011	0.003	0.079	0.451
$\hat{p}_{m44}$	0.005	0.018	0.060	0.207	0.712	0.900	0.519

5.2.3 THE MULTISECTORAL PROBLEM

Consider next the problem of recovering estimates of the elements a_{ij} of a $(K \times K)$ multisectoral SAM matrix A that contains $K(K-1)$ unknown parameters. Building on the formulation in Section 4.3.2 and in Golan *et al.* (1994) involving the inverse problem

$$\mathbf{y} = A\mathbf{x} \tag{5.2.11}$$

where $\mathbf{y}$ and $\mathbf{x}$ are K-dimensional vectors of known data and A is an unknown $(K \times K)$ matrix that must satisfy the following consistency and adding-up conditions:

$$\sum_i a_{ij} = 1, \qquad \text{for all } j = 1, 2, \ldots, K \tag{5.2.12}$$

$$\sum_j a_{ij} x_j = y_i, \qquad \text{for } i = 1, 2, \ldots, K \tag{5.2.13}$$

along with the non-negativity restrictions

$$a_{ij} \geq 0, \qquad \text{for } i, j = 1, 2, \ldots, K \tag{5.2.14}$$

We now generalize the problem such that each a_{ij} element is defined, over the parameter space $[0, 1]$, by a set of $M \geq 2$ discrete points $\mathbf{z} = [z_1, z_2, \ldots, z_M]'$, with corresponding unknown probabilities $\mathbf{p}_{ij} = [\mathbf{p}_{ij1}, p_{ij2}, \ldots, p_{ijM}]'$. Thus, we let

$$A = ZP \tag{5.2.15}$$

where

$$ZP = \begin{bmatrix} \mathbf{z}' & & & \\ & \mathbf{z}' & & \\ & & \ddots & \\ & & & \mathbf{z}' \end{bmatrix} \begin{bmatrix} \mathbf{p}_{11} & \mathbf{p}_{12} & \cdots & \mathbf{p}_{1K} \\ \mathbf{p}_{21} & \mathbf{p}_{22} & \cdots & \mathbf{p}_{2K} \\ \vdots & \vdots & \ddots & \vdots \\ \mathbf{p}_{K1} & \mathbf{p}_{K2} & \cdots & \mathbf{p}_{KK} \end{bmatrix} \tag{5.2.16}$$

The $\mathbf{z}$ vector specifies the M discrete points in the $[0, 1]$ parameter space for each a_{ij}, and the M dimensional vector $\mathbf{p}_{ij}$, for fixed M, specifies the corresponding distribution of discrete probabilities for each a_{ij}. The natural bound points in the support $\mathbf{z}$ are 0 and 1 and should be included in $\mathbf{z}$.

Given the reparameterized pure inverse problem, the generalized ME formulation may be posed as

$$\max_{\mathbf{p}} H(\mathbf{p}) = -\sum_m \sum_i \sum_j p_{mij} \ln(p_{mij}) \tag{5.2.17}$$

subject to

$$\sum_i \sum_m z_m p_{mij} = 1, \qquad \text{for all } j \tag{5.2.18}$$

$$\sum_m p_{mij} = 1, \qquad \text{for all } i \text{ and } j \tag{5.2.19}$$

$$\sum_j \sum_m z_m p_{mij} x_j = y_i, \qquad \text{for all } i \tag{5.2.20}$$

The p_{mij} provide a probability measure over the specified M-dimensional parameter space for each $\hat{a}_{ij}$. Based on the above set of equations and parameters, and following the same optimization procedure as in Chapter 3 and Section 5.1, the ME estimates $\hat{a}_{ij}$, are

$$\hat{a}_{ij} = \sum_m z_m \hat{p}_{mij} \tag{5.2.21}$$

where the $\hat{a}_{ij}$ are *equivalent* to those of the non-generalized ME formulation of Chapter 4, and demonstrates the consistency of the generalized framework. *Now, however, we have the $\hat{p}_{mij}$, which provide a probability distribution and an uncertainty measure for each of the $\hat{a}_{ij}$.* This additional information may be useful when working with real data. An additional measure of diversity or uncertainty, the normalized entropy, for each $\hat{a}_{ij}$ is

$$S(\hat{a}_{ij}) = -\sum_m \hat{p}_{mij} \ln \hat{p}_{mij} / \ln(M) \tag{5.2.22}$$

We now discuss the normalized entropy measures within the generalized ME framework by comparing the measures S, S_j and $S(\hat{a}_{ij})$. The normalized entropy measures S and S_j capture the information content of the whole set of recovered coefficients and of each column (sector) $j = 1, 2, \ldots, K$, respectively. The lower the value of S, or S_j, the lower the uncertainty and the sharper the inference for the recovered coefficients. As is expected, with the proper normalization, the value of S is invariant to the generalized ME problem formulated here. On the other hand, $S(\hat{a}_{ij})$ reflects a measure of uncertainty that is attached to each coefficient. The more uniform the distribution of probabilities associated with a certain coefficient ($\hat{a}_{ij}$), the higher $S(\hat{a}_{ij})$ and the higher the level of uncertainty associated with that coefficient.

To indicate the reach of the generalized ME–CE formulations in recovering the $MK(K-1)$ unknown parameters for sectoral matrices, we use, as in Chapter 4, artificial data for a four-dimensional A matrix. The sectoral data flows, the row and column totals, and the corresponding coefficient matrix for these artificial data are presented in Table 4.3.1. In the experiment below the parameter space used was $\mathbf{z} = (0, 0.25, 0.50, 0.75, 1.00)'$ where $\mathbf{M} = 5$. Using priors q_{mij} consistent with the a_{ij}^0 priors of Section 4.3.3, the generalized CE

Table 5.2.4 $\tilde{p}_{mij}$, $\tilde{a}_{ij}$ and $S(\tilde{a}_{ij})$ in the generalized CE case with the informative prior q_{ijm}

	$m=1$	$m=2$	$m=3$	$m=4$	$m=5$	$\sum_m \tilde{p}_{mij} z_m = \tilde{a}_{ij}$	$S(\tilde{a}_{ij})$
z_m	0	0.25	0.50	0.75	1.0		
$\tilde{p}_{m11}$	0.054	0.091	0.154	0.261	0.442	0.735	0.853
$\tilde{p}_{m21}$	0.618	0.239	0.093	0.036	0.014	0.156	0.646
$\tilde{p}_{m31}$	0.676	0.221	0.072	0.024	0.008	0.109	0.567
$\tilde{p}_{m41}$	1	0	0	0	0	0	0.000
$\tilde{p}_{m12}$	1	0	0	0	0	0	0.000
$\tilde{p}_{m22}$	0.481	0.260	0.141	0.076	0.041	0.249	0.812
$\tilde{p}_{m32}$	0.064	0.102	0.162	0.259	0.414	0.699	0.881
$\tilde{p}_{m42}$	0.830	0.141	0.024	0.004	0.001	0.052	0.341
$\tilde{p}_{m13}$	0.574	0.250	0.109	0.047	0.021	0.179	0.702
$\tilde{p}_{m23}$	1	0	0	0	0	0	0.000
$\tilde{p}_{m33}$	0.076	0.114	0.171	0.256	0.384	0.673	0.907
$\tilde{p}_{m43}$	0.636	0.234	0.086	0.032	0.012	0.149	0.623
$\tilde{p}_{m14}$	0.402	0.258	0.166	0.106	0.068	0.254	0.892
$\tilde{p}_{m24}$	0.232	0.215	0.199	0.184	0.170	0.509	0.996
$\tilde{p}_{m34}$	1	0	0	0	0	0	0.000
$\tilde{p}_{m44}$	0.469	0.261	0.145	0.081	0.045	0.238	0.825

estimation formalism yields $\tilde{p}_{ijm}$, which in turn, yield the point estimates $\tilde{a}_{ij}$ which are almost identical to 4.3.22.

Note that the $\tilde{a}_{ij}$ estimates are very close to those of the standard cross-entropy case (Section 4.3.3), but now we have a measure of uncertainty or reliability about each a_{ij} that is given in terms of the distribution of the probabilities over the $\mathbf{z}$ parameter space. Further, the generalized CE (or ME) estimates are *superior* to those of the classical ME since we are now able to capture the whole distribution of each a_{ij} and not just the point estimate. Comparing the SE of these two cases confirms the argument since SE = 0.0038 for Table 5.2.4 while SE = 0.004 for (4.3.23). In Chapter 7 we discuss this in great detail. The corresponding normalized entropy values $S(\tilde{a}_{ij})$ for the $\tilde{a}_{ij}$ are given in the last column of Table 5.2.4.

A few comments regarding $S(\tilde{a}_{ij})$ are in order. Note that $\tilde{a}_{22}$ and $\tilde{a}_{14}$ have approximately the same values (0.249 and 0.254) but differ greatly regarding the distribution of probabilities and entropy values (0.812 and 0.892). Also, $\tilde{a}_{32}$ and $\tilde{a}_{14}$ have almost the same entropy values (0.881 and 0.892) but differ in regard to the distribution of probabilities and value of the estimated parameter. The $\tilde{a}_{ij} = 0$ have probability mass concentrated at zero and an entropy value of zero.

In regard to $S(\tilde{\mathbf{p}})$, the normalized entropy values may be partitioned by column (sectors) with the following outcomes: $S_1 = 0.547$, $S_2 = 0.528$, $S_3 =$

0.600, $S_4 = 0.765$. This indicates a larger degree of uncertainty, regarding the $\tilde{a}_{i4}$, for sector 4 than for the other sectors and this result suggests where the emphasis should be placed in terms of data collection.

5.3 A NON-TRADITIONAL GENERAL CROSS-ENTROPY PURE INVERSE FORMULATION

Consider the pure inverse problem in Section 5.1

$$\mathbf{y} = X\boldsymbol{\beta} \tag{5.1.1$'$}$$

where all definitions remain the same *except that the elements of the unknown* $\boldsymbol{\beta}$ *vector are no longer required to retain the properties of probabilities.* This means, following Judge *et al.* (1993), that the coordinates β_k are now *unconstrained.* To reflect this, the parameter space $\mathbf{z}_k$ defines the conceptual playing field for each β_k, for $k = 1, 2, \ldots, K$, and, consistent with our expectations for the unknown coefficients, may take on positive and/or negative values.

In this context, (5.1.2) and (5.1.3) are redefined such that

$$\beta_k = \sum_m z_{km} p_{km}, \qquad \text{for } k = 1, 2, \ldots, K, \quad \text{and } m = 1, 2, \ldots, M \tag{5.3.1}$$

If we let $\{z_{km}\}$ be the possible realizations of β_k defined on a compact subset of $\mathbb{R}^K$ with corresponding probabilities p_{km}, the generalized CE problem may be specified as

$$\min_{\mathbf{p}} I(\mathbf{p}, \mathbf{q}) = \sum_k \sum_m p_{km} \ln(p_{km}/q_{km}) \tag{5.3.2}$$

subject to

$$\sum_k \sum_m x_{tk} z_{km} p_{km} = y_t, \qquad \text{for } t = 1, 2, \ldots, T \tag{5.3.3}$$

$$\sum_m p_{km} = 1, \qquad \text{for all } k \tag{5.3.4}$$

The Lagrangian, the optimality conditions and the solution follow those of Section 5.1, except that the adding up constraints on the β_k are omitted in this case, and the support space $\mathbf{z}_k$ appears in a more general form. For example, in most cases where researchers are uninformed as to the sign and magnitude of the unknown β_k, they should specify a support that is *uniformly symmetric around zero* with endpoints of large magnitude, say $\mathbf{z}_k = (-C, -C/2, 0, C/2, C)'$ for $M = 5$ and for some scalar C. This formulation permits the traditional categories, x_{tk}, to take on different definitions and increases the range of conformable problems.

From the corresponding Lagrangian, the generalized CE solution is

$$\tilde{p}_{km} = \frac{q_{km}}{\Omega_k(\hat{\boldsymbol{\lambda}})} \exp\left(z_{km} \sum_t \tilde{\lambda}_t x_{tk} \right) \tag{5.3.5}$$

where

$$\Omega_k(\tilde{\boldsymbol{\lambda}}) = \sum_m q_{km} \exp\left(z_{km} \sum_t \tilde{\lambda}_t x_{tk} \right) \tag{5.3.6}$$

is the normalization factor for each coefficient, $\tilde{\beta}_k$. Finally, a point estimate of each coefficient is recovered through the relation

$$\tilde{\beta}_k = \sum_m \tilde{p}_{km} z_{km}, \qquad k = 1, 2, \ldots, K \tag{5.3.7}$$

The reparameterization of the $\boldsymbol{\beta}$ parameter space has been accomplished through a set of linear restrictions. Consequently, these linear restrictions along with the consistency-data restrictions (5.3.3), maintain the stability of the CE solution. A further discussion of $\mathbf{z}_k$ and M, within the general linear statistical model with noise, is given in Chapters 6 and 7 where the sensitivity of the recovered unknowns to the specification of Z is analyzed.

5.4 A NON-STATIONARY, NON-TRADITIONAL GENERAL CROSS-ENTROPY PURE INVERSE FORMULATION

In Section 5.3 we considered the recovery of a fixed coefficient vector $\boldsymbol{\beta}$. Consider now the pure inverse problem

$$\mathbf{y}_t = \mathbf{x}_t'\boldsymbol{\beta}_t, \qquad \text{for } t = 1, 2, \ldots, T \tag{5.4.1}$$

where all definitions remain as in Section 5.3 but the $\boldsymbol{\beta}$ vector is no longer fixed but may change over the data points. Given the existence of a unique relationship between $\boldsymbol{\beta}_t$ and $\boldsymbol{\beta}_{t-\tau}$, for $\tau = 1, 2, \ldots,$ the generalized ME–CE method can be applied to recover the changing parameters of the system where now the $\boldsymbol{\beta}$ are defined as $\boldsymbol{\beta}_t = (\beta_{t1}, \beta_{t2}, \ldots, \beta_{tK})'$. Having reparameterized $\boldsymbol{\beta}$ and imposing a relationship over time on the $\boldsymbol{\beta}_t$, the generalized cross-entropy problem may be specified as

$$\min_{\mathbf{p}} I(\mathbf{p}, \mathbf{q}) = \sum_t \sum_k \sum_m p_{tkm} \ln(p_{tkm}/q_{km}) \tag{5.4.2}$$

subject to

$$\sum_k \sum_m x_{tk} z_{tkm} p_{tkm} = y_t, \qquad \text{for } t = 1, 2, \ldots, T \tag{5.4.3}$$

$$\sum_m p_{tkm} = 1, \qquad \text{for all } t \text{ and } k \tag{5.4.4}$$

and the dynamic relations

$$\beta_{tk} = \mathbf{f}_t(\beta_{(t-1),k}, \beta_{(t-2),k}, \ldots, \beta_{(t-\tau),k}) \tag{5.4.5}$$

The prior distribution q_{ij} can be specified as uniform for all t or individually for each t in terms of q_{tkm} where specific prior information exists. The solution to this non-linear optimization procedure provides the general non-stationary cross-entropy point estimates

$$\tilde{\beta}_{tk} = \sum_m z_{tkm}\tilde{p}_{tkm} \tag{5.4.6}$$

that are consistent with the information contained in the prior, the data (5.4.3) and the dynamic process underlying the system (5.4.5). In addition, the normalized entropy (uncertainty) measures and the $\tilde{p}_{tkm}$ are recovered. Removing equation (5.4.5) from the constraint set yields estimates for t independent systems where, as was shown in Section 5.3, each can be optimized independently.

As before, the Lagrangian yields the corresponding generalized non-stationary, cross-entropy solution

$$\tilde{p}_{tkm} = \frac{q_{tkm}}{\Omega_{tk}(\tilde{\lambda}_t, \tilde{\theta}_{t+1,i}, \tilde{\theta}_{tk})} \exp[\tilde{\lambda}_t x_{tk} z_{tkm} + \tilde{\theta}_{t+1,k}\mathbf{f}'_t(\tilde{\beta}_{t-1,k}) z_{tkm} - \tilde{\theta}_{tk} z_{tkm}] \tag{5.4.7}$$

with

$$\Omega_{tk}(\tilde{\lambda}_t, \tilde{\theta}_{t+1,k}, \tilde{\theta}_{tk}) = \sum_m q_{tkm} \exp[\tilde{\lambda}_t x_{tk} z_{tkm} + \tilde{\theta}_{t+1,k}\mathbf{f}'_t(\tilde{\beta}_{t-1,k}) z_{tkm} - \tilde{\theta}_{tk} z_{tkm}] \tag{5.4.8}$$

where constraint (5.4.5) is represented, for simplicity, as $\beta_{tk} = \mathbf{f}_t(\beta_{t-1,k})$, and $\mathbf{f}'_t(\tilde{\beta}_{t-1,k})$ is $\partial f / \partial \beta_{t-1,k}$.

For the special case where the number of observations (data points) equals the number of constraints (e.g. $\beta_{tk} = \alpha_k \beta_{t-1,k}$ for some $\boldsymbol{\alpha} = (\alpha_1, \alpha_2, \ldots, \alpha_K)'$ and $T = 2K$), this method yields a solution equal to the mathematical inversion, implying there is a unique solution that satisfies the constraints. Within the context of optimal control theory, equation (5.4.5) may be identified as the equation of motion, and $\tilde{\beta}_{1k}$ of equation (5.4.6) is the estimated state of the system in period 1 (initial condition). A further discussion and generalization of dynamic and control (linear and non-linear) problems is given in Part V of this monograph. In Part V we also generalize the type of non-stationary problems developed here to include noisy data and demonstrate the generalized ME performance with a large number of linear and non-linear examples.

5.5 REMARKS

The focus of this chapter, and indeed all of the chapters in Part I, has been to suggest an analytical basis and corresponding empirical solution for a range of ill-posed, pure inverse problems in economics. In particular, we note that

- The classical maximum entropy formalism is traditionally used, via an optimization framework, to recover a distribution(s) of probabilities in the case of ill-posed, underdetermined pure inverse problems. Only information from the data (moment-consistency) and the adding up constraints is used.
- The maximum entropy formalism can be reparameterized to be useful as a general non-linear inversion procedure.
- A distribution of probabilities or uncertainty measure (normalized entropy), relating to the sharpness of the inference, may be recovered for each of the coordinates.
- Under the general entropy formulations, the normalized entropy measure provides a basis for evaluating the informational content of each additional constraint or data point.
- The entropy and cross-entropy procedures are, like Bayes rule, efficient information processing rules.
- In the cross entropy formulations the discrete prior probability densities appear in the objective function and not in the constraints.
- Non-stationary general cross-entropy formulations provide information concerning initial conditions and the equation of motion and thus have implications for recovering unknown parameters in optimal control problems that are to be discussed in Chapter 14.

The ME and CE procedures discussed in Chapters 3, 4 and 5 provide a basis for recovering information and making inferences in ill-posed inverse problems, especially when one is restricted by limited non-experimental social or economic data. Efficient algorithms exist for solving the resulting non-linear optimization problems and these are discussed in the chapters to come. Again, we emphasize that the focus of the chapters in Part I is directed to recovering (in the form of a frequency function) whatever information exists in the data and the prior. The proposed information measures provide a basis for assessing the uncertainty that exists after the evidence is in. In contrast to traditional ways of inference when dealing with ill-posed, underdetermined problems, the ME procedure *does not* introduce *convenient assumptions* to form a tractable well posed problem with a unique solution.

Finally, within the class of ME–CE models we have discussed, there are formulations that fit a large number of problems in the natural sciences where one searches for the most probable distribution consistent with data and conservation rules. In such problems, the Lagrange parameters represent basic quantities of the system.

REFERENCES

Golan, A. and Judge, G. (1992) Recovering and processing information in the case of underdetermined economic models. Unpublished manuscript, University of California, Berkeley.

Golan, A., Judge, G. and Robinson, S. (1994) Recovering information from incomplete or partial multisectoral economic data. *Review of Economics and Statistics* **76,** 541–9.

Judge, G., Golan, A. and Miller, D. (1993) Recovering information in the case of ill-posed inverse problems with noise. Unpublished manuscript, University of California, Berkeley.

PART II

Linear inverse problems with noise

In Part I, we focused on economic systems that could be represented as pure inverse relations. That is, the underlying inverse relation is non-stochastic, and the indirect observations (e.g. moments) are assumed to be free of measurement errors or other disturbances. Given the characteristics of economic data and the nature of economic processes, few observations are without measurement errors and few economic relations are free of shocks. In the presence of these disturbances, the task of information recovery becomes an inverse problem *with noise.* Many linear inverse problems with noise may be written in terms of the general linear model (GLM)

$$\mathbf{y} = \mathbf{X}\boldsymbol{\beta} + \mathbf{e}$$

Here, $\mathbf{y}$ is a T-vector of noisy observations, $\mathbf{X}$ is a $(T \times K)$ design matrix composed of explanatory variables, and $\boldsymbol{\beta}$ is a K-vector of unknown response parameters. Although $\boldsymbol{\beta}$ is typically taken to be a real-valued vector (as in Chapter 5), it may belong to a more specialized parameter space. For example, $\boldsymbol{\beta}$ may represent one or more discrete probability distributions supported on the elements of $\mathbf{X}$ (as in Chapters 3 and 4).

The unobservable disturbance vector, $\mathbf{e}$, may represent one or more sources of noise in the observed system, including sample and non-sample errors in the data, randomness in the behavior of the economic agents, and specification or modeling errors if $\mathbf{X}\boldsymbol{\beta}$ is a convenient approximation of the underlying system. In general, we consider the equation errors to be uncharacterized deviations. In many situations, we will assume that the error 'distribution' is in some way centered about the origin, $\mathbf{0}$. Further, we assume that either the domain (support) of the distribution is bounded or that the errors have a finite, positive definite variance–covariance matrix, $\Sigma_{\mathbf{e}}$.

CHAPTER 6

Generalized maximum entropy (GME) and cross-entropy (GCE) formulations

6.1 INTRODUCTION

Given the flexibility and simplicity of linear forms, the general linear model (GLM)

$$\mathbf{y} = \mathbf{X}\boldsymbol{\beta} + \mathbf{e} \tag{6.1.1}$$

is a popular and convenient means of formulating inverse problems with noise. However, economic processes are typically dynamic, interdependent, and stochastic, and the available economic data are often composed of limited, non-experimental observations. Hence, the associated economic-statistical models may be ill-posed or underdetermined unless researchers impose strong simplifying assumptions. If traditional methods are applied to the resulting GLM-based inverse problems with noise, the solutions are often infeasible or inadmissible. Consequently, an alternate basis of information recovery must be employed to solve many problems found in practice.

As demonstrated in Chapters 3–5, the generalized entropy formalism is a feasible approach for *pure* linear inverse problems. In the present chapter, the generalized maximum entropy (GME) and generalized cross-entropy (GCE) treatment of the GLM parameters will be formalized. Further, this approach will be extended to account for the presence of the unknown disturbances, which have typically presented a challenge to other entropy-based methods. The following discussion assumes analysts are able to bound the unknown parameters and disturbances, and the bounds are used to specify a finite and discrete support for each of the unknowns. Additional information about the unknowns may be expressed in the form of prior probability distributions on these supports. Then, the entropy objective is used to find the set of 'posterior' distributions on the supports that satisfy the observations *and* are 'closest' to the prior distributions.

After presenting the generalized entropy formulations for various cases of the GLM, we will demonstrate the analytical properties of the resulting GME–GCE solutions. For a broad class of the GME–GCE formulations, we also prove that the generalized entropy point estimators of $\boldsymbol{\beta}$ exist in large samples and are consistent and asymptotically normal. The associated finite sample properties are discussed in Chapter 7.

6.2 REPARAMETERIZATION OF THE GLM

To extend the Chapter 5 results to inverse problems with noise, suppose we have limited prior or non-sample information about the unknown signal and noise components, $\boldsymbol{\beta}$ and $\mathbf{e}$. For example, we often encounter problems in practice for which we have prior beliefs about the signs, magnitudes, or ranges of plausible values for each of the unknowns. Conceptually, we may compose discrete random variables with prior weights and finite supports that reflect our non–sample information about $\boldsymbol{\beta}$ and $\mathbf{e}$. Accordingly, the linear inverse model may be written in terms of the random variables, and the estimation problem is to recover probability distributions for $\boldsymbol{\beta}$ and $\mathbf{e}$ that reconcile the available prior information with the observed sample information. It is important to note that the random variables are merely conceptual devices used to express the prior and sample knowledge in a mutually compatible format.

In particular, we treat each β_k as a discrete random variable with a compact support and $2 \leq M < \infty$ possible outcomes. If z_{k1} and z_{kM} are the plausible extreme values (upper and lower bounds) of β_k, we can express β_k as a convex combination of these two points. That is, there exists $p_k \in [0, 1]$ such that, for $M = 2$,

$$\beta_k = p_k z_{k1} + (1 - p_k) z_{kM} \tag{6.2.1}$$

We can do this for each element of $\boldsymbol{\beta}$, and the parameter space, $\mathscr{B}$, may be represented by a compact hyperrectangle, $\mathscr{Z} \subset \mathbb{R}^K$.

To express the parameters in a more general fashion, let z_k be a set of M points that span the kth dimension of $\mathscr{Z}$. Given an M-dimensional vector of positive weights that sum to one, $\mathbf{p}_k \gg \mathbf{0}$, the kth parameter can be expressed as a convex combination of points $\mathbf{z}_k$ with weights $\mathbf{p}_k$. Further, these convex combinations may be assembled in matrix form so that any $\boldsymbol{\beta} \in \text{int}(\mathscr{Z})$ may be written as

$$\boldsymbol{\beta} = \mathbf{Z}\mathbf{p} = \begin{bmatrix} \mathbf{z}_1' & \mathbf{0} & \cdot & \mathbf{0} \\ \mathbf{0} & \mathbf{z}_2' & \cdot & \mathbf{0} \\ \cdot & \cdot & \cdot & \cdot \\ \mathbf{0} & \mathbf{0} & \cdot & \mathbf{z}_K' \end{bmatrix} \begin{bmatrix} \mathbf{p}_1 \\ \mathbf{p}_2 \\ \cdot \\ \mathbf{p}_K \end{bmatrix} \tag{6.2.2}$$

Here, $\mathbf{Z}$ is a $(K \times KM)$ matrix and $\mathbf{p} \gg \mathbf{0}$ is a KM-dimensional vector of weights. For example, suppose β_1 is an elasticity of supply, and we believe $\beta_1 \in [0, 2]$ with a prior expectation of $\beta_1 = 1$. Then, $z_{11} = 0$ and $z_{12} = 2$ may be used as supports on β_1, and uniform prior weights on these points reflect the prior expected elasticity. As in Chapter 5, the number of support points for each parameter, M, may be increased to reflect higher moments or more refined prior knowledge about $\boldsymbol{\beta}$. Practical issues and empirical results related to the choice of M are outlined in Chapter 8.

The vector of disturbances, $\mathbf{e}$, is assumed to be a random vector with finite location and scale parameters. Accordingly, we represent our uncertainty about the outcome of the error process by treating each e_t as a finite and discrete random variable with $2 \leq J < \infty$ possible outcomes. Suppose there exist sets of error bounds, v_{t1} and v_{tJ}, for each e_t so that $\Pr[v_{t1} < e_t < v_{tJ}]$ may be made arbitrarily small. With positive probability, for $J = 2$, each disturbance may be written as

$$e_t = w_t v_{t1} + (1 - w_t) v_{tJ} \tag{6.2.3}$$

for some $w_t \in (0, 1)$. As above, $J \geq 2$ points may be used to express or recover additional information about e_t (e.g. skewness or kurtosis). If we assume the error distribution is symmetric and centered about $\mathbf{0}$, we can specify a symmetric support, $v_{t1} = -v_{tJ}$, for each t.

The T unknown disturbances may be written in matrix form as

$$\mathbf{e} = \mathbf{V}\mathbf{w} = \begin{bmatrix} \mathbf{v}_1' & \mathbf{0} & \cdot & \mathbf{0} \\ \mathbf{0} & \mathbf{v}_2' & \cdot & \mathbf{0} \\ \cdot & \cdot & \cdot & \cdot \\ \mathbf{0} & \mathbf{0} & \cdot & \mathbf{v}_T' \end{bmatrix} \begin{bmatrix} \mathbf{w}_1 \\ \mathbf{w}_2 \\ \cdot \\ \mathbf{w}_T \end{bmatrix} \tag{6.2.4}$$

where $\mathbf{V}$ is a $(T \times TJ)$ matrix and $\mathbf{w}$ is a TJ-dimensional vector of weights. As before, we restrict the weights to be strictly positive and to sum to 1 for each t.

Using the reparameterized unknowns, $\boldsymbol{\beta} = \mathbf{Z}\mathbf{p}$ and $\mathbf{e} = \mathbf{V}\mathbf{w}$, Judge and Golan (1992) rewrite the GLM, equation (6.1.1), as

$$\mathbf{y} = \mathbf{X}\boldsymbol{\beta} + \mathbf{e} = \mathbf{X}\mathbf{Z}\mathbf{p} + \mathbf{V}\mathbf{w} \tag{6.2.5}$$

Table 6.2.1 Cases of the generic GLM problem

Model	$\boldsymbol{\alpha}$	$\boldsymbol{\Gamma}$	$\boldsymbol{\varepsilon}$
ME	$\mathbf{y}$	$\mathbf{X}$	$\mathbf{0}$
GME-D	$\mathbf{y}$	$\mathbf{X}$	$\mathbf{e}$
GME-M	$\mathbf{X'y}$	$\mathbf{X'X}$	$\mathbf{X'e}$
GME-NM	$(\mathbf{X'y}/T)$	$(\mathbf{X'X}/T)$	$(\mathbf{X'e}/T)$

Given that a large number of linear models may be written in the GLM form, we rewrite equation (6.2.5) as a generic linear model

$$\boldsymbol{\alpha} = \boldsymbol{\Gamma\beta} + \boldsymbol{\varepsilon} \tag{6.2.6}$$

and the associated generic GME formulation of the GLM is

$$\boldsymbol{\alpha} = \boldsymbol{\Gamma}\mathbf{Zp} + \mathbf{Vw} \tag{6.2.7}$$

Special cases of the generic GLM are presented in Table 6.2.1. The suffixes D, M, and NM denote the data, moment, and normed-moment formulations, respectively. For example, the dice example from Chapter 2 is a case of the ME model where $\mathbf{y}$ is the observed mean, $\mathbf{X}$ is the support of the die, and the noise term is excluded.

Provided $\boldsymbol{\beta} \in \mathscr{L}$ is the same for each version of the generic GME problem, the choice of $\mathbf{Z}$ should not change under various forms of the consistency or model constraints. However, the choice of $\mathbf{V}$ clearly depends on the properties of $\boldsymbol{\varepsilon}$. For example, Chebychev's inequality may be used as a conservative means of specifying sets of error bounds. For any random variable, $\mathbf{x}$, such that $\mathrm{E}(\mathbf{x}) = 0$ and $\mathrm{Var}(\mathbf{x}) = \sigma^2$, the inequality provides

$$\Pr[|\mathbf{x}| < v\sigma] \geq v^{-2} \tag{6.2.8}$$

for arbitrary $v > 0$. Given some excluded tail probability, v^{-2}, the Chebychev error bounds are $v_{t1} = -v\sigma$ and $v_{tJ} = v\sigma$. An example is the familiar 3σ rule that excludes at most one-ninth of the mass for $v = 3$. For a recent discussion of probability bounds and the 3σ rule, refer to Pukelsheim (1994). The choice of $\mathbf{V}$ will be considered in greater detail later. For now, it is important to note that the elements of $\mathbf{V}$ reflect the variation (e.g. variance, support) of the underlying errors, and the bounds may be functions of T.

6.3 PRIMAL GME PROBLEM

Following the ME formalism outlined in Chapter 3, the objective of the generalized entropy problem is to recover the unknown parameters through the sets of probabilities, $\mathbf{p}$ and $\mathbf{w}$. At the optimal solution, the probabilities must satisfy the model or consistency constraints, Equation (6.2.7), and the associated additivity constraints. Accordingly, we propose a generalized maximum entropy (GME) solution to the linear inverse problem with noise that selects $\mathbf{p}, \mathbf{w} \gg \mathbf{0}$ to maximize

$$H(\mathbf{p}, \mathbf{w}) = -\mathbf{p}' \ln(\mathbf{p}) - \mathbf{w}' \ln(\mathbf{w}) \tag{6.3.1}$$

subject to

$$\boldsymbol{\alpha} = \boldsymbol{\Gamma}\mathbf{Z}\mathbf{p} + \mathbf{V}\mathbf{w} \tag{6.3.2}$$

$$\mathbf{1_K} = (\mathbf{I}_K \otimes \mathbf{1}'_\mathbf{M})\mathbf{p} \tag{6.3.3}$$

$$\mathbf{1_T} = (\mathbf{I}_T \otimes \mathbf{1}'_\mathbf{J})\mathbf{w} \tag{6.3.4}$$

Here, equation (6.3.2) is the model or consistency constraint, and equations (6.3.3) and (6.3.4) provide the required additivity or normalization constraints for $\mathbf{p}$ and $\mathbf{w}$, respectively. Recall that $\otimes$ is the Kronecker product and that $\mathbf{1_T}$ is a T-dimensional vector of ones.

As in the pure ME formulations, the GME objective is strictly concave on the interior of the additivity constraint set, and a unique solution exists if the intersection of the consistency and additivity constraint sets is non-empty. Analogous to Jaynes' motivation of the maximum entropy formalism, GME selects probabilities on supports $\mathbf{Z}$ and $\mathbf{V}$ that are most 'uniform' (i.e. uncertain) *and* satisfy the observed information. The optimal probability vectors, $\hat{\boldsymbol{p}}$ and $\hat{\boldsymbol{w}}$, may be used to form point estimates of the unknown parameter vector, $\hat{\boldsymbol{\beta}} = \mathbf{Z}\hat{\boldsymbol{p}}$, and the unknown disturbances, $\hat{\mathbf{e}} = \mathbf{V}\hat{\boldsymbol{w}}$. If the prior distributions are non-uniform, the problem may be restated in terms of the generalized cross-entropy criterion. The generic GCE problem is defined and solved in the next section, and the generic GME problem is a special case (i.e. uniform priors).

6.4 PRIMAL GCE PROBLEM AND SOLUTION

As in the CE formalism introduced in Chapter 3, prior information about the unknown parameters and disturbances may be expressed as a set of subjective probability distributions. In the supply elasticity example discussed in Section 6.2, suppose $\beta_1 \in [0, 2]$, but we expect $\beta_1 = 0.5$ *a priori*. Here, for $M = 2$ we can use prior weights $\mathbf{q_1} = [0.75, 0.25]'$ on the support $\mathbf{z_1} = [0, 2]$ to reflect this information about the unknown parameter. In general, we will let $\mathbf{q}$ be the KM-dimensional vector of prior weights for the K unknown parameters, $\boldsymbol{\beta}$, and the prior mean for $\boldsymbol{\beta}$ is $\mathbf{Zq}$. Accordingly, let $\mathbf{u}$ be the TJ-dimensional vector of prior weights on disturbances $\mathbf{e}$ with prior mean $\mathbf{Vu}$.

At times, researchers may have very little (if any) prior information about the unknown parameters. To reflect a general lack of prior knowledge, the support for the unknown parameters may be allocated across a broad portion of the parameter space. For example, suppose we have very little knowledge about plausible values for β_2. We may center the corresponding support about zero and use bounds that are very large in magnitude. A more complex approach is to use several support points (centered about zero) and place almost all of the prior mass at the points nearest to zero. For example, the support on β_2 may be specified as $\mathbf{z}_2 = [-20, -10, 0, 10, 20]'$ with prior weights, $\mathbf{q}_2 = [0.05, 0.2, 0.5, 0.2, 0.05]'$. In this way, the prior mean is still zero, but the cross-entropy objective strongly *shrinks* the posterior distribution to have more mass near zero (as shown in Section 3.3.2). A related approach is used to identify extraneous regressors in variable selection problems (Chapter 10).

Given informative prior distributions on $\mathbf{Z}$ and $\mathbf{V}$ (i.e. $\mathbf{q}$ and $\mathbf{u}$), the cross entropy formalism may be extended to form the generalized cross-entropy (GCE) problem. For greatest generality, we will specify and solve the GCE problem based on the generic consistency constraint, equation (6.2.7). The generic GCE problem selects $\mathbf{p}, \mathbf{w} \gg \mathbf{0}$ to minimize

$$I(\mathbf{p}, \mathbf{q}, \mathbf{w}, \mathbf{u}) = \mathbf{p}' \ln(\mathbf{p}/\mathbf{q}) + \mathbf{w}' \ln(\mathbf{w}/\mathbf{u}) \tag{6.4.1}$$

subject to

$$\boldsymbol{\alpha} = \boldsymbol{\Gamma}\mathbf{Z}\mathbf{p} + \mathbf{V}\mathbf{w} \tag{6.4.2}$$

$$\mathbf{1_K} = (\mathbf{I}_K \otimes \mathbf{1}'_\mathbf{M})\mathbf{p} \tag{6.4.3}$$

$$\mathbf{1_T} = (\mathbf{I}_T \otimes \mathbf{1}'_\mathbf{J})\mathbf{w} \tag{6.4.4}$$

Note that the additivity constraint set, equations (6.4.3) and (6.4.4), is composed of K unit simplices of dimension $M \geq 2$ and T unit simplices of dimension $J \geq 2$. If we denote the individual simplices as $\mathscr{S}_M$ and $\mathscr{S}_J$, respectively, we can write the additivity constraint set as the Cartesian product of these sets, $\mathscr{A} = \mathscr{S}_M^K \times \mathscr{S}_J^T$. Clearly, $\mathscr{A}$ is a non-empty and compact set because each of the component simplices is non-empty and compact. Further, we only consider the interior of the additivity constraint set, $\text{int}(\mathscr{A})$, which contains all $(\mathbf{p}, \mathbf{w}) \gg \mathbf{0}$. The model constraint set (6.4.2) further restricts $\mathscr{A}$ to those probability distributions that are 'consistent' with the data. Let the fully restricted constraint set be

$$\mathscr{A}^* = \{(\mathbf{p}, \mathbf{w}) \in \text{int}(\mathscr{A}) \colon \boldsymbol{\alpha} = \boldsymbol{\Gamma}\mathbf{Z}\mathbf{p} + \mathbf{V}\mathbf{w}\} \tag{6.4.5}$$

Assuming $\mathscr{A}^* \neq \varnothing$, we can use the Lagrangian equation

$$\begin{aligned}\mathscr{L} = I(\mathbf{p}, \mathbf{q}, \mathbf{w}, \mathbf{u}) &+ \boldsymbol{\lambda}'[\boldsymbol{\alpha} - \boldsymbol{\Gamma}\mathbf{Z}\mathbf{p} - \mathbf{V}\mathbf{w}] + \boldsymbol{\theta}'[\mathbf{1_K} - (\mathbf{I_K} \otimes \mathbf{1}'_\mathbf{M})\mathbf{p}] \\ &+ \boldsymbol{\tau}'[\mathbf{1_T} - (\mathbf{I_T} \otimes \mathbf{1}'_\mathbf{J})\mathbf{w}]\end{aligned} \tag{6.4.6}$$

to find the interior solution. Here, $\boldsymbol{\lambda} \in \mathbb{R}^T$, $\boldsymbol{\theta} \in \mathbb{R}^K$, and $\boldsymbol{\tau} \in \mathbb{R}^T$ are the associated vectors of Lagrange multipliers. Taking the gradient of $\mathscr{L}$ to derive the first-order conditions (FOC), we have

$$\nabla_p \mathscr{L} = \mathbf{1_{KM}} + \ln(\tilde{\boldsymbol{p}}/\mathbf{q}) - \mathbf{Z}'\boldsymbol{\Gamma}'\tilde{\boldsymbol{\lambda}} - (\mathbf{I_K} \otimes \mathbf{1_M})\tilde{\boldsymbol{\theta}} = \mathbf{0} \tag{6.4.7}$$

$$\nabla_w \mathscr{L} = \mathbf{1_{TJ}} + \ln(\tilde{\boldsymbol{w}}/\mathbf{u}) - \mathbf{V}'\tilde{\boldsymbol{\lambda}} - (\mathbf{I_T} \otimes \mathbf{1_J})\tilde{\boldsymbol{\tau}} = \mathbf{0} \tag{6.4.8}$$

$$\nabla_\lambda \mathscr{L} = \boldsymbol{\alpha} - \boldsymbol{\Gamma}\mathbf{Z}\tilde{\boldsymbol{p}} - \mathbf{V}\tilde{\boldsymbol{w}} = \mathbf{0} \tag{6.4.9}$$

$$\nabla_\theta \mathscr{L} = \mathbf{1_K} - (\mathbf{I_K} \otimes \mathbf{1'_M})\tilde{\boldsymbol{p}} = \mathbf{0} \tag{6.4.10}$$

$$\nabla_\tau \mathscr{L} = \mathbf{1_T} - (\mathbf{1_T} \otimes \mathbf{1'_J})\tilde{\boldsymbol{w}} = \mathbf{0} \tag{6.4.11}$$

Solving equations (6.4.7) and (6.4.8) for $\tilde{\boldsymbol{p}}$ and $\tilde{\boldsymbol{w}}$, respectively, yield

$$\tilde{\boldsymbol{p}} = \mathbf{q} \odot \exp(\mathbf{Z}'\boldsymbol{\Gamma}'\tilde{\boldsymbol{\lambda}}) \odot \exp[-\mathbf{1_{KM}} + (\mathbf{I_K} \otimes \mathbf{1_M})\tilde{\boldsymbol{\theta}}] \tag{6.4.12}$$

$$\tilde{\boldsymbol{w}} = \mathbf{u} \odot \exp(\mathbf{V}'\tilde{\boldsymbol{\lambda}}) \odot \exp[-\mathbf{1_{TJ}} + (\mathbf{I_T} \otimes \mathbf{1_J})\tilde{\boldsymbol{\tau}}] \tag{6.4.13}$$

where $\odot$ is the Hadamard (elementwise) product. To simplify matters, consider the intermediate solution for $\tilde{\boldsymbol{p}}_k$, the GCE distribution for β_k

$$\tilde{\boldsymbol{p}}_k = \mathbf{q}_k \odot \exp(\mathbf{z}'_k \boldsymbol{\Gamma}'_k \tilde{\boldsymbol{\lambda}}) \odot \exp[-\mathbf{1_M}(\mathbf{1} - \tilde{\theta}_\mathbf{k})]$$

Note that the term

$$\exp[-\mathbf{1_M}(\mathbf{1} - \tilde{\theta}_\mathbf{k})]$$

is the same for each m. So,

$$\hat{p}_{km} \propto q_{km} \cdot \exp(z_{km} \boldsymbol{\Gamma}'_k \tilde{\boldsymbol{\lambda}}) \tag{6.4.14}$$

for all M probabilities in the distribution of each β_k. This implies that we can find probabilities that satisfy the additivity constraints by eliminating the common terms and using the sum of the remaining kernels to normalize each $\tilde{\boldsymbol{p}}_{km}$.

More formally, substitute equations (6.4.12) and (6.4.13) into equations (6.4.10) and (6.4.11), respectively. Considering just $\tilde{\boldsymbol{p}}$, the normalization factor may be identified by further premultiplication

$$\begin{aligned}
(\mathbf{I}_K \otimes \mathbf{1_M})\mathbf{1_K} &= (\mathbf{I}_K \otimes \mathbf{1_M})(\mathbf{I_K} \otimes \mathbf{1'_M})\tilde{\boldsymbol{p}} \\
\mathbf{1_{KM}} &= (\mathbf{I}_K \otimes \mathbf{1_M}\mathbf{1'_M})\tilde{\boldsymbol{p}} \\
\mathbf{1_{KM}} &= (\mathbf{I}_K \otimes \mathbf{1_M}\mathbf{1'_M})[\mathbf{q} \odot \exp(\mathbf{Z}'\boldsymbol{\Gamma}'\tilde{\boldsymbol{\lambda}}) \odot \exp(-\mathbf{1_{KM}} + (\mathbf{I_K} \otimes \mathbf{1_M})\tilde{\boldsymbol{\theta}})] \\
\mathbf{1_{KM}} &= \{(\mathbf{I}_K \otimes \mathbf{1_M}\mathbf{1'_M})[\mathbf{q} \odot \exp(\mathbf{Z}'\boldsymbol{\Gamma}'\tilde{\boldsymbol{\lambda}})]\} \odot \exp(-\mathbf{1_{KM}} + (\mathbf{I_K} \otimes \mathbf{1_M})\tilde{\boldsymbol{\theta}})
\end{aligned} \tag{6.4.15}$$

where $\mathbf{1_M}\mathbf{1'_M}$ is an $(M \times M)$ matrix of ones. By inverting the bracketed term, the result may be rewritten as

$$\exp(-\mathbf{1_{KM}} + (\mathbf{I_K} \otimes \mathbf{1_M})\tilde{\boldsymbol{\theta}}) = \{(\mathbf{I_K} \times \mathbf{1_M}\mathbf{1'_M})[\mathbf{q} \odot \exp(\mathbf{Z}'\boldsymbol{\Gamma}'\tilde{\boldsymbol{\lambda}})]\}^{-1} \tag{6.4.16}$$

and substituting this result into equation (6.4.12) provides

$$\tilde{\boldsymbol{p}} = \mathbf{q} \odot \exp(\mathbf{Z}'\boldsymbol{\Gamma}'\tilde{\boldsymbol{\lambda}}) \odot \{(\mathbf{I}_K \otimes \mathbf{1_M 1'_M})[\mathbf{q} \odot \exp(\mathbf{Z}'\boldsymbol{\Gamma}'\tilde{\boldsymbol{\lambda}})]\}^{-1} \tag{6.4.17}$$

The individual probabilities take the form

$$\tilde{p}_{km} = \frac{q_{km} \exp(z_{km} \Gamma'_k \tilde{\boldsymbol{\lambda}})}{\Omega_k(\tilde{\boldsymbol{\lambda}})} \tag{6.4.18}$$

where Γ_k is the kth column of Γ. The normalization factor for $\tilde{p}_{km}$ is

$$\Omega_k(\tilde{\boldsymbol{\lambda}}) = \sum_n q_{kn} \exp(z_{kn} \Gamma'_k \tilde{\boldsymbol{\lambda}}) \tag{6.4.19}$$

which is known as the *partition function.* In similar fashion, the vector of optimal noise probabilities is

$$\tilde{\boldsymbol{w}} = \mathbf{u} \odot \exp(\mathbf{V}'\tilde{\boldsymbol{\lambda}}) \odot \{(\mathbf{I}_T \otimes \mathbf{1_J 1'_J})[\mathbf{u} \odot \exp(\mathbf{V}'\tilde{\boldsymbol{\lambda}})]\}^{-1} \tag{6.4.20}$$

with individual elements

$$\tilde{w}_{tj} = \frac{u_{tj} \exp(v_{tj} \tilde{\boldsymbol{\lambda}})}{\Psi_t(\tilde{\boldsymbol{\lambda}}_t)} \tag{6.4.21}$$

The partition function for $\tilde{\boldsymbol{w}}$ is

$$\Psi_t(\tilde{\boldsymbol{\lambda}}) = \sum_n u_{tn} \exp(v_{tn} \tilde{\boldsymbol{\lambda}}_t) \tag{6.4.22}$$

To verify the uniqueness of the solution, note that the Hessian matrix of the objective function is

$$\nabla_{(p,\, w)(p',\, w')} I(\mathbf{p}, \mathbf{w}) = \begin{bmatrix} \mathbf{P}^{-1} & \mathbf{0} \\ \mathbf{0} & \mathbf{W}^{-1} \end{bmatrix} \tag{6.4.23}$$

where $\mathbf{P}^{-1}$ is a $(KM \times KM)$ diagonal matrix with elements p_{km}^{-1}, and $\mathbf{W}^{-1}$ is a $(TJ \times TJ)$ diagonal matrix with elements w_{tj}^{-1}. The matrix is positive definite for $\mathbf{p}, \mathbf{w} \gg \mathbf{0}$, which satisfies the sufficient condition for strict convexity. So, there is a unique global minimum for the problem if $\mathscr{A}^* \neq \varnothing$.

Clearly, the GCE solutions, $\tilde{\boldsymbol{p}}$ and $\tilde{\boldsymbol{w}}$, satisfy the additivity constraints, (6.4.3) and (6.4.4), and are strictly positive. However, the GCE solution depends on the Lagrange multipliers for the model or consistency constraints, $\tilde{\boldsymbol{\lambda}}$. The only remaining information in the FOC is the set of model constaints (6.4.2), which are not a function of $\boldsymbol{\lambda}$. As in Jaynes' dice problem, the GME–GCE problems have no closed-form solution. The GCE solution must be found numerically, and an efficient computing algorithm is presented in the next section.

The normalized entropy measure developed in Chapter 3 may be extended to the more general setting of Chapter 6. Further, we can now measure the relative informational content of the signal and noise components through $\tilde{p}$ and $\tilde{w}$, respectively. For the signal, $\mathbf{X\beta}$, the normalized entropy of $\tilde{p}$ is defined as

$$S(\tilde{p}) = \frac{-\tilde{p}' \ln(\tilde{p})}{-\mathbf{q}' \ln(\mathbf{q})} \tag{6.4.24}$$

Similarly, the normalized entropy for the noise, $\mathbf{e}$, is

$$S(\tilde{w}) = \frac{-\tilde{w}' \ln(\tilde{w})}{-\mathbf{u}' \ln(\mathbf{u})} \tag{6.4.25}$$

As before, $S(\cdot) \in [0, 1]$ where $S(\cdot) = 0$ implies no uncertainty (i.e. a degenerate distribution) and $S(\tilde{\boldsymbol{\beta}}) = 1$ implies $\tilde{p} = \mathbf{q}$. Whereas the variance of a discrete distribution measures the concentration of mass about the mean, $S(\cdot)$ measures the concentration of mass over the support of the distribution.

In the GME case, note that these measures reduce to

$$S(\hat{p}) = \frac{-\hat{\mathbf{p}}' \ln(\hat{\mathbf{p}})}{K \ln(M)} \tag{6.4.26}$$

and

$$S(\hat{w}) = \frac{-\hat{\mathbf{w}}' \ln(\hat{\mathbf{w}})}{T \ln(J)} \tag{6.4.27}$$

where $S(\cdot) = 1$ implies that the posterior distribution is identical to the uniform prior. Later in the monograph, the normalized entropy measures are further discussed in the context of specific applications, and they are especially useful criteria for solving variable selection problems (see Chapter 10).

6.5 AN UNCONSTRAINED DUAL GCE PROBLEM

Although computing power is no longer a serious limitation to empirical research, there are clear advantages to using efficient techniques that may be employed in a broad set of computing environments. The purpose of this section is to specify a dual version of the generic GCE problem which may be solved with simpler and more widely available unconstrained numerical methods. The results also apply to the GME case, which is a special case of the GCE formulation. Further, the dual formulation is a valuable tool for evaluating the statistical properties of the GME–GCE solution.

For arbitrary $\boldsymbol{\lambda} \in \mathbb{R}^T$, let $\mathbf{p}(\boldsymbol{\lambda})$ and $\mathbf{w}(\boldsymbol{\lambda})$ represent the functional form of the optimal GCE probabilities, equations (6.4.17) and (6.4.20). If we substitute these into the original Lagrangian expression, (6.4.6), we form the *minimal value* function. Given that the optimal probabilities satisfy the additivity constraints

$\forall \boldsymbol{\lambda} \in \mathbb{R}^T$, the terms associated with these constraints may be dropped from the Lagrangian to yield

$$\begin{aligned}\mathscr{L}(\boldsymbol{\lambda}) &= \mathbf{p}(\boldsymbol{\lambda})' \ln(\mathbf{p}(\boldsymbol{\lambda})) + \mathbf{w}(\boldsymbol{\lambda})' \ln(\mathbf{w}(\boldsymbol{\lambda})) + \boldsymbol{\lambda}'[\boldsymbol{\alpha} - \boldsymbol{\Gamma}\mathbf{Z}\mathbf{p}(\boldsymbol{\lambda}) - \mathbf{V}\mathbf{w}(\boldsymbol{\lambda})] \quad (6.5.1)\\ &= \mathbf{p}(\boldsymbol{\lambda})'[\mathbf{Z}'\boldsymbol{\Gamma}'\boldsymbol{\lambda} - \ln(\boldsymbol{\Omega}(\boldsymbol{\lambda}))] + \mathbf{w}(\boldsymbol{\lambda})'[\mathbf{V}'\boldsymbol{\lambda} - \ln(\boldsymbol{\Psi}(\boldsymbol{\lambda}))]\\ &\quad + [\boldsymbol{\alpha}' - \mathbf{p}(\boldsymbol{\lambda})'\mathbf{Z}'\boldsymbol{\Gamma}' - \mathbf{w}(\boldsymbol{\lambda})'\mathbf{V}']\boldsymbol{\lambda}\\ &= \boldsymbol{\alpha}'\boldsymbol{\lambda} - \mathbf{p}(\boldsymbol{\lambda})' \ln(\boldsymbol{\Omega}(\boldsymbol{\lambda})) - \mathbf{w}(\boldsymbol{\lambda})' \ln(\boldsymbol{\Psi}(\boldsymbol{\lambda}))\\ &= \boldsymbol{\alpha}'\boldsymbol{\lambda} - \sum_k \ln(\Omega_k(\boldsymbol{\lambda})) - \sum_t \ln(\Psi_t(\boldsymbol{\lambda})) \equiv M(\boldsymbol{\lambda})\end{aligned}$$

The minimal value function, $M(\boldsymbol{\lambda})$, may be interpreted as a constrained expected log-likelihood function. To see this, recall that we have expressed our uncertainty about $\boldsymbol{\beta}$ and $\mathbf{e}$ by viewing them as random variables on supports $\mathbf{Z}$ and $\mathbf{V}$, respectively. If we view $\mathbf{p}(\boldsymbol{\lambda})$ and $\mathbf{w}(\boldsymbol{\lambda})$ as families of parametric probability mass functions for these random variables, the joint log-likelihood function may be written in multinomial form as

$$N^{-1} l(\boldsymbol{\lambda}) = \sum_k \sum_m f_{km} \ln(p_{km}(\boldsymbol{\lambda})) + \sum_t \sum_j g_{tj} \ln(w_{tj}(\boldsymbol{\lambda})) \quad (6.5.2)$$

for a sample of size N. Here, f_{km} and g_{tj} are the observed frequencies of outcomes z_{km} and v_{tj}, respectively.

Clearly, the frequency and probability distributions are merely conceptual devices used to represent our uncertainty, and the frequency distributions do not exist. However, we can form an analog version of the log-likelihood function by replacing the frequencies with the associated probabilities. By substitution, equation (6.5.2) becomes the *expected* log-likelihood function

$$\mathrm{E}[l(\boldsymbol{\lambda})] = \mathbf{p}(\boldsymbol{\lambda})' \ln(\mathbf{p}(\boldsymbol{\lambda})) + \mathbf{w}(\boldsymbol{\lambda})' \ln(\mathbf{w}(\boldsymbol{\lambda})) \quad (6.5.3)$$

To ensure that $\mathrm{E}[l(\boldsymbol{\lambda})]$ satisfies the properties of the observed sample, we will maximize the expected log-likelihood function subject to the consistency constraints, equation (6.4.2). After simplifying the expression (as in 6.5.1) and imposing the consistency constraints by substitution, we can see that the constrained expected log-likelihood function is simply $M(\boldsymbol{\lambda})$.

Thus, the dual version of the GCE problem is to choose $\boldsymbol{\lambda}$ to maximize the constrained expected log-likelihood function. A related discussion of the entropy-likelihood duality is provided by Brown (1986, Chapter 6). Note that $M(\boldsymbol{\lambda})$ is a generalization of the dual ME–CE objective function presented in Chapter 3. It was originally developed by Alhassid *et al.* (1978) and Agmon *et al.* (1979), who view it as a generalized potential function of the underlying system. Regardless of interpretation, the unconstrained dual GCE problem is equivalent to the constrained primal GCE problem if the following property is satisfied.

Proposition 6.1 *If $\mathcal{A}^* \neq \emptyset$, the optimal solution to the GCE problem, $(\tilde{\boldsymbol{p}}, \tilde{\boldsymbol{w}}, \tilde{\boldsymbol{\lambda}})$, satisfies the saddlepoint (SP) property:*

$$\mathcal{L}(\mathbf{p}, \mathbf{w}, \tilde{\boldsymbol{\lambda}}) \geq \mathcal{L}(\tilde{\boldsymbol{p}}, \tilde{\boldsymbol{w}}, \tilde{\boldsymbol{\lambda}}) \geq \mathcal{L}(\tilde{\boldsymbol{p}}, \tilde{\boldsymbol{w}}, \boldsymbol{\lambda})$$

A proof of the saddlepoint property appears in Appendix A at the end of this chapter. The proposition implies that the Lagrangian equation is a concave function of the unknown Lagrange multipliers, $\boldsymbol{\lambda}$. In terms of $M(\boldsymbol{\lambda})$, SP implies

$$M(\tilde{\boldsymbol{\lambda}}) \geq M(\boldsymbol{\lambda}) \,\forall\, \boldsymbol{\lambda} \in \mathbb{R}^T \tag{6.5.4}$$

The inequality is *strict* if there exists an interior solution to the problem, and that solution is unique. Thus, we can maximize $M(\boldsymbol{\lambda})$ over $\boldsymbol{\lambda}$ without constraints to find the optimal Lagrange multipliers. Then, we can compute $\tilde{\boldsymbol{p}}$, $\tilde{\boldsymbol{w}}$, $\tilde{\boldsymbol{\beta}}$, and $\tilde{\mathbf{e}}$ by substitution.

The computational properties of the dual GCE problem are very attractive. The objective function, equation (6.5.1), is easily formed and is readily conformable for numerical evaluation of the gradient. Alternately, the analytical gradient of the dual problem

$$\nabla_{\lambda} M(\boldsymbol{\lambda}) = \boldsymbol{\alpha} - \boldsymbol{\Gamma}\mathbf{Z}\mathbf{p}(\boldsymbol{\lambda}) - \mathbf{V}\mathbf{w}(\boldsymbol{\lambda}) \tag{6.5.5}$$

is simply the model or consistency constraint, equation (6.4.2), in homogeneous form. Given the objective function and analytical or numerical gradients, the dual GCE problem may be solved with the same methods used for maximum likelihood and non-linear least squares problems.

The Hessian matrix of $M(\boldsymbol{\lambda})$ takes the form

$$\begin{aligned} \nabla_{\lambda\lambda'} M(\boldsymbol{\lambda}) &= -\boldsymbol{\Gamma}\mathbf{Z}\nabla_{\lambda'}\mathbf{p}(\boldsymbol{\lambda}) - \mathbf{V}\nabla_{\lambda'}\mathbf{w}(\boldsymbol{\lambda}) \\ &= -\boldsymbol{\Gamma}\boldsymbol{\Sigma}_{\mathbf{Z}}(\boldsymbol{\lambda})\boldsymbol{\Gamma}' - \boldsymbol{\Sigma}_{\mathbf{V}}(\boldsymbol{\lambda}) \end{aligned} \tag{6.5.6}$$

where $\boldsymbol{\Sigma}_{\mathbf{Z}}(\boldsymbol{\lambda})$ and $\boldsymbol{\Sigma}_{\mathbf{V}}(\boldsymbol{\lambda})$ are the *variance–covariance* matrices for distributions $\mathbf{p}(\boldsymbol{\lambda})$ and $\mathbf{w}(\boldsymbol{\lambda})$. To evaluate the Hessian matrix, note that the tth equation in $\nabla_{\lambda} M(\boldsymbol{\lambda})$ is

$$\alpha_t - \boldsymbol{\Gamma}_t \mathbf{Z}\mathbf{p}(\boldsymbol{\lambda}) - \mathbf{V}_t \mathbf{w}_t(\boldsymbol{\lambda}) \tag{6.5.7}$$

The second-partial derivative of this equation with respect to λ_s is

$$\frac{\partial^2 M}{\partial \lambda_s \partial \lambda_t} = -\sum_k \Gamma_{tk} \sum_k z_{km} \frac{\partial p_{km}(\lambda)}{\partial \lambda_s} - \sum_j v_{tj} \frac{\partial w_{tj}(\lambda_t)}{\partial \lambda_s} \tag{6.5.8}$$

where

$$\frac{\partial p_{km}(\boldsymbol{\lambda})}{\partial \lambda_s} = \Gamma_{sk}\left[z_{km}p_{km} - p_{km}\sum_n z_{kn}p_{kn}\right] \tag{6.5.9}$$

and

$$\frac{\partial w_{tj}(\lambda_t)}{\partial \lambda_s} = \begin{cases} v_{tj}w_{tj} - w_{tj}\sum_n v_{tn}w_{tn}, & s = t \\ 0, & s \neq t \end{cases} \tag{6.5.10}$$

Finally, note that

$$\sigma_{zk}^2 = \sum_m p_{km} z_{km}^2 - \left[\sum_m p_{km} z_{km} \right]^2 \tag{6.5.11}$$

$$\sigma_{vt}^2 = \sum_j w_{tj} v_{tj}^2 - \left[\sum_j w_{tj} v_{tj} \right]^2 \tag{6.5.12}$$

which implies

$$\frac{\partial^2 M}{\partial \lambda_s \partial \lambda_t} = - \sum_k \Gamma_{tk} \Gamma_{sk} \sigma_{zk}^2 - \sigma_{vt}^2 \tag{6.5.13}$$

For any interior solution, $(\tilde{\boldsymbol{p}}, \tilde{\boldsymbol{w}})$, each of these variance terms is strictly positive, and thus $\boldsymbol{\Sigma}_{\mathbf{Z}}$ and $\boldsymbol{\Sigma}_{\mathbf{V}}$ are positive definite matrices.

Assembled in matrix form, the second-partials take the form of equation (6.5.6). Although $\boldsymbol{\Gamma\Sigma}_{\mathbf{Z}}\boldsymbol{\Gamma}'$ is positive semi-definite when $T > K$, $\boldsymbol{\Sigma}_{\mathbf{V}}$ is a positive definite matrix. Hence, $\boldsymbol{\Gamma\Sigma}_{\mathbf{Z}}\boldsymbol{\Gamma}' + \boldsymbol{\Sigma}_{\mathbf{V}}$ is positive definite, and (6.5.6) is a negative definite matrix. By the sufficient condition for strict concavity, $M(\boldsymbol{\lambda})$ is strictly concave in $\boldsymbol{\lambda}$, and choosing $\boldsymbol{\lambda}$ to maximize $M(\boldsymbol{\lambda})$ will yield the unique solution, $\tilde{\boldsymbol{\lambda}}$. Thus, the unique GCE solution may be computed with *unconstrained* techniques, and the gradient vector and Hessian matrix for the problem are convenient and inexpensive to form. In general, the unconstrained solutions may be computed as efficiently as related ML or LS problems. For more details, refer to Miller (1994) or to Chapter 17.

6.6 LARGE SAMPLE PROPERTIES

As discussed in the preceding chapters, the entropy-based methods of information recovery are not directly motivated by standard sampling theory. However, large and small sample properties are useful measures of performance and may be used to compare competing estimators. For example, researchers may compute the bias and variance of a Bayesian point estimator in order to compare its mean squared error (MSE) with a sampling theoretic alternative. Although the GME–GCE solution does not have a closed-form, the dual formulation of the problem may be used to evaluate the behavior of the solutions within the context of extremum or M-estimators (Huber, 1981; Newey and McFadden, 1994). The large sample properties of the GME–GCE solutions are outlined in this section, and the small sample properties are discussed in Chapter 7.

The model constraints used in Jaynes' classical ME problems were implicitly assumed to be consistent empirical analogs to the underlying population moments. If the empirical moments are drawn from very large samples, the remaining noise should be negligible. For example, the observed sample average in the dice example represents such a large sample that the average is assumed to have converged to the population mean. Thus, the problem is asymptotically non-stochastic and may be treated as a pure inverse problem (as in Chapters 3–5).

Accordingly, we will examine the properties of a generalized entropy formulation that employs convergent functions of the sample information. In particular, consider the vector of weighted averages formed by dividing $\mathbf{X}'\mathbf{y} = \mathbf{X}'\mathbf{X}\boldsymbol{\beta} + \mathbf{X}'\mathbf{e}$ by the sample size, T. Under fairly mild regularity conditions, these normed moments converge in probability. The GCE problem using the normed moments as model or consistency constraints, is identified as the GCE–NM problem in Table 6.2.1. Our goal is to outline conditions on the components of the GCE–NM model that provide a non-stochastic problem in very large samples. To do so, we must first show that there exists a solution to the GCE–NM problem in large samples – a property we have implicitly assumed to this point. Then, we show that the GME–GCE solutions are consistent and asymptotically normal as the sample size, T, becomes infinitely large. Although the following discussion is rather informal, we provide detailed proofs of these propositions in the Appendices to this chapter.

For the purpose of the large sample analysis, the solution to the GCE–NM problem is computed by choosing $(\mathbf{p}, \mathbf{w}) \gg \mathbf{0}$ to minimize

$$I(\mathbf{p}, \mathbf{q}, \mathbf{w}, \mathbf{u}) = \mathbf{p}' \ln(\mathbf{p}/\mathbf{q}) + \mathbf{w}' \ln(\mathbf{w}/\mathbf{u}) \tag{6.6.1}$$

subject to

$$\frac{\mathbf{X}'\mathbf{y}}{T} = \left(\frac{\mathbf{X}'\mathbf{X}}{T}\right)\mathbf{Z}\mathbf{p} + \mathbf{V}\mathbf{w} \tag{6.6.2}$$

$$\mathbf{1_K} = (\mathbf{I}_K \otimes \mathbf{1}'_\mathbf{M})\mathbf{p} \tag{6.6.3}$$

$$\mathbf{1_K} = (\mathbf{I}_K \otimes \mathbf{1}'_\mathbf{J})\mathbf{w} \tag{6.6.4}$$

where $\mathbf{V}$ redefined as is a $(K \times KJ)$ matrix that specifies a finite and discrete support for each of the K residuals, $T^{-1}\mathbf{X}'\mathbf{e}$. Based on the results of the preceding section, the dual formulation of the problem is

$$\max_{\lambda} M_T(\boldsymbol{\lambda}) = \left(\frac{\mathbf{y}'\mathbf{X}}{T}\right)\boldsymbol{\lambda} - \sum_k \ln[\Omega_k(\boldsymbol{\lambda})] - \sum_k \ln[\Psi_k(\boldsymbol{\lambda})] \tag{6.6.5}$$

where $\boldsymbol{\lambda} \in \mathbb{R}^K$ and the associated partition functions are

$$\Omega_k(\boldsymbol{\lambda}) = \sum_n q_{kn} \exp\left(z_{kn}\left(\frac{\mathbf{X_k}\mathbf{X}'}{T}\right)\boldsymbol{\lambda}\right) \tag{6.6.6}$$

$$\Psi_k(\boldsymbol{\lambda}) = \sum_n u_{kn} \exp(V_{kn}\lambda_k) \tag{6.6.7}$$

For a sample of size T, the solution to the dual problem is denoted $\tilde{\boldsymbol{\lambda}}_T$, and the associated point estimate of the unknown parameter vector is $\tilde{\boldsymbol{\beta}}_T = \mathbf{Z}\mathbf{p}(\tilde{\boldsymbol{\lambda}}_T)$.

Before examining the properties of the GCE solution, we must specify the regularity conditions assumed for the underlying empirical moments. In this context, we make the following assumptions.

(6.A1) There exists a finite, positive definite matrix $\mathbf{Q}$ such that

$$\lim_T \left(\frac{\mathbf{X}'\mathbf{X}}{T}\right) = \mathbf{Q}$$

(6.A2) $\mathrm{E}(\mathbf{e}) = \mathbf{0}$, $\mathrm{Var}(\mathbf{e}) = \mathbf{\Sigma_e}$, and $F(\mathbf{e})$ satisfies the Lindeberg condition (Billingsley 1986, equation 27.8)

$$T^{-1} \sum_{t=1}^{T} \int_{\mathscr{E}} \|\mathbf{e}\|^2 \, dF(\mathbf{e}) \to 0$$

where $\mathscr{E} = \{\mathbf{e}: \|\mathbf{e}\| > \varepsilon\sqrt{T}\}$ for $\varepsilon > 0$.

(6.A3) The variance–covariance matrix of $\boldsymbol{\varepsilon} = \mathbf{X}'\mathbf{e}/\sqrt{T}$ converges to a finite, positive definite matrix

$$\lim_T \left(\frac{\mathbf{X}'\mathbf{\Sigma_e X}}{T}\right) = \mathbf{\Sigma}^*$$

Given these assumptions, we can prove the following result.

Lemma 6.1

$$\lim_T \Pr\left(\frac{\mathbf{X}'\mathbf{e}}{T}\right) = \mathbf{0}$$

Proof. By Assumptions 6.A2 and 6.A3, $\mathrm{E}[\mathbf{X}'\mathbf{e}] = \mathbf{0} \; \forall T$, and

$$\lim_T \mathrm{Var}\left(\frac{\mathbf{X}'\mathbf{e}}{T}\right) = \lim_T T^{-1}\mathbf{\Sigma}^* = \mathbf{0} \tag{6.6.8}$$

So, $T^{-1}\mathbf{X}'\mathbf{e}$ converges (in quadratic mean) to a null vector, which implies $T^{-1}\mathbf{X}'\mathbf{e} \xrightarrow{p} \mathbf{0}$ by Chebychev's inequality. □

Accordingly, the components of the GCE–NM formulation should be specified to exhibit similar behavior. To ensure a feasible solution in large samples, the bounded parameter space, $\mathscr{Z}$, should contain the true parameter vector, $\boldsymbol{\beta}_0$. Also, the error bounds, $\mathbf{V}$, should mimic the convergent behavior of their sample analogs. Following Chebychev's inequality and other rules, the error bounds should be proportional to the standard errors of the underlying disturbances. From Lemma 6.1, we can see that the standard errors of the

GCE–NM disturbances are $O_p(^{-1}\sqrt{T})$. Thus, we make two additional assumptions.

(6.A4) $\boldsymbol{\beta}_0 \in \text{int}(\mathscr{Z})$

(6.A5) $\mathbf{V} = O(^{-1}\sqrt{T})$

Assumption 6.A5 implies that the error bounds converge pointwise on $\mathbf{0}$ at the same rate as the underlying disturbances converge stochastically. Later, we will increase the rate at which $\mathbf{V}$ converges in order to achieve asymptotically normal GCE solutions.

Given that the elements of $\mathbf{y}$ are the only stochastic components of the GCE–NM consistency constraints, Lemma 6.1 and Assumption 6.A1 imply that the problem becomes asymptotically non-stochastic with limiting gradient $\mathbf{Q}\boldsymbol{\beta}_0 - \mathbf{QZp}$. By 6.A1, we can premultiply the FOC by $\mathbf{Q}^-$, which is a full-rank matrix. By 6.A4, there exists some set of weights, $\mathbf{p}^*$, such that $\boldsymbol{\beta}_0 = \mathbf{Zp}^*$, and a solution to the problem exists in sufficiently large samples. Further, $\mathbf{p}(\tilde{\boldsymbol{\lambda}}_T) \xrightarrow{p} \mathbf{p}^*$, and the solution is consistent. However, the dual GCE–NM problem is actually solved for the Lagrange multipliers, $\boldsymbol{\lambda}$, not the probability distributions. Fortunately, the Lagrange multipliers and the original parameters, $\boldsymbol{\beta}$, have a unique relationship which is demonstrated in Appendix B. Thus, the solution to the unconstrained problem, $\tilde{\boldsymbol{\lambda}}_T$, provides the correct probabilities, $\mathbf{p}^*$ in large samples. As well, the point estimator, $\tilde{\boldsymbol{\beta}}_T$, exhibits related behavior, and proofs of the existence and consistency properties appear in Appendices C and D.

Finally, we prove that the GCE–NM solution is asymptotically normal under a refined version of 6.A5. The central idea behind our proof is based on a familiar result

$$\left(\frac{\mathbf{X}'\mathbf{e}}{\sqrt{T}}\right) \Rightarrow \text{N}[\mathbf{0}, \boldsymbol{\Sigma}^*]$$

which follows from Assumptions 6.A2 and 6.A3 and implicitly from the Lindeberg–Feller central limit theorem (Spanos, 1986, p. 177). Given that the consistency constraints (empirical moments) are asymptotically normal, we can show that the GME–GCE analogs exhibit equivalent behavior. Further, the optimal Lagrange multipliers and the ultimate point estimator are accordingly Gaussian in large samples. The large-sample distribution of the GCE–NM solution is

$$\sqrt{T}(\tilde{\beta}_T - \beta_0) \Rightarrow \text{N}[\mathbf{0}, \mathbf{Q}^{-1}\boldsymbol{\Sigma}^*\mathbf{Q}^{-1}] \tag{6.6.9}$$

where $\boldsymbol{\Sigma}^*$ is defined in 6.A3. Note that this is identical to the limiting distribution of the sampling theoretic LS estimator. A proof of the asymptotic distribution of the GCE–NM solution appears in Appendix E.

Intuitively, the GCE–NM solution is asymptotically equivalent to the LS estimator because the FOC (normal equations) are identical in the limit of T. In the pure formulation of the GCE–NM problem, $\mathbf{V} = \mathbf{0}$ for all T and the model constraint is

$$\frac{\mathbf{X}'\mathbf{y}}{T} = \left(\frac{\mathbf{X}'\mathbf{X}}{T}\right)\mathbf{Z}\mathbf{p}(\boldsymbol{\lambda}) \tag{6.6.10}$$

If $\tilde{\boldsymbol{\beta}}_{LS} \in \mathscr{Z}$ for a particular T, then $\tilde{\boldsymbol{\beta}}_T = \tilde{\boldsymbol{\beta}}_{LS}$; otherwise, there is no interior solution. Note that interior solutions are more probable for the noise formulation, which employs a less restrictive set of model constraints. However, the same large-sample properties also characterize the pure GCE–NM problem.

6.7 REMARKS

In this chapter, we have formalized and extended the generalized entropy framework for pure inverse problems introduced in Chapter 5. By reparameterizing the unknown parameters *and* disturbances of the GLM in terms of finite and discrete probability distributions, Jaynes' entropy formalism may be used to solve linear inverse problems with noise. Using a dual approach to the constrained GME–GCE problem, we derive an algorithm for computing the GME–GCE solution by unconstrained numerical techniques. Under fairly mild regularity conditions, we also prove that some members of the GME–GCE family of solutions are consistent and normal in large samples. The results of this chapter are basic to the formulations and estimators developed and evaluated in Chapters 9 through 16.

In Chapter 7, we explore additional extensions and refinements of the GME–GCE framework. The topics covered include the finite sample properties of the GME–GCE solutions and a more general version of the entropy objective. We conclude Chapter 7 and Part II with an application of GME–GCE to a familiar problem in the statistics literature, recovering a bounded mean.

REFERENCES

Agmon, N., Alhassid, Y. and Levine, R. D. (1979) An algorithm for finding the distribution of maximal entropy. *Journal of Computational Physics* **30**, 250–8.

Alhassid, Y., Agmon, N. and Levine, R. D. (1978) An upper bound for the entropy and its applications to the maximal entropy problem. *Chemical Physics Letters* **53**, 22–6.

Billingsley, P. (1986) *Probability and Measure.* John Wiley, New York.

Brown, L. D. (1986) *Fundamentals of Statistical Exponential Families,* Vol. 9, Institute of Mathematical Statistics Lecture Notes-Monograph Series, Hayward, CA.

Huber, P. (1981) *Robust Statistics.* John Wiley, New York.

Johansen, S. (1979) *Introduction to the Theory of Regular Exponential Families.* Lecture Notes, Vol. 3. Institute of Mathematical Statistics, Copenhagen, Denmark.

Judge, G. G. and Golan, A. (1992) Recovering information in the case of ill-posed inverse problems with noise. Unpublished paper, University of California at Berkeley.

Miller, D. (1994) Solving generalized maximum entropy problems with unconstrained numerical techniques. Unpublished paper, University of California at Berkeley.

Newey, W. K. and McFadden, D. L. (1994) Large sample estimation and hypothesis testing. In R. F. Engle and D. L. McFadden (eds.), *Handbook of Econometrics,* Vol. 4. Elsevier, Amsterdam.

Pukelsheim, F. (1994) The three sigma rule. *American Statistician* **48**(4), 88–91.

Spanos, A. (1986) *Statistical Foundations of Econometric Modelling.* Cambridge University Press.

Takayama, A. (1985) *Mathematical Economics.* Cambridge University Press.

APPENDIX

A. PROOF OF PROPOSITION 6.1

If $\mathscr{A}^* \neq \varnothing$, the strict convexity of $I(\mathbf{p}, \mathbf{w})$ ensures that the GCE problem has a unique global minimum (GM), $(\tilde{\mathbf{p}}, \tilde{\mathbf{w}}, \tilde{\boldsymbol{\lambda}})$. Clearly, a GM is also a local minimum (LM). The linearity of the constraint set defined by equations (6.4.2), (6.4.3), and (6.4.4) satisfies the second condition of the Arrow–Hurwicz–Uzawa constraint qualification (Takayama, 1985, Theorem 1.D.4), and the LM is also a quasi-saddlepoint by the Kuhn–Tucker theorem (Takayama, 1985, Theorem 1.D.3). Finally, the linearity (hence concavity) of the constraints satisfies result (ii) of Theorem 1.D.1 in Takayama (1985). Therefore, the unique GM for the GCE problem also satisfies SP. □

B. RELATING THE PARAMETER SPACES

As previously noted, we are interested in the properties of the GCE–NM point estimator, $\tilde{\boldsymbol{\beta}}_T$, although we actually solve GME–GCE problems for the optimal

Lagrange multipliers, $\tilde{\boldsymbol{\lambda}}_T$. The following result allows us to define $\boldsymbol{\lambda}_0 \in \mathbb{R}^K$, which is uniquely and implicitly defined as $\boldsymbol{\beta}_0 = \mathbf{Zp}(\boldsymbol{\lambda}_0)$ for some $\boldsymbol{\beta}_0 \in \text{int}(Z)$. Consequently, we can relate the original constrained parameter space, $\mathscr{Z}$, to the space of Lagrange multipliers, Λ. In the mathematical statistics literature, similar operations are used to relate the original and canonical parameter spaces in exponential families (Brown, 1986; Johansen, 1979).

Before proceeding, define the following parameter spaces.

(6.D1) For some $\boldsymbol{\lambda} \in \mathbb{R}^K$, Λ is an open neighborhood of $\boldsymbol{\lambda}$ with topological closure $\bar{\Lambda}$.

(6.D2) $\mathscr{Z}_\Lambda$ is the range of $\mathbf{Zp}(\boldsymbol{\lambda})$ for all $\boldsymbol{\lambda} \in \Lambda$.

(6.D3) $\mathscr{Y}_\Lambda$ is the range of $\mathbf{QZp}(\boldsymbol{\lambda})$ for all $\boldsymbol{\lambda} \in \Lambda$.

Lemma 6.2 *$\omega(\boldsymbol{\lambda}) \equiv \mathbf{Zp}(\boldsymbol{\lambda})$ is a diffeomorphism from Λ to $\mathscr{Z}_\Lambda$ for all sufficiently large T.*

Proof. A *diffeomorphism* is a mapping from one set to another that is one-to-one, onto, and continuous in each direction. The one-to-one property may be demonstrated by contradiction. Suppose there exists two vectors, $\boldsymbol{\lambda}_1 \neq \boldsymbol{\lambda}_2$, such that

$$\boldsymbol{\beta}_0 = \mathbf{Zp}(\boldsymbol{\lambda}_1) = \mathbf{Zp}(\boldsymbol{\lambda}_2) \tag{6.A.1}$$

The equality holds for both distributions on $\mathbf{Z}$, so the analysis may be restricted to the probabilities. Without loss of generality, let $\boldsymbol{\lambda}_1 = \mathbf{0}$, and note that z_{km} in each term in the denominator does not cancel. Consequently, just consider the numerator of the individual probabilities

$$q_{km} \exp\left(z_{km} \left(\frac{\mathbf{X}_\mathbf{k}' \mathbf{X}}{T} \right) \boldsymbol{\lambda}_2 \right) = q_{km} \exp(0) \tag{6.A.2}$$

This only holds for $\boldsymbol{\lambda}_2 \neq \mathbf{0}$ if $\mathbf{X}'\mathbf{X}$ is rank deficient, which contradicts 6.A1 in large samples.

Also, $\omega: \bar{\Lambda} \rightarrow \mathscr{Z}_{\bar{\Lambda}}$ is onto by construction. Finally, $\omega(\boldsymbol{\lambda})$ is clearly a continuous function of $\boldsymbol{\lambda}$. Thus, each of the required properties of a homeomorphism from Λ to $\mathscr{Z}_\Lambda$ are satisfied. When moving in the opposite direction, the continuity and onto properties hold as before. A violation of the one-to-one property requires a single vector of Lagrange multipliers, $\boldsymbol{\lambda}_0$, to be associated with two vectors in the original parameter space, $\boldsymbol{\beta}_1$ and $\boldsymbol{\beta}_2$. However, this implies that a single probability distribution, $\mathbf{p}(\boldsymbol{\lambda}_0)$, has two means, which is inconsistent with the properties of full-rank exponential families. □

Before concluding, we should identify the local properties of the functions relating the two parameter spaces. Note that $\omega(\boldsymbol{\lambda})$ is continuously differentiable with Jacobian matrix

$$\omega'(\boldsymbol{\lambda}) = \nabla_{\lambda'}\mathbf{Z}\mathbf{p}(\boldsymbol{\lambda}) = \left(\frac{\mathbf{X}'\mathbf{X}}{T}\right)\boldsymbol{\Sigma}_{\mathbf{Z}}(\boldsymbol{\lambda}) \tag{6.A.3}$$

as a special case of equation (6.5.5). For all sufficiently large T, ω' is positive definite for all $\boldsymbol{\lambda} \in \Lambda$ by Assumption 6.A1. By the inverse function theorem, ω has a unique continuously differentiable inverse, ρ: $\mathscr{Z}_\Lambda \to \Lambda$, with Jacobian matrix

$$\left[\left(\frac{\mathbf{X}'\mathbf{X}}{T}\right)\boldsymbol{\Sigma}_{\mathbf{Z}}(\boldsymbol{\lambda})\right]^{-1} \tag{6.A.4}$$

which is also positive definite in large samples. Thus, ρ also satisfies the inverse function theorem.

C. EXISTENCE

We now prove that an interior solution to the GCE–NM problem exists for all sufficiently large samples.

Proposition 6.2 *Under Assumptions 6.A1–6.A3,*

$$\lim_T \Pr[\tilde{\boldsymbol{\lambda}}_T \in \Lambda] = 1$$

for all sufficiently large T.

Proof. By Lemma 6.2, the event

$$\left(\frac{\mathbf{X}'\mathbf{y}}{T}\right) \in \mathscr{Y}_\Lambda$$

is equivalent to the event of interest, $\tilde{\boldsymbol{\lambda}}_T \in \Lambda$, in sufficiently large samples. Assumption 6.A1 and Lemma 6.1 imply

$$\frac{\mathbf{X}'\mathbf{y}}{T} = \left(\frac{\mathbf{X}'\mathbf{X}}{T}\right)\boldsymbol{\beta}_0 + \left(\frac{\mathbf{X}'\mathbf{e}}{T}\right)$$
$$\xrightarrow{p} \mathbf{Q}\boldsymbol{\beta}_0 \tag{6.A.5}$$

by Slutsky's theorem. Lemma 6.2 and Definition 6.D3 further provide

$$\mathbf{Q}\boldsymbol{\beta}_0 \equiv \mathbf{Q}\mathbf{Z}\mathbf{p}(\boldsymbol{\lambda}_0) \in \mathscr{Y}_\Lambda \tag{6.A.6}$$

Thus,

$$\lim_T \Pr\left[\frac{\mathbf{X}'\mathbf{y}}{T} \in \mathcal{Y}_\Lambda\right] = 1 \tag{6.A.7}$$

and the equivalence of the events proves the proposition. □

D. CONSISTENCY

Proposition 6.3 *Under Assumptions 6.A1–6.A3,*

$$\text{plim}(\tilde{\boldsymbol{\beta}}_T) = \boldsymbol{\beta}_0$$

Proof. First, show that $\tilde{\boldsymbol{\lambda}}_T \xrightarrow{p} \boldsymbol{\lambda}_0$. To do this, evaluate the three sets of terms in the GCE–NM dual objective function, equation (6.6.5). Following equation (6.A.6),

$$\left(\frac{\mathbf{y}'\mathbf{X}}{T}\right)\boldsymbol{\lambda} \xrightarrow{p} \boldsymbol{\beta}_0'\mathbf{Q}'\boldsymbol{\lambda} \tag{6.A.8}$$

By Assumption 6.A2 and Slutsky's theorem,

$$\begin{aligned} \Omega_k(\boldsymbol{\lambda}) &= \sum_n q_{kn} \exp\left[z_{kn}\left(\frac{\mathbf{X}_\mathbf{k}'\mathbf{X}}{T}\right)\boldsymbol{\lambda}\right] \\ &\to \sum_n q_{kn} \exp[z_{kn}\mathbf{Q}_k'\boldsymbol{\lambda}] \end{aligned} \tag{6.A.9}$$

Given $\mathbf{V} = O(\sqrt[-1]{T})$, Slutsky's theorem implies

$$\begin{aligned} \Psi_k(\boldsymbol{\lambda}) &= \sum_j u_{kj} \exp[\mathbf{v}_k'\boldsymbol{\lambda}] \\ &\to \sum_j u_{kj} \exp[0] = 1 \end{aligned} \tag{6.A.10}$$

By additional application of Slutsky's theorem, the three results may be combined to yield

$$\begin{aligned} M_T(\boldsymbol{\lambda}) &\xrightarrow{p} \boldsymbol{\beta}_0'\mathbf{Q}\boldsymbol{\lambda} - \sum_k \ln\left[\sum_m q_{km} \exp(z_{km}\mathbf{Q}_k'\boldsymbol{\lambda})\right] - \sum_k \ln[1] \\ &= \boldsymbol{\beta}_0'\mathbf{Q}\boldsymbol{\lambda} - \sum_k \ln\left[\sum_m q_{km} \exp(z_{km}\mathbf{Q}_k'\boldsymbol{\lambda})\right] \\ &\equiv M_\infty(\boldsymbol{\lambda}) \end{aligned} \tag{6.A.11}$$

The limiting objective function, $M_\infty(\boldsymbol{\lambda})$, is non-stochastic, strictly concave in $\boldsymbol{\lambda}$, and has gradient

$$\nabla_\lambda M_\infty(\boldsymbol{\lambda}) = \mathbf{Q}\boldsymbol{\beta}_0 - \mathbf{QZp}(\boldsymbol{\lambda}) \tag{6.A.12}$$

By Lemma 6.2, $\boldsymbol{\lambda}_0 \in \Lambda$ is the unique solution to the FOC for the limiting objective function. Further,

$$\lim_T \Pr[\tilde{\boldsymbol{\lambda}}_T \in \partial(\bar{\Lambda})] = 0 \qquad (6.A.13)$$

by Proposition 6.2.

Given that $M_T(\boldsymbol{\lambda})$ is uniformly continuous in $\boldsymbol{\lambda}$ for all sufficiently large T, $M_T(\boldsymbol{\lambda}) \xrightarrow{p} M_\infty(\boldsymbol{\lambda})$ necessarily implies $\tilde{\boldsymbol{\lambda}}_T \xrightarrow{p} \boldsymbol{\lambda}_0$. Further, $\mathbf{Zp}(\boldsymbol{\lambda})$ is a continuous function of $\boldsymbol{\lambda}$, and Slutsky's theorem implies that $\mathbf{Zp}(\tilde{\boldsymbol{\lambda}}_T) \xrightarrow{p} \mathbf{Zp}(\boldsymbol{\lambda}_0) \equiv \boldsymbol{\beta}_0$. Thus, $\tilde{\boldsymbol{\beta}}_T \xrightarrow{p} \boldsymbol{\beta}_0$. □

E. ASYMPTOTIC NORMALITY

The asymptotic distribution of the GCE–NM solution can be derived by finding the distribution of $\tilde{\boldsymbol{\lambda}}_T$. Given that $\tilde{\boldsymbol{\beta}}_T = \mathbf{Zp}(\tilde{\boldsymbol{\lambda}}_T)$ is a continuous function of $\tilde{\boldsymbol{\lambda}}_T$, the δ-method (Spanos, 1986, p. 201) may be used to approximate the distribution of $\tilde{\boldsymbol{\beta}}_T$.

Proposition 6.4 *Under Assumptions 6.A1–6.A4,*

$$\sqrt{T}(\tilde{\boldsymbol{\beta}}_T - \boldsymbol{\beta}_0) \Rightarrow \mathrm{N}[\mathbf{0}, \mathbf{Q}^{-1}\boldsymbol{\Sigma}^*\mathbf{Q}^{-1}]$$

if the GCE–NM error bounds are $\mathbf{V} = O(T^{-1})$.

Proof. If $\tilde{\boldsymbol{\lambda}}_T \in \Lambda$, the first-order Taylor expansion of the FOC is

$$\nabla_\lambda M_T(\tilde{\boldsymbol{\lambda}}_T) = \nabla_\lambda M_T(\boldsymbol{\lambda}_0) + \nabla_{\lambda\lambda'} M_T(\boldsymbol{\lambda}_T^*)(\tilde{\boldsymbol{\lambda}}_T - \boldsymbol{\lambda}_0) \qquad (6.A.14)$$

for some $\boldsymbol{\lambda}_T^*$ between $\tilde{\boldsymbol{\lambda}}_T$ and $\boldsymbol{\lambda}_0$ by the mean value theorem. By solving the FOC, $\tilde{\boldsymbol{\lambda}}_T$ ensures that the left-hand side is $\mathbf{0}$. Then, the approximation may be rewritten as

$$\sqrt{T}(\tilde{\boldsymbol{\lambda}}_T - \boldsymbol{\lambda}_0) = -[\nabla_{\lambda\lambda'} M(\boldsymbol{\lambda}_T^*)]^{-1} \cdot [\sqrt{T}\nabla_\lambda M(\boldsymbol{\lambda}_0)] \qquad (6.A.15)$$

Note that the inverse of the Hessian matrix exists because it is a positive definite matrix for all T and $\boldsymbol{\lambda}_T^*$ by the previous discussion.

To evaluate this expression, note that

$$\sqrt{T}\nabla_\lambda M_T(\boldsymbol{\lambda}_0) = \sqrt{T}\left[\frac{\mathbf{X}'\mathbf{y}}{T} - \left(\frac{\mathbf{X}'\mathbf{X}}{T}\right)\mathbf{Zp}(\boldsymbol{\lambda}_0) - \mathbf{Vw}(\boldsymbol{\lambda}_0)\right] \qquad (6.A.16)$$

$$= \sqrt{T}\left[\frac{\mathbf{X}'(\mathbf{y} - \mathbf{X}\boldsymbol{\beta}_0)}{T} + O(T^{-1})\right]$$

$$= \left(\frac{\mathbf{X}'\mathbf{e}}{\sqrt{T}}\right) + O(^{-1}\!\!\sqrt{T})$$

which converges in law to $N[\mathbf{0}, \boldsymbol{\Sigma}^*]$ by Assumptions 6.A2 and 6.A3. Further, $\text{plim}(\tilde{\boldsymbol{\lambda}}_T) = \boldsymbol{\lambda}_0$ implies $\text{plim}(\boldsymbol{\lambda}_T^*) = \boldsymbol{\lambda}_0$, which provides

$$\begin{aligned} \text{plim } \nabla_{\lambda\lambda'} M_T(\boldsymbol{\lambda}^*) &= \lim_T \nabla_{\lambda\lambda'} M(\boldsymbol{\lambda}_0) \\ &= \lim_T \left[\left(\frac{\mathbf{X}'\mathbf{X}}{T}\right) \boldsymbol{\Sigma}_{\mathbf{Z}}(\boldsymbol{\lambda}_0) \left(\frac{\mathbf{X}'\mathbf{X}}{T}\right)' + \boldsymbol{\Sigma}_{\mathbf{V}} \right] \\ &= \mathbf{Q}\boldsymbol{\Sigma}_{\mathbf{Z}}\mathbf{Q}' \end{aligned} \tag{6.A.17}$$

because $\mathbf{V} = O(T^{-1})$. The limiting distribution for $\tilde{\boldsymbol{\lambda}}_T$ is

$$\begin{aligned} \sqrt{T}(\tilde{\boldsymbol{\lambda}}_T - \boldsymbol{\lambda}_0) &\Rightarrow N[\mathbf{0}, (\mathbf{Q}\boldsymbol{\Sigma}_{\mathbf{Z}}\mathbf{Q}')^{-1}\boldsymbol{\Sigma}^*(\mathbf{Q}\boldsymbol{\Sigma}_{\mathbf{Z}}\mathbf{Q}')^{-1}] \\ &\equiv N[\mathbf{0}, \boldsymbol{\Sigma}_{\boldsymbol{\lambda}_0}] \end{aligned} \tag{6.A.18}$$

Now, the continuity of $\mathbf{Zp}(\boldsymbol{\lambda})$ and the δ-method may be used. For $\boldsymbol{\beta}_0 \equiv \mathbf{Zp}(\boldsymbol{\lambda}_0)$,

$$\sqrt{T}(\mathbf{Zp}(\tilde{\boldsymbol{\lambda}}_T) - \boldsymbol{\beta}_0) \Rightarrow N[\mathbf{0}, \nabla_{\lambda'}\mathbf{Zp}(\boldsymbol{\lambda})\boldsymbol{\Sigma}_{\boldsymbol{\lambda}_0}\nabla_{\lambda}\mathbf{Zp}(\boldsymbol{\lambda})] \tag{6.A.19}$$

By the GCE–NM version of equation (6.5.6),

$$\nabla_{\lambda'}\mathbf{Zp}(\boldsymbol{\lambda}) = \mathbf{Q}\boldsymbol{\Sigma}_{\mathbf{Z}} \tag{6.A.20}$$

which yields the desired result by substitution. □

Specifying $\mathbf{V} = O(T^{-1})$ only affects the existence of an interior solution for a finite sample, and does not change the existence or consistency results as $T \to \infty$. If the rate of convergence was not changed, the remainder in equation (6.A.16) would be $O(\sqrt[-1]{T})$, and multiplying by $\sqrt{T}$ yields a remainder that is $O(1)$. Thus, the asymptotic bias in $\tilde{\boldsymbol{\lambda}}_T$ would be

$$-(\mathbf{Q}\boldsymbol{\Sigma}_{\mathbf{Z}}\mathbf{Q}')^{-1}\mathbf{Vw}(\boldsymbol{\lambda}_0) \tag{6.A.21}$$

where $\mathbf{Vw}(\boldsymbol{\lambda}_0)$ is a vector of constants.

CHAPTER 7

Finite sample extensions of GME–GCE

7.1 INTRODUCTION

In Chapter 6, the analytical properties of a generic GCE problem were developed, and these extend to most of the applications used throughout the book. For a special case, the normed moment (GCE–NM) problem, the large-sample properties were derived in a sample theoretic framework. In general, we found that the specification of the parameter and error bounds, **Z** and **V**, do not affect the large sample properties of the GCE–NM rule.

In the present chapter, we consider the analytical and sampling properties of the GME–GCE problems in a more realistic setting with finite samples. First, we return to the GCE–NM problem and outline the approximate finite-sample behavior of the associated point estimators, which now depend on **Z** and **V**. Given the joint impact of the signal and noise terms, we extend the GME–GCE framework to allow for generic weights on the parameter and error entropies in the objective function. Finally, we use a simple example, the bounded mean problem, to demonstrate the finite-sample properties of the GME–GCE solutions under normal and non-normal errors.

7.2 FINITE SAMPLE PROPERTIES

Although the large-sample properties of the GME–GCE solution are useful, the entropy formalisms were developed to solve ill-posed or underdetermined problems using limited or incomplete data and available prior information. Consequently, researchers may be more concerned about the properties of GME–GCE under finite samples and other conditions typically found in practice.

7.2.1 APPROXIMATE DISTRIBUTIONS

The asymptotic normality property from Chapter 6 may be used to approximate the distribution of the GME–GCE point estimate for finite samples. Based on the limiting distribution of $\tilde{\boldsymbol{\beta}}_T$, the finite-sample approximation is

$$\tilde{\boldsymbol{\beta}}_T \sim \mathrm{N}[\boldsymbol{\beta}, \boldsymbol{\Sigma}_Z(\tilde{\boldsymbol{\lambda}}_T)(\mathbf{X}'\mathbf{X})\mathbf{C}^{-1}\mathbf{D}(\mathbf{C}')^{-1}(\mathbf{X}'\mathbf{X})\boldsymbol{\Sigma}_Z(\tilde{\boldsymbol{\lambda}}_T)] \tag{7.2.1}$$

where

$$\mathbf{C} = \mathbf{X}'\mathbf{X}\boldsymbol{\Sigma}_\mathbf{Z}(\tilde{\boldsymbol{\lambda}}_T)\mathbf{X}'\mathbf{X} + \boldsymbol{\Sigma}_\mathbf{V}(\tilde{\boldsymbol{\lambda}}) \tag{7.2.2}$$

$$\mathbf{D} = \mathbf{X}'\boldsymbol{\Sigma}_\mathbf{e}\mathbf{X} \tag{7.2.3}$$

If the GCE–NM problem is specified as a pure inverse problem, the $\boldsymbol{\Sigma}_\mathbf{V}$ terms disappear. In this case, the approximate variance–covariance matrix of $\tilde{\boldsymbol{\beta}}_T$ is

$$(\mathbf{X}'\mathbf{X})^{-1}\mathbf{X}'\boldsymbol{\Sigma}_\mathbf{e}\mathbf{X}(\mathbf{X}'\mathbf{X})^{-1} \tag{7.2.4}$$

if $\boldsymbol{\Sigma}_\mathbf{Z}$ is full-rank (i.e. an interior solution exists). Given the relationship between the pure GCE–NM consistency constraints and the LS–ML normal equations, it is no surprise that this matrix is identical to the variance–covariance structure of the LS estimator.

In general, the presence of $\boldsymbol{\Sigma}_\mathbf{V}$ in the inverted terms reduces the variance of $\tilde{\boldsymbol{\beta}}_T$ under the noise specification. To see this, consider a special case in which $\Sigma_e = \sigma^2\mathbf{I}_T$ (i.e. the Gauss–Markov setting) and $\mathbf{X}$ is orthogonal. Now, the approximate variance–covariance matrix for $\tilde{\boldsymbol{\beta}}_T$ is

$$\sigma^2\boldsymbol{\Sigma}_\mathbf{Z}(\boldsymbol{\Sigma}_\mathbf{Z} + \boldsymbol{\Sigma}_\mathbf{V})^{-2}\boldsymbol{\Sigma}_\mathbf{Z} \tag{7.2.5}$$

This is a diagonal matrix, and the kth element is

$$\sigma^2\left(\frac{\sigma^2_{z_k}}{\sigma^2_{z_k} + \sigma^2_{v_k}}\right)^2 \tag{7.2.6}$$

Clearly, the approximate variance of $\tilde{\boldsymbol{\beta}}_T$ is smaller than the variance of the LS–ML estimator, $\tilde{\boldsymbol{\beta}}_{LS}$, which is $\sigma^2\mathbf{I}_K$.

Given that $\boldsymbol{\Sigma}_\mathbf{Z}$ and $\boldsymbol{\Sigma}_\mathbf{V}$ are functions of $\boldsymbol{\lambda}$, the approximate variance of $\tilde{\boldsymbol{\beta}}_T$ depends on $\tilde{\boldsymbol{\lambda}}_T$. We will show that maximizing the parameter and error entropies yields a GME estimator, $\tilde{\boldsymbol{\beta}}_T$, that has minimum variance. First, we must show that there is a unique relationship between the entropy objective and $\boldsymbol{\Sigma}_\mathbf{Z} + \boldsymbol{\Sigma}_\mathbf{V}$.

Proposition 7.1. *For $M = 2$, there is a unique relationship between $S = S(\tilde{\boldsymbol{p}}) + S(\tilde{\boldsymbol{w}})$ and the denominator of the approximate covariance matrix, $\boldsymbol{\Sigma}_\mathbf{Z} + \boldsymbol{\Sigma}_\mathbf{V}$ in the GME case.*

Proof. The denominator of the approximate covariance matrix is $\boldsymbol{\Sigma}_\mathbf{Z} + \boldsymbol{\Sigma}_\mathbf{V}$, which is the sum of the covariance matrices for distributions $\tilde{\boldsymbol{p}}$ and $\tilde{\boldsymbol{w}}$. For $M = 2$, rewrite $S(\tilde{\boldsymbol{p}})$ from equation (6.4.26) in terms of $\hat{p}_k$ and $(1 - \hat{p}_k)$. It then follows that maximizing $S(\mathbf{p}_k)$ to choose the GME solutions also maximizes the σ_{z_k}, the variance of the distribution on $\mathbf{z}_k$. Using the same arguments with $S(\tilde{w})$ completes the proof. □

Thus, the maximum entropy solution corresponds with the maximum denominator for the approximate variance of $\tilde{\boldsymbol{\beta}}_T$, which minimizes the approximate variance. It is important to note that this property does not extend to the GCE problems, in general. Given an informative prior distribution, the GCE objective shrinks the posterior distribution to the prior subject to the consistency constraints. If the prior has limited variance (e.g. heavily skewed), then the posterior will be selected to reflect the prior distribution, and it may have limited variance, as well.

Although the finite sample GME solution is almost certainly biased, the consistency constraints must be satisfied and the bias cannot become very large. Given the properties of limited bias and minimum variance, GME solutions exhibit reduced mean squared error relative to the traditional competitors. In the following chapters, we focus on estimation precision and favorable sampling performance of the GME–GCE solutions under squared error loss measures.

7.2.2 IMPACT OF ERROR BOUNDS, V

The noise terms, $\mathbf{Vw}$, effectively 'loosen' the model constraints for a given set of observations, and an interior solution is more likely. If we view the GME–GCE objective as a directed divergence function, wider error bounds provide posterior distributions that are 'closer' to the prior distributions. The magnitudes of the error bounds affect the amount of shrinkage toward the prior distributions, and the degree of shrinkage may be measured in the Lagrange multipliers. Recall that $\tilde{\boldsymbol{\lambda}} = \mathbf{0}$ yields $\tilde{\boldsymbol{p}} = \mathbf{q}$, which implies there is no additional information in the consistency constraints (i.e. the data).

To demonstrate a simple example of the shrinkage property, consider a noise formulation of Jaynes' dice problem from Chapter 2. Let the bounds on the noise term be $[-v, v]$ for some $v > 0$. Then, the GME probability of observing i on the next roll of the die is

$$\hat{p}_i = \frac{\exp(-x_i\hat{\lambda})}{\Omega(\hat{\lambda})} \tag{7.2.7}$$

with the associated error probability

$$\hat{w} = \frac{\exp(-v\hat{\lambda})}{\exp(v\hat{\lambda}) + \exp(-v\hat{\lambda})} \tag{7.2.8}$$

$$= \frac{\exp(-v\hat{\lambda})}{2\cdot\cosh(-v\hat{\lambda})} \tag{7.2.9}$$

by employing the definition of the hyperbolic cosine. As before, $\hat{\lambda}$ is the optimal Lagrange multiplier.

To compute the impact of a change in v on $\hat{\lambda}$, write the dual objective function as

$$M(\lambda) = y\lambda + \ln[\Omega(\lambda)] + \ln[2\cdot\cosh(-v\lambda)] \tag{7.2.10}$$

The FOC for the unconstrained problem is

$$\nabla_{\lambda} M(\hat{\lambda}) = y - \sum_i x_i p_i(\hat{\lambda}) - v\cdot\tanh(-v\hat{\lambda}) = 0 \tag{7.2.11}$$

Now, take the total differential of the FOC

$$\mathrm{d}\hat{\lambda}\{\nabla^2_{\hat{\lambda}} M(\hat{\lambda})\} + \mathrm{d}v\{\tanh(-v\hat{\lambda}) - v\lambda[1 - \tanh^2(-v\hat{\lambda})]\} = 0 \tag{7.2.12}$$

where $\nabla^2_{\hat{\lambda}} M(\hat{\lambda}) > 0$ because $M(\lambda)$ is strictly convex. Finally, solve for the desired ratio

$$\frac{\mathrm{d}\hat{\lambda}}{\mathrm{d}v} = \frac{\tanh(-v\hat{\lambda}) - v\hat{\lambda}[1 - \tanh^2(-v\hat{\lambda})]}{\nabla^2_{\hat{\lambda}} M(\hat{\lambda})} \tag{7.2.13}$$

To evaluate this term, note that the denominator is simply the second order condition, which is strictly positive. Further, $\tanh(\cdot)$ is an odd function, and $\tanh(x) \in [-1, 1]\,\forall\, x$. We find that

$$\frac{\mathrm{d}\hat{\lambda}}{\mathrm{d}v} = \begin{cases} >0, & \forall\hat{\lambda} < 0 \\ =0, & \hat{\lambda} = 0 \\ <0, & \forall\hat{\lambda} > 0 \end{cases} \tag{7.2.14}$$

As expected, 'widening' the error bound by increasing v reduces the absolute value of $\hat{\lambda}$. This action corresponds with a solution that is 'more uniform', or closer to the prior distribution. By considering the potential noise in the observed average, the posterior distribution is 'shrunk' toward the prior. Although many robust estimation schemes use the signal–noise ratio to derive a shrinkage factor, the GME–GCE error bounds include this information in a direct and natural fashion.

Given our ignorance regarding the error distribution, one way of determining the error bounds, v_1 and v_j, is to calculate the sample scale parameter and use this with the three-sigma rule.

7.3 A WEIGHTED GME–GCE OBJECTIVE FUNCTION

In Chapter 6, the traditional entropy formalisms were extended under the GME–GCE framework to solve linear inverse problems with noise. Given appropriate supports and prior distributions, the primal GME–GCE dual loss objective function

$$I(\mathbf{p}, \mathbf{q}, \mathbf{w}, \mathbf{u}) = \mathbf{p}' \ln(\mathbf{p}/\mathbf{q}) + \mathbf{w}' \ln(\mathbf{w}/\mathbf{u}) \tag{7.3.1}$$

includes entropies for the parameter *and* disturbance distributions. By accounting for the unknown signal and noise components in the consistency relations, GME–GCE estimates of the unknown parameters, $\boldsymbol{\beta}$, and disturbances, $\mathbf{e}$, are jointly determined. As a result, the entropy-based objective reflects statistical losses in the sample space (prediction) and in the parameter space (precision). Although we will explore the precision–prediction loss trade-off in the following chapters, it is important to note that the GME–GCE formulations employed to this point have implicitly placed equal weight on the parameter and error entropies.

Depending on the problem at hand, we may wish to recover an image of the underlying system that reflects greater prediction or precision fidelity. As such, we may wish to place relatively more or less weight on the parameter and error components of the objective function in order to reflect the relative importance of these components. Given that the entropies may be viewed as measures of the divergence between $\mathbf{p}$ and $\mathbf{q}$ and between $\mathbf{w}$ and $\mathbf{u}$, various weights will reflect the relative importance of these 'distances' in the parameter and sample spaces.

To extend the GME and GCE methods to reflect more general weighting schemes, consider placing weights $\gamma \in (0, 1)$ and $1 - \gamma$ on the error and parameter entropies, respectively. Following Section 6.4, we can solve the generic GCE problem by choosing $\mathbf{p}, \mathbf{w} \gg \mathbf{0}$ to minimize the weighted objective

$$I(\mathbf{p}, \mathbf{w}, \mathbf{q}, \mathbf{u}) = (1 - \gamma)\mathbf{p}' \ln(\mathbf{p}/\mathbf{q}) + \gamma \mathbf{w}' \ln(\mathbf{w}/\mathbf{u}) \tag{7.3.2}$$

subject to the appropriate consistency and additivity constraints. From the associated Lagrangian equation, the first-order conditions corresponding to $\mathbf{p}$ and $\mathbf{w}$ are

$$\nabla_p \mathscr{L} = (1 - \gamma)[\mathbf{1_{KM}} + \ln(\tilde{\boldsymbol{p}}/\mathbf{q})] - \mathbf{Z}'\mathbf{\Gamma}'\tilde{\boldsymbol{\lambda}} - (\mathbf{I_K} \otimes \mathbf{1_M})\tilde{\boldsymbol{\theta}} = \mathbf{0} \tag{7.3.3}$$

$$\nabla_w \mathscr{L} = \gamma[\mathbf{1_{TJ}} + \ln(\tilde{\boldsymbol{w}}/\mathbf{u})] - \mathbf{V}\tilde{\boldsymbol{\lambda}} - (\mathbf{I_T} \otimes \mathbf{1_J})\tilde{\boldsymbol{\tau}} = \mathbf{0} \tag{7.3.4}$$

As before, the FOC may be solved for the GCE probability vectors

$$\tilde{\boldsymbol{p}} = \mathbf{q} \odot \exp(\mathbf{Z}'\mathbf{\Gamma}'\tilde{\boldsymbol{\lambda}}/(1 - \gamma)) \odot \{(\mathbf{I}_K \otimes \mathbf{J}_M)[\mathbf{q} \odot \exp(\mathbf{Z}'\mathbf{\Gamma}'\tilde{\boldsymbol{\lambda}}/(1 - \gamma))]\}^{-1} \tag{7.3.5}$$

$$\tilde{\boldsymbol{w}} = \mathbf{u} \odot \exp(\mathbf{V}'\tilde{\boldsymbol{\lambda}}/\gamma) \odot \{(\mathbf{I}_T \otimes \mathbf{J}_J)[\mathbf{u} \odot \exp(\mathbf{V}'\tilde{\boldsymbol{\lambda}}/\gamma)]\}^{-1} \tag{7.3.6}$$

Individual elements of these vectors take the form

$$\tilde{p}_{km} = \frac{q_{km} \exp(z_{km}\Gamma_k'\tilde{\boldsymbol{\lambda}}/(1 - \gamma))}{\Omega_k(\tilde{\boldsymbol{\lambda}}, \gamma)} \tag{7.3.7}$$

$$\tilde{w}_{tj} = \frac{u_{tj} \exp(v_{tj}\tilde{\lambda}_t/\gamma)}{\Psi_t(\tilde{\boldsymbol{\lambda}}, \gamma)} \tag{7.3.8}$$

with partition functions

$$\Omega_k(\tilde{\boldsymbol{\lambda}}, \gamma) = \sum_n q_{kn} \exp(z_{kn}\Gamma'_k\tilde{\boldsymbol{\lambda}}/(1-\gamma)) \tag{7.3.9}$$

$$\Psi_t(\tilde{\boldsymbol{\lambda}}, \gamma) = \sum_n u_{tn} \exp(v_{tn}\tilde{\lambda}_t/\gamma) \tag{7.3.10}$$

Following Chapters 3 and 6, the dual or unconstrained GCE(γ) objective function is

$$M(\boldsymbol{\lambda}, \gamma) = \boldsymbol{\alpha}'\boldsymbol{\lambda} - (1-\gamma)\sum_k \ln(\Omega_k(\boldsymbol{\lambda}, \gamma)) - \gamma \sum_t \ln(\Psi_t(\boldsymbol{\lambda}, \gamma)) \tag{7.3.11}$$

For $\gamma \in (0, 1)$, $M(\boldsymbol{\lambda}, \gamma)$ retains all the properties outlined in Chapter 6. As before, we can maximize $M(\boldsymbol{\lambda}, \gamma)$ to find $\tilde{\boldsymbol{\lambda}}$, and the parameter and error estimates may be derived by substitution. To denote the presence of unequal weights, we will refer to the generalized entropy methods as GME(γ) and GCE(γ). The impact of choosing γ for specific models is demonstrated in Chapter 15.

Given that $\tilde{\boldsymbol{\lambda}}$ is now an implicit function of γ, changes in the precision–prediction loss trade-off will alter the magnitude of the optimal Lagrange multipliers and the corresponding GCE(γ) solution. As in most constrained optimization problems, 'smaller' Lagrange multipliers for the GCE solution imply that the constraints have a smaller impact on the objective. Hence, the GCE posterior distributions are 'closer' to the prior distributions. In the GME setting, intuition implies that placing less weight on the errors in the consistency constraints (i.e. smaller γ) will allow for larger disturbances. As such, the Lagrange multipliers will shrink because we have effectively made the constraint less binding. However, we can show that this intuition does not hold in general.

Following Section 6.7.2, we can examine the impact of an increase in γ on the magnitude of $\tilde{\boldsymbol{\lambda}}$ by totally differentiating the FOC for the unconstrained problem. To simplify matters, consider the GCE–NM model in which $\boldsymbol{\Gamma}$ is an identity matrix (e.g. $\mathbf{X}$ is orthogonal). In this case, the kth equation in the FOC is

$$\frac{\mathrm{d}M(\boldsymbol{\lambda}, \gamma)}{\mathrm{d}\lambda_k} = \alpha_k - \mathbf{z}'_k\tilde{\mathbf{p}}_k(\lambda_k, \gamma) - \mathbf{v}'_k\tilde{\mathbf{w}}_k(\lambda_k, \gamma) = 0 \tag{7.3.12}$$

where

$$\tilde{p}_{km}(\lambda_k, \gamma) = \frac{q_{km}\exp(z_{km}\lambda_k)}{\Omega_k(\lambda_k, \gamma)} \tag{7.3.13}$$

$$\tilde{w}_{kj}(\lambda_k, \gamma) = \frac{u_{kj}\exp(v_{kj}\lambda_k)}{\Psi_k(\lambda_k, \gamma)} \tag{7.3.14}$$

The total differential of the FOC provides the following result:

$$\frac{\mathrm{d}\tilde{\lambda}_k}{\mathrm{d}\gamma} = \left(\frac{\tilde{\lambda}_k}{\sigma_{z_k}^2 + \sigma_{v_k}^2}\right)\cdot\left(\frac{\sigma_{z_k}^2}{(1-\gamma)^2} - \frac{\sigma_{V_k}^2}{\gamma^2}\right) \tag{7.3.15}$$

$$\propto \tilde{\lambda}_k \cdot [\gamma^2\sigma_{z_k}^2 - (1-\gamma)^2\sigma_{v_k}^2] \tag{7.3.16}$$

The bracketed term may be either positive or negative, as can $\tilde{\lambda}_k$. Given that the sign on $\tilde{\lambda}_k$ depends on the magnitude of the kth consistency constraint, and not on γ, these terms have *a priori* indeterminant signs.

For a more concrete special case, consider the dice problem with noise examined in Section 7.2.2. The FOC for the dual problem is

$$\nabla_\lambda M(\lambda, \gamma) = y - \sum_i x_i p_i(\hat{\lambda}, \gamma) - v \cdot \tanh(-v\hat{\lambda}/\gamma) = 0 \tag{7.3.17}$$

The total differential of the FOC is then

$$\{\nabla_\lambda^2 M(\lambda)\}\mathrm{d}\hat{\lambda} + \{-(1-\gamma)^{-2}\sigma_x^2 + v\hat{\lambda}\gamma^{-2}[1 - \tanh^2(-v\hat{\lambda}/\gamma)]\}\mathrm{d}\gamma = 0 \tag{7.3.18}$$

By rearranging terms to derive the desired ratio, we find

$$\frac{\mathrm{d}\hat{\lambda}}{\mathrm{d}\gamma} = \frac{(1-\gamma)^{-2}\sigma_X^2 - \gamma^2 v\hat{\lambda}[1 - \tanh^2(-v\hat{\lambda}/\gamma)]}{\nabla_\lambda^2 M(\lambda)} \tag{7.3.19}$$

which may be positive or negative.

We can evaluate the sign of this expression numerically for a particular case of the dice problem. Let the observed mean of the die be $y = 3$ and the error bounds be $v = \pm 0.5$. For various values of γ, the associated optimal value of $\hat{\lambda}$ was computed, and the relationship is plotted in Figure 7.3.1 below and the corresponding data are given in Table 7.3.1. Clearly, increasing γ from 0.5 does decrease $\hat{\lambda}$, but the impact of changes in the weight is not uniform. Although they are not included here, a family of curves relating γ and $\hat{\lambda}$ was derived for

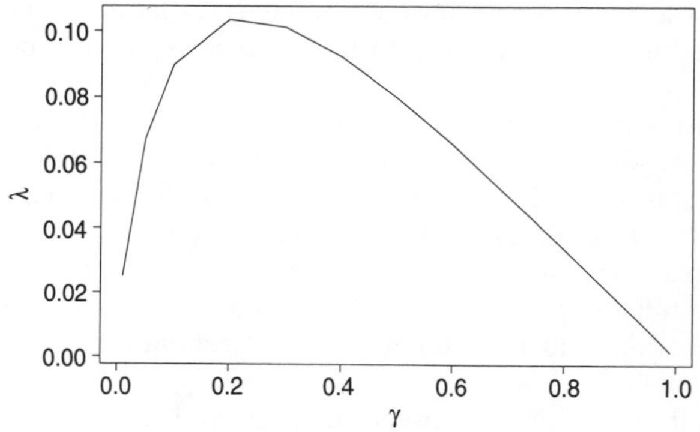

Figure 7.3.1 Solution to the dice problem as changes in γ

Table 7.3.1 Sensitivity of $\hat{\lambda}$ with respect to γ

γ	$\hat{\lambda}(\gamma)$
0.01	0.0252
0.05	0.0674
0.10	0.0898
0.20	0.1035
0.30	0.1012
0.40	0.0924
0.50	0.0800
0.60	0.0660
0.70	0.0500
0.80	0.0340
0.90	0.0170
0.95	0.0087
0.99	0.0017

various values of y and v. In general, the direction of change in $\hat{\lambda}$ is indeterminant.

7.4 A COMMENT ON THE CHOICE OF CONSISTENCY CONSTRAINTS

As in the ME–CE formalism, the GME–GCE consistency constraints are selected to reflect all of the available information for a particular problem. For example, the single consistency constraint for Jaynes' dice problem reflects the only available information, the empirical mean of the die. In practical applications of the GLM, researchers usually have all T observations consistent with the underlying data generating process, $\mathbf{y} = \mathbf{X}\boldsymbol{\beta} + \mathbf{e}$. Hence, each observation may be used as a single constraint (i.e. the GCE–D model from Table 6.2.1), or the moments or other functions of the data may be used as constraints (i.e. the GCE–M or GCE–NM models).

In the traditional econometric world, samples are often assumed to be Gaussian, and the sample moments are minimal sufficient statistics. In this case, no information is lost by reducing the data to the moments, and many estimators are functions of the sample moments. Outside the Gaussian setting, the moments may be poor sources of information, and using them may be wasteful of the full sample information (Koenker *et al.*, 1994). For example, moment-based estimators may suffer a loss of estimation precision in finite samples.

Given the full set of sample observations, it is always possible to use the moments as the GME–GCE consistency constraints. In order to make the best use of limited sample and non-sample information, we use the full set of observations as consistency constraints whenever possible. A notable exception occurs in our analysis of discrete choice problems (Chapter 15) where it is more natural to use the moment formulations. In other problems, we present sampling results based on the data and moment formulations in order to demonstrate the information loss.

7.5 RECOVERING A BOUNDED MEAN

The basic properties of the generalized entropy solutions derived in Chapters 6 and 7 may be demonstrated with a simple problem. Consider a single observation, $x = \beta + e$, where $e \sim \mathrm{N}[0, 1]$ and $\beta \in [-c, c]$ are unknown. The problem of recovering an image of β from x is a familiar linear inverse problem in statistics.

The standard sampling theory estimator is the restricted ML rule

$$\hat{\beta}_{\mathrm{ML}} = \begin{cases} -c & \text{if } x < -c \\ x & \text{if } x \in [-c, c] \\ c & \text{if } x > c \end{cases} \tag{7.5.1}$$

In this case, the ML estimator is equivalent to the restricted LS estimator (RLS), which does not require the normality assumption.

Alternately, consider a Bayesian version of the problem. As in the GME–GCE reparameterization of real-valued unknowns, Casella and Strawdermann (1981) specify a discrete prior distribution with equal mass on points $-c$ and c. Using this prior and the normal likelihood function, Casella and Strawdermann show that the Bayesian posterior mean under squared-error loss (SEL) is

$$\hat{\beta}_{\mathrm{B}} = c \tanh(cx) \tag{7.5.2}$$

By applying an earlier result from Ghosh (1964), they also show that $\hat{\beta}_{\mathrm{B}}$ is minimax if $c < 1.06$. For larger values of c, the minimax property may be extended by increasing the number of elements in the support of β. Bickel (1981) examines the minimax character of the problem for $\boldsymbol{\beta} \in \mathbb{R}^K$.

As in the LS case, the generalized entropy approach does not require the normality assumption. Using the Bayes support, $\beta \in \{-c, c\}$, to represent our uncertainty about β, the GME model constraint may be written as

$$\begin{aligned} x &= \mathbf{Zp} + \mathbf{Vw} \\ &= -cp + c(1-p) - vw + v(1-w) \end{aligned} \tag{7.5.3}$$

where $v \geq 0$ is the error bound. Taken as a special case of the generic GCE solution, the GME probability is

$$\hat{p} = \frac{\exp(c\hat{\lambda})}{\exp(c\hat{\lambda}) + \exp(-c\hat{\lambda})} \tag{7.5.4}$$

where $\hat{\lambda}$ is the optimal Lagrange multiplier on the model constraint. Accordingly, the GME posterior mean is

$$\begin{aligned} \hat{\beta}_{\text{GME}} &= \frac{-c\exp(c\hat{\lambda}) + c\exp(-c\hat{\lambda})}{\exp(c\hat{\lambda}) + \exp(-c\hat{\lambda})} \\ &= c\tanh(-c\hat{\lambda}) \end{aligned} \tag{7.5.5}$$

Clearly, the GME and Bayes solutions are related through their common functional form. The estimates are equal if $\hat{\lambda} = -x$, which only occurs when $x = 0$. If the GME problem is treated as a pure inverse problem (i.e. $v = 0$), the GME solution is the posterior distribution on $-c$ and c with a mean of x. For $x \in (-c, c)$, the pure GME solution is simply x. If the violated boundary is used in case of an infeasible solution, the pure GME solution is identical to $\hat{\beta}_{\text{ML}}$. Thus, the ML approach is a special case of generalized entropy.

For $v > 0$, the GME solution behaves like a shrinkage rule. To see this, we follow Section 7.2 and compute the impact of a change in v on $\hat{\lambda}$ by writing the dual objective function as

$$\begin{aligned} M(\lambda) &= y\lambda + \ln[\Omega(\lambda)] + \ln[\Psi(\lambda)] \\ &= y\lambda + \ln[2\cdot\cosh(-x\lambda)] + \ln[2\cdot\cosh(-v\lambda)] \end{aligned} \tag{7.5.6}$$

by employing the definition of the hyperbolic cosine. The FOC for the unconstrained problem is

$$\nabla_\lambda M(\hat{\lambda}) = y - c\cdot\tanh(-x\hat{\lambda}) - v\cdot\tanh(-v\hat{\lambda}) = 0 \tag{7.5.7}$$

Now, take the total differential of the FOC

$$\mathrm{d}\hat{\lambda}\{\nabla^2_\lambda M(\hat{\lambda})\} + \mathrm{d}v\{\tanh(-v\hat{\lambda}) - v\hat{\lambda}[1 - \tanh^2(-v\hat{\lambda})]\} = 0 \tag{7.5.8}$$

where $\nabla^2_\lambda M(\hat{\lambda}) > 0$ because $M(\lambda)$ is strictly convex. Finally, solve for the desired ratio

$$\frac{\mathrm{d}\hat{\lambda}}{\mathrm{d}v} = \frac{\tanh(-v\hat{\lambda}) - v\hat{\lambda}[1 - \tanh^2(-v\hat{\lambda})]}{\nabla^2_\lambda M(\hat{\lambda})} \tag{7.5.9}$$

To sign this term, note that $\tanh(\cdot)$ is an odd function and that $\tanh(x) \in [-1, 1]$ for all x. We find that

$$\frac{\mathrm{d}\hat{\lambda}}{\mathrm{d}v} \begin{cases} >0, & \forall\hat{\lambda} < 0 \\ =0, & \hat{\lambda} = 0 \\ <0, & \forall\hat{\lambda} > 0 \end{cases} \tag{7.5.10}$$

As expected, 'widening' the error bound by increasing v reduces the absolute value of $\hat{\lambda}$. This action corresponds with a solution that is 'more uniform', or closer to the prior distribution. By considering the potential noise in the observed average, the posterior distribution is 'shrunk' toward the prior.

7.5.1 NORMAL ERRORS

To compare the competing rules, let $c = 1$ so that $\hat{\beta}_B$ is minimax. For the GME with noise formulation, specify $v = 3$ according to the 3σ rule. Also, infeasible solutions will be evaluated at the violated bound. The risk functions of the three estimators were recovered as the mean SEL (MSEL), $\|\hat{\beta} - \beta\|^2$, and the results for $\beta \in [0, 1]$ are plotted in Figure 7.5.1. The risk functions for the ML and Bayes estimators are nearly identical to those presented in Figure 2 of Casella and Strawdermann (1981), and the Bayes estimator risk-dominates the ML solution. The GME solution risk-dominates the Bayes solution for most of the parameter space, and only surrenders its advantage for very large values of β.

In the present example, an error bound of $v = 3$ allows for a feasible solution if $x \in (-4, 4)$, and the probability of a boundary solution is nearly zero. As v decreases, the GME solution will behave more like the restricted sampling estimator, $\hat{\beta}_{ML}$. For $v \in \{0.5, 1, 3\}$, the empirical risk functions of the GME and Bayes solutions are also presented in Figure 7.5.1. As expected, the wider error bounds allow for a GME solution that is 'closer' to the prior distribution. As v decreases, the GME risk becomes 'flatter' as it uses less of the prior information. Note that for $v = 0.5$, the GME solution behaves very much like the Bayes estimator.

Again, the analysis of $d\hat{\lambda}/dv$ implies that increasing v shrinks the pure GME solution away from the sample and toward the prior mean. In this example,

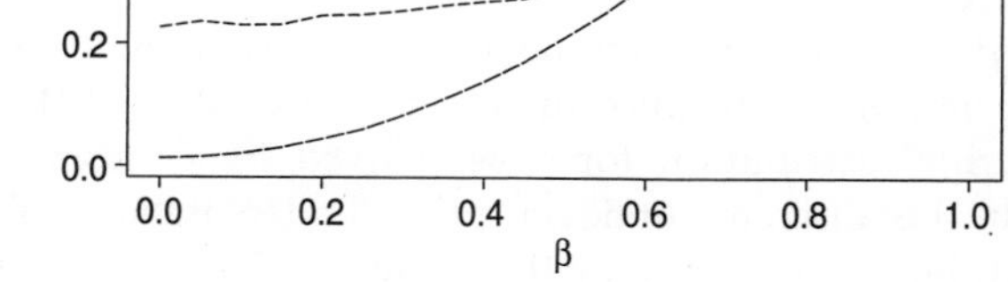

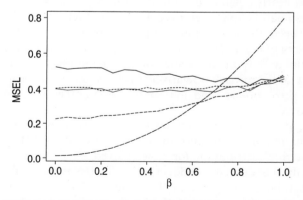

Figure 7.5.1 Empirical risk of bounded normal mean estimators. ____, LS-ML; ....., Bayes; _ _ _, GME ($v = 0.5$); _ _ _ _ _, GME ($v = 1$); __ __, GME ($v = 3$)

Table 7.5.1 Data for Figure 7.5.1

β	RLS–ML	Bayes	GME, $v = 0.5$	GME, $v = 1$	GME, $v = 3$
0.00	0.52348	0.39834	0.40169	0.22587	0.01231
0.05	0.51075	0.39114	0.40612	0.23520	0.01407
0.10	0.51671	0.39567	0.40692	0.22947	0.02035
0.15	0.51893	0.39974	0.40664	0.23055	0.02991
0.20	0.51883	0.40028	0.38872	0.24492	0.04438
0.25	0.48987	0.38062	0.39627	0.24664	0.06046
0.30	0.50892	0.39902	0.39963	0.25324	0.08381
0.35	0.50591	0.39897	0.39373	0.26188	0.11036
0.40	0.48206	0.38278	0.40841	0.26848	0.13922
0.45	0.48239	0.38600	0.39776	0.27359	0.17097
0.50	0.48368	0.39481	0.40735	0.29138	0.20993
0.55	0.46854	0.38778	0.40945	0.29742	0.25042
0.60	0.47610	0.39893	0.40145	0.31767	0.29767
0.65	0.45731	0.39008	0.40433	0.33211	0.34512
0.70	0.44370	0.38526	0.41903	0.35814	0.39760
0.75	0.46337	0.41055	0.41591	0.36327	0.45674
0.80	0.46291	0.41856	0.41526	0.37631	0.52165
0.85	0.42433	0.39262	0.42273	0.40259	0.57940
0.90	0.45881	0.43065	0.44012	0.43040	0.65217
0.95	0.45316	0.43627	0.45544	0.44878	0.72446
1.00	0.47412	0.46133	0.44398	0.48520	0.80321

the prior mean is 0, and the pure or sample solution is $\hat{\beta}_{\mathrm{ML}}$. As the error bounds increase, we rely on the prior mean with decreasing regard for the sample information. In the limit, $\hat{\lambda} \to 0$ as $v \to \infty$, and we completely ignore the sample and choose $\hat{\beta}_{\mathrm{GME}} = 0$ with certainty. Further, the risk of our strategy is simply β^2. In our example, the error bound, $v = 3$, is large enough so that the empirical risk function is nearly equal to the limiting risk. As such, GME–GCE provides a family of estimators (parameterized by v) that reflect varying degrees of shrinkage between the prior and sample information. In other inferential settings, a variety of methods have been devised for choosing shrinkage factors, and most methods rely on the underlying signal–noise ratio for the model. However, the GME approach is relatively easy to implement because v is simply viewed as an error bound, and information about the signal–noise ratio is directly employed.

Alternately, the performance of the GME solution may be explained by considering the minimum distance interpretation of the GME problem. The Bayesian posterior distribution for β is derived by combining the normal likelihood with the discrete, uniform prior under Bayes' rule. Without a likelihood function, GME solves for the posterior that is 'closest' to the prior and satisfies the model constraint (7.5.3). By using $v > 0$, the constraint is effectively loosened, and the posterior may be 'shrunk' closer to the prior.

Consequently, GME will do very well when the prior information is correct, but the other estimators dominate GME when $\boldsymbol{\beta}$ is large. In this example, an error bound of $v = 0.5$ provides a GME posterior distribution that is nearly equivalent to using Bayes' rule and a normal likelihood function to evaluate the sample information. Although it is not a true Bayesian method, GME may be informally viewed as a non-parametric (i.e. *sans* likelihood) Bayesian technique.

7.5.2 ALTERNATE ERROR DISTRIBUTIONS

Given that the restricted ML approach may be viewed as a restricted LS estimator, the Bayes estimator is the only rule based on a distributional assumption. To examine the robustness of the competing methods, the sampling experiments were repeated using two non-normal alternatives. First, the Student-t distribution with three degrees of freedom was used to evaluate performance under a heavy-tailed distribution. To maintain a unit variance, all of the drawings from the $t(3)$ pseudo-random number generator were divided by $\sqrt{3}$. The risk functions of the restricted ML, Bayes, and GME estimators appear in Figure 7.5.2.

The risk functions for the ML and Bayes solutions maintain the same

Table 7.5.2 Data for Figure 7.5.2

β	RLS–ML	Bayes	GME, $v = 3$
0.00	0.36144	0.28011	0.01574
0.05	0.36533	0.28243	0.01929
0.10	0.35639	0.27604	0.02311
0.15	0.35539	0.27809	0.03274
0.20	0.35377	0.27432	0.04811
0.25	0.36270	0.28371	0.06745
0.30	0.35273	0.27615	0.08932
0.35	0.34711	0.27377	0.11508
0.40	0.34255	0.27315	0.14333
0.45	0.34043	0.27252	0.17788
0.50	0.33083	0.26673	0.21453
0.55	0.33089	0.27314	0.25882
0.60	0.30835	0.25741	0.30135
0.65	0.32475	0.27679	0.34974
0.70	0.29292	0.25666	0.40397
0.75	0.30310	0.27356	0.46562
0.80	0.29381	0.27240	0.52393
0.85	0.30025	0.28573	0.58958
0.90	0.30842	0.30161	0.66098
0.95	0.30209	0.30482	0.72824
1.00	0.29330	0.30717	0.80535

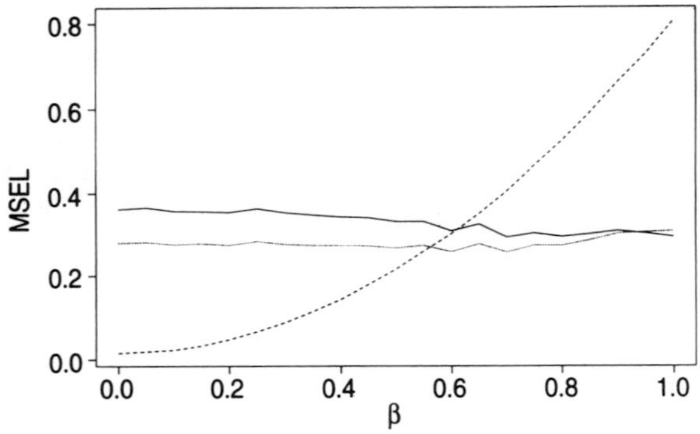

Figure 7.5.2 Empirical risk of bounded $t(3)$ mean estimators. ____, RLS; ....., Bayes; _ _ _, GME ($v = 3$)

relationship, but the GME solutions for $v = 0.5, 1, 3$ do not shrink the sample as strongly as before, and the risk functions appear in Figure 7.5.3. As before, decreasing v provides less shrinkage toward the prior, and the risk function is 'flatter' as it uses more of the sample information.

Another variation is to consider a skewed error distribution. The following

Table 7.5.3 Data for Figure 7.5.3

β	Bayes	GME, $v = 0.5$	GME, $v = 1$	GME, $v = 3$
0.00	0.28011	0.27865	0.15349	0.01574
0.05	0.28243	0.27776	0.15192	0.01929
0.10	0.27604	0.26581	0.15119	0.02311
0.15	0.27809	0.27190	0.16175	0.03274
0.20	0.27432	0.27095	0.15857	0.04811
0.25	0.28371	0.27040	0.16655	0.06745
0.30	0.27615	0.28375	0.17482	0.08932
0.35	0.27377	0.27917	0.18271	0.11508
0.40	0.27315	0.27803	0.19467	0.14333
0.45	0.27252	0.27490	0.20693	0.17788
0.50	0.26673	0.28241	0.20384	0.21453
0.55	0.27314	0.27974	0.23015	0.25882
0.60	0.25741	0.26951	0.24127	0.30135
0.65	0.27679	0.28737	0.26292	0.34974
0.70	0.25666	0.26702	0.27672	0.40397
0.75	0.27356	0.27743	0.29049	0.46562
0.80	0.27240	0.28341	0.32223	0.52393
0.85	0.28573	0.28577	0.34472	0.58958
0.90	0.30161	0.30325	0.35972	0.66098
0.95	0.30482	0.31771	0.39344	0.72824
1.00	0.30717	0.32307	0.41841	0.80535

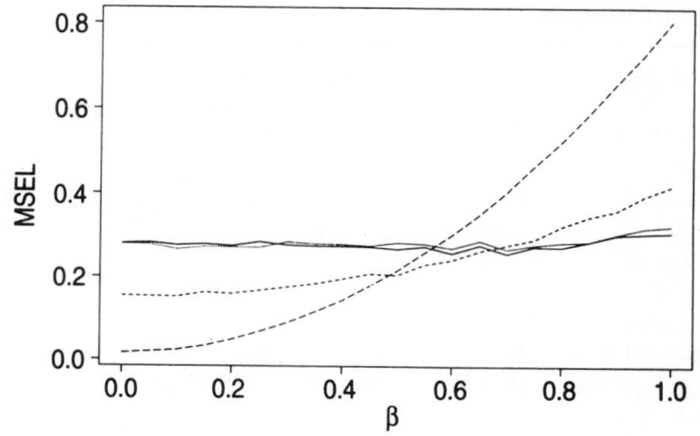

Figure 7.5.3 GME risk under various error bounds. ____, Bayes; ....., GME ($v = 0.5$); _ _ _, GME ($v = 1$); __ __, GME ($v = 3$)

results are based on errors drawn from a $\chi^2(4) - 4$ distribution, which has a mean of 0 due to mean-centering. As before, the disturbances were scaled to have a unit variance by dividing the centered drawings by $\sqrt{8}$. By incorrectly assuming that the errors are standard normal, the GME solutions for $v = 3$ were computed. Given that the error distribution is no longer symmetric, Figure 7.5.4 now includes the risk functions for $\boldsymbol{\beta} \in [-1, 1]$.

Again, the restricted ML and Bayes estimators maintain the same relative performance, although the risk functions take a different general shape. Further, the GME solution continues to dominate both ML and Bayes over much of the parameter space. Intuitively, the favorable performance of the GME solution follows from its reliance on sample *and* prior information. Although

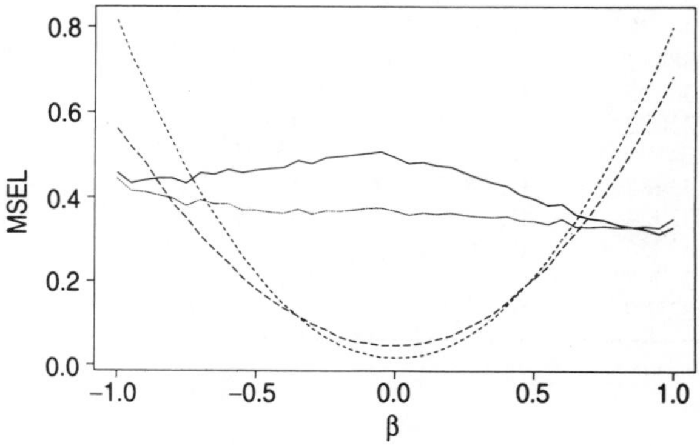

Figure 7.5.4 Empirical risk of bounded $\chi^2(4)$ mean estimators. ____, RLS; ....., Bayes; _ _ _, GME ($v = 3$); __ __, GME ($v = [-1.4, 2.8]$)

Table 7.5.4 Data for Figure 7.5.4

β	RLS–ML	Bayes	GME, $v = 3$	GME, $v = [-\sqrt{2}, 2\sqrt{2}]$
−1.00	0.45790	0.44432	0.81562	0.56151
−0.95	0.43319	0.41498	0.73280	0.51864
−0.90	0.44056	0.41221	0.66502	0.48249
−0.85	0.44501	0.40432	0.59054	0.43282
−0.80	0.44444	0.39751	0.52902	0.38476
−0.75	0.43251	0.37875	0.46599	0.35068
−0.70	0.45768	0.39336	0.41060	0.30772
−0.65	0.45371	0.38366	0.35911	0.27428
−0.60	0.46512	0.38393	0.31019	0.24464
−0.55	0.45776	0.36838	0.26041	0.20894
−0.50	0.46361	0.36865	0.22013	0.18102
−0.45	0.46778	0.36362	0.17823	0.15697
−0.40	0.47005	0.36133	0.14445	0.13539
−0.35	0.48673	0.37103	0.11695	0.11759
−0.30	0.47895	0.35935	0.08822	0.09847
−0.25	0.49274	0.36749	0.06623	0.08462
−0.20	0.49578	0.36637	0.04846	0.06667
−0.15	0.49935	0.36966	0.03487	0.05679
−0.10	0.50302	0.37343	0.02577	0.05221
−0.05	0.50674	0.37448	0.01822	0.04702
0.00	0.49448	0.36762	0.01748	0.04668
0.05	0.48027	0.35816	0.01848	0.04782
0.10	0.48301	0.36355	0.02338	0.05193
0.15	0.47486	0.36052	0.03310	0.06126
0.20	0.47216	0.36342	0.04700	0.06997
0.25	0.45840	0.35823	0.06402	0.08653
0.30	0.44605	0.35513	0.08650	0.10420
0.35	0.43498	0.35323	0.11035	0.12304
0.40	0.42778	0.35567	0.14253	0.14913
0.45	0.40799	0.34574	0.17557	0.17978
0.50	0.38750	0.34396	0.21167	0.20648
0.55	0.38179	0.33654	0.25153	0.23560
0.60	0.38473	0.34858	0.30095	0.27940
0.65	0.35933	0.33037	0.34418	0.31596
0.70	0.35022	0.32911	0.40125	0.35842
0.75	0.34591	0.33099	0.45821	0.40659
0.80	0.33488	0.32803	0.51604	0.45512
0.85	0.32924	0.32939	0.58399	0.50772
0.90	0.32366	0.33078	0.65041	0.56883
0.95	0.31267	0.32731	0.72144	0.62131
1.00	0.32770	0.34878	0.79901	0.68490

the ML result is also the restricted LS rule, which does not require normality, the shrinkage behavior of the GME rule improves the risk of the estimator.

Finally, suppose we suspect the disturbances are skewed and use this information to specify the error supports within the GCE framework. Using an informative prior distribution of $u = [0.667, 0.333]$ on $\mathbf{v} = [-\sqrt{2}, 2\sqrt{2}]$, the inverse problem may be solved under the GCE framework. The resulting risk function is also presented in Figure 7.5.4. In this case, the additional information used in the GCE problem uniformly improves the entropy risk.

Based on these limited results, the GME–GCE formulations for the bounded mean problem are robust alternatives to the traditional RLS–ML and Bayes estimators. By accounting for the noise in the system, the GME solution to the inverse problem with noise is superior to the Bayesian and frequentist rules over a large portion of the parameter space. Also, the magnitude of the error bound allows for varying degrees of shrinkage based on the underlying signal–noise ratio. Finally, the GME–GCE framework does not rely on the likelihood assumption and is robust to alternate error distributions.

7.6 REMARKS

In this chapter, we have refined and extended the GME–GCE formulations and have explored some of the important finite-sample properties. In general, we find that the GME–GCE solutions to 'classical' versions of the GLM are robust alternatives to traditional estimators for a range of data generating processes. As such, the GME–GCE framework permits us to avoid making unwanted distributional assumptions. In Part III, we consider a range of statistical models, some of which are ill-posed, and present GME–GCE formulations for these problems. For each, we compare the GME–GCE results with the performance of the traditional estimators.

REFERENCES

Bickel, P. J. (1981) Minimax estimation of the mean of a normal distribution when the parameter space is restricted. *Annals of Statistics* **9**, 1301–9.

Casella, G. and Strawdermann, W. E. (1981) Estimating a normal bounded mean. *Annals of Statistics* **9**, 870–8.

Ghosh, M. N. (1964) Uniform approximation of minimax point estimates. *Annals of Mathematical Statistics* **35**, 1031–47.

Koenker, R., Machado, J. A. F., Keels, C. L. S. and Welsh, A. H. (1994) Momentary lapses: Moment expansions and the robustness of minimum distance estimation. *Econometric Theory* **10**, 172–97.

PART III

General linear model applications of GME–GCE

In Part III we consider a range of problems that are encountered in practice when using the general linear statistical model and demonstrate with sampling experiments the performance of the GME–GCE estimator. In particular, we consider the statistical implications of using GME–GCE when:

- the design matrix is ill-conditioned
- the underlying data generation process is possibly non-Gaussian
- the equation errors are possibly heteroskedastic and/or autocorrelated
- there is uncertainty regarding the form and content of the design matrix (variable selection).

In each of these potential problem areas, use is made of GME–GCE procedures to mitigate the statistical consequences of these possible model specification problems and to compare them with their traditional counterparts.

CHAPTER 8

GME–GCE solutions to ill-conditioned problems

8.1 INTRODUCTION

To this point, we have focused much of our attention on ill-posed inverse problems resulting from limited, partial or incomplete sample information. For example, we have noted that the traditional methods of information recovery are undefined or non-unique if the number of unknown parameters exceeds the number of observations. However, it is also important to note that traditional methods may encounter difficulties even if there are enough observations to form a fundamentally well-posed inverse problem. Given the shortcomings of the non-experimental observations commonly available to economists and other social scientists, solutions to seemingly well-posed inverse problems may be undefined or non-unique. Further, the estimators may have inflated variance or low precision for the recovered parameters, and the estimates may be highly unstable and perhaps inadmissible. In the literature on inverse problems, these are known as ill-conditioned problems.

To mitigate the impact of poor data, researchers typically use existing prior or non-sample information to augment or regularize traditional estimation procedures. Accordingly, the generalized entropy formalisms also provide a useful basis for reconciling sample and non-sample information in ill-conditioned inverse problems. In this chapter, we review the impact of ill-conditioning on traditional methods, and we present two sampling experiments to demonstrate the favorable performance of GME–GCE relative to the traditional alternatives.

8.2 THE ILL-EFFECTS OF ILL-CONDITIONING

In experimental applications of the general linear model (GLM)

$$\mathbf{y} = \mathbf{X}\boldsymbol{\beta} + \mathbf{e}$$

the explanatory variables, $\mathbf{X}$, are selected or controlled to provide an effective (i.e. orthogonal) experimental design. In economic applications, the explanatory variables are often passively observed responses and are not subject to experimental controls. Consequently, there may exist one or more exact or near-exact linear dependencies among the explanatory variables, and the linear inverse problem is ill-conditioned. Also, linear dependencies may be induced in finite samples by certain data transformations (e.g. linear spline models). In either case, the design matrix, **X**, does not have full column rank or a numerically stable inverse matrix and the explanatory variables are said to be collinear. For example, the set of explanatory variables in consumer demand models often includes real income as well as real prices of related goods, all of which tend to move together over time and may be linearly related. In the next section, we use a production example to illustrate the ill-effects of ill-conditioning on traditional inversion techniques.

For the GLM, the impact of ill-conditioned data is commonly demonstrated through the sampling performance of the least squares (LS) estimator. If we assume $\mathbf{e} \sim (\mathbf{0}, \sigma^2\mathbf{I}_T)$, then

$$\hat{\boldsymbol{\beta}}_{LS} = (\mathbf{X}'\mathbf{X})^{-1}\mathbf{X}'\mathbf{y} \sim (\boldsymbol{\beta}, \sigma^2(\mathbf{X}'\mathbf{X})^{-1}) \tag{8.2.1}$$

If we further assume normality of the errors, $\hat{\boldsymbol{\beta}}_{LS}$ is also the maximum likelihood (ML) estimator of $\boldsymbol{\beta}$ and exhibits the corresponding sampling properties. Clearly, the LS estimator is not uniquely defined if the problem is severely ill-conditioned and **X** does not have full column rank.

In moderately ill-conditioned problems, the inverse matrix, $(\mathbf{X}'\mathbf{X})^{-1}$, may exist, but $\hat{\boldsymbol{\beta}}_{LS}$ may have very large elements in its variance–covariance matrix. To see this, consider the singular value decomposition (SVD) of the design matrix, $\mathbf{X} = \mathbf{QLR}'$, where **Q** is a $(T \times K)$ orthogonal matrix, **L** is a $(K \times K)$ diagonal matrix, and **R** is a $(K \times K)$ orthogonal matrix. The diagonal elements of **L**, $\{\pi_{(i)}\}$, are the singular values of **X**, and the columns of **R** are the associated eigenvectors of **X**. Using the spectral decomposition of $(\mathbf{X}'\mathbf{X})^{-1}$, the covariance matrix may be written as

$$\text{Var}(\hat{\boldsymbol{\beta}}_{LS}) = \sigma^2(\mathbf{X}'\mathbf{X})^{-1} = \sum_k \frac{\sigma^2}{\pi_k^2} \mathbf{R}_k\mathbf{R}_k' \tag{8.2.2}$$

if $\boldsymbol{\Sigma}_e \equiv \sigma^2\mathbf{I}_T$. As the problem becomes more ill-conditioned, one or more of the $\{\pi_k\}$ approaches 0, and the variance of $\hat{\boldsymbol{\beta}}_{LS}$ increases. In the econometrics literature, the singular values have been used to form diagnostic tools known as variance inflation factors (VIFs).

Although the degree of collinearity present in a given design matrix may be measured with VIF's and other diagnostic tools, Belsley (1991) recommends another function of the singular values known as the condition number

$$\kappa(\mathbf{X}'\mathbf{X}) = \frac{\pi_{(1)}}{\pi_{(K)}} \tag{8.2.3}$$

which is the ratio of the largest and smallest singular values of **X** (with columns scaled to unit length). If the design matrix is orthogonal and the columns of $\mathbf{X}$ are linearly independent, $\pi_{(i)} = 1\ \forall i$ and $\kappa(\mathbf{X}'\mathbf{X}) = 1$. As the degree of collinearity increases, $\pi_{(K)} \to 0$ and $\kappa(\mathbf{X}'\mathbf{X}) \to \infty$.

Belsley notes that potentially harmful collinearity may arise if $\kappa(\mathbf{X}'\mathbf{X})$ is as small as 25, but such cases are rarely encountered in practice. Although $\kappa(\mathbf{X}'\mathbf{X})$ is only an ordinal measure of collinearity, Belsley recommends using $\kappa(\mathbf{X}'\mathbf{X}) >$ 900 as a sign that potentially harmful collinearity may be present. Given that $\kappa(\mathbf{X}'\mathbf{X})$ only measures the most severe linear relationship in $\mathbf{X}$, he further recommends examining the full set of K condition indices

$$\left\{\frac{\pi_{(i)}}{\pi_{(1)}}\right\}$$

for the presence of two or more potential harmful linear dependencies. Throughout the remainder of this chapter, we will use the condition number, $\kappa(\mathbf{X}'\mathbf{X})$, to measure the ill-conditioned nature of a given inverse problem.

8.3 REGULARIZATION METHODS FOR ILL-CONDITIONED PROBLEMS–A SHORT REVIEW

In practice, the condition indices and other useful diagnostic tools for detecting collinearity are typically consulted *after* preliminary estimates of $\boldsymbol{\beta}$ do not conform to prior beliefs. A more reasonable approach to solving economic inverse problems is to use the available prior information to augment or 'regularize' the problem. In general, solutions to the regularized problems will be unique or more stable and will reflect the sample and non-sample information. Robust estimation methods based on the regularization approach have a long history in science and engineering fields. Recently, the techniques were formalized by Tikhonov (Tikhonov and Arsenin, 1977) and are collectively known as the method of regularization (MOR); for an overview, see O'Sullivan (1986).

For the GLM, the MOR objective may be written in a generic form

$$\mathscr{L} = \|\mathbf{y} - \mathbf{X}\boldsymbol{\beta}\| + \eta\phi(\boldsymbol{\beta}) \tag{8.3.1}$$

where $\|\cdot\|$ is some norm on the sample space, $\phi(\cdot)$ is a penalty function that reflects information about the plausible values of $\boldsymbol{\beta}$, and the trade-off between the components is provided by η. The objective reflects the fidelity of the recovered system to the indirect observations and to the regularity conditions, which may represent prior information, dual objectives for the recovered information (Zellner, 1993), or merely convenient assumptions.

Linear inverse problems associated with the GLM may be regularized or augmented in a variety of ways. The parameter space may be restricted to subsets of $\mathbb{R}^K$ under the restricted GMM (e.g. LS) or ML approaches. Here, η may be set to some very large value, and $\phi(\boldsymbol{\beta})$ is simply an indicator function for values of $\boldsymbol{\beta}$ that violate the restrictions. A boundary solution indicates that the sample is not consistent with the prior information. Another familiar case of regularized GMM is quadratic regularization (QR) which chooses $\boldsymbol{\beta}$ to minimize

$$\mathscr{L} = \|\mathbf{y} - \mathbf{X}\boldsymbol{\beta}\|^2 + \eta\boldsymbol{\beta}'\mathbf{C}\boldsymbol{\beta} \tag{8.3.2}$$

Here, $\mathbf{C}$ is a positive definite matrix, and $\boldsymbol{\beta}'\mathbf{C}\boldsymbol{\beta}$ is the square of the weighted Euclidean norm of $\boldsymbol{\beta}$. In effect, we are penalizing solutions whose 'norm' exceeds some prior bound. The penalized solution

$$\boldsymbol{\beta}_{\mathbf{QR}} = (\mathbf{X}'\mathbf{X} + \eta\mathbf{C})^{-1}\mathbf{X}'\mathbf{y} \tag{8.3.3}$$

is commonly known as the *ridge regressor*. The QR problem may be further generalized to include weights on the first component (e.g. regularized weighted LS) or distances from some non-null point in the parameter space (e.g. generalized ridge regressor).

In effect, Bayesian inference is a form of regularization that uses Bayes' rule to process the sample and prior information. Using subjective probabilities, an informative prior distribution for $\boldsymbol{\beta}$ may be used to regularize the likelihood function in a formal or empirical Bayesian analysis. To reflect bounds on the unknown parameters, the Bayesian prior distributions may have a discrete or bounded support. For example, the support of a Lebesgue prior density may be truncated, and the posterior distribution may be evaluated as shown by Geweke (1986). From the Bayesian perspective, $\boldsymbol{\beta}_{\mathrm{QR}}$ is the posterior mean associated with a $\mathrm{N}[\mathbf{X}\boldsymbol{\beta}, \mathbf{I}_T]$ likelihood function and prior distribution $g(\boldsymbol{\beta}) = \mathrm{N}[\mathbf{0}, (\eta\mathbf{C})^{-1}]$. Accordingly, James–Stein and other Stein–like shrinkage rules have been motivated as empirical Bayes estimators and may be viewed as methods of regularization. Conceptually, minimax estimation is also a form of regularization that restricts the Bayesian point estimate to have the 'worst' prior (i.e. maximum risk).

In either the frequentist or Bayesian world, the researcher must still choose the smoothing or prior parameters to reflect the available non-sample information for a particular problem. For example, the prior variance–covariance structure implicit in $\boldsymbol{\beta}_{\mathrm{QR}}$ is analogous to the QR 'norm' restriction. Unfortunately, economists rarely have information about the 'norm' of their parameter vectors. Further, the choice of a likelihood function is typically a matter of convenience rather than an expression of actual prior knowledge. Finally, the set of available non-sample information for economic inverse problems is often limited to *signs* or *magnitudes* of individual parameters (e.g. elasticities). Thus, the traditional methods of regularizing linear inverse problems are not well-suited to economic inverse problems.

8.4 THE GME–GCE APPROACH

Within the generalized entropy framework, limited non-sample information may be used to solve ill-conditioned inverse problems, but additional or unnatural assumptions are not required to generate a solution. In particular, prior information about unknown economic parameters is usually limited to bounds, signs, or expected magnitudes. These components may be directly specified in the supports on the constrained parameter space, $\mathbf{Z}$, or in the associated discrete prior distribution, $\mathbf{q}$. If appropriate information is available to specify the QR roughness penalty, $\boldsymbol{\beta}'\mathbf{C}\boldsymbol{\beta}$, or to restrict the least squares parameter space, it may also be expressed in $\mathbf{Z}$ or $\mathbf{q}$.

Further, GME–GCE does not employ a likelihood function and only requires modest assumptions on the underlying error structure. Information about the signal–noise ratio may be expressed in the set of error bounds, V. Prior beliefs about other properties of the disturbances (e.g. skewness or kurtosis) may be expressed in the prior weights, $\mathbf{u}$. Finally, the weighted entropy objective (Section 7.2) may be used to reflect trade-offs in the prediction–precision character of the inverse problem. Thus, GME–GCE problems may be adapted to reflect various regularity conditions or types of prior information.

It is important to note that the entropy criterion may be used in other MOR settings. By dropping the additivity constraint, Donoho *et al.* (1992) show that $I(\mathbf{p}, \mathbf{q})$ may be used as an MOR penalty function to solve inverse problems with noise for $\mathbf{p} \in \mathbb{R}_{+}^{K}$. Although this approach has been used to solve many signal recovery problems in the physical and social sciences, it does not extend to problems with negative unknowns. This difficulty may be overcome by incorporating the parameter supports, $\mathbf{Z}$, and solving the related MOR objective

$$\mathscr{L} = \|\mathbf{y} - \mathbf{XZp}\| + \eta I(\mathbf{p}, \mathbf{q}) \tag{8.4.1}$$

subject to additivity constraints. Although this formulation avoids error bounds, the optimal probabilities do not take a closed form, even as functions of the Lagrange multipliers. This alternate formulation is not consistent with the GME–GCE framework and is only included here for completeness.

8.5 AN ILLUSTRATIVE ECONOMIC EXAMPLE

To motivate the generalized entropy methods of solving ill-conditioned linear inverse problems, consider the following economic example. Suppose we observe levels of fertilizer inputs (nitrogen, phosphorus, and potassium) which are used to produce a single output, corn. If the underlying production technology is Cobb–Douglas

$$\mathbf{y} = \alpha \mathbf{X}_2^{\beta_2} \mathbf{X}_3^{\beta_3} \mathbf{X}_4^{\beta_4} \tag{8.5.1}$$

we can use the log-transformation of the observations to specify the statistical model in linear form

$$\ln \mathbf{y} = \beta_1 + \mathbf{X}_2\beta_2 + \mathbf{X}_3\beta_3 + \mathbf{X}_4\beta_4 + \mathbf{e} \tag{8.5.2}$$

For this model, we conducted a sampling exercise to examine the behavior of the GME–CGE solution relative to some traditional competitors. First, 30 observations of nitrogen and phosphorus data were taken from Table 11.5 in Griffiths *et al.* (1993, p. 387) and used to generate the potassium data. To represent a poor experimental design, a near-linear dependency between potassium and phosphorus was formed by generating potassium ($\mathbf{X}_4$) as one-half of the tabulated phosphorus ($\mathbf{X}_3$) input value plus pseudo-random noise from an i.i.d. $N(0, \sigma^2)$ distribution with $\sigma = 0.2$. After using the logarithmic transformation, the condition number of the design matrix is $\kappa(\mathbf{X}'\mathbf{X}) = 7899$, which is exceptionally large. The associated pure signal for corn production, $\mathbf{X}\boldsymbol{\beta}$, was formed with parameters $\beta = [0.45, 0.35, 0.40, 0.50]'$ and the logarithmic form of the independent variables. Then for each of 5000 Monte Carlo trials, the new set of noisy observations was formed by adding i.i.d. standard normal disturbances to the pure signal.

Using the familar LS–ML estimator, the parameters for the production model were recovered for each of the Monte Carlo data sets. The average of each estimated parameter and the empirical mean squared error loss, MSEL $= E\|\hat{\boldsymbol{\beta}} - \hat{\boldsymbol{\beta}}_0\|^2$, are presented in Table 8.5.1. Although the LS–ML estimator should be roughly unbiased in a large number of trials, the condition number is so large that the average point estimates are not very close to the true values. As well, the large precision measure reflects the unstable nature of the data. Two robust alternatives to the LS–ML estimator, the ridge and the restricted LS–ML (RLS) estimators, were also used to recover $\boldsymbol{\beta}$ from the Monte Carlo data. The ridge parameter was set at 0.06 for each trial, and this value was iteratively computed (Hoerl *et al.*, 1975) from the data for the first trial. Although 0.06 is a small value for the smoothing parameter, the precision of the corresponding estimates is much improved. By further restricting the response parameters to the closed unit interval, [0, 1], the RLS estimator has even greater precision than the competing ridge estimator.

Table 8.5.1 Average estimates of the production parameters

Method	$\bar{\beta}_1$	$\bar{\beta}_2$	$\bar{\beta}_3$	$\bar{\beta}_4$	MSEL
LS–ML	0.4417	0.1422	0.6369	0.4775	13.1363
Ridge	0.6172	0.3127	0.3590	0.5532	4.0695
RLS	0.4315	0.4183	0.4569	0.3492	0.3472
GME–D	0.4821	0.4086	0.4139	0.4247	0.0114
True	0.45	0.35	0.40	0.50	

The entropy-based estimate of the production model was derived using the GME–D form of the consistency constraints. The parameter space was restricted to the unit interval, as in the RLS case, and vector of supports on each parameter was $\mathbf{Z}_k = [0, 0.25, 0.5, 0.75, 1]$. To refect the disturbances, the error bounds were set to $\mathbf{V}_t = [-5, 0, 5]$. Based on the results of this limited sampling experiment, it appears that the GME–D method has exceptional precision and recovers considerably more accurate information about the underlying production system. However, GME–D requires no more information than is used by the traditional regularization methods. Although the results of the exercise are based on a design matrix with a very large condition number, we will show that the GME–GCE methods exhibit similar performance for smaller, more realistic values of $\kappa(\mathbf{X}'\mathbf{X})$. In the next section, we employ a more detailed sampling experiment to demonstrate the performance of the GME–GCE solutions for a broad range of ill-conditioned problems.

8.6 AN EXTENSIVE SAMPLING EXPERIMENT

The results in the preceding section suggest that GME–GCE performs very well when the condition number is very large. However, it is important to assess the relative performance of GME–GCE in more realistic settings. Given that we do not know the exact finite-sample properties of many robust estimators (including GME–GCE) we use Monte Carlo sampling experiments to compare GME–GCE with the least squares (LS), restricted LS (RLS) and ridge (QR) estimators. The experimental design is outlined in the following subsections, and the competing estimators are compared according to the empirical risk measures (precision and prediction). As before, each experiment is based on 5000 Monte Carlo trials.

8.6.1 THE EXPERIMENTAL DESIGN

To form the signal for the Monte Carlo experiment, a (10×4) design matrix was drawn from an i.i.d. N(0, 1) pseudo-random number generator. To form a design matrix with a desired condition number, $\kappa(\mathbf{X}'\mathbf{X}) = \mu$, the singular value decomposition of $\mathbf{X}$ was recovered. Then, the eigenvalues in $\mathbf{L}$ were replaced with the K-vector

$$a = \left[\sqrt{\frac{2}{1+\mu}},\ 1,\ 1,\ \sqrt{\frac{2\mu}{1+\mu}}\right] \tag{8.6.1}$$

which has length $K = 4$. The new design matrix, $\mathbf{X}_a = \mathbf{Q}\mathbf{L}_a\mathbf{R}$, is characterized by $\kappa(\mathbf{X}_a'\mathbf{X}_a) = \mu$, and the condition number may be specified *a priori*. Given that each column of $\mathbf{X}$ has the same *expected* length, the columns of $\mathbf{X}_a$ are not scaled to unit length, as suggested by Belsley (1991). For $\boldsymbol{\beta} = [2, 1, -3, 2]'$, the signal was formed as $\mathbf{X}_a\boldsymbol{\beta}$, and T i.i.d. N(0, 1) pseudo-random errors, $\mathbf{e}$, were added to form vector of noisy observations, $\mathbf{y}$.

For each Monte Carlo trial, the LS, RLS, and ridge methods were used to estimate $\boldsymbol{\beta}$ from the associated sample information, $\mathbf{X}_a$ and $\mathbf{y}$. The RLS estimates were restricted to $\beta_k \in [-10, 10]$ for each k, and the Hoerl *et al.* (1975) iterative ridge estimator was used with $\mathbf{C} \equiv \mathbf{I}_K$ and

$$\hat{\eta} = \frac{\hat{\sigma}^2(K-2)}{\hat{\boldsymbol{\beta}}'\hat{\boldsymbol{\beta}}} \tag{8.6.2}$$

Entropy-based estimates of $\boldsymbol{\beta}$ were recovered by the GME–D method with parameter supports $\mathbf{z}_k = [-10, -5, 0, 5, 10]$ for each k. The choice of the parameter supports is discussed in greater detail in Sections 8.7.1 and 8.7.2. The 3σ rule was used to form the error supports, $\mathbf{V}$, and $\mathbf{v}_t = [-3, 0, 3]$ for each t.

8.6.2 EMPIRICAL RISK FUNCTIONS

To gauge the performance of the competing methods, the precision of each estimator was computed under squared error loss, SEL $= \|\boldsymbol{\beta} - \hat{\boldsymbol{\beta}}\|^2$. The average SEL (MSEL) is then an estimate of the empirical precision risk for each of the competing methods of information recovery. Accordingly, the prediction risk is computed as the average sum of squared errors, SSE $= \|\mathbf{y} - \mathbf{X}\boldsymbol{\beta}\|^2$. The risk results for the experiment are presented in Figures 8.6.1 and 8.6.2. The horizontal axis of each plot is expressed in units of $\kappa(\mathbf{X}'\mathbf{X})$, which ranges from 1 to 100.

Note that the empirical risk of the LS estimator is 4.02 when $\kappa(\mathbf{X}'\mathbf{X}) = 1$, which is very close to its theoretical value of 4. The empirical risk of RLS is close to the LS risk in the nearly orthogonal case, but it declines relative to LS as $\kappa(\mathbf{X}'\mathbf{X})$ increases. Clearly, the variance inflation effect increases the probability that the LS estimates fall outside the restricted parameter space. Further, the iterative ridge estimator is biased, and its empirical risk is 4.4 when $\kappa(\mathbf{X}'\mathbf{X}) = 1$. As the

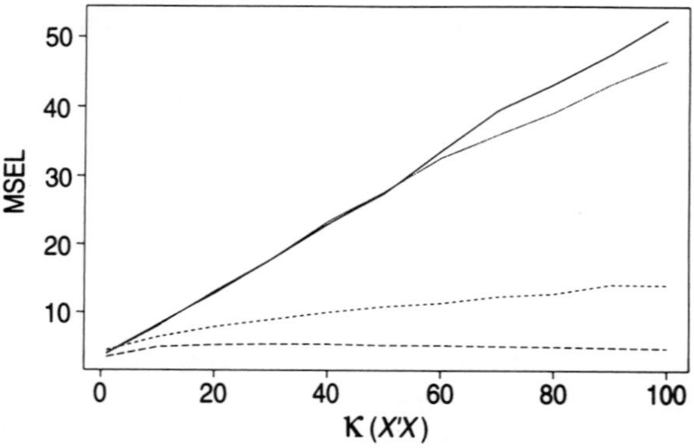

Figure 8.6.1 MSEL in ill-conditioned problems. ____, LS; ....., RLS; _ _ _, ridge; __ __, GME

Table 8.6.1 Data for Figure 8.6.1

$\kappa(\mathbf{X}'\mathbf{X})$	LS	RLS	Ridge	GME–D
1	4.08657	4.02271	4.54300	3.57897
10	8.22531	7.93210	6.45564	4.99437
20	12.75875	13.08564	7.91884	5.32732
30	17.73376	17.78132	8.98486	5.45113
40	22.83802	23.24995	10.00941	5.44312
50	27.36695	27.59951	10.86021	5.27084
60	33.56641	32.57188	11.38744	5.27865
70	39.40164	35.93276	12.37142	5.17348
80	43.18114	39.13230	12.79996	5.08621
90	47.47539	43.14750	14.11707	4.98305
100	52.46118	46.54126	14.06549	4.89986

condition number increases, the LS and ridge empirical risk functions cross, and the ridge estimator risk-dominates LS. Again, the regularity (shrinkage) conditions reduce the risk of the ridge estimator relative to LS.

In contrast, the empirical risk of GME–D is nearly invariant to the degree of ill-conditioning, and it dominates the traditional estimators over the range of $\kappa(\mathbf{X}'\mathbf{X})$. The superior performance of the entropy-based method in the region of very slight collinearity was unexpected, especially given the 'best unbiased' property of the LS estimator. The parameter restrictions implied in $\mathbf{Z}$ are equivalent to the RLS restrictions, and these should provide very similar estimates. Given the shrinkage property of GME–GCE when the noise terms, $\mathbf{Vw}$, are included, we may loosely view the noise version of GME–D as a shrinkage version of RLS. Hence, the GME–D risk is lower than the RLS risk for all values of $\kappa(\mathbf{X}'\mathbf{X})$.

The ridge estimator is often viewed as a variance-reduction technique that restricts the LS solution to an ellipsoid in the parameter space

$$\{\mathbf{x} \in \mathbb{R}^K : \|\mathbf{x}\|^2 \leq \boldsymbol{\beta}'\mathbf{C}\boldsymbol{\beta}\}$$

As the degree of collinearity increases, the sample and prior information are less likely to be consistent, and the restriction becomes relatively more binding. However, the ellipsoid expands with the data-based ridge parameter, η, and the risk increases with the condition number. However, the GME–D parameter vector is restricted to a fixed hypercube, as in the RLS case, and there is no risk penalty for using a data-driven regularization method. Finally, GME–D guarantees that the estimates are consistent with the sample yet reflect the prior information, and the performance is not affected by the condition number.

It is important to note that some of the precision (risk)-gains of the GME–D estimator are offset in the empirical prediction risk (MSSE) (see Figure 8.6.2).

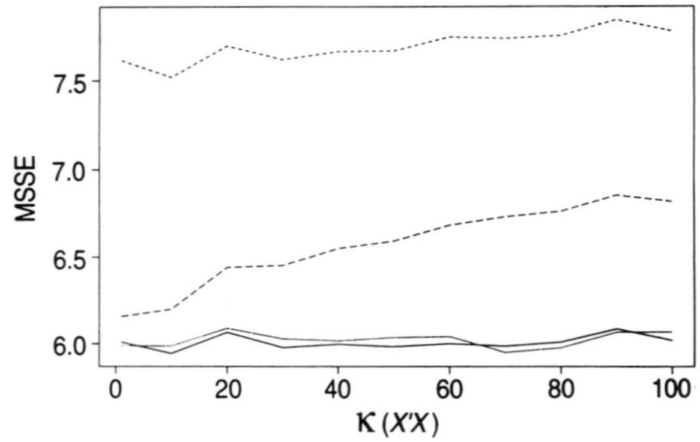

Figure 8.6.2 MSEL in ill-conditioned problems. ____, LS; ....., RLS; _ _ _, ridge; __ __, GME

As expected, the least squares rules (LS and RLS) dominate GME–D and ridge under this measure because the estimates are selected to minimize SSE. However, the GME–D prediction risk is smaller than the ridge MSSE, and GME–D dominates ridge under both loss measures.

8.6.3 THE EMPIRICAL DISTRIBUTION OF β_3

Although the exact finite-sample properties of the RLS, ridge, and GME methods are unknown, especially in the ill-conditioned cases, the empirical distribution of the recovered parameters may provide some information. Figures 8.6.3 and 8.6.4 present smoothed densities of the LS, ridge, and GME point estimates for β_3. The RLS estimates are excluded given their relation to the LS rule. The impact of the condition number is represented by a well-conditioned (orthogonal) design matrix, $\kappa(\mathbf{X}'\mathbf{X}) = 1$, and a moderately ill-conditioned design matrix, $\kappa(\mathbf{X}'\mathbf{X}) = 90$.

In the orthogonal case, the mean (-3.02) and variance (0.99) of the LS estimator are very close to their theoretical values. As expected, the data-based, iterative method of selecting the ridge parameter provides for some bias and variance-reduction relative to LS (mean $= -2.54$, variance $= 0.96$). However, the GME–D distribution is centered between the true value ($\beta_3 = -3$) and the center of its parameter support, 0. Consequently, the shrinkage property of the GME solution provides less bias (mean $= -2.78$) *and* less variance (0.83).

As the condition number increases, the LS estimator exhibits greater variance (as expected) but remains unbiased as the distribution is centered over the true parameter value, $\beta_3 = -3$ (mean $= -3.05$, variance $= 21.18$). The ridge and GME–D distributions shift right as the degree of shrinkage (toward zero)

Table 8.6.2 Data for Figure 8.6.2

$\kappa(\mathbf{X'X})$	LS	RLS	Ridge	GME–D
1	6.00994	5.98864	7.61309	6.15874
10	5.94337	5.98739	7.51699	6.20075
20	6.06601	6.09004	7.69560	6.44064
30	5.97812	6.02895	7.61679	6.45209
40	5.99669	6.01632	7.66320	6.55045
50	5.98180	6.03587	7.66625	6.59210
60	5.99993	6.04206	7.74654	6.68149
70	5.98637	5.94897	7.73824	6.72939
80	6.00983	5.97600	7.75349	6.76028
90	6.08708	6.06819	7.84309	6.85182
100	6.02083	6.06912	7.77747	6.81382

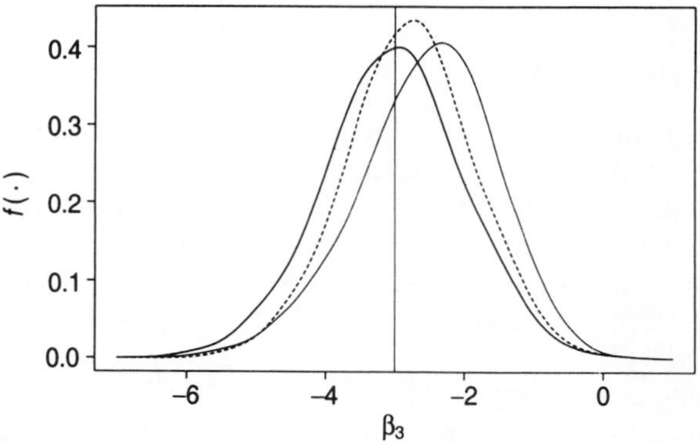

Figure 8.6.3 Empirical distribution of β_3, $\kappa(X'X) = 1$. ____, LS; ....., ridge; _ _ _, GME

increases, and their sample means are -1.82 and -2.17, respectively. Further, the ridge technique has a greater sample variance (4.77) than GME–D (1.33). Consequently, the entropy technique continues to reflect less bias than the ridge estimator, and it has smaller variance than either of the traditional methods in this sampling study.

8.7 ALTERNATE ENTROPY FORMULATIONS

In this section, we examine some of the practical issues related to the choice of parameter supports and prior weights. We present sampling results to demonstrate the impact of the breadth of the parameter bounds, the number of support points, and the sign of the prior mean.

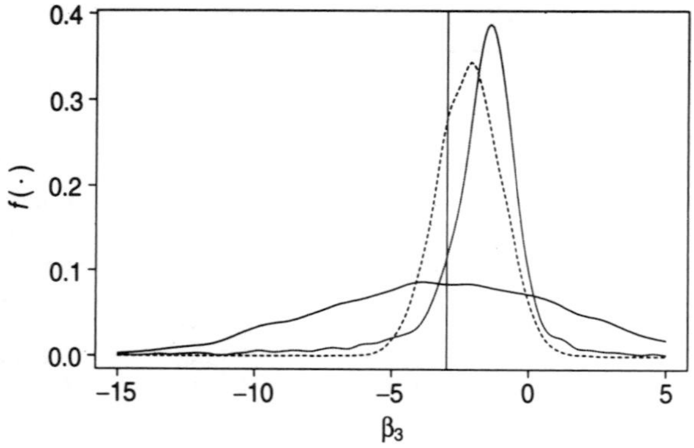

Figure 8.6.4 Empirical distribution of β_3, $\kappa(X'X) = 90$. ____, LS; ....., ridge; _ _ _, GME

8.7.1 THE CHOICE OF Z

The restrictions imposed on the parameter space through $\mathbf{Z}$ reflect prior knowledge about the unknown parameters. However, such knowledge is not always available, and researchers may want to entertain a variety of plausible bounds on $\boldsymbol{\beta}$. The preceding sampling experiments were repeated using two additional $\mathbf{Z}$ matrices, $\mathbf{Z}_k=[-5, -2.5, 0, 2.5, 5]$ and $\mathbf{Z}_k=[-15, -7.5, 0, 7.5, 15]$ for each k. The empirical risk functions for these alternatives are presented in Figure 8.7.1.

As the parameter supports are widened, the GME risk functions modestly shift upward reflecting the reduced constraints on the parameters space, Hence, wide bounds may be used without extreme risk consequences if our knowledge is minimal and we want to ensure that $\mathbf{Z}$ contains $\boldsymbol{\beta}$. Intuitively, increasing the bounds increases the impact of the data and decreases the impact of the support. Of course, narrowing the parameter supports only improves the risk as long as the true parameter vector is well in the interior of $\mathscr{Z}$. It is important to note that for $\kappa(X'X) = 1$, even if the bounds of $\mathbf{Z}$ are increased to $(-1060, -500, 0, 500, 1000)$ the empirical MSE = 3.90 and is thus below its ML-LS counterpart. This is also true over the range of $\kappa(X'X) = 1$, ---, 100. Although the results are not included here, the corresponding MSSE moves in the opposite direction, further highlighting the trade-off between the precision and prediction losses.

8.7.2 THE CHOICE OF M AND J

At this point, it is important to comment on our choice of the number of points used to form the parameter and error supports, $\mathbf{Z}$ and $\mathbf{V}$. Recall from Chapters

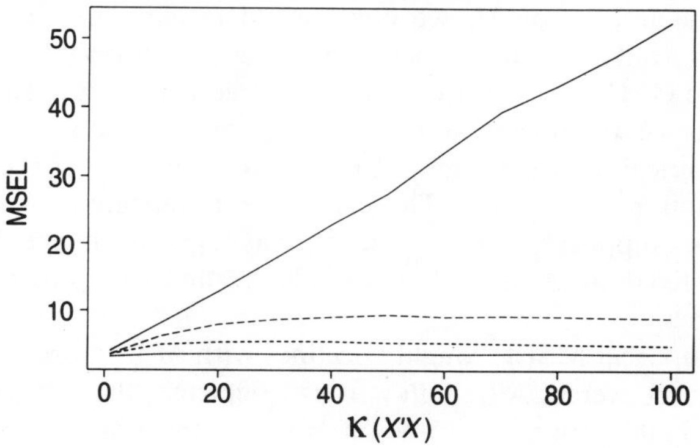

Figure 8.7.1 GME risk under alternate **Z**. ____, LS; ....., GME ($z = 5$); ___, GME ($z = 10$); ____, GME ($z = 15$)

Table 8.7.1 Data for Figure 8.7.1

$\kappa(\mathbf{X'X})$	LS	GME, $z = 5$	GME, $z = 10$	GME, $z = 15$
1	4.08657	3.24878	3.57897	3.59601
10	8.22531	3.58411	4.99437	6.26713
20	12.75875	3.64336	5.32732	7.93725
30	17.73376	3.61772	5.45113	8.68749
40	22.83802	3.66083	5.44312	9.04058
50	27.36695	3.64942	5.27084	9.39303
60	33.56641	3.64038	5.27865	9.10160
70	39.40164	3.69548	5.17348	9.22596
80	43.18114	3.75824	5.08621	9.17489
90	47.47539	3.68518	4.98305	9.02410
100	52.46118	3.69216	4.89986	8.93665

6 and 7 that $\mathbf{\Sigma_Z}$ and $\mathbf{\Sigma_V}$ are prominent components in the approximate variance of the GME–GCE point estimators. Consequently, the dimensions of the supports may affect the sampling properties of the entropy-based rules. For example a discrete uniform distribution supported on $\mathbf{z} = [-c, c]$ (i.e. $M = 2$) has a variance of $\sigma_z^2 = c^2$. If we increase the number of points in the support and allocate them in an equidistant fashion, the variance of the uniform distribution decreases. As the number of points becomes infinitely large and the uniform distribution becomes continuous, the variance drops to $\sigma_z^2 = c^2/3$. Hence, adding more points to the support of $\mathbf{Z}$ should decrease the variance of the associated point estimator in GME problems. Of course, this increases the computational burden of the problem.

To check the impact of M, we constructed a sampling experiment based on 10000 MC trials and the experimental design outlined above. For each of the trials, the GME–D estimates were recovered using supports on $[-10, 10]$ for each unknown parameter and $[-3, 0, 3]$ for each unknown disturbance. Then the empirical precision loss (SEL) was computed for each trial (see the next subsection for details). The exercise was repeated for $M = 3, \ldots, 10$ by shifting the support points to be equally spaced in the $[-10, 10]$ interval; J was fixed at 3 in each case. The results are presented in Figure 8.7.2.

Note that empirical MSEL roughly declines with M as more refined information about $\boldsymbol{\beta}$ is recovered. Although it is not depicted, the empirical prediction risk increases, highlighting the trade-off between the precision and prediction losses. Depending on the weights used to form the risk trade-off, the gains in the parameter space may offset the losses in the sample space. However, based on these limited results, it appears that the greatest improvement in precision comes from using $M = 5$ and $\mathbf{Z}_k = [-10, -5, 0, 5, 10]$ for each k. The choice of J may be made on a similar basis.

8.7.3 THE IMPACT OF PARAMETER SIGN INFORMATION

Finally, the cross-entropy criterion may be used to recover information about $\boldsymbol{\beta}$ by employing non-uniform prior distributions on $\mathbf{Z}$. Using the GME–D formulation and $\mathbf{Z}_k = [-10, 10]$ for each k, the Monte Carlo trials were repeated under two conflicting priors. First, the correct sign of the true parameters was included by specifying prior weights of $\mathbf{q}_k = [0.375, 0.625]$ for $\beta_k > 0$, and $\mathbf{q}_3 = [0.625, 0.375]$ for β_3. Thus, the prior mean of each parameter is 2.5 in absolute value. Next, the prior weights were transposed so that the prior means are also 2.5 in absolute value, but with the wrong sign. The empirical risk functions appear in Figure 8.7.3.

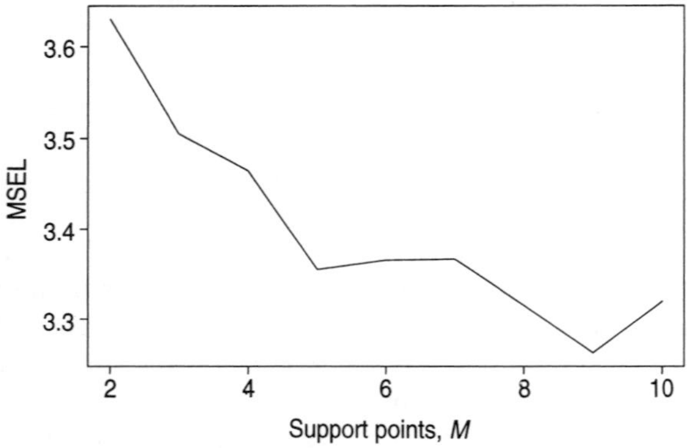

Figure 8.7.2 MSEL of GME–D as M increases

Table 8.7.2 Data for Figure 8.7.2

M	MSEL	MSSE
2	3.62962	6.06953
3	3.50504	6.12467
4	3.46418	6.14822
5	3.35443	6.18797
6	3.36486	6.21447
7	3.36594	6.27556
8	3.31543	6.25810
9	3.26225	6.21410
10	3.31973	6.28666

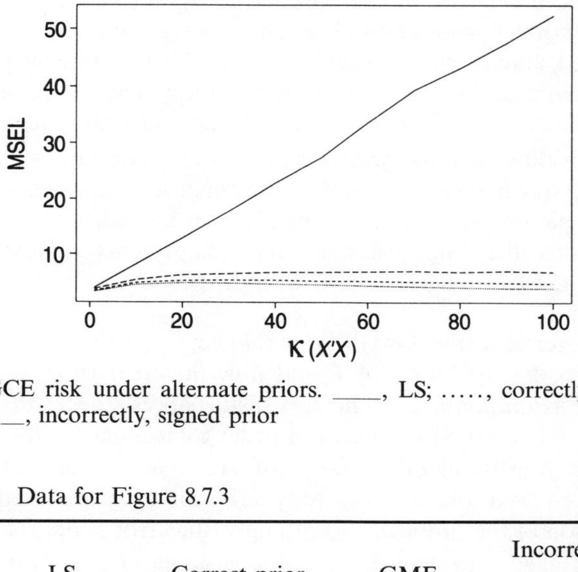

Figure 8.7.3 GCE risk under alternate priors. ____, LS; ....., correctly, signed prior; _ _ _, GME; __ __, incorrectly, signed prior

Table 8.7.3 Data for Figure 8.7.3

κ(**X′X**)	LS	Correct prior	GME	Incorrectly signed prior
1	4.08657	3.39558	3.57897	3.89273
10	8.22531	4.63228	4.99437	5.49821
20	12.75875	4.91015	5.32732	6.31644
30	17.73376	4.89968	5.45113	6.54100
40	22.83802	4.72740	5.44312	6.80651
50	27.36695	4.62097	5.27084	6.82707
60	33.56641	4.47631	5.27865	6.95539
70	39.40164	4.33548	5.17348	7.05679
80	43.18114	4.15830	5.08621	6.89581
90	47.47539	4.03034	4.98305	7.07840
100	52.46118	4.03178	4.89986	6.91289

As expected, including the correct prior signs improves risk for all values of $\kappa(\mathbf{X}'\mathbf{X})$. However, the penalty for using the wrong prior information is not very large relative to the risk of the alternate estimators. The reason undoubtedly lies in the model constraint, which must be satisfied for any interior solution to the GME–D problem. Although the incorrect prior weights affect the results, the entropy method cannot stray too far from the true parameters because it *must* also satisfy the sample information. This property is another benefit of the generalized entropy approach – *incorrect prior information is effectively discounted by the GCE criterion if it does not agree with the sample.*

8.8 NON-NORMAL ERRORS

As in the bounded mean example from Chapter 7, we will show that the GME–D solutions are robust under non-Gaussian error structures. Using the sample design outlined above, we generated observations by drawing pseudo-random disturbances from a $t(3)$ and a $\chi^2(4)$ distribution. The chi-square errors were centered by subtracting the mean (4), and all drawings were scaled to have unit variance by dividing each by the associated standard deviation (i.e. $\sqrt{3}$ and $\sqrt{8}$, respectively). To conserve space, the RLS estimator is omitted, and estimates of the unknown parameters were computed for the LS, ridge, and GME–GCE–D rules. As before, the empirical risk functions were computed by averaging the precision (SEL) and prediction (SSE) losses over all 5000 Monte Carlo trials.

For both exercises, the GME–D parameter supports were maintained at $\mathbf{z}_k = [-10, -5, 0, 5, 10]'$ for each k, but now the error supports vary with the distributional assumption. For the $t(3)$ disturbances, the error supports were widened to $\mathbf{v}_t = [-5, 0, 5]$ for each t in order to account for the thicker tails of the t-distribution. Although the chi-square errors were centered, the distribution remains skewed and the cross-entropy criterion may be used to solve the GCE–D version of the problem. Accordingly, the error supports were shifted to $\mathbf{v}_t = [-\sqrt{2}, 0, 2\sqrt{2}]'$ for each t, and prior weights of $\mathbf{q}_t = [4/9, 1/3, 2/9]'$ were assigned to reflect a skewed, mean-zero distribution.

The precision risk (MSEL) results are presented in Figures 8.8.1 and 8.8.2. Although the magnitude of the risks are different under the non-normal errors, the relative behavior of the three estimators remains the same. The ridge estimator improves upon the LS result, and the GME–GCE–D solution out-performs both competitors. The prediction risk (MSSE) functions are not included here, but they depict the same relationship as found in the normal case. That is, the LS estimator has smallest prediction risk, but the GME–GCE–D rule performs better than the ridge estimator. Thus, the GME–D and GCE–D formulations may be adapted to reflect subjective information about the error distribution, and the resulting solutions are robust and superior relative to the traditional

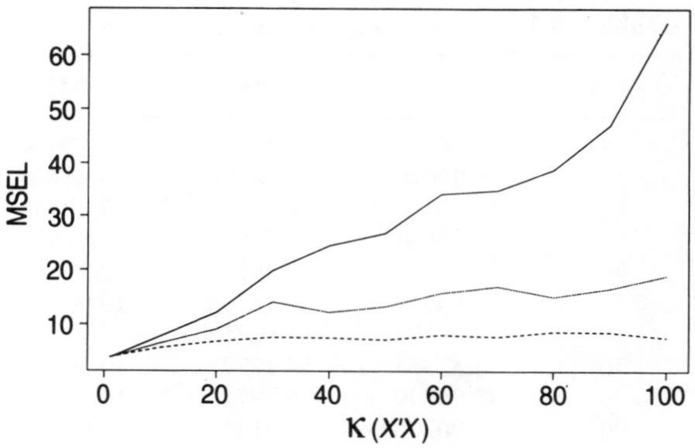

Figure 8.8.1 GME risk under $t(3)$ disturbances. ____, LS; ....., ridge; _ _ _, GME

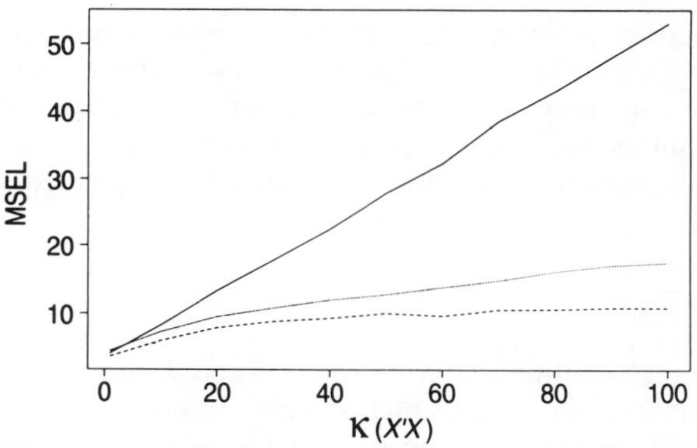

Figure 8.8.2 GCE risk under centered $\chi^2(4)$ disturbances. ____, LS; ....., ridge; _ _ _, GME

Table 8.8.1 Data for Figure 8.8.1

$\kappa(\mathbf{X}'\mathbf{X})$	LS	Ridge	GME
1	3.95558	3.96302	4.04143
10	7.83964	6.58930	5.76529
20	12.16706	9.09495	6.88685
30	19.91341	14.13076	7.68336
40	24.52322	12.24956	7.58442
50	26.81259	13.29359	7.26093
60	34.14352	15.82557	8.14501
70	34.82527	17.02269	7.83677
80	38.80454	15.11180	8.71352
90	47.04659	16.63191	8.64879
100	66.19146	19.01172	7.67507

Table 8.8.2 Data for Figure 8.8.2

$\kappa(\mathbf{X}'\mathbf{X})$	LS	Ridge	GME
1	4.06432	4.46875	3.62079
10	8.28040	7.28096	5.94976
20	13.30136	9.50738	7.86865
30	17.73664	10.77814	8.81874
40	22.42951	11.98120	9.31785
50	27.88518	12.75790	10.00706
60	32.26527	13.80714	9.63731
70	38.53353	14.82771	10.56522
80	42.96299	16.09723	10.62896
90	48.06205	17.01336	10.85206
100	53.00933	17.41067	10.85184

rules of information recovery. Additional evidence concerning the robustness of GME–GCE to distributional specifications is presented in Chapters 15 and 16.

Finally, we emphasize again, that in most cases where the underlying distribution is unknown, one conservative way of choosing the error support $\mathbf{V}$ is by using the empirical standard deviation of the observed $\mathbf{y}$.

8.9 REMARKS

Following the analytical results in Chapters 6 and 7, the Monte Carlo results provide information about the small-sample properties of GME–GCE. As expected, the traditional least squares (LS, RLS, and ridge) techniques provide smaller average prediction losses (MSSE). However, the prediction and precision risks of the entropy-based methods are nearly invariant as the condition number increases. In moderately ill-conditioned problems, GME–GCE also provides smaller average precision loss (MSEL).

The generalized entropy formulations are feasible alternatives to the standard methods of information recovery in ill-conditioned linear inverse problems. The required prior information is limited to bounds on the unknown parameters, but more complex prior knowledge may be incorporated in a number of ways. For example, additional information about the signs of the unknown parameters may be included by shifting the support space, $\mathbf{Z}$, or by using non-uniform prior weights, $\mathbf{q}$. By choosing posterior probability distributions that satisfy the consistency constraints *and* are most similar to the prior weights, the GME–GCE solutions are improved by correct prior information, but remain robust if the prior information is incorrect. Finally, the dual GME–GCE formulation (Chapter 6) reduces the computational burden of the problems to be roughly the same as required for the RLS and ridge estimators.

REFERENCES

Belsley, D. (1991) *Conditioning Diagnostics: Collinearity and Weak Data in Regressions.* John Wiley, New York.

Donoho, D., Johnstone, I., Hoch, J. and Stern, A. (1992) Maximum entropy and the near black object. *Journal of the Royal Statistical Society, Series B* **54,** 41–81.

Geweke, J. (1986) Exact inference in the inequality constrained normal linear regression model. *Journal of Applied Econometrics* **1,** 127–42.

Griffiths, W. E., Hill, R. C. and Judge, G. G. (1993) *Learning and Practicing Econometrics.* John Wiley, New York.

Hoerl, A., Kennard, R. and Baldwin, K. (1975) Ridge regression: Some simulations. *Communications in Statistics* **5,** 105–23.

O'Sullivan, F. (1986) A statistical perspective on ill-posed inverse problems. *Statistical Science* **1,** 502–27.

Tikhonov, A. N. and Arsenin, V. Y. (1977) *Solutions of Ill-Posed Problems.* Winston, Washington, DC.

Zellner, A. (1993) Bayesian and non-Bayesian estimation using balanced loss functions. In Gupta, S. S. and Berger, J. O. (eds) *Statistical Decision Theory: Theory and Related Topics:* 377–390. Springer Verlag, New York.

CHAPTER 9

General linear statistical model with a non-scalar identity covariance matrix

9.1 INTRODUCTION

It is conventional when specifying a linear statistical model for an economic problem to use the simplifying assumption that the elements of the error vector are uncorrelated and have identical variances. In terms of the inverse problem with noise, introduced in Chapter 6, this implies the linear statistical model

$$\mathbf{y} = X\boldsymbol{\beta} + \mathbf{e} \tag{9.1.1}$$

where $\mathbf{y}$ is a T-dimensional vector of observables, X is a $(T \times K)$ design matrix and $\boldsymbol{\beta}$ is a K dimensional vector of unknown coefficients, and $\mathbf{e}$ is a T-dimensional unobservable random vector with mean vector $\mathbf{0}$ and covariance matrix $\mathrm{E}[\mathbf{ee}'] = \Phi = \sigma^2 I_T$. If the elements of the error vector $\mathbf{e}$ are drawing from distributions that have different variances, the errors are said to be heteroskedastic. If the elements of the error vector $\mathbf{e}$ are correlated from drawing to drawing, they are said to be autocorrelated. In either case, Φ is no longer scalar-identity and under conditions normally found in practice, each of these error structures may be consistent with data generating processes in economics (see Judge *et al.*, 1988, pp. 351–419).

If the error covariance matrix Φ is known, it is traditional to use the generalized least squares (GLS) rule

$$\boldsymbol{\beta}_g = [X'\Phi^{-1}X]^{-1}X'\Phi^{-1}\mathbf{y} \tag{9.1.2}$$

which is unbiased and efficient, with covariance matrix $(X'\Phi^{-1}X)^{-1}$. If instead of the GLS rule, the least squares (LS) rule

$$\mathbf{b} = (X'X)^{-1}X'\mathbf{y} \tag{9.1.3}$$

is used, the LS rule is unbiased but inefficient because its covariance matrix

$$(X'X)^{-1}X'\Phi X(X'X)^{-1} \tag{9.1.4}$$

exceeds $(X'\Phi^{-1}X)^{-1}$, the covariance of $\boldsymbol{\beta}_g$ in the sense that

$$\Delta = (X'X)^{-1}X'\Phi X(X'X)^{-1} - (X'\Phi X)^{-1} \tag{9.1.5}$$

is a positive semi-definite matrix.

If Φ is unknown, which is the case normally found in practice, the GLS estimator $\boldsymbol{\beta}_g$ is no longer feasible. In this case it is conventional to replace Φ with a consistent estimate of the covariance matrix, Φ. This leads to the two-stage EGLS or feasible GLS estimator

$$\boldsymbol{\beta}_{\hat{g}} = (X'\hat{\Phi}^{-1}X)^{-1}X'\hat{\Phi}^{-1}\mathbf{y} \tag{9.1.6}$$

With this estimator the large number of $T(T+1)/2$ unknown parameters in Φ cannot be satisfactorily recovered from the T data points. Consequently, in order to cope with inconvenient data generation processes and to achieve a tractable statistical model, it is customary to make creative assumptions about the structure of the error covariance matrix, Φ.

In terms of the statistical properties of the EGLS estimator, it is possible to show that although it is unbiased, it is neither best nor linear. In general, it can be shown (Judge *et al.*, 1988, p. 354) that $\boldsymbol{\beta}_g$ and $\boldsymbol{\beta}_{\hat{g}}$ have the same limiting distribution if the unknown parameters of Φ are consistently estimated.

In the sections ahead we investigate, within the context of Chapter 6 and a general linear model formulation, an efficient basis for recovering the unknown $\boldsymbol{\beta}$ vector where Φ is unknown and the diagonal elements are not identical (heteroskedasticity) and the off diagonal elements are non-zero (autocorrelated).

9.2 AUTOCORRELATED ERRORS

There are many possible reasons for, and forms of, autocorrelation and each one leads to a different structure for the error covariance matrix (see Judge *et al.*, 1985, pp. 275–8). In econometrics one popular structure for autocorrelation is a first-order autoregressive process. To reflect this error covariance structure, we write the general linear model in scalar form as

$$y_t = \mathbf{x}_t'\boldsymbol{\beta} + e_t \tag{9.2.1}$$

where

$$e_t = \rho e_{t-1} + a_t \tag{9.2.2}$$

and a_t is white noise that is assumed to have mean zero, constant variance and is uncorrelated over t. Thus,

$$\mathrm{E}[\mathbf{a}] = \mathbf{0} \quad \text{and} \quad \mathrm{E}[\mathbf{aa}'] = \sigma_a^2 I_T \tag{9.2.3}$$

and in terms of (9.1.1)

$$\mathrm{E}[\mathbf{e}] = \mathbf{0}, \qquad \mathrm{E}[\mathbf{ee}'] = \Phi = \sigma_a^2 \Psi \tag{9.2.4}$$

where

$$\Psi = \frac{1}{1 - p^2} \begin{bmatrix} 1 & \rho & \cdots & \rho^{T-1} \\ \rho & 1 & \cdots & \rho^{T-2} \\ \vdots & \vdots & \ddots & \vdots \\ \rho^{T-1} & \rho^{T-2} & \cdots & 1 \end{bmatrix} \tag{9.2.5}$$

Since ρ is unknown, a consistent estimator of ρ is traditionally obtained from least squares residuals e_t and a two-stage GLS estimator is used. The finite sample properties of $\boldsymbol{\beta}_{\hat{g}}$ are unknown but $\boldsymbol{\beta}_g$ and $\boldsymbol{\beta}_{\hat{g}}$ have the same asymptotic distribution.

To indicate how the problem of autocorrelation may be handled in the context of a GME linear statistical model formulation, we start with a first-order specification and then generalize it to higher-order autocorrelation.

9.2.1 A GME FORMULATION OF FIRST-ORDER AUTOCORRELATION

Within the context of Chapter 6, the reparameterized general linear statistical model with first-order autoregressive errors may be specified as

$$y_t = \mathbf{x}_t'\boldsymbol{\beta} + e_t = \mathbf{x}_t' Z\mathbf{p} + e_t \tag{9.2.6}$$

$$e_t = \rho e_{t-1} + a_t = \rho e_{t-1} + \mathbf{v}'\mathbf{w}_t \tag{9.2.7}$$

where the stochastic characteristics of e_t and a_t are given in (9.2.3)–(9.2.5). Under this specification a GME formulation is

$$\max_{\mathbf{p},\mathbf{w},\rho} H(\mathbf{p}, \mathbf{w}) = \{-\mathbf{p}' \ln \mathbf{p} - \mathbf{w}' \ln \mathbf{w}\} \tag{9.2.8}$$

subject to

$$y_t = \mathbf{x}_t'\mathbf{z}_k'\mathbf{p}_k + e_t \tag{9.2.9}$$

$$\mathbf{1}_K = (I_K \otimes \mathbf{1}_M')\mathbf{p} \tag{9.2.10}$$

$$\mathbf{1}_T = (I_T \otimes \mathbf{1}_J')\mathbf{w} \tag{9.2.11}$$

$$\begin{cases} e_t = a_t = \sum_j v_j w_{1j}, & \text{for } t = 1 \\ e_t = \rho e_{t-1} + a_t = \rho e_{t-1} + \sum_j v_j w_{tj}, & \text{for } t = 2, 3, \ldots, T \end{cases} \tag{9.2.12}$$

Under this framework we recover simultaneously the unknown β_k's (or the corresponding probabilities $\mathbf{p}_k$), the unknown errors e_t and a_t and the unknown first-order autocorrelation coefficients ρ. The unknown errors e_t and a_t are related through the autocorrelation relations (9.2.2), or (9.2.12). Consequently, it is sufficient to reparameterize only the errors $a_t = \sum_j v_j w_{tj}$ and impose the additional constraints (9.2.12) on the linear-GME model. Proceeding in the way introduced in Chapters 3 and 6, the resulting solution yields estimates of both the unknown e_t and the ρ. In more general terms, the solution to (9.2.8)–(9.2.12) has to satisfy the set of autocorrelation restrictions. Consequently, the set of optimal solutions consistent with (9.2.2), allows for first-order autocorrelation, while in the linear model of Chapter 6 it is assumed that $\rho = 0$.

Forming the Lagrangian and solving for the optimal solution yields $\hat{\mathbf{p}}$, $\hat{\mathbf{w}}$ and $\hat{\rho}$, which in turn yield $\hat{\boldsymbol{\beta}}$, $\hat{\mathbf{e}}$ and $\hat{\mathbf{a}}$. As in the previous linear models (Chapters 3 and 6) the Hessian is negative-definite assuring a unique global solution. In Section 9.5 we show that $\text{plim}(\hat{\boldsymbol{\beta}}) = \boldsymbol{\beta}$ for this model.

9.2.2 HIGHER-ORDER AUTOCORRELATION

It is straightforward to generalize the previous model to accommodate the fact that some economic data generating processes are consistent with the possibility of higher-order autocorrelation. Higher-order autocorrelations may be specified as

$$e_t = \rho_1 e_{t-1} + \rho_2 e_{t-2} + \ldots + \rho_\tau e_{t-\tau} + a_t \qquad \text{for } t = \tau + 1, \tau + 2, \ldots, T \quad \text{and } T > \tau \tag{9.2.13}$$

The higher-order autocorrelation–GME model is

$$\max_{\mathbf{p}, \mathbf{w}, \boldsymbol{\rho}} H(\mathbf{p}, \mathbf{w}) = \{-\mathbf{p}' \ln \mathbf{p} - \mathbf{w}' \ln \mathbf{w}\} \tag{9.2.14}$$

subject to (9.2.9)–(9.2.11) and

$$\begin{cases} e_t = a_t = \sum_j v_j w_{1j}, & \text{for } t = 1 \\ e_t = \rho_1 e_{t-1} + a_t = \rho_1 e_{t-1} + \sum_j v_j w_{2j}, & \text{for } t = 2 \\ e_t = \rho_1 e_{t-1} + \rho_2 e_{t-2} + \sum_j v_j w_{3j}, & \text{for } t = 3 \\ \vdots & \\ e_t = \rho e_{t-1} + \rho_2 e_{t-2} + \ldots + \rho_\tau e_{t-\tau} + \sum_j v_j w_{tj}, & \text{for } t = \tau + 1, \tau + 2, \ldots, T \end{cases} \tag{9.2.15}$$

Proceeding as before, the optimal solution simultaneously yields estimates of $\hat{\mathbf{p}}$, $\hat{\mathbf{w}}$ and $\hat{\boldsymbol{\rho}} = (\hat{\rho}_1, \hat{\rho}_2, \ldots, \hat{\rho}_\tau)'$, which in turn yield $\hat{\boldsymbol{\beta}}$, $\hat{\mathbf{e}}$ and $\hat{\mathbf{a}}$.

9.2.3 SAMPLING RESULTS

To indicate finite sample performance of the GME estimator, the results of a limited set of sampling experiments are presented. The experiments used 2000 replications of $T = 10$ and $T = 20$ observations, a parameter vector $\boldsymbol{\beta} = (1, 2, -3, 2)'$ and the a_t were drawings from a N(0, 1) distribution. In Table 9.2.1 we present the empirical MSE($\hat{\boldsymbol{\beta}}$), MSE($\hat{\boldsymbol{\rho}}$), mean of $\bar{\hat{\rho}}$ and tr(cov($\hat{\boldsymbol{\beta}}$)) for a first-order autocorrelated statistical model with $T = 10$ and an orthonormal design matrix X (condition number $\kappa(X'X) = 1$). A similar experiment, but with a design matrix with condition number $\kappa(X'X) = 90$, is presented in Table 9.2.2. In Tables 9.2.3 and 9.2.4 the sampling results of a similar experiment are presented where the number of observations is increased to $T = 20$. In all experiments the 3σ rule was used in specifying $\mathbf{v}_j$.

In Table 9.2.1, where the focus is on the possibility of positive first-order autocorrelated errors and an orthonormal linear statistical model, the empirical results for the LS estimator $\boldsymbol{\beta}_{\text{LS}}$ follows expectations. When $\rho = 0$ the LS empirical risk is 3.92 and near its theoretical risk of 4.0. As ρ increases the risk of the LS estimator rises exponentially. In contrast, for the GME estimator, if it is correctly assumed that $\rho = 0$, then the empirical MSE($\hat{\boldsymbol{\beta}}$) is 3.48 and thus much below both the empirical and theoretical LS risk. Further, if it is incorrectly assumed that $\rho = 0$, then the empirical risk for the GME estimator remains below the empirical risk of the LS estimator. For example if $\rho = 0.8$ and we assume $\rho = 0$, the empirical risk of GME is 5.4. This is in contrast to an empirical risk of 12.67 for ($\hat{\boldsymbol{\beta}}_{\text{LS}}$).

When positive first-order autocorrelated errors are assumed and the GME formulation (9.2.8)–(9.2.12) is used, the empirical MSE($\hat{\boldsymbol{\beta}}$), when $\rho = 0$, is 3.79. This empirical risk is below both the empirical and theoretical LS risk and only marginally higher ($3.79 - 3.48 = 0.31$) than knowing $\rho = 0$. As ρ increases to $\rho = 0.5$, the empirical MSE($\hat{\boldsymbol{\beta}}$) increases and reaches 4.0 the theoretical risk of

Table 9.2.1 Results of 2000 replications of a sampling experiment for a first-order autocorrelated statistical model with $T = 10$, $\kappa(X'X) = 1$, $\mathbf{z}_k = (-10, 0, 10)'$ and $\mathbf{v}_j = (-3, 0, 3)'$

	$\rho = 0$	$\rho = 0.2$	$\rho = 0.5$	$\rho = 0.8$	$\rho = 0.9$
MSE($\hat{\boldsymbol{\beta}}$)	3.79	3.78	4.00	4.61	6.61
tr(cov($\hat{\boldsymbol{\beta}}$))	3.69	3.75	3.97	4.59	6.58
MSE($\hat{\boldsymbol{\rho}}$)	0.14	0.13	0.13	0.13	0.11
$\bar{\hat{\boldsymbol{\rho}}}$	0.22	0.31	0.48	0.69	0.76
MSE($\hat{\boldsymbol{\beta}}_{\text{LS}}$)	3.92	4.12	5.45	12.67	25.33
MSE($\hat{\boldsymbol{\beta}}_{\text{GLS}}$) ($\Phi$ known)	4.00	4.11	4.35	4.30	4.13

Table 9.2.2 Results of 2000 replications of a sampling experiment for a first-order autocorrelated statistical model with $T = 10$, $\kappa(X'X) = 90$, $\mathbf{z}_k = (-10, 0, 10)'$ and $\mathbf{v}_j = (-3, 0, 3)'$

	$\rho = 0$	$\rho = 0.2$	$\rho = 0.5$	$\rho = 0.8$	$\rho = 0.9$
$\text{MSE}(\hat{\boldsymbol{\beta}})$	4.29	4.08	3.93	4.71	10.46
$\text{tr}(\text{cov}(\hat{\boldsymbol{\beta}}))$	4.20	3.95	3.83	4.61	10.37
$\text{MSE}(\hat{\boldsymbol{\rho}})$	0.14	0.11	0.10	0.07	0.06
$\bar{\hat{\boldsymbol{\rho}}}$	0.23	0.33	0.53	0.74	0.83
$\text{MSE}(\hat{\boldsymbol{\beta}}_{\text{LS}})$	48.31	51.89	78.17	265.37	668.67
$\text{MSE}(\hat{\boldsymbol{\beta}}_{\text{GLS}})$ (Φ known)	48.01	49.00	50.44	50.48	49.84

the LS estimator when $\rho = 0$. Finally, at $\rho = 0.9$ the empirical risk of GME reaches 6.61. Again this is much below 25.33 the empirical $\text{MSE}(\boldsymbol{\beta}_{\text{LS}})$. The empirical $\text{tr}(\text{cov}(\hat{\boldsymbol{\beta}}))$ of the GME estimator is fairly stable over the range $0 \leq \rho \leq 0.8$.

In Table 9.2.2 under possible first-order autocorrelation and an ill-conditioned design ($\kappa(X'X) = 90$), the empirical MSE results for the LS estimator are in line with the results reported in Chapter 8 for the statistical model when $\rho = 0$. As ρ increases the empirical risk of the LS estimator rises dramatically. In contrast, for $0 \leq \rho \leq 0.8$, the empirical risk of the GME estimator only increases to 4.71, not greatly in excess of a theoretical risk for the LS estimator when $\rho = 0$ and $\kappa(X'X) = 1.0$. Also, in line with the $\text{MSE}(\hat{\boldsymbol{\beta}})$, the $\text{tr}(\text{cov}(\hat{\boldsymbol{\beta}}))$ is stable although $\kappa(X'X) = 90$ and $\rho \neq 0$. In both Tables 9.2.1 and 9.2.2, note that since positive autocorrelation is assumed, the empirical average GME estimates of ρ are biased upward when $\rho < 0.5$ and biased downward when $\rho > 0.5$.

In Tables 9.2.3 and 9.2.4 the results for $T = 20$ are reported. In general, although the empirical risk values are different for the $T = 10$ case, the relative GME–LS sampling performance is the same. It is interesting to note that when

Table 9.2.3 Results of 2000 replications of a sampling experiment for a first-order autocorrelated statistical model with $T = 20$, $\kappa(X'X) = 1$, $\mathbf{z}_k = (-10, 0, 10)'$ and $\mathbf{v}_j = (-3, 0, 3)'$

	$\rho = 0$	$\rho = 0.2$	$\rho = 0.5$	$\rho = 0.8$	$\rho = 0.9$
$\text{MSE}(\hat{\boldsymbol{\beta}})$	3.77	3.67	3.22	3.18	5.87
$\text{tr}(\text{cov}(\hat{\boldsymbol{\beta}}))$	3.69	3.59	3.17	3.15	5.85
$\text{MSE}(\hat{\boldsymbol{\rho}})$	0.05	0.05	0.05	0.03	0.03
$\bar{\hat{\boldsymbol{\rho}}}$	0.13	0.26	0.51	0.77	0.84
$\text{MSE}(\hat{\boldsymbol{\beta}}_{\text{LS}})$	4.05	4.22	5.16	8.05	10.39

Table 9.2.4 Results of 2000 replications of a sampling experiment for a first-order autocorrelated statistical model with $T = 20$, $\kappa(X'X) = 90$, $\mathbf{z}_k = (-10, 0, 10)'$ and $\mathbf{v}_j = (-3, 0, 3)'$

	$\rho = 0$	$\rho = 0.2$	$\rho = 0.5$	$\rho = 0.8$	$\rho = 0.9$
$\text{MSE}(\hat{\boldsymbol{\beta}})$	5.95	5.71	5.39	5.99	12.71
$\text{tr}(\text{cov}(\hat{\boldsymbol{\beta}}))$	4.33	4.23	4.18	5.02	11.88
$\text{MSE}(\hat{\boldsymbol{\rho}})$	0.04	0.05	0.05	0.03	0.02
$\bar{\hat{\boldsymbol{\rho}}}$	0.12	0.25	0.51	0.77	0.85
$\text{MSE}(\hat{\boldsymbol{\beta}}_{\text{LS}})$	46.92	47.36	60.35	115.23	162.87

$\rho = 0.5$, on average the GME estimator of ρ is on target and this is reflected in a favorable $\text{MSE}(\hat{\boldsymbol{\beta}})$ and excellent sampling precision.

In contrast to EGLS, two-stage estimation procedures that are traditionally used to mitigate the impact of autocorrelated errors, the GME formulation is a *one*-stage procedure and it is straightforward to handle the possibility of higher-order autocorrelated errors.

9.3 HETEROSKEDASTICITY

The scalar identity error covariance assumption may also be violated if the diagonal elements of Φ are *not* identical. This error covariance violation, where the e_t's are drawings from distributions that have different scale parameters, is commonly found in applied econometric studies that make use of cross-section data (see Judge *et al.*, 1988, pp. 366, 367). Often, this involves a statistical model in which one or more of the explanatory variables is a direct or indirect measure of size, and the errors have scale parameters, σ_t^2, that also vary by size.

The problem of detecting and mitigating heteroskedasticity has been considered by many econometricians. In spite of their efforts, there is still not a consensus as to how to test and correct for it. Traditionally, it has been popular to devise an estimate of σ_t^2 as some function of one or more explanatory variables and then to use a two-stage GLS estimator. Recent wisdom, on which the jury is still out, seems to suggest using the LS estimator, but to estimate the variances with a heteroskedastic consistent estimator (White, 1980; Davidson and MacKinnon, 1993). In general, if one takes the two-stage route the statistical model is

$$y_t = \mathbf{x}_t'\boldsymbol{\beta} + e_t \tag{9.3.1}$$

with

$$\text{E}[e_t^2] = \sigma_t^2 = f(\mathbf{s}_t'\boldsymbol{\alpha}), \qquad \text{for } t = 1, 2, \ldots, T \tag{9.3.2}$$

where σ_t^2 is a function $f(\cdot)$ of τ explanatory variables. For example, if we assume that heteroskedasticity is of a multiplicative form, then we may specify σ_t^2 as an exponential function of τ explanatory variables, and the statistical model is (9.3.1) with

$$E[e_t^2] = \sigma_t^2 = \exp[\mathbf{s}_t'\boldsymbol{\alpha}], \qquad \text{for } t = 1, 2, \ldots, T \tag{9.3.3}$$

where $\mathbf{s}_t' = [s_{t1}, s_{t2}, \ldots, s_{t\tau}]$ is a $(1 \times \tau)$ dimensional vector of explanatory variables and $\boldsymbol{\alpha}$ is a τ dimensional vector of unknown coefficients. Because σ_t^2 is unknown, it is customary to use estimated LS residuals, $\hat{e}_t$, and to rewrite (9.3.3) as

$$\ln \hat{e}_t^2 + \ln \sigma_t^2 = \mathbf{s}_t'\boldsymbol{\alpha} + \ln \hat{e}_t^2 \tag{9.3.4}$$

or

$$\ln \hat{e}_t^2 = \mathbf{s}_t'\boldsymbol{\alpha} + u_t$$

where $u_t = \ln(\hat{e}_t^2/\sigma_t^2)$. One way to estimate $\boldsymbol{\alpha}$ is to apply the LS rule to (9.3.4). Unfortunately, the finite sample properties of u_t, and thus the LS estimator, are complicated.

9.3.1 A GME FORMULATION

Consider the general heteroskedastic linear statistical model

$$y_t = \mathbf{x}_t'\boldsymbol{\beta} + e_t \tag{9.3.5}$$

with

$$E[e_t^2] = e_t^2 = \sigma_t^2 = f(\mathbf{s}_t'\boldsymbol{\alpha}), \qquad \text{for } t = 1, 2, \ldots, T \tag{9.3.6}$$

and $\mathbf{s}_t = (s_{t1}, s_{t2}, \ldots, s_{t\tau})$ is a $(1 \times \tau)$ vector containing the tth observation on τ non-stochastic explanatory variables $\mathbf{s}_t$, $\boldsymbol{\alpha} = (\alpha_1, \alpha_2, \ldots, \alpha_\tau)'$ is a $(\tau \times 1)$ vector of unknown coefficients and $\mathbf{u}$ (defined in equations 9.3.4 and 9.3.9) is a noise vector. In order to recover the unknown $\boldsymbol{\beta}$, we follow the procedure introduced in Chapter 6 and reparameterize the unknown and unobservables $\boldsymbol{\beta}$, $\boldsymbol{\alpha}$ and $\mathbf{u}$ and form the heteroskedastic–GME model as

$$\max_{\mathbf{p}, \mathbf{p}^\alpha, \mathbf{w}} H(\mathbf{p}, \mathbf{p}^\alpha, \mathbf{w}) = \{-\mathbf{p}' \ln \mathbf{p} - \mathbf{p}^{\alpha\prime} \ln \mathbf{p}^\alpha - \mathbf{w}' \ln \mathbf{w}\} \tag{9.3.7}$$

subject to

$$y_t = \mathbf{x}_t'\boldsymbol{\beta} + e_t = \mathbf{x}_t'\mathbf{z}_k'\mathbf{p}_k + e_t \tag{9.3.8}$$

$$e_t^2 = f(\mathbf{s}_t'\boldsymbol{\alpha} + u_t) = f(\mathbf{s}_t'\mathbf{z}_\tau^\alpha\mathbf{p}_\tau^\alpha + \mathbf{v}_t'\mathbf{w}_t) \tag{9.3.9}$$

$$\mathbf{1}_K = (I_K \otimes \mathbf{1}_M')\mathbf{p} \tag{9.3.10}$$

$$\mathbf{1}_T = (I_T \otimes \mathbf{1}_J')\mathbf{w} \tag{9.3.11}$$

$$\mathbf{1}_\tau = (I_\tau \otimes \mathbf{1}_H')\mathbf{p}^\alpha \tag{9.3.12}$$

where $\beta_k = \sum_m z_{km} p_{km}$, $\alpha_\tau = \sum_h z_{\tau h}^\alpha p_{\tau h}^\alpha$ and $u_t = \sum_j v_j w_{tj}$. Solving for the optimal solution yields $\hat{\mathbf{p}}$, $\hat{\mathbf{p}}^{\alpha}$ and $\hat{\mathbf{w}}$ which in turn yield $\hat{\boldsymbol{\beta}}$, $\hat{\boldsymbol{\alpha}}$ and $\hat{\mathbf{u}}$. The Hessian is negative definite and the optimal solution is globally unique.

If for example we assume the popular multiplicative-heteroskedasticity (9.3.3) or (9.3.4), then $f(\mathbf{s}_t'\boldsymbol{\alpha}) = \exp(\mathbf{s}_t'\boldsymbol{\alpha})$ and consequently (9.3.9) becomes

$$e_t^2 = \exp(\mathbf{s}_t'\mathbf{z}_\tau^\alpha\mathbf{p}_\tau^\alpha + \mathbf{v}_t'\mathbf{w}_t) \tag{9.3.13}$$

As the heteroskedastic restriction (9.3.9) is in most cases nonlinear, computational limits may preclude reaching an optimal solution. We therefore reformulate (9.3.9), or (9.3.13), in a general flexible way which is consistent with the theory (Model 9.3.7–9.3.12), and always yields the numerical optimal values of the unknown $\mathbf{p}$'s and β_k's, and is formulated in terms of e_t instead of e_t^2. To do so, we rewrite constraint (9.3.9) in a general polynomial form as

$$\begin{aligned} e_t = f(\mathbf{s}_t'\boldsymbol{\alpha} + u_t) &= \alpha_1 s_1 + \alpha_2 s_2 + \cdots + \alpha_\tau s_\tau \\ &+ \alpha_{\tau+1} s_1^2 + \alpha_{\tau+2} s_2^2 + \cdots + \alpha_{2\tau} s_\tau^2 \\ &+ \alpha_{2\tau+1} s_1^3 + \alpha_{2\tau+2} s_2^3 + \cdots + \alpha_{3\tau} s_\tau^3 + \cdots + u_t \end{aligned} \tag{9.3.14}$$

where $\boldsymbol{\alpha}$ is a degree of polynomial dimensional vector of unknown parameters. From a computational point of view, the quadratic form is sufficient for (9.3.14). Thus, the specification has 2τ unknown α's and is a good approximation for almost any non-linear heteroskedastic process. This quadratic form is used in the sampling experiments to follow.

However, it is important to note that, under the above GME formulation, we are not restricted to a specific $f(\mathbf{x}_t'\boldsymbol{\alpha})$. This specification should be determined according to our knowledge of the underlying data generation process for the problem under study. In Section 9.3.2, an example is given to illustrate the methodology and to report the results of a corresponding sampling experiment.

A two-scale parameter problem. In investigating the statistical consequence of heteroskedasticity it has been popular (Taylor, 1978; Yancey *et al.*, 1984) to suppose a sample can be partitioned into two subsets of observations where the variance may be different for each subset. This leads to the statistical model

$$y = \begin{bmatrix} \mathbf{y}_1 \\ \mathbf{y}_2 \end{bmatrix} = \begin{bmatrix} X_1 \\ X_2 \end{bmatrix} \boldsymbol{\beta} + \begin{bmatrix} \mathbf{e}_1 \\ \mathbf{e}_2 \end{bmatrix} = X\boldsymbol{\beta} + \mathbf{e} \tag{9.3.15}$$

where

$$\mathrm{E}[\mathbf{ee}] = \begin{bmatrix} \sigma_1^2 I_{T_1} & 0 \\ 0 & \sigma_2^2 I_{T_2} \end{bmatrix} = \Phi \tag{9.3.16}$$

a $(T \times T)$ error covariance matrix and $\boldsymbol{\beta}$ is a $(K \times 1)$-dimensional unknown coefficient vector.

To provide a two-stage estimator for this formulation, estimates $\hat{\sigma}_1^2$, $\hat{\sigma}_2^2$ are computed from separate regressions on each of the subsets and an EGLS estimator is used. Alternatively, under a GME formulation, the linear model formulation of Chapter 6 would be used with error parameter supports, V, that accommodate the variability of both $\mathbf{e}_1$ and $\mathbf{e}_2$. The GME formulation also remains unchanged for the case of multiple scale parameters. If knowledge existed that $\sigma_1^2 \lesseqqgtr \sigma_2^2$ this information could be taken into account in specifying the error parameter support or in a cross-entropy context.

9.3.2 SAMPLING EXPERIMENTS

1. *The general heteroskedastic model.* To illustrate a GME heteroskedastic formulation and to give an indication of sampling performance we use the following sample design given in Judge *et al.* (1988, p. 374):

$$y_t = \beta_1 + \beta_2 x_{t2} + \beta_3 x_{t3} + e_t \tag{9.3.17}$$

where the e_t are normally and independently distributed with $\mathrm{E}[e_t] = 0$, $\mathrm{E}[e_t^2] = \sigma_t^2$ and $\sigma_t^2 = \exp\{\alpha_1 + \alpha_2 x_{t2}\}$. The (20×1) observation vector $\mathbf{y}$ was generated using the parameters $\boldsymbol{\beta} = (\beta_1, \beta_2, \beta_3)' = (10, 1, 1)'$ and $\boldsymbol{\alpha} = (\alpha_1, \alpha_2)' = (-3, 0.3)'$. In a real world problem, only $\mathbf{y}$, $\mathbf{x}_2$, $\mathbf{x}_3$ are observed along with the knowledge that heteroskedasticity may be a problem and that the multiplicative process is a reasonable way to represent it. In the reparameterized GME model, when assuming no knowledge of both the β's and the α's, the $\mathbf{z}_k$ in (9.3.8) is

$$Z = \begin{bmatrix} -50 & 0 & 50 & & & & & & \\ & & & -5 & 0 & 5 & & & \\ & & & & & & -5 & 0 & 5 \end{bmatrix} \tag{9.3.18}$$

The $\mathbf{z}^\alpha$ in (9.3.9) is

$$Z^\alpha = \begin{bmatrix} -20 & 0 & 20 & & & \\ & & & -4 & 0 & 4 \end{bmatrix} \tag{9.3.19}$$

and $\mathbf{v}_t = (-25, 0, 25)'$.

Given this experimental design, 1000 replications of the experiment were performed and the results are reported in Table 9.3.1. Even though we know the correct model for the σ_t^2, the results presented here are based on the quadratic relations (9.3.14).

Table 9.3.1 Results of 1000 replications of a heteroskedastic experiment with $T = 20$

Estimator	MSE($\hat{\boldsymbol{\beta}}$)	tr(cov($\hat{\boldsymbol{\beta}}$))	$\hat{\beta}_1$	$\hat{\beta}_2$	$\hat{\beta}_3$
GME	12.42	10.53	8.63	0.92	1.00
LS	141.43	85.88	10.19	1.00	0.98
EGLS (Φ unknown)	61.03	44.45	9.98	1.00	0.99
GLS (Φ known)	39.21	39.21	–	–	–

Table 9.3.2 Results of 1000 replications for the two scale parameter experiment

Estimator	MSE($\hat{\boldsymbol{\beta}}$)	tr(cov($\hat{\boldsymbol{\beta}}$))
GME	7.32	6.25
LS	17.21	17.19
GLS (Φ known)	7.59	7.59

The sampling results for the traditional estimators are on target with theoretical expectations. The least squares estimator produces estimates that are on average approximately equal to β_k. However, relative to GLS with known Φ the least squares estimator produces very large MSEs and variances. When Φ is unknown and the EGLS estimator is used, its MSE($\boldsymbol{\beta}$) greatly exceeds that of the GLS estimator. Alternatively, for the GME estimator the MSE($\hat{\boldsymbol{\beta}}$) is about one-third that of the GLS estimator when Φ is known. Furthermore, the tr(cov($\hat{\boldsymbol{\beta}}$)) is about one-fourth that of the GLS estimator with known Φ. Thus, under a MSE measure of performance the choice of the GME estimator is an easy one.

2. *A two-scale parameter experiment.* To provide some information about the sampling performance of the GME estimator for the two-scale parameter problem specified in statistical model (9.3.15) and (9.3.16), the following experiment was carried through with 1000 replications: $T = 20$, $T_1 = T_2 = 10$, $X'X = I_{20}$, $\boldsymbol{\beta} = (1, 2, -3, 2)'$, $\mathbf{e}_1 \sim \mathrm{N}(\mathbf{0}, I_{10})$, $\mathbf{e}_2 \sim \mathrm{N}(\mathbf{0}, 9I_{10})$, and

$$\mathrm{E}[\mathbf{ee}'] = \begin{bmatrix} I_{10} & 0 \\ 0 & 9I_{10} \end{bmatrix} = \Phi,$$

$\mathbf{z}_k = (-10, 0, 10)$ for all $k = 1, 2, 3, 4$ and $\mathbf{v}_t = (-9, -4.5, 0, 4.5, 9)$ for all t. The results are reported in Table 9.3.2. Again the empirical results are in line with theoretical expectations. In terms of a squared error measure of performance the GME estimator is superior to the LS estimator and to the GLS estimator when the error covariance is known. The variances for GME and GLS with Φ known are approximately equal.

9.4 POOLING CROSS-SECTION AND TIME SERIES DATA

In Sections 9.2 and 9.3 we have discussed situations involving autocorrelated and heteroskedastic equation errors. Heteroskedastic errors are reasonable when using cross-section–longitudinal-panel data and autocorrelated errors may be a reasonable assumption when using time series data. When combining or pooling cross-section–time series data it is necessary to specify a data generation model that captures both effects (Judge *et al.*, 1985, pp. 515–560; Kmenta, 1986, p. 616; Hsiao, 1992).

Working in this direction consider the model

$$y_{it} = \beta_1 x_{it,1} + \beta_2 x_{it,2} + \cdots + \beta_K x_{it,k} + e_{it} \tag{9.4.1}$$

that is cross-sectionally heteroskedastic $\mathrm{E}[e_{it}^2] = \sigma_i^2$ timewise autoregressive $e_{it} = \rho_i e_{i,t-1} + a_{it}$ and cross-sectional independent $\mathrm{E}[e_{it}e_{jt}] = 0$ for $i \neq j$ and $i = 1, 2, \ldots, N$ and $t = 1, 2, \ldots, T$. Making the appropriate substitutions results in the error covariance matrix

$$\Phi = \begin{bmatrix} \sigma_1^2\Psi_1 & & & 0 \\ & \sigma_2^2\Psi_2 & & \\ & & \ddots & \\ 0 & & & \sigma_N^2\Psi_N \end{bmatrix} \tag{9.4.2}$$

where Ψ is of the form of (9.2.5). Other variants of the model (9.4.1) include assuming ρ has the same value for all cross-sectional observations or leaving the block diagonal error covariance world and dropping the assumption that the cross-sectional units are mutually independent.

9.4.1 A GME FORMULATION

A main advantage of the GME formalism is its flexibility to accommodate a range of specifications. This flexibility is especially important in the case of pooling time-series and cross-section data. To illustrate the methodology, consider the case where we assume the parameter ρ has the same value over all cross-sectional units and the diagonal of the error covariance is $\sigma_t^2 P$. In this case the GME formulation is

$$\max_{\mathbf{p},\mathbf{p}^\alpha,\mathbf{w}_1,\mathbf{w}_2,\rho} \quad H(\mathbf{p}, \mathbf{p}^\alpha, \mathbf{w}_1, \mathbf{w}_2) = \{-\mathbf{p}'\ln\mathbf{p} - \mathbf{p}^{\alpha\prime}\ln\mathbf{p}^\alpha - \mathbf{w}_1'\ln\mathbf{w}_1 - \mathbf{w}_2'\ln\mathbf{w}_2\} \tag{9.4.3}$$

subject to

$$y_t = \mathbf{x}_t'\boldsymbol{\beta} + e_t = \mathbf{x}_t'\mathbf{z}_k'\mathbf{p}_k + e_t \tag{9.4.4}$$

$$\begin{aligned} e_t = f(\mathbf{s}_t'\boldsymbol{\alpha} + u_t) &= \alpha_1 s_1 + \alpha_2 s_2 + \cdots + \alpha_\tau s_\tau \\ &+ \alpha_{\tau+1}s_1^2 + \alpha_{\tau+2}s_2^2 + \cdots + \alpha_{2\tau}s_\tau^2 + \mathbf{v}_t^{1\prime}\mathbf{w}_t^1 \end{aligned} \tag{9.4.5}$$

$$e_t = \rho e_{t-1} + a_t = \rho e_{t-1} + \mathbf{v}_t^{2\prime}\mathbf{w}_t^2, \qquad t = 2, 3, \ldots, T \tag{9.4.6}$$

$$\mathbf{1}_K = (I_K \otimes \mathbf{1}_M')\mathbf{p} \tag{9.4.7}$$

$$\mathbf{1}_D = (I_D \otimes \mathbf{1}_H')\mathbf{p}^\alpha, \qquad \text{for } D = 2\tau \tag{9.4.8}$$

$$\mathbf{1}_T = (I_T \otimes \mathbf{1}_J')\mathbf{w}^i, \qquad i = 1, 2 \tag{9.4.9}$$

Table 9.4.1 Results of 1000 replications of a heteroskedastic–autocorrelated experiment with $T = 20$, $\sigma^2 = \exp(\mathbf{s}'\boldsymbol{\alpha})$ with $\boldsymbol{\alpha} = (-3, 0.03)'$ and with $\rho = 0.5$ and $\rho = 0.8$

	$\text{MSE}(\hat{\boldsymbol{\beta}})$	$\text{tr}(\text{cov}(\hat{\boldsymbol{\beta}}))$	$\bar{\hat{\beta}}_1$	$\bar{\hat{\beta}}_2$	$\bar{\hat{\beta}}_3$
$\rho = 0.5$					
GME estimator	14.43	9.16	7.71	0.81	1.02
LS estimator	300.41		9.86	1.00	1.01
$\rho = 0.8$					
GME estimator	22.94	17.97	7.78	0.80	1.03
LS estimator	489.97		9.80	1.00	1.01

Solving for the optimal solution yields $\hat{\mathbf{p}}$, $\hat{\mathbf{p}}^{\alpha}$, $\mathbf{w}^1$, $\mathbf{w}^2$ and $\hat{\rho}$, which in turn yield $\hat{\boldsymbol{\beta}}$, $\hat{\boldsymbol{\alpha}}$, $\hat{\mathbf{u}}$ and $\hat{a}$. The Hessian is negative definite and the optimal solution is globally unique.

9.4.2 A SAMPLING EXPERIMENT

To illustrate the methodology and the inferential reach of the GME formulation, consider the following sampling experiment. The first sampling experiment is an extension of the heteroskedastic experiment presented in Table 9.3.1. Using the same design we now add first order autocorrelation of $\rho = 0.5$ and $\rho = 0.8$. The results are presented in Table 9.4.1, where the parameter supports are symmetric around zero as is given in Section 3.3. The GME estimator yields, in both cases, $\text{MSE}(\hat{\boldsymbol{\beta}})$ and $\text{tr}(\text{cov}(\hat{\boldsymbol{\beta}}))$ that are significantly smaller than the LS estimator. Further, in both cases the estimated $\text{MSE}(\hat{\boldsymbol{\beta}})$ for the GME are smaller than those of the theoretical GLS when Φ is known. In fact, the GME estimators are even superior to the GLS with known Φ for the heteroskedastic case with $\rho = 0$ (Table 9.3.1).

The second sampling experiment, consisting of 1000 replications, is an extension of the autocorrelation example presented in Table 9.2.3 with $\rho = 0.5$, $T = 20$, condition number $\kappa(X'X) = 1$ and heteroskedastic variances generated by the process $\sigma^2 = \exp(\mathbf{s}'\boldsymbol{\alpha})$, where $\boldsymbol{\alpha} = (-3, 0.03)'$ and $\mathbf{s}$ is taken from the previous heteroskedastic examples (Tables 9.3.1 and 9.4.1). In that case the $\text{MSE}_{\text{GME}}(\hat{\boldsymbol{\beta}}) = 13.08$ while $\text{MSE}_{\text{LS}}(\hat{\boldsymbol{\beta}}) = 36.32$.

9.5 LARGE SAMPLE PROPERTIES

Next it is relevant to raise the consistency question and to inquire if $\text{plim}(\hat{\boldsymbol{\beta}}) = \boldsymbol{\beta}$ for the different statistical models discussed in this chapter. Fortunately, this question is easily answered for the GME formulations. Looking back at assumptions (6.A2)–(6.A3), which were imposed on the error terms in Chapter 6, reveals that these assumptions hold for any variance–covariance structure. Thus, we conjecture the consistency properties of the moment GME estimator relative to the β_k's hold for all the models discussed in this chapter.

9.6 OTHER ERROR STRUCTURES

The GME formulations introduced in this chapter can readily be extended to reflect other error covariance structures. Two error structures popular in the literature are the moving average MA($\cdot$) and the autoregressive–conditional heteroskedasticity (ARCH) process. The moving average process follows directly from the autocorrelated GME formulation in Section 9.3. For example, under a MA(1) error process $e_t = \varepsilon_t + \alpha\varepsilon_{t-1}$ and $\varepsilon_t \sim$ i.i.d.$(0, \omega^2)$, the ε_t affects both e_t and e_{t+1}, but not e_{t+j} for $j > 1$. Also, it is expected that $|\alpha| < 1$ in such a process where $\sigma^2 = \omega^2 + \alpha^2\omega^2 = \omega^2(1 + \alpha^2)$ with covariance $\mathrm{E}(e_t + \alpha e_{t-1})(e_{t-1} + \alpha e_{t-2}) = \alpha\omega^2$. Consequently, the covariance matrix of e_t is

$$\omega^2 \begin{bmatrix} 1+\alpha^2 & \alpha & & & 0 \\ \alpha & 1+\alpha^2 & \alpha & & \\ & & \ddots & & \\ & & \alpha & 1+\alpha^2 & \alpha \\ 0 & & & \alpha & 1+\alpha^2 \end{bmatrix} \tag{9.6.1}$$

Traditional specifications of the MA($\cdot$) process result in a non-linear regression formulation.

The GME–MA formulation is closely related to the first-order autocorrelation GME model of Section 9.2, and is formulated as follows:

$$\max_{\mathbf{p}, \mathbf{w}, \alpha} H(\mathbf{p}, \mathbf{w}) = -\{\mathbf{p}' \ln \mathbf{p} - \mathbf{w}' \ln \mathbf{w}\} \tag{9.6.2}$$

subject to

$$y_t = \mathbf{x}_t' \mathbf{z}_k' \mathbf{p}_k + e_t \tag{9.6.3}$$

$$\begin{cases} e_1 = \varepsilon_1 = \sum_j v_j w_{1j} & \text{for } t = 1 \\ e_t = \varepsilon_t + \alpha\varepsilon_{t-1} = \sum_j v_j w_{tj} - \alpha \sum_j v_j w_{t-1,j}, & \text{for } t = 2, 3, \ldots, T \end{cases} \tag{9.6.4}$$

$$\mathbf{1}_K = (I_K \otimes \mathbf{1}_M')\mathbf{p} \tag{9.6.5}$$

$$\mathbf{1}_T = (I_T \otimes \mathbf{1}_J')\mathbf{w} \tag{9.6.6}$$

where α is recovered without a support. The optimal solution is globally unique and yields $\hat{\mathbf{p}}$, $\hat{\mathbf{w}}$ and a point estimate of $\hat{\alpha}$, which in turn yields $\hat{\boldsymbol{\beta}}$ and $\hat{\mathbf{e}}$.

When analyzing time series data it is not uncommon to have residuals that vary in magnitude over time. To handle situations like this Engle (1982) proposed a process known as ARCH, where the variance of e_t depends on the size of the squared errors in previous periods. Thus,

$$\sigma_t^2 \equiv \mathrm{E}[e_t^2 \mid \Phi_t] = \alpha + \delta_1 e_{t-1}^2 + \delta_2 e_{t-2}^2 \ldots \tag{9.6.7}$$

where $\alpha, \delta_1 > 0$. The simple conditional variance ARCH(1) process, $\sigma_t^2 = \alpha + \delta e_{t-1}^2$, is often used.

To handle such a process, within the GME formulation, we adjust the autocorrelated model of Section 9.2 as follows

$$\max_{\mathbf{p}, \mathbf{w}, \alpha, \delta} \; H(\mathbf{p}, \mathbf{w}) = \{-\mathbf{p}' \ln \mathbf{p} - \mathbf{w}' \ln \mathbf{w}\} \tag{9.6.8}$$

subject to

$$y_t = \mathbf{x}_t' \mathbf{z}_k' \mathbf{p}_k + e_t \tag{9.6.9}$$

$$\begin{cases} e_1 = u_1 = \sum_j v_j w_{1j}, & \text{for } t = 1 \\ e_t^2 = \alpha + \delta e_{t-1}^2 + u_t = \alpha + \delta e_{t-1}^2 + \sum_j v_j w_{tj}, & \text{for } t = 2, 3, \ldots, T \end{cases} \tag{9.6.10}$$

$$\mathbf{1}_K = (I_K \otimes \mathbf{1}_M')\mathbf{p} \tag{9.6.11}$$

$$\mathbf{1}_T = (I_T \otimes \mathbf{1}_J')\mathbf{w} \tag{9.6.12}$$

where $u_t = \sum_j v_j w_{tj}$. The optimal solution yields the vectors $\hat{\mathbf{p}}$ and $\hat{\mathbf{w}}$ and the point estimates $\hat{\alpha}$ and $\hat{\delta}$, which in turn yield $\hat{\boldsymbol{\beta}}$ and $\hat{\mathbf{e}}$. Again the optimal solution is globally unique.

9.7 REMARKS

In this chapter we have focused on GME formulations ranging from pure autocorrelated or heteroskedastic errors to a more complex error process that results when time series–cross-section data are pooled. In each case GME formulations were proposed and sampling procedures were used to evaluate estimator performance. Under a MSE the GME estimates exhibited superior performance in each of the cases analyzed. In situations where autocorrelated and heteroskedastic error processes exist and are ignored, the GME estimator is uniformly superior to its LS counterpart. The GME formulations involving statistical models with non-scalar identity error covariances, are easily reformulated to reflect a range of error processes that are consistent with the way economic data are generated. In this regard MA and ARCH processes are two popular examples.

REFERENCES

Davidson, R. and MacKinnon, J. H. (1993) *Estimation and Inference in Econometrics.* Oxford University Press, New York.

Engle, R. F. (1982) Autoregressive conditional heteroskedasticity with estimates of the variance of United Kingdom inflation. *Econometrica* **50**, 987–1007.

Hsiao, C. (1992) *Analysis of Panel Data.* Cambridge University Press.

Judge, G. G., Griffiths, W. E., Hill, R. C., Lütkepohl, H., and Lee, T.-C. (1985) *The Theory and Practice of Econometrics*, 2nd edn. John Wiley, New York.

Judge, G. G., Hill, R. C., Griffiths, W. E., Lütkepohl, H., and Lee, T.-C. (1988) *Introduction to the Theory and Practice of Econometrics*, 2nd edn. John Wiley, New York.

Kmenta, J. (1986) *The Elements of Econometrics.* Macmillan, New York.

Taylor, W. E. (1978) The heteroskedastic linear model: exact finite sample results. *Econometrica* **46**, 663–675.

White, H. (1980) A heteroskedasticity–consistent covariance matrix estimator and a direct test for heteroskedasticity. *Econometrica* **48**, 817–838.

Yancey, T. A., Judge, G. and Miyazaki, S. (1984) Some improved estimators in the case of possible heteroskedasticity. *Journal of Econometrics* **25**, 133–150.

CHAPTER 10

Statistical model selection

10.1 INTRODUCTION

Selecting the appropriate statistical model from a large class of competing models is one of the most important problems in inferential statistics. For example, in applied econometrics, implementing a linear statistical model based on a *finite* sample of data involves the following basic decisions:

- specifying a statistical model that describes the sampling process underlying the data generation
- choosing a rule to estimate the unknowns in the corresponding parameterized statistical model.

Although uncertainty is usually present in all aspects of statistical model specification, perhaps the most attention has been paid to developing a basis for selecting the optimal set of right-hand side explanatory variables in regression analysis. Thus, given an outcome vector $\mathbf{y}$ and a collection of possible ancillary variables $\mathbf{x}_1, \mathbf{x}_2, \ldots, \mathbf{x}_K$, the problem is to select the true (optimal) subset K_0 of x's, where $K - K_0$ extraneous x's appear with zero coefficients.

The literature contains many references on classical and Bayesian procedures relating to this problem (see, for example, Mallows, 1973; Hocking, 1976; Mitchell and Beauchamp, 1988; Miller, 1990). Variable selection criteria that have been proposed include C_p (Mallows, 1973) and AIC (Akaike, 1974). Under these criteria, in determining the optimal subset one considers jointly the 'goodness of fit' of a model and a complexity factor usually related to the number of x covariates. The optimal subset model is the one that minimizes the sum of these two measures. Unfortunately, use of these criteria can lead to over fitting and, thus, inconsistent estimates (Shibata, 1981; Zhang, 1992). Furthermore, criteria such as SC (Schwarz, 1978) or the Zheng and Loh (1993) generalization of C_p rely on asymptotic considerations, and when K is large the computing requirements are prohibitive. Cross-validation has also been offered as a possible solution, but it is of limited usefulness with small samples of data. None of the above variable selection techniques permit the use of prior or non-sample information. This is addressed in the Bayesian approach to model selection, but this involves setting prior probabilities over the large class of models being considered and the corresponding priors for the parameters of each model. With a large number of competing models, the Bayesian solution requires a lot of information one may not have (see, for example, George and McCulloch, 1993; Geweke, 1994).

In this chapter we investigate the use of GME and GCE as a basis for model (variable) selection. These procedures have the following advantages:

- they are simple to perform (even for a large number of ancillary variables)
- they permit the use of prior-non-sample information
- they are free of asymptotic requirements
- they involve a shrinkage rule that focuses on estimation precision and prediction
- they perform well when the equation errors are non-normal and the design matrix is ill-conditioned.

In the next two sections we formulate a basis for variable selection within the GME–GCE formalism. Using the dual precision-prediction criterion, in Sections 10.4 and 10.5, we report the results of several sampling experiments and empirical examples. In Section 10.6 we discuss statistical model selection and uncertainty and then present some sampling experiments.

10.2 VARIABLE SELECTION PROBLEM AND NOTATION

Consider the variable selection problem for the linear statistical model

$$\mathbf{y} = X\boldsymbol{\beta} + \mathbf{e} \qquad (10.2.1)$$

where $\mathbf{y}$ is a T-dimensional vector of observations, X is a $(T \times K)$ matrix of *potential* explanatory variables, $\boldsymbol{\beta}$ is a $(K \times 1)$ vector of unknown coefficients and $\mathbf{e}$ is a $(T \times 1)$ vector of random variables with mean zero and precision matrix $\sigma^2 I_T$. Within this context the model selection component may be couched as follows. An investigator has a single sample of data and wants to estimate the parameters of a linear statistical model that are known to lie within the high-dimensional parameter space $\boldsymbol{\beta}$. However, the investigator suspects the relationship may be characterized by a lower-dimensional parameter space $\boldsymbol{\beta}_0$, where $\boldsymbol{\beta}_0$ is a proper subspace of $\boldsymbol{\beta}$. Consequently, within a linear statistical model framework we visualize a K-dimensional parameter space that includes the set of K_0 relevant variables, plus possibly $K - K_0$ extraneous ones. Therefore, the true model is a proper subset of the included variables. In terms of variable selection, there are 2^K possible models that can be obtained from the general model (10.2.1). The problems faced in implementing a statistical model based on a sample of data are:

- to determine the dimension of the parameter space and identify the true variables, K_0
- to determine the underlying statistical model that forms the basis for choosing the estimation rule.

10.3 THE TRADITIONAL AND GME CRITERIA

10.3.1 A TRADITIONAL CRITERION

Under traditional variable selection procedures there are two elements in the criterion function. Relative to (10.2.1), one element involves a measure of goodness of fit and the other involves a penalty for complexity that is some function of the number of variables K_0 in one of the competing models. If, following Zheng and Loh (1993), we let $MG(K_0)$ be the measure of goodness for the competing model K_0, the various estimators $\tilde{K}_0$ are asymptotically equivalent to

$$\tilde{K}_0 = \arg \min_{0 \leq K_0 \leq K} \{MG(K_0) + \lambda K \hat{\sigma}^2\} \tag{10.3.1}$$

where $\hat{\sigma}^2$ is a consistent estimate of σ^2. For example, if $\lambda = 2$ and $MG(K_0) = \|\mathbf{y} - X\boldsymbol{\beta}_{K0}\|^2$, equation 10.3.1 leads to the AIC criterion-estimator. Under this specification that uses a linear function of $\lambda K \hat{\sigma}^2$, the estimator $\tilde{K}_0$ is inconsistent and tends to overfit the data.

10.3.2 A GME–GCE CRITERION

In Chapter 6 we reparameterized the linear statistical model (10.2.1) as

$$\mathbf{y} = XZ\mathbf{p} + V\mathbf{w} \tag{10.3.2}$$

where $\boldsymbol{\beta} = Z\mathbf{p}$ and $\mathbf{e} = V\mathbf{w}$ are defined in (6.2.2) and (6.2.4). Under the GME formulation, (10.3.2) is the data-consistency relation and the objective is to maximize

$$H(\mathbf{p}, \mathbf{w}) = -\mathbf{p}' \ln \mathbf{p} - \mathbf{w}' \ln \mathbf{w} \tag{10.3.3}$$

subject to the data-consistency and the adding-up constraints. The dual-balanced objective function (10.3.3) identifies both the estimation and prediction objectives in model selection that are important in applied econometric work. Although we will not use it in this chapter, we note that if, for a particular problem, one of these objectives is deemed more important than the other, the weighted dual-criterion objective function discussed in Chapter 7

$$H(\mathbf{p}, \mathbf{w}_j, \gamma) = -(1 - \gamma)\mathbf{p}' \ln \mathbf{p} - \gamma \mathbf{w}' \ln \mathbf{w} \tag{10.3.4}$$

where $\gamma \in (0, 1)$, may be used. In applied econometric problems, it would seem that either the weighted or unweighted criterion is more useful than the traditional objective (10.3.1) that includes the fuzzy component identified as parsimony. If prior-non-sample information is available concerning the unknown $\mathbf{p}$ and $\mathbf{w}$ in (10.3.2), this information may, as in Chapter 6, be introduced in the GCE criterion function

$$I(\mathbf{p}, \mathbf{w}, \mathbf{q}, \mathbf{u}) = \mathbf{p}' \ln(\mathbf{p}/\mathbf{q}) + \mathbf{w}' \ln(\mathbf{w}/\mathbf{u}) \tag{10.3.5}$$

where $\mathbf{q}$ and $\mathbf{u}$ are prior probabilities for $\mathbf{p}$ and $\mathbf{w}$. Under this GCE formulation, (10.3.5) is minimized subject to the data-consistency and adding-up constraints.

Given these criterion functions and the normalized entropy measures developed in Chapters 3 and 6, we make use of the fact that $\beta_k = \mathbf{z}_k' \mathbf{p}_k$ and $e_t = \mathbf{v}_t' \mathbf{w}_t$ and employ the normalized entropy measures $S(\hat{\mathbf{p}})$ and $S(\hat{\mathbf{w}})$ as the identifying criteria for excluding a variable. In this case, where model selection is the objective, $\mathbf{z}_k$ is specified to be uniformly symmetric around zero for all $k = 1, 2, \ldots, K$. As discussed earlier, in terms of the information measures $S(\hat{\mathbf{p}}) \in [0, 1]$ and $S(\hat{\mathbf{w}}) \in [0, 1]$, zero reflects no uncertainty while one reflects total uncertainty in the sense that $\mathbf{p}$ or $\mathbf{w}$ are uniformly distributed. In terms of the GCE criterion (10.3.5), it means that the posteriors and priors are equivalent. Thus, for the GME $S(\hat{\mathbf{p}}_k) \cong 1$ implies $\hat{\boldsymbol{\beta}}_k \cong 0$. Keeping this in mind, a natural criterion for identification of the information content of a given x_k is just the normalized entropy. Given a potential set of K right-hand side X variables, the $K - K_0$ extraneous variables with normalized entropy of 1 have no information value for this given sample, and as such should be excluded from the model. However, in order to avoid computational difficulties and problems arising from computer rounding effects, a variable K is excluded if $S(\hat{\mathbf{p}}_k) > 0.99$. Using this simple criterion we now present the results of some illustrative sampling experiments.

10.4 SIMULATED EXAMPLES

In this section we use sampling experiments to illustrate and compare the performance of GME and GCE estimators with a range of sampling theory and Bayesian variable selection procedures.

10.4.1 EXAMPLE 1

This experiment duplicates the one carried out by Judge *et al.* (1987) and involves the linear statistical model $\mathbf{y} = X\boldsymbol{\beta} + \mathbf{e}$ with nine location parameters $\boldsymbol{\beta} = (5, 4, 3, 2, 1, 0, 0, 0, 0)'$, four extraneous variables, a (20×9) design matrix X, where $XX' = I_9$, an error process $\mathbf{e} \sim \mathrm{N}(\mathbf{0}, \sigma^2 I_{20} = I_{20})$ and

500 replications of samples of size 20. The parameter supports for the $\boldsymbol{\beta}_k$ are $\mathbf{z}_k = (-10, 0, 10)$, and the parameter supports for e_t are $\mathbf{v}_t = (-3, 0, 3)$.

First, using all nine variables and a squared error loss measure (MSE), we compared the empirical risk of the eight estimators ML, GME–GCE, partitioned Stein, $\boldsymbol{\beta}^{(\cdot)}$, and the positive part Stein (1981), $\boldsymbol{\beta}^+$, that shrinks all coefficients toward zero (see Judge *et al.*, 1987). These empirical risk results are presented in Table 10.4.1. The ML estimator is close to the theoretical risk of 9. Both the Stein and GME estimators, as expected, have empirical risks superior to ML. The traditional variable selection estimators, Akaike (AIC) (1974), Schwarz (SC) (1978) and Mallows (C_p) (1973), have empirical risks that are only slightly superior to ML, are risk inferior to $\boldsymbol{\beta}^+$, and are significantly (more than 10%) inferior to GME that shrinks but does not eliminate variables.

1. *A GCE estimator.* The GME estimator is identical to the GCE estimator when the prior probabilities $\mathbf{q}_k$ in (10.3.5) are uniform. If we believe that potential extraneous variables with zero coefficients exist in the linear statistical model specifications, it would seem reasonable to shrink those close to zero more than others. With this in mind, since we do not know *a priori* which variables are extraneous, we use for the parameter support space $\mathbf{z}_k = (-10, 0, 10)$, the cross-entropy probability vector $\mathbf{q}_k = (0.25, 0.5, 0.25)'$ for all k, which shrinks those close to zero twice as much as the other points in the parameter space, we obtain in Table 10.4.1 an empirical risk of 7.67, which is superior to GME and the other competing estimators.

2. *A GME–GCE variable selection estimator.* A characteristic of the GCE estimator is that when the prior $\mathbf{q}_k$ are consistent with the data, the prior takes over as the solution. If the prior knowledge led us to use a point mass probability at zero for the extraneous variables, and a uniform distribution for the other variables, we obtain the results given in Table 10.4.2. The empirical risk is now 4.45 and thus, as expected, there is a drastic reduction in empirical risk relative to GME and GCE in Table 10.4.1. Also note the normalized entropy values $S(\hat{\mathbf{p}}_k)$ give an indication of the departure of the distribution of probabilities for each of the β_k from uniformity, and thus contain useful information in discriminating between the extraneous and real variables. Note if one worked through all the 2^K possible subset models that can be obtained

Table 10.4.1 Empirical risks of a range of estimators

Empirical risk of							
ML	$\boldsymbol{\beta}^+$	$\boldsymbol{\beta}^{(\cdot)}$	GME	GCE	AIC	SC	C_p
8.77	8.18	7.97	7.78	7.67	8.50	8.73	8.64

Table 10.4.2 Sampling results for the GCE estimator with a point mass prior at zero for the extraneous variables

	MSE	β_1	β_2	β_3	β_4	β_5	β_6	β_7	β_8	β_9
	4.45	4.59	3.65	2.82	1.76	0.88	0	0	0	0
$S(\hat{\mathbf{p}}_k)$		0.84	0.80	0.94	0.97	0.989	1	1	1	1

from the general model using the GCE estimator with point mass at zero for the $K - K_0$ extraneous variables, the minimum MSE result of Table 10.4.2 would be achieved.

To get an idea of the use of $S(\hat{\mathbf{p}}_k)$ in identifying the extraneous variables, we continue the experiment introduced in Section 10.4.1 and report the results of an experiment with 500 replications. In this experiment, which uses a parameter support space symmetric around zero, under GME or GCE with a prior probability vector $\mathbf{q}_k = (0.1, 0.25, 0.30, 0.25, 0.1)'$, variables that have an $S(\hat{\mathbf{p}}_k) > 0.99$ were excluded from the statistical model. Thus, under this rule, variables that reflected an almost uniform distribution of estimated probabilities are excluded. These results, along with that of the partitioned Stein estimator $\boldsymbol{\beta}^{(\cdot)}$, are given in Table 10.4.3. The strong variable identification criterion of $S(\hat{\mathbf{p}}_k) > 0.99$ has led to the extraneous variables being identified a high percentage of the time, for example, in the case of GCE, about 88% of the time. However, it has also led to underfitting in that the variable x_5 was included only 26–33% of the time. Both the GME ($S(\hat{\mathbf{p}}_k) > 0.99$) and GCE ($S(\hat{\mathbf{p}}_k) > 0.99$) are uniformly superior to the partitioned Stein estimator in excluding the extraneous variables.

10.4.2 EXAMPLE 2

This example involves two problems and duplicates the sampling designs used by George and McCulloch (1993). In the first experiment (Problem 1), there

Table 10.4.3 Using an exclusion criterion of $S(\hat{\mathbf{p}}_k) > 0.99$, the number of times each variable was included in the model in 500 trials, with $\mathbf{z}_k = (-10, 5, 0, 5, 10)$ and $\mathbf{q}_k = (0.1, 0.25, 0.30, 0.25, 0.1)'$

		Variables								
Estimator	MSE	x_1	x_2	x_3	x_4	x_5	x_6	x_7	x_8	x_9
GME ($M = 5$)	7.66	500	498	477	349	164	81	80	78	73
GCE ($M = 5$)	7.64	500	498	470	330	131	60	65	59	59
$\boldsymbol{\beta}^{(\cdot)}$	7.97	500	497	468	370	194	93	91	90	85

are five x's that were obtained as independent standard normal vectors $\mathbf{x}_1, \mathbf{x}_2, \ldots, \mathbf{x}_5$. The y's were generated from the statistical model

$$\mathbf{y} = \mathbf{x}_4 + 1.2\mathbf{x}_5 + \mathbf{e} \tag{10.4.1}$$

where $\mathbf{e}$ is a normally distributed random vector with mean zero and covariance $\sigma^2 I_T$. With $\sigma = 2.5$ and $\boldsymbol{\beta} = (0, 0, 0, 1, 1.2)'$, the ML estimator has theoretical MSE $= 0.567$. In a second sampling design (Problem 2) that was designed to reflect extreme collinearity, $\mathbf{x}_3$ is replaced by

$$\mathbf{x}_3^* = \mathbf{x}_5 + 0.15\mathbf{e}^* \tag{10.4.2}$$

where $\mathbf{e}^*$ is a normal (0, 1) random vector.

Using 500 replications we applied the GME and GCE estimators and ME (pure moment) estimators to the sample observations for both problems. In the pure GME version we used the ME (pure moment) formulation discussed in Chapter 6 that we restate as

$$\max H(\mathbf{p}) = -\mathbf{p}' \ln \mathbf{p} \tag{10.4.3}$$

subject to the pure moment condition

$$X'\mathbf{y} = X'XZ\mathbf{p} \tag{10.4.4}$$

and the adding-up condition

$$\mathbf{1} = (I_K \otimes \mathbf{1}_M)\mathbf{p} \tag{10.4.5}$$

For-interior solutions the moment condition (10.4.4) is identical to the first-order conditions for the LS–ML estimator for the linear model. However, formulating the problem in this way makes it possible to employ the information measures $S(\hat{\mathbf{p}}_k)$ to the more traditional ML estimator, which is just a special case of the GME–exact moment estimator. The sampling results for the well-posed problem (Problem 1) are given in Table 10.4.4.

A variable exclusion criterion of $S(\hat{\mathbf{p}}_k) > 0.99$ performs well with all three of the entropy estimators (including the GME-pure moment estimator). The number of times the correct model was chosen by each estimator was around 68%. Under the $S(\hat{\mathbf{p}}_k) > 0.99$ criterion, the extraneous variables would have been included only 7–8% of the time. The non-extraneous variables were identified more than 86% of the time. These results were obtained when there were $M = 3$ points in the $\mathbf{2}_k$ parameter space and a GCE prior of $\mathbf{q}_k = (0.25, 0.5, 0.25)'$. Almost identical sampling results were obtained when the experiment was rerun with $M = 5$ and $\mathbf{q}_k = (0.1, 0.25, 0.3, 0.25, 0.1)'$.

An alternative to 2^K. Instead of following the traditional variable selection procedures and evaluating 2^K subset models or using GME on the complete

Table 10.4.4 Sampling results for Problem 1 and a variable exclusion criterion of $S(\hat{\mathbf{p}}_k) > 0.99$ and $\mathbf{z}_k = (-5, 0, 5)'$

			Variables included					
Estimator	MSE	$S(\hat{\mathbf{p}})$	x_1	x_2	x_3	x_4	x_5	Number of times correct model chosen
GME	0.591	0.984	27	38	35	431	483	339
		$S(\hat{\mathbf{p}}_k)$	0.997	0.997	0.997	0.970	0.957	
Pure moment GME	0.568	0.983	23	40	36	429	485	340
		$S(\hat{\mathbf{p}}_k)$	0.997	0.997	0.997	0.970	0.956	
GCE	0.579	0.985	21	30	30	418	477	337
		$S(\hat{\mathbf{p}}_k)$	0.998	0.997	0.997	0.973	961	

set of variables, let us consider an in-between strategy where we use the information measures $S(\hat{\mathbf{p}}_k)$ from the set of one predictor variable models. If we use the data from this five-variable sample design to form five single variable models, and use the pure moment–GME (LS–ML) estimator, we obtain the results reported in Table 10.4.5. Under the selection criterion of $S(\hat{\mathbf{p}}_k) > 0.99$, and a design matrix X that is nearly orthonormal, the correct model would be identified 71.8% of the time. The correct variables would be identified over 98% of the time and the extraneous variables would be excluded over 90% of the time. Thus, this is slightly superior to the variable selection rule reported in Table 10.4.4.

Sample size $T = 10$. To get an idea of the impact of sample size on estimator performance, the Problem 1 experiment was rerun with $T = 10$ observations. The GME ($M = 3$) and pure moment–GME ($M = 3$) sampling results for 500 replications of the experiment are reported in Table 10.4.6. As expected, decreasing the size of the sample also decreased the sampling performance of the $S(\hat{\mathbf{p}}_k)$ criterion in identifying and excluding the extraneous

Table 10.4.5 Sampling analysis of the five single-variable models, $\mathbf{z}_k = (-5, 0, 5)'$, GME–moment estimator

	x_1	x_2	x_3	x_4	x_5
$S(\hat{\mathbf{p}}_k)$	0.996	0.997	0.997	0.946	0.940
Times included	58	36	37	492	498

Table 10.4.6 Sampling results for problem 1, with $T = 10$, $\mathbf{z}_k = (-5, 0, 5)'$ and 500 replications

			Variables included					
Estimator	MSE	$S(\hat{\mathbf{p}})$	x_1	x_2	x_3	x_4	x_5	Correct model
GME	1.507	0.981	139	129	83	345	402	121
		$S(\hat{\mathbf{p}}_k)$	0.992	0.992	0.995	0.966	0.958	
Pure moment GME	2.00	0.975	169	155	100	355	400	113
		$S(\hat{\mathbf{p}}_k)$	0.989	0.990	0.994	0.956	0.949	

variables. Still GME, with the rule $S(\mathbf{p}_k) > 0.99$, chose the correct model over 24% of the time. Due to the shrinkage character, with the small sample size the MSE of GME was superior to pure moment–GME in identifying the extraneous variables.

Collinear design matrix X. The sampling results for the highly collinear Problem 2 (10.4.2) are presented in Table 10.4.7. In terms of variable identification, all three models continued to perform well. The extraneous variables x_1 and x_2 are sharply identified (excluded) using the $S(\mathbf{p}_k) > 0.99$ criterion. The x_3 and x_5 variables that are nearly identical are included with approximately the same frequency in the pure moment–GME case. Note, consistent with Chapter 8,

Table 10.4.7 Sampling results for Problem 2, with 500 replications, $\mathbf{z}_k = (-5, 0, 5)'$ and $\mathbf{q}_k = (0.25, 0.5, 0.25)'$

			Variables included					
Estimator	MSE	$S(\hat{\mathbf{p}})$	x_1	x_2	x_3	x_4	x_5	Correct model
GME	1.572	0.983	22	35	225	429	310	175
		$S(\hat{\mathbf{p}}_k)$	0.997	0.997	0.982	0.970	0.970	
GCE	1.373		20	28	205	416	296	181
		$S(\hat{\mathbf{p}}_k)$	0.999	0.998	0.984	0.985	0.975	
Pure moment GME	9.497	0.962	6	5	359	319	377	63
		$S(\hat{\mathbf{p}}_k)$	0.999	0.998	0.927	0.984	0.903	

case. The large increase relative to Problem 1 in MSE for the pure moment–GME estimator. In spite of the high collinearity, under GME and GCE, the correct model is chosen over 35% of the time. With pure moment–GME estimator and the $S(\mathbf{p}_k) > 0.99$ rule, the correct model appears about 12% of the time.

10.4.3 EXAMPLE 3

A large portion of the variable selection research focuses on situations involving 50 or more predictor variables. To investigate this many possible predictor variable situation, we duplicated the sampling experiment proposed by George and McCulloch (1993) and generated sample observations from 200 replications. This experiment involved 60 standard normal predictor variables partitioned into 4 groups of 15 variables each, with corresponding coefficients of $\boldsymbol{\beta} = (\mathbf{0}', \mathbf{1}', \mathbf{2}', \mathbf{3}')$, $T = 120$ and $\mathbf{e} \sim N_{120}(\mathbf{0}, 4I)$. If we again use the $S(\hat{\mathbf{p}}_k) > 0.99$ criterion, $\mathbf{z}_k = (-10, 0, 10)'$, $\mathbf{v}_t = (-6, 0, 6)'$, along with either GME or pure moment–GME as a basis for variable selection, the results can be summarized as follows:

- the 15 extraneous variables are almost perfectly identified
- the 15 variables that have a coefficient of one were included in the model over 70% of the time
- the remaining 30 variables with coefficients 2 and 3 were always included

Two things stand out from these sampling results. First, the ease with which these procedures handle variable situations involving a large number of predictor variables, and second, out of the 2^{60} possible models the $S(\hat{\mathbf{p}}_k)$ criterion permits the correct model to be chosen a high percentage of the time, based on only *one* analysis of the sample data.

10.5 EMPIRICAL EXAMPLES

10.5.1 EXAMPLE 1

In the model selection literature, it is popular to use the Hald data set presented in Draper and Smith (1981). For a discussion and comparison of different model selection formulations see Geweke (1994) and George and McCulloch (1993). With this data set there are five variables: $\mathbf{y}$ (heat produced in the hardening of cement), and the potential explanatory variables, $\mathbf{x}_1$ (percentage of input composed of tricalcium aluminate), $\mathbf{x}_2$ (percentage of input composed of silicate), $\mathbf{x}_3$ (percentage of input composed of tetracalcium aluminoferrite) and $\mathbf{x}_4$ (percentage of input composed of dicalcium silicate). There are $T = 13$ observations.

Within the GME–GCE formulations we specified $\mathbf{z}_1 = (-100, 0, 100)'$, $\mathbf{z}_k = (-2, 0, 2)$ for $k = (2, \ldots, 4)$ and $\mathbf{v}_t = (-3.5, 0, 3.5)$ for all t. The results for the different models, where all include an intercept, $\mathbf{x}_5$, are presented in Table 10.5.1. These results indicate that, for the GME and GCE estimators, and an exclusion criterion of $S(\hat{\mathbf{p}}_k) > 0.99$, the variables $\mathbf{x}_3$ and $\mathbf{x}_4$ are identified as extraneous. Thus, the information they contribute to reducing the uncertainty about of $\mathbf{y}$ is practically zero. However, it is interesting to note that, using the pure moment-GME (ML) estimator and $S(\hat{\mathbf{p}}_k) > 0.99$, one concludes that $\mathbf{x}_2$, $\mathbf{x}_3$ and $\mathbf{x}_4$ are all extraneous variables. From the Draper and Smith (1981) conventional variable selection analysis of this problem, the model $\mathbf{x}_1$, $\mathbf{x}_4$ was favored by all subsets regression. In terms of the three-predictor model, George and McCulloch (1993) were unable to discriminate between $(\mathbf{x}_1, \mathbf{x}_2, \mathbf{x}_3)$, $(\mathbf{x}_1, \mathbf{x}_2, \mathbf{x}_4)$ and $(\mathbf{x}_1, \mathbf{x}_3, \mathbf{x}_4)$. Geweke (1994) concludes that the favored models should incorporate $\mathbf{x}_1$ and $\mathbf{x}_2$ or $\mathbf{x}_1, \mathbf{x}_2, \mathbf{x}_3$ or $\mathbf{x}_1, \mathbf{x}_2, \mathbf{x}_4$, or all four regressors. In contrast we note again that, under the GME or GCE estimator and a $S(\hat{\mathbf{p}}_k) > 0.99$ criterion, $\mathbf{x}_3$ and $\mathbf{x}_4$ should not be incorporated. Since this is real data and we do not know the underlying data generation mechanism, no bets can be collected. However, the results for the entropy based estimators provide strong evidence that $\mathbf{x}_1$ and $\mathbf{x}_2$ should be included and $\mathbf{x}_3$ and $\mathbf{x}_4$ should be excluded.

To check the GME–GCE results, an additional GCE experiment was done. In that case, a point mass prior of $\mathbf{q}_k = (0, 1, 0)'$ was specified for each k. This means that a prior of unit mass on zero is given for $\mathbf{x}_1$, $\mathbf{x}_2$, $\mathbf{x}_3$ and $\mathbf{x}_4$. If this prior is correct, all coefficients should be zero. Using this prior yields the following results: $\hat{\boldsymbol{\beta}} = (1.44, 0.66, 0, 0)'$ with $S(\hat{\mathbf{p}}_k) = (0.46, 0.42, 1, 1)'$. Again, the same variables $(\mathbf{x}_3, \mathbf{x}_4)$ were identified as extraneous variables. If the same GME estimator is applied to the chosen model $\mathbf{x}_1$ and $\mathbf{x}_2$, this yields $\hat{\boldsymbol{\beta}} = (1.44, 0.66)'$, where, under the $S(\hat{\mathbf{p}}_k)$ criterion, the conclusion is that both variables should be incorporated in the model. To conclude, unlike other estimators, the GME and GCE results are conclusive and suggest that $\mathbf{x}_3$ and $\mathbf{x}_4$ are extraneous variables.

10.5.2 EXAMPLE 2

These data, called the Happiness Data and reported by George and McCulloch (1993), were collected from 39 MBA students at the University of Chicago. There are five variables: $\mathbf{y}$ (happiness), on a 10-point scale ranging from 1 to 10; $\mathbf{x}_1$ (money), in thousands of dollars; $\mathbf{x}_2$ (sex), measured by 0 or 1; $\mathbf{x}_3$ (love), measured on a 3-point scale 1–3; $\mathbf{x}_4$ (work), measured on a 5-point scale 1–5.

The results for the GME–GCE estimators with $\mathbf{z}_k = (-3, 0, 3)'$, for all k, $\mathbf{z}_0 = (-10, 0, 10)'$, for the intercept and with $\mathbf{v}_t = (-2.5, 0, 2.5)$ for all t, are presented in Table 10.5.2. In statistical model selection, we must be concerned with all components of the statistical model. For example, if the error process is

Table 10.5.1 Results of the Hald data for pure moment–GME, GME and GCE, with $q_k = (0.25, 0.5, 0.25)'$ and $k = (1, 2, 3, 4)$

	Pure moment–GME				GME				GCE			
$\hat{\boldsymbol{\beta}}_k$	1.551	0.510	0.102	−0.144	1.53	0.484	0.040	−0.180	1.53	0.496	0.046	−0.168
$S(\hat{\mathbf{p}}_k)$	0.930	0.993	1.00	0.999	0.540	0.960	1.00	0.994	0.560	0.961	1.00	0.996
$S(\hat{\mathbf{p}})$		0.927				0.833				0.843		

Table 10.5.2 Results of the happiness data for pure moment–GME, GME and GME ($\rho \neq 0$)

	Pure moment–GME				GME				GME ($\rho \neq 0$)			
$\hat{\boldsymbol{\beta}}$	0.010	−0.149	1.919	0.476	0.011	−0.025	1.860	0.580	0.003	−0.944	2.22	−0.037
$S(\hat{\mathbf{p}}_k)$	1.0	0.998	0.69	0.98	1.0	1.0	0.72	0.97	1.0	0.93	0.57	1.0
$S(\hat{\mathbf{p}})$		0.935				0.938				0.893		
$\hat{\rho}$		–				–				0.28		

incorrectly specified, this may have an impact on variable selection. Keeping this in mind, in reformulating the entropy estimators we allowed for the possibility of first-order autocorrelated errors (see Chapter 9) in the underlying statistical model. Under this formulation, we seek to recover information about the autocorrelation process and also to identify the extraneous variables. The results are presented in the right hand side of Table 10.5.2. If one ignores the autocorrelation, the variables x_3 and $\mathbf{x}_4$ are chosen in both models. These results are somewhat comparable to George and McCulloch (1993) and Geweke (1994) who chose $\mathbf{x}_3$ among all one-variable models, $\mathbf{x}_3$, $\mathbf{x}_4$ among all two-variable models and $\mathbf{x}_1$, $\mathbf{x}_3$, $\mathbf{x}_4$ among all three-variable models.

Allowing for the possibility of autocorrelated errors within the GME model reveals that the errors are moderately correlated. After accounting for this correlation, the optimal model should incorporate variables $\mathbf{x}_2$ and $\mathbf{x}_3$. As in all the other studies, $\mathbf{x}_3$ is also included. However, with the generalized GME estimator instead of $\mathbf{x}_4$, the corrected model includes $\mathbf{x}_2$ (sex). Finally, note that $S(\hat{\mathbf{p}})$ of the ρ corrected model is the smallest one, indicating that it has the lowest uncertainty of all models considered. These results indicate the sensitivity of variable selection relative to correctly specifying the underlying data generation mechanism. With real data it is important to account for departures from the conventional scalar identity error covariance assumption when considering variable selection. In other words, there are many ways to specify a statistical model and these specification errors may be interdependent. The GME formulation is one way to account for these potential model specification errors. Some evidence in this area is presented in the next section.

10.6 STATISTICAL MODEL UNCERTAINTY

The game usually played in sampling experiments, as it relates to variable selection, is to work with a perfectly specified statistical model that involves some extraneous predictor variables. In the real world, models possibly involving two or more incorrectly specified components are the rule rather than the exception (see, for example, Draper, 1995). Consequently, we need some way needed to measure the uncertainty relative to a model that may reflect two or more model misspecifications. Toward this end, in this section we report the results of a sampling experiment when the statistical model may have extraneous predictor variables *and* autocorrelated errors.

10.6.1 EXTRANEOUS PREDICTORS AND AUTOCORRELATED ERRORS

The one-stage GME–GCE formulations, as evidenced by Chapters 6–9, are general enough to also account for a range of misspecifications such as the functional form, heteroskedasticity and non-stationary parameters (Chapters 13 and 14). Within the context of Section 9.2, consider the linear statistical model

$$y_t = \mathbf{x}_t \boldsymbol{\beta} + e_t \tag{10.6.1}$$

where

$$e_t = \rho e_{t-1} + a_t \tag{10.6.2}$$

with

$$\mathrm{E}[\mathbf{a}] = \mathbf{0} \quad \text{and} \quad \mathrm{E}[\mathbf{aa}'] = \sigma^2 I_T \tag{10.6.3}$$

and

$$\mathrm{E}[\mathbf{e}] = \mathbf{0} \quad \text{and} \quad \mathrm{E}[\mathbf{ee}'] = \sigma_a^2 \Psi = \Phi \tag{10.6.4}$$

with

$$\Psi = \frac{1}{1-\rho^2} \begin{bmatrix} 1 & \rho & \cdots & \rho^{T-1} \\ \rho & 1 & \cdots & \rho^{T-2} \\ \vdots & \vdots & \ddots & \vdots \\ \rho^{T-1} & \rho^{T-2} & \cdots & 1 \end{bmatrix} \tag{10.6.5}$$

Continuing with the autocorrelated specification of Chapter 9, data for the GME statistical model may be reparameterized as

$$y_t = \mathbf{x}_t' Z \mathbf{p} + e_t \tag{10.6.6}$$

$$\begin{cases} e_t = a_t = v'\mathbf{w}_1, & \text{for } t = 1 \\ e_t = \rho e_{t-1} + a_t = \rho e_{t-1} + \mathbf{v}'\mathbf{w}_t, & \text{for } t = 2, 3, \ldots, T \end{cases} \tag{10.6.7}$$

and results in the GME formulation (9.2.6)–(9.2.10).

10.6.2 SAMPLING EXPERIMENT

To generate observations consistent with extraneous predictors and autocorrelated errors, we use the sample design of Example 2 of Section 10.4.2 with $\boldsymbol{\beta} = (0, 0, 0, 1, 1.2)'$, $T = 20$ and an autocorrelated error process with $\rho = 0.8$, and with a as a standard normal random variable. Observations from 500 replications were generated and coefficient estimates and variable selection counts were obtained from pure moment–GME and GME estimators, ignoring the fact that the errors were uncorrelated. Alternatively, for the GME estimator, the possibility of autocorrelated errors is taken into account and an estimate of ρ is obtained along with that of the coefficients of the predictor variables and the information measures $S(\hat{\mathbf{p}})$ and $S(\hat{\mathbf{p}}_k)$. The results of the sampling experiment are presented in Table 10.6.1. If one ignores the possibility that $\rho \neq 0$ and uses the pure moment–GME estimator with the rule $S(\hat{\mathbf{p}}_k) > 0.99$, the correct model is identified 61% of the time, the true variables are included

Table 10.6.1 Variable selection with possibly autocorrelated errors

Estimator	MSE	$S(\hat{\mathbf{p}})$	Number of times variables included x_1	x_2	x_3	x_4	x_5	Number of times correct model chosen
GME (ρ)	0.397	0.986	4	20	3	461	456	403
$S(\hat{\mathbf{p}}_k)$			0.999	0.998	0.999	0.973	0.960	
Pure moment	1.171	0.980	12	23	25	420	400	306
$S(\hat{\mathbf{p}}_k)$			0.998	0.997	0.997	0.969	0.939	

over 80% of the time and the extraneous variables are correctly excluded over 90% of the time.

If the possibility that $\rho \neq 0$ is recognized and the GME(ρ) estimator is used, the true model is identified over 81% of the time. Furthermore, the true variables are included over 90% of the time, and the extraneous variables are excluded over 90% of the time. Moreover, the MSE of the GME is much superior to the pure moment GME–ML estimator that ignores the possibility of $\rho \neq 0$.

These results are *suggestive* relative to the statistical consequences of pursuing variable selection under false model assumptions. If traditional variable selection procedures such as AIC or SC had been used as a basis for comparison, our expectation is that large performance differences from GME(ρ) would have been observed.

10.7 REMARKS

Within a general linear statistical model context, and the GME–GCE formulations of Chapter 6, we have suggested a simple variable selection criterion and have compared, through sampling experiments and the use of real data, the performance of the entropy-based estimators and traditional variable selection procedures. In general, for all the situations we investigated, the GME–GCE formulations that used a normalized information measure criterion performed, in a superior way relative to traditional variable selection procedures. In practice the procedure

- is simple to apply
- permits the use of non-sample information
- is free of asymptotic requirements
- involves a shrinkage rule that reduces MSE

- permits multiple areas of model uncertainty to be taken into account simultaneously
- uses a criterion function emphasizing precision and prediction
- does not require the evaluation of 2^K models.

It is time we questioned the traditional criterion of goodness of fit and complexity as the basis for variable selection. It is also time to admit there is usually uncertainty about a range of statistical model assumptions and to recognize it is somewhat restrictive to choose a particular form for the set of underlying statistical model assumptions and then to proceed with estimation, inference and variable selection as if these data generation foundations hold. With the limited or partial non-experimental data that we use in practice, they seldom do. It is time to seek a measure that expresses general model uncertainty and that can handle and mitigate statistical model specification errors. The model selection procedures developed in this chapter, within the GME-GCE framework β provide one basis for such a measure.

REFERENCES

Akaike, H. (1974) A new look at the statistical model identification. *IEEE Transactions on Automatic Control* **19**, 716–23.

Draper, D. (1995) Assessment and propagation of model uncertainty. *Journal of the Royal Statistical Society, Series B* **57**, 47–97.

Draper, N. and Smith H. (1981) *Applied Regression Analysis*, 2nd edn. John Wiley, New York.

George, E. and McCulloch, R. (1993) Variable selection in Gibbs sampling. *Journal of the American Statistical Association* **88**, 881–9.

Geweke, J. (1994) Variable selection and model comparison in regression. Working Paper 539, Federal Reserve Bank of Minneapolis.

Hocking, R. R. (1976) The analysis and selection of variables in linear regression. *Biometrics* **32**, 1–51.

Judge, G., Yi, G. Yancey, T. and Teräsvirta, T. (1987) The extended Stein procedure for simultaneous model selection and parameter estimation. *Journal of Econometrics* **35**, 375–91.

Mallows, C. L. (1973) Some comments on C_p. *Technometrics* **15**, 661–5.

Miller, A. J. (1990) *Subset Selection in Regression*. Chapman & Hall, London.

Mitchell, T. J. and Beauchamp, J. J. (1988) Bayesian variable selection in linear regression (with discussion). *Journal of the American Statistical Association* **83**, 1023–36.

Schwarz, G. (1978) Estimating the dimensions of a model. *Annals of Statistics* **6**, 461–4.

Shibata, R. (1981) An optimal selection of regression variables. *Biometrika* **68**, 45–54.

Stein, C. (1981) Estimation of the mean of a multivariate normal distribution *Annals of Statistics* **9**, 1135–51.

Zhang, P. (1992) On the distributional properties of model selection criteria. *Journal of the American Statistical Association* **87**, 732–7.

Zheng, X. and Loh, W.-Y. (1993) Consistent variable selection in linear models. *Journal of the American Statistical Association* **90**, 151–6.

PART IV

A system of economic-statistical relations

In Part III we relaxed the assumption that the covariance matrix for the error vector $\mathbf{e}$ was of a scalar identity form. In Part IV we recognize:

- that the error vectors between equations may be contemporaneously correlated
- the simultaneous nature of the economic data generation process and the possibility of an instantaneous-feedback mechanism operating between some of the variables

  and
- we develop a GME–GCE system of equations, formulation and estimator.

Sampling experiments are used to illustrate the sampling performance of the GME–GCE estimators and to make comparisons with traditional counterparts.

CHAPTER 11

Sets of linear statistical models

11.1 INTRODUCTION

To this point we have considered estimation and inference procedures for a single statistical relation and one sample of data. In Chapter 9, depending on the assumptions made about the data generation process and the resulting error covariance matrix, different formulations of the single-sample model were considered. In this chapter we follow the lead of Zellner (1962) and extend our analysis to consider two or more economic and statistical relations and correspondingly, two or more samples of data. Developing methods to cope with formulations of this type, which Zellner labeled seemingly unrelated regressions (SUR), is important because a large part of non-experimentally generated economic data cannot be pooled into a single equation and are more consistent with economic-statistical models describing processes that vary over time, space and agents. For a discussion of the types of data generation schemes and corresponding statistical models, see Judge *et al.* (1988, pp. 443–96) and Srivastava and Giles (1988). In this chapter we suggest a range of formulations and present some sampling experiments to suggest the potential sampling performance of the GME–SUR model.

11.1.1 GENERAL MODEL AND TRADITIONAL ESTIMATES

To develop notation and a basis for estimation and inference in the set of equations area, consider N linear statistical models where the ith model (equation) is given by

$$\mathbf{y}_i = X_i \boldsymbol{\beta}_i + \mathbf{e}_i, \qquad \text{for } i = 1, 2, \ldots, N \tag{11.1.1}$$

where $\mathbf{y}_i$ and $\mathbf{e}_i$ are of dimension $(T \times 1)$, X_i is $(T \times K_i)$ and $\boldsymbol{\beta}_i$ is $(K_i \times 1)$. We write the complete model as

$$\begin{bmatrix} \mathbf{y}_1 \\ \mathbf{y}_2 \\ \vdots \\ \mathbf{y}_N \end{bmatrix} = \begin{bmatrix} X_1 & & & \\ & X_2 & & \\ & & \ddots & \\ & & & X_N \end{bmatrix} \begin{bmatrix} \boldsymbol{\beta}_1 \\ \boldsymbol{\beta}_2 \\ \vdots \\ \boldsymbol{\beta}_N \end{bmatrix} + \begin{bmatrix} \mathbf{e}_1 \\ \mathbf{e}_2 \\ \vdots \\ \mathbf{e}_N \end{bmatrix} \tag{11.1.2}$$

or compactly as

$$\mathbf{y} = X\boldsymbol{\beta} + \mathbf{e} \tag{11.1.3}$$

where $\mathbf{y}$ and $\mathbf{e}$ are of dimensions $(NT \times 1)$. For this model it is customary to assume that the equation errors e_{it} are contemporaneously correlated but uncorrelated over time. Thus, $\mathrm{E}[e_{ti}e_{sj}] = \sigma_{ij}$ if $t = s$ and 0 if $t \neq s$ or, in vector form, $\mathrm{E}[\mathbf{e}_i\mathbf{e}_j'] = \sigma_{ij}I_T$. Consequently, the covariance matrix for $\mathbf{e}$ may be written as

$$\Phi = \mathrm{E}[\mathbf{ee}'] = \begin{bmatrix} \sigma_{11}I_T & \sigma_{12}I_T & \cdots & \sigma_{1N}I_T \\ \sigma_{21}I_T & \sigma_{22}I_T & \cdots & \sigma_{2N}I_T \\ \vdots & \vdots & \ddots & \vdots \\ \sigma_{N1}I_T & \sigma_{N2}I_T & \cdots & \sigma_{NN}I_T \end{bmatrix} \tag{11.1.4}$$

or

$$\Phi = \Sigma \otimes I_T \tag{11.1.5}$$

where Σ is an $(N \times N)$ positive definite symmetric matrix, $\otimes$ is the Kronecker product operator and I_T is an identity matrix of dimension T.

If Φ is known then we may, as in the context of Chapter 9, use the GLS estimator

$$\boldsymbol{\beta}_{\mathrm{GLS}} = [X'\Phi^{-1}X]^{-1}X'\Phi^{-1}\mathbf{y} = [X'(\Sigma^{-1} \otimes I)X]^{-1}X'(\Sigma^{-1} \otimes I)\mathbf{y} \tag{11.1.6}$$

with $\Sigma_{\boldsymbol{\beta}_{\mathrm{GLS}}} = [X'(\Sigma^{-1} \otimes I)X]^{-1}$. If the error covariance is unknown, consistent estimates of the variances and covariances are used to form the EGLS estimator

$$\boldsymbol{\beta}_{\mathrm{EGLS}} = [X'(\hat{\Sigma}^{-1} \otimes I)X]^{-1}X'(\hat{\Sigma}^{-1} \otimes I)\mathbf{y} \tag{11.1.7}$$

with covariance matrix that is consistently estimated by $[X'(\hat{\Sigma}^{-1} \otimes I)X]^{-1}$.

11.2 STATISTICAL MODEL 1

Consider first the following special case heteroskedastic version of the set of equations model that is popular in the literature (Taylor, 1977, 1978), and discussed briefly in Chapter 9,

$$\mathbf{y} = \begin{bmatrix} \mathbf{y}_1 \\ \mathbf{y}_2 \end{bmatrix} = \begin{bmatrix} X_1 \\ X_2 \end{bmatrix} \boldsymbol{\beta} + \begin{bmatrix} \mathbf{e}_1 \\ \mathbf{e}_2 \end{bmatrix} \equiv X\boldsymbol{\beta} + \mathbf{e} \tag{11.2.1}$$

where the pooled observations $\mathbf{y}_1$ and $\mathbf{y}_2$ each have dimension $(T \times 1)$ and $\boldsymbol{\beta}$ is an unknown $(K \times 1)$ vector. The unobservable $(T \times 1)$ error vectors $\mathbf{e}_1$ and $\mathbf{e}_2$ have mean $\mathbf{0}$ and covariance

$$\mathrm{E}[\mathbf{ee}'] = \begin{bmatrix} \sigma_{11} I_T & 0 \\ 0 & \sigma_{22} I_T \end{bmatrix} \tag{11.2.2}$$

If we assume the design matrices X_1 and X_2 satisfy the orthonormal condition $X'_1 X_1 = X'_2 X_2 = I_K$ and if $\sigma_{11} = \sigma_{22} = \sigma^2$ the least squares estimator $\boldsymbol{\beta}_{\mathrm{LS}}$ has mean $\boldsymbol{\beta}$, covariance $(\sigma^2/2)I_K$ and risk, or squared error loss, $\rho(\boldsymbol{\beta}, \boldsymbol{\beta}_{\mathrm{LS}}) = (\sigma^2/2)K$. If we let $\omega = \sigma_{11}/\sigma_{22}$, then if $\omega \neq 1$ the least squares estimator has mean $\boldsymbol{\beta}$, covariance $\sigma_{22}((1 + \omega)/4)I_K$ and risk $\sigma_{22}((1 + \omega)/4)K = \rho(\boldsymbol{\beta}, \boldsymbol{\beta}_{\mathrm{LS}})$.

If the scale parameters are known, the GLS estimator has mean $\boldsymbol{\beta}$ and covariance $(\sigma_{22}\omega/(1 + \omega))I_K$ and under a squared error measure, risk $(\sigma_{22}\omega/(1 + \omega))K = \rho(\boldsymbol{\beta}, \boldsymbol{\beta}_{\mathrm{GLS}})$. These results imply for $0 \leq \omega < \infty$ that $\rho(\boldsymbol{\beta}, \boldsymbol{\beta}_{\mathrm{LS}})/\rho(\boldsymbol{\beta}, \boldsymbol{\beta}_{\mathrm{GLS}}) \geq 1$. If the scale parameters are unknown and the EGLS estimator $\boldsymbol{\beta}_{\mathrm{EGLS}}$ is used, Kariya (1981) has shown that $\mathrm{Cov}(\boldsymbol{\beta}_{\mathrm{EGLS}}) \geq \mathrm{Cov}(\boldsymbol{\beta}_{\mathrm{GLS}})$. In Section 11.2.1 a general N-equation version of the special case model (11.2.1) is specified and a GME basis for estimation is proposed.

11.2.1 A GME FORMULATION

Within the context of Chapter 6, the reparameterized set of N equations model version of (11.2.1) may be specified as

$$\begin{aligned} \mathbf{y} = \begin{bmatrix} \mathbf{y}_1 \\ \mathbf{y}_2 \\ \vdots \\ \mathbf{y}_N \end{bmatrix} &= \begin{bmatrix} X_1 \\ X_2 \\ \vdots \\ X_N \end{bmatrix} \boldsymbol{\beta} + \begin{bmatrix} \mathbf{e}_1 \\ \mathbf{e}_2 \\ \vdots \\ \mathbf{e}_N \end{bmatrix} \equiv X\boldsymbol{\beta} + \mathbf{e} \\ &= \begin{bmatrix} X_1 \\ X_2 \\ \vdots \\ X_N \end{bmatrix} Z\mathbf{p} + \begin{bmatrix} V_1 \mathbf{w}_1 \\ V_2 \mathbf{w}_2 \\ \vdots \\ V_N \mathbf{w}_N \end{bmatrix} \equiv XZ\mathbf{p} + V\mathbf{w} \end{aligned} \tag{11.2.3}$$

where $\mathrm{E}[\mathbf{ee}'] = \Sigma \otimes I_T$, Σ is a $(N \times N)$ diagonal matrix, $\mathbf{p} = (\mathbf{p}_1, \mathbf{p}_2, \ldots, \mathbf{p}_K)'$ and $\mathbf{w} = (\mathbf{w}_1, \mathbf{w}_2, \ldots, \mathbf{w}_N)'$ are the unknown signal and noise probabilities we wish to recover, and Z, V_1, $V_2, \ldots, V_N$ are, as defined in Chapter 6, the corresponding parameter supports for $\boldsymbol{\beta}$ and $\mathbf{e}$. Given $\mathbf{p}$ and $\mathbf{w}$, the unknown probabilities associated with Z and V, a corresponding GME formulation is

$$\max_{\mathbf{p}, \mathbf{w}} H(\mathbf{p}, \mathbf{w}) = -\mathbf{p}' \ln \mathbf{p} - \mathbf{w}' \ln \mathbf{w} \tag{11.2.4}$$

subject to the data-consistency relations

$$\mathbf{y} = \begin{bmatrix} X_1 \\ X_2 \\ \vdots \\ X_N \end{bmatrix} Z\mathbf{p} + \begin{bmatrix} V_1 \mathbf{w}_1 \\ V_2 \mathbf{w}_2 \\ \vdots \quad \vdots \\ V_N \mathbf{w}_N \end{bmatrix} \tag{11.2.3'}$$

and the adding-up conditions

$$\mathbf{1}_K = (I_K \otimes \mathbf{1}'_M)\mathbf{p} \tag{11.2.5}$$

$$\mathbf{1}_{T_i} = (I_{T_i} \otimes \mathbf{1}'_J)\mathbf{w}_i, \qquad \text{for } i = 1, 2, \ldots, N; \quad T = \sum_i T_i. \tag{11.2.6}$$

As this model is just a linear extension of the GME linear model developed in Chapter 6, the same statistical properties hold and the recovered $\hat{\boldsymbol{\beta}}$ vector is a consistent estimator of $\boldsymbol{\beta}$. When we have some knowledge of the magnitude of the scale parameters in this model, we can specify a different error support, V_i, for each one of the different N equations or introduce this knowledge in a GCE context. For example, using the sample standard deviation of $\mathbf{y}_i$, together with the 3σ rule for each $i = 1, \ldots, N$, is one simple rule for changing each $\mathbf{v}_i$. When we do not wish to use the estimated sample scale parameter for each i, a unique set of symmetric around zero parameters supports, V, for all the N equations should be specified.

11.2.2 SAMPLING EXPERIMENTS

To illustrate sampling performance and applicability of this statistical model, in this section we report the results of a limited set of sampling experiments. In the experiments we used 1000 replications of $T_1 = T_2 = 10$ observations, a parameter vector $\boldsymbol{\beta} = (1, 2, -3, 2)'$ and scale parameters $\sigma_{11} = 1$ and $\sigma_{22} = 9$. Both X_1 and X_2 are orthonormal with condition number $\kappa(X'_1X_1) = \kappa(X'_2X_2) = 1$. The support space Z for the unknown parameters $\boldsymbol{\beta}$ is $z_k = (-10, 0, 10)'$ for all $k = 1, 2, 3, 4$. Using the 3σ rule and prior information consistent with that normally found in practice, the error support for $\mathbf{e}_1$ is $\mathbf{v}_1 = (-3, 0, 3)'$ for $\mathbf{e}_2$ is $\mathbf{v}_2 = (-9, 0, 9)'$. The sampling results are presented in Table 11.2.1.

Table 11.2.1 Results of 1000 replications of SUR–GME experiments with orthonormal X's, $\boldsymbol{\beta} = (1, 2, -3, 2)'$, $\sigma_{11} = 1$ and $\sigma_{12} = 9$

Estimator	MSE ($\hat{\boldsymbol{\beta}}$)	tr(Cov($\hat{\boldsymbol{\beta}}$))
GME	3.42	3.38
GLS (Φ known)	3.60	3.60

The GME experiment with different error supports for σ_{11} and σ_{22}, yields MSE ($\hat{\boldsymbol{\beta}}$) sampling results that are superior to the GLS with a known covariance matrix. Similar results for this model, but for $X'X = I_{20}$, are reported in Section 9.3. We note again that this is just a two-equation variation of the heteroskedastic statistical model considered in Chapter 9 and the alternative formulations, and sampling results, considered there are applicable here.

11.3 STATISTICAL MODEL 2

In this section we consider the traditional seemingly unrelated regression (SUR) model. First, for expository purposes, and without loss of generality, we start with the following two equation version of the SUR model:

$$\mathbf{y} = \begin{bmatrix} \mathbf{y}_1 \\ \mathbf{y}_2 \end{bmatrix} = \begin{bmatrix} X_1 & \\ & X_2 \end{bmatrix} \begin{bmatrix} \boldsymbol{\beta}_1 \\ \boldsymbol{\beta}_2 \end{bmatrix} + \begin{bmatrix} \mathbf{e}_1 \\ \mathbf{e}_2 \end{bmatrix} \equiv X\boldsymbol{\beta} + \mathbf{e} \qquad (11.3.1)$$

In this formulation the location parameters may differ from equation to equation, and the error covariances may possibly be non-zero. If $\sigma_{11} \neq \sigma_{22}$ and $\sigma_{ij} \neq 0$, the GLS estimator (11.1.6) and the EGLS estimator (11.1.7) are traditionally used to recover estimates of the location and scale parameters. In the next section a general version of the SUR model is specified and a GME formulation for estimation purposes is suggested.

11.3.1 A GME FORMULATION

Building on the previous section, we now generalize the GME model to include N coefficient vectors $\boldsymbol{\beta}_i$, $i = 1, 2, \ldots, N$, and N different scale parameters and possibly non-zero covariance elements. Reparameterizing the set of equations

(11.3.1) yields

$$\mathbf{y} = \begin{bmatrix} \mathbf{y}_1 \\ \mathbf{y}_2 \\ \vdots \\ \mathbf{y}_N \end{bmatrix} = \begin{bmatrix} X_1 & & & \\ & X_2 & & \\ & & \ddots & \\ & & & X_N \end{bmatrix} \begin{bmatrix} \boldsymbol{\beta}_1 \\ \boldsymbol{\beta}_2 \\ \vdots \\ \boldsymbol{\beta}_N \end{bmatrix} + \begin{bmatrix} \mathbf{e}_1 \\ \mathbf{e}_2 \\ \vdots \\ \mathbf{e}_N \end{bmatrix} \equiv X\boldsymbol{\beta} + \mathbf{e}$$

$$= \begin{bmatrix} X_1 & & & \\ & X_2 & & \\ & & \ddots & \\ & & & X_N \end{bmatrix} \begin{bmatrix} Z_1\mathbf{p}_1 \\ Z_2\mathbf{p}_2 \\ \vdots \\ Z_N\mathbf{p}_N \end{bmatrix} + \begin{bmatrix} V_1\mathbf{w}_1 \\ V_2\mathbf{w}_2 \\ \vdots \\ V_N\mathbf{w}_N \end{bmatrix} \qquad (11.3.2)$$

where $\mathrm{E}[\mathbf{ee}'] = \Sigma \otimes I_T$ and Σ is an $(N \times N)$ symmetric positive definite matrix, where $\mathbf{p}_i$, $\mathbf{w}_i$, Z_i and V_i $(i = 1, 2, \ldots, N)$ are as previously defined.

To allow the possibility of non-zero covariances we follow the formulations of Chapter 9 and specify, within the GME formulation, an additional set of restrictions which is based on the relations $\delta_{ij}^2 = (\sigma_{ij})^2/\sigma_{ii}\sigma_{jj}$. These additional consistency relations are

$$\frac{1}{T}\sum_{t=1}^{T} e_{ti}e_{tj} = \delta_{ij}\left[\left(\frac{1}{T}\sum_{t=1}^{T} e_{ti}e_{ti}\right)\left(\frac{1}{T}\sum_{t=1}^{T} e_{tj}e_{tj}\right)\right]^{1/2}, \qquad \text{for } i \neq j \qquad (11.3.3)$$

where $\mathbf{e}_i = \mathbf{v}_i'\mathbf{w}_i$.

These $(N^2 - N)$ additional consistency relations reflect the possibility of non-zero covariances through the coefficient δ_{ij}. Note that divisors other than T^{-1} can be specified. Given the data consistency (11.3.2) and the covariance's interrelationship (11.3.3), the one-step GME–SUR model may be formulated as

$$\max_{\{\mathbf{p}_i\},\{\mathbf{w}_i\},\boldsymbol{\delta}} \quad H(\mathbf{p}, \mathbf{w}) = \{-\mathbf{p}' \ln \mathbf{p} - \mathbf{w}' \ln \mathbf{w}\} \qquad (11.3.4)$$

subject to the data-consistency relations

$$\begin{bmatrix} \mathbf{y}_1 \\ \mathbf{y}_2 \\ \vdots \\ \mathbf{y}_N \end{bmatrix} = \begin{bmatrix} X_1 & & & \\ & X_2 & & \\ & & \ddots & \\ & & & X_N \end{bmatrix} \begin{bmatrix} Z_1\mathbf{p}_1 \\ Z_2\mathbf{p}_2 \\ \vdots \\ Z_N\mathbf{p}_N \end{bmatrix} + \begin{bmatrix} V_1\mathbf{w}_1 \\ V_2\mathbf{w}_2 \\ \vdots \\ V_N\mathbf{w}_N \end{bmatrix} \qquad (11.3.2')$$

the covariance consistency relations (11.3.3) and the adding up-normalization

$$\mathbf{1}_{K_i} = (I_{K_i} \otimes \mathbf{1}_M')\mathbf{p}_i, \qquad \text{for } i = 1, 2, \ldots, N;\ K = \sum_i K_i \qquad (11.3.5)$$

$$\mathbf{1}_{T_i} = (I_{T_i} \otimes \mathbf{1}_J')\mathbf{w}_i, \qquad \text{for } i = 1, 2, \ldots, N;\ T = \sum_i T_i \qquad (11.3.6)$$

where $\mathbf{p} = (\mathbf{p}_1, \mathbf{p}_2, \ldots, \mathbf{p}_N)'$ and $\mathbf{w} = (\mathbf{w}_1, \mathbf{w}_2, \ldots, \mathbf{w}_N)'$.

Under this framework we recover simultaneously the unknowns $\boldsymbol{\beta} = (\boldsymbol{\beta}_{K_1}, \boldsymbol{\beta}_{K_2}, \ldots, \boldsymbol{\beta}_{K_N})'$, the unknown errors $\mathbf{e}_i$ and the unknown covariance correlation coefficients δ_{ij}, for each pair $i \neq j$, $i, j = 1, 2, \ldots, N$. Similar to the autocorrelation–GME model presented in Section 9.2 of Chapter 9, the unknown δ_{ij} are not reparameterized and are recovered directly through the consistency relations (11.3.3). Finally, any prior cross-equation information concerning the $\boldsymbol{\beta}_i$, such as $\boldsymbol{\beta}_{ik} = \boldsymbol{\beta}_{jk}$ for some $i \neq j$, can be introduced as an additional consistency relation.

Before presenting some sampling experiments we note the following. First, in many cases found in practice, the off-diagonal elements in the covariance matrix are relatively small and as such δ_{ij} is practically zero. In that case the GME formulation with, or without (11.3.3) yields the *same* result. That is, the Lagrange multipliers associated with (11.3.3) are zero. However, for those cases where the δ_{ij} are significantly different than zero these restrictions are valuable. In terms of the model selection discussed in Chapter 10, it means that the normalized entropy $S(\hat{\mathbf{p}})$ decreases as a result of adding equations (11.3.3). Second, following Chapter 6, it is possible to derive the dual GME formulation. Specifically, following the notation introduced in (11.3.1) where $\mathbf{y}$ and $\mathbf{e}$ are each of dimensions $(NT \times 1)$, X is a block diagonal matrix of dimension $(NT \times K)$ with $K = \sum_{i=1}^{N} K_i$ and $\boldsymbol{\beta} = (\boldsymbol{\beta}_1, \boldsymbol{\beta}_2, \ldots, \boldsymbol{\beta}_N)'$ is an unknown vector of dimension NK, the dual SUR–GME has the same basic three components developed in Chapter 6. The only difference is that the optimal $\mathbf{w}$ and Ψ_t already include the interrelationship among the equations.

11.3.2 SAMPLING EXPERIMENTS

In this section we consider two different formulations of the SUR model. In the first case we investigate the consequences of a general error covariance matrix and an orthonormal design matrix. In the second case we investigate the consequences of a design matrix with a high condition number. In the sampling experiments, there are three sets of equations ($N = 3$), $T_1 = T_2 = T_3 = 10$, $\boldsymbol{\beta}_2 = (1, 2, -3, 2)'$, $\boldsymbol{\beta}_2 = (2, -3, 2, 1)'$, $\boldsymbol{\beta}_3 = (-1, 1, 1, -1)'$ and

$$\Sigma = \begin{bmatrix} 1 & 2.62 & 0.81 \\ 2.62 & 4 & 9 \\ 0.81 & 9 & 9 \end{bmatrix}.$$

The first set of experiments involves orthonormal X's with condition numbers $\kappa(X_1'X_1) = \kappa(X_2'X_2) = \kappa(X_3'X_3) = 1$. In the second set of the experiments we present the results of a similar experiment except that X_2 and X_3 are ill-conditioned with condition numbers $\kappa(X_2'X_2) = 50$ and $\kappa(X_3'X_3) = 90$. In

Table 11.3.1 Results of two sampling experiments of the SUR-statistical model with three equations and a general error covariance matrix

	MSE ($\hat{\boldsymbol{\beta}}$)	tr(Cov($\hat{\boldsymbol{\beta}}$))
GME orthonormal X's	36.63	25.3
GLS (Φ known) orthonormal X's	30.43	
GME $\kappa_i(X_i'X_i) = 1, 50, 90$	40.75	35.3
GLS (Φ known) $\kappa_i(X_i'X_i) = 1, 50, 90$	1478.14	

both cases $Z_k = (-10, 0, 10)'$ for all k and $\mathbf{v}_i = (-12, -6, 0, 6, 12)'$ for all $i = 1, 2, 3$. The results for each experiment based on 1000 replications are presented in Table 11.3.1. In these experiments the GME estimates are stable and have empirical MSE that is only *slightly* inferior to the GLS (Φ known) estimator in the well posed case and much superior to the GLS (Φ known) estimator in the ill-posed case.

11.3.3 A SPECIAL CASE SUR MODEL

We now discuss a variation of the previous model where we know that

$$\boldsymbol{\beta}_{ik} = \boldsymbol{\beta}_{jk}, \qquad \text{for some } i \neq j \quad \text{and } i, j = 1, 2, \ldots, N; \\ k = 1, 2, \ldots, K_i \quad \text{and } K = \sum_i K_i. \tag{11.3.7}$$

If such cases arises, we can incorporate the restriction(s) (11.3.7) within the GME–SUR model of Section 11.3.1, where the corresponding support matrices Z_{ik} and Z_{jk} are specified to be similar.

However, if we do not wish to impose restriction(s) (11.3.7), we may just impose the less restrictive (assumption) requirement of

$$Z_{ik} = Z_{jk}, \qquad \text{for some } i \neq j \tag{11.3.8}$$

within a GCE or GME–SUR formulation of Section 11.3.1.

Based on the orthonormal X's experimental design discussed in Section 11.3.2, we present here the results of a 1000 replication sampling experiment, where $\beta_{11} = \beta_{21} = \beta_{31}$. The correct $\boldsymbol{\beta}_i$'s are $\boldsymbol{\beta}_1 = (1, 2, -3, 2)'$, $\boldsymbol{\beta}_2 = (1, -3, 2, 1)'$, $\boldsymbol{\beta}_3 = (1, 1, -1, -1)$, and the error covariance Σ and Z and V are specified as in Section 11.3.2. The GME MSE ($\hat{\boldsymbol{\beta}}$) = 23.56 and tr(cov($\hat{\boldsymbol{\beta}}$)) = 21.44 in that case. Adding the cross-equation restrictions reduces both the MSE($\hat{\boldsymbol{\beta}}$) and the tr(cov($\hat{\boldsymbol{\beta}}$)) relative to the unconstrained results of Table 11.3.1. If, within the GME formulation, we are not sure that $\beta_{11} = \beta_{21} = \beta_{31}$ and therefore *do not* impose these additional restrictions, the GME yields a MSE

($\hat{\boldsymbol{\beta}}$) and tr(cov($\hat{\boldsymbol{\beta}}$)) which are approximately the same as the GME results presented in Table 11.3.1.

11.4 POOLING TIME SERIES–CROSS-SECTION USING AN ERROR COMPONENTS MODEL

In many cases (see Judge *et al.*, 1988), when dealing with pooled time series and cross-sectional data, use is made of the following model:

$$y_{it} = \beta_{1i} + \sum_{k=2}^{K} \beta_k X_{kit} + e_{it} \qquad (11.4.1)$$

which involves specifying a different intercept coefficient for each cross-sectional unit (equation). An alternative formulation is to assume that the intercept coefficients β_{1i} are independent random variables with mean $\bar{\beta}$ and variance σ_u^2. Thus, $\beta_{1i} = \bar{\beta}_1 + u_i$, where $\mathrm{E}[u_i] = 0$, $\mathrm{E}[u_i^2] = \sigma^2$, $\mathrm{E}[u_i u_j] \equiv 0$ for $i \neq j$, and u_i are uncorrelated with the e_{jt}. Under this formulation, model (11.4.1) becomes

$$y_{it} = \bar{\beta}_1 + \sum_{k=2}^{K} \beta_k X_{kit} + u_i + e_{it} \qquad (11.4.2)$$

or in matrix form the ith equation (individual) is

$$\mathbf{y}_i = X_i \boldsymbol{\beta} + u_i \mathbf{j}_T + \mathbf{e}_i \qquad (11.4.3)$$

where $\mathbf{j}_T = (1, 1, \ldots, 1)'$ a $(T \times 1)$ vector of ones, and $u_i \mathbf{j}_T + \mathbf{e}_i$ is a composite error vector with mean zero and covariance matrix $\sigma_u^2 \mathbf{j}_T \mathbf{j}_T' + \sigma_e^2 I_T$. The complete system of N separameterized equations may be written compactly as

$$\mathbf{y} = \mathbf{x}\boldsymbol{\beta} + \mathbf{u} \otimes \mathbf{j}_T + \mathbf{e} = xz\mathbf{p} + (V^{\mathrm{u}}\mathbf{w}^{v}) \otimes \mathbf{j}_T + V^{e}\mathbf{w}^{e} \qquad (11.4.4)$$

where $u \otimes \mathbf{J}_T + \mathbf{e}$ has mean vector $\mathbf{0}$ and covariance $I_N \otimes [\sigma_u^2 \mathbf{j}_T \mathbf{j}_T' + \sigma_e^2 I_T]$, which is a block diagonal matrix.

In this form (11.4.4) is just a variant of the linear statistical models developed in Chapters 6 and 9 and can be estimated within a GME context by putting parameter supports on $\boldsymbol{\beta}$, $\mathbf{u}$ and $\mathbf{e}$ and using the GME formulation of Section 11.2.1 with the $\mathbf{u}$ component added in terms of probabilities in the objective, consistency relation and adding up conditions.

Another alternative for the error component model is to transform the statistical model (11.4.4) (see Judge *et al.*, 1988, pp. 482–3) so that the error covariance is of a diagonal form and thus we can estimate one equation at a time. This leads, via a transformation, to a statistical model for the ith equation of an α difference form

$$y_{it} - \alpha \mathbf{y}_i = (1 - \alpha)\bar{\beta}_1 + \sum_{k=2}^{K} (X_{kit} - \alpha \bar{X}_{ki})\beta_k + e_{it} \qquad (11.4.5)$$

where $0 \leq \alpha \leq 1$. Under the GME formulation, support parameters would be specified for the unknown $\bar{\beta}_1$, β_k, for $k = 2, 3, \ldots, K$ and e_{it}, and the optimization would be carried through in terms of the corresponding probabilities.

Other more complicated variants of the SUR error components model could, of course, be modeled and estimated. For example, if the correlation between time periods varies with time, the error covariance that results is more general than the block diagonal structure we have considered. In that case, within the GME formulation, we use a variation of (11.3.3) to capture the different covariances for each period. The new set of equations is

$$e_{ti}e_{tj} = \delta_{tij}[(e_{ti}e_{ti})(e_{tj}e_{tj})]^{1/2}, \qquad \text{for all } t = 1, 2, \ldots, T \quad \text{and for } i \neq j \qquad (11.3.3a)$$

11.5 REMARKS

Our objective in this chapter has been to extend the GME methodology so that it can be used to estimate the unknown $\boldsymbol{\beta}$ parameters for a seemingly unrelated regression (SUR) model. Several variants of the SUR models have been specified and corresponding GME formulations for estimating the unknown parameters have been noted. Sampling experiments of traditional and GME estimators have been presented. In most of the cases evaluated, the GME estimator reflected a superior sampling performance to traditional estimators with *known* covariance. However, when the covariance is not assumed to be known and when the covariates are moderately collinear, the risk gains of the GME estimator are even more significant relative to the more traditional estimators. Finally, we note that the GME formulation permits the sample data to determine the structure of the traditional elements of the covariance. Once again, the GME-SUR formulation demonstrates the flexibility of the GME–GCE approach for a range of data generation processes.

REFERENCES

Judge, G. G., Hill, R. C., Griffiths, W. E., Lütkepohl, H. and Lee, T.-C. (1988) *Introduction to the Theory and Practice of Econometrics*, 2nd edn. John Wiley, New York.

Kariya, T. (1981) Bounds for the covariance matrices of Zellner's estimator in the SUR model and the 2SAE in a heteroscedastic model. *Journal of the American Statistical Association* **76**, 975–9.

Srivastava, V.K. and Giles, D. E. (1988) *Seemingly Unrelated Regression Equation Models: Estimation and Inference.* Marcel Dekker, New York.

Taylor, W. E. (1977) Small sample properties of a class of two stage Aitken estimators. *Econometrica* **45**, 497–508.

Taylor, W. E. (1978) The heteroskedastic linear model: exact finite sample results. *Econometrica* **46**, 663–75.

Zellner, A. (1962) An efficient method of estimating seemingly unrelated regressions and tests of aggregation bias. *Journal of the American Statistical Association* **57**, 348–68.

CHAPTER 12

Simultaneous equations statistical model

12.1 INTRODUCTION

In Chapter 11 we considered the problem of estimation and inference for a set of regression equations that were related through the equation errors. In this chapter we extend this model to include an instantaneous feedback mechanism between some of the variables in the system and this leads us to the traditional simultaneous equations statistical model (SESM). To provide a format for analyzing the SESM, consider the ith equation of a set of N simultaneous equations,

$$\mathbf{y}_i = [Y_i, E_i^*]\begin{bmatrix}\boldsymbol{\alpha}_i \\ \boldsymbol{\beta}_i\end{bmatrix} + \mathbf{e}_i$$

$$= X_i\boldsymbol{\delta}_i + \mathbf{e}_i \tag{12.1.1}$$

where $\mathbf{y}_i$ and Y_i represent the endogenous-jointly determined variables in the ith equation and E_i^* represents the exogenous-predetermined variables in ith equation. Here $E_i^* + E_i^{**} = E$ represent the $R_i^* + R_i^{**} = R$ exogenous-predetermined variables in the *system* of equations. Let X_i be a $(T \times K_i)$ matrix representing the endogenous Y_i and exogenous-predetermined E_i^* variables that appear in the ith equation with non-zero coefficients. Further, $\boldsymbol{\delta}_i = (\boldsymbol{\alpha}_i', \boldsymbol{\beta}_i')'$ is a K_i dimensional vector of unknown and unobservable parameters corresponding to the endogenous and exogenous variables in the ith equation, and $\mathbf{e}_i$ is a T-dimensional random vector for the ith equation that is traditionally assumed to have mean $\mathbf{0}$ and scale parameter σ_{ii}. The variables $\mathbf{y}_i$, Y_i, E_i^*, E_i^{**} are observed, and $\boldsymbol{\delta}_i$ and $\mathbf{e}_i$ are unobserved and unobservable.

Given the ith equation (12.1.1), the *complete* system of N equations may be written as

$$\begin{bmatrix}\mathbf{y}_1 \\ \mathbf{y}_2 \\ \vdots \\ \mathbf{y}_N\end{bmatrix} = \begin{bmatrix}X_1 & & & \\ & X_2 & & \\ & & \ddots & \\ & & & X_N\end{bmatrix}\begin{bmatrix}\boldsymbol{\delta}_1 \\ \boldsymbol{\delta}_2 \\ \vdots \\ \boldsymbol{\delta}_N\end{bmatrix} + \begin{bmatrix}\mathbf{e}_1 \\ \mathbf{e}_2 \\ \vdots \\ \mathbf{e}_N\end{bmatrix} \tag{12.1.2}$$

or compactly as

$$\mathbf{y} = X\boldsymbol{\delta} + \mathbf{e} \tag{12.1.3}$$

where, in the context of the SUR statistical model of Chapter 11 and the traditional SESM, $\mathbf{y}$ and $\mathbf{e}$ are NT-dimensional random vectors. Traditionally $\mathbf{e}$ has mean $\mathbf{0}$ and $\text{Cov}(\mathbf{e}) = \Sigma \otimes I_T$, where Σ is an $(N \times N)$ unknown covariance matrix.

Given the SESM, the problem before us is to develop a GME–GCE basis for estimating the unknown and unobservable parameters, $\boldsymbol{\delta}_i$ or $\boldsymbol{\delta}$, and to compare the sampling performance of the GME–GCE and the traditional simultaneous equation estimators.

12.2 ESTIMATING δ_i

In this section our main focus is on the ith equation and the problem of recovering an estimate of the unknown vector $\boldsymbol{\delta}_i$. The ith equation (12.1.1) has the same general form as the linear statistical model considered in Chapter 6, except that now the Y_i variables may no longer be considered uncorrelated with the equation noise $\mathbf{e}_i$. In this situation, the traditional least squares rule is biased, a fate generally viewed with distaste by those from asymptopia. To cope with the fact that the random variables Y_i and $\mathbf{e}_i$ may not be uncorrelated, instrumental variable (IV), general method of moments (GMM) and two-stage least squares (2SLS) estimators

$$\boldsymbol{\delta}_i^* = [X_i'E(E'E)^{-1}E'X_i]^{-1}X_i'E(E'E)^{-1}E'\mathbf{y}_i \tag{12.2.1}$$

have been proposed to provide at least a rule with the consistency property (see Hansen, 1982; Judge *et al.*, 1988, pp. 636–50; Davidson and MacKinnon, 1993, pp. 209–42). One interesting aspect of the 2SLS estimator is that, in order to achieve the consistency goal, observables are treated as unobservables.

The unknown and unobservable $\boldsymbol{\delta}_i$ and $\mathbf{e}_i$ may take on values over the real line. To specify a GME formulation for estimating the unknown parameters in an equation from a simultaneous system of equations we view the unknowns probablistically and reparameterize (12.1.1). To do this we use the logic and the reparameterizations (6.2.3) and (6.2.5) that were developed in Chapter 6. This reparameterization results in the following respecification of (12.1.1):

$$\mathbf{y}_i = X_i\boldsymbol{\delta}_i + \mathbf{e}_i = X_iZ_i\mathbf{p}_i + V_i\mathbf{w}_i \tag{12.2.2}$$

where Z_i and V_i are the matrices representing the discrete random variables support spaces for $\boldsymbol{\delta}_i$ and $\mathbf{e}_i$ and $\mathbf{p}_i$ while $\mathbf{w}_i$ are the corresponding vectors of unknown probabilities. Given the results of Chapters 6 and 7 and reparameterization (12.2.2), it is possible to specify different GME–GCE formulations based on the observed data or moments. For generality, we present all the models within the GCE formulation and remind the reader that GME is just a special case of GCE where all the prior probabilities are uniform.

12.2.1 GCE FORMULATION 1

Given the reparameterization (12.2.2), one natural GCE formulation for recovering the unknown $\boldsymbol{\delta}_i$ parameter vector for the ith equation is to make use of (12.2.2) as a consistency relation since it makes use of the information for *all* the data points. Using (12.2.2) as the consistency relation leads to the problem

$$\min I(\mathbf{p}_i, \mathbf{q}_i, \mathbf{w}_i, \mathbf{u}_i) = \mathbf{p}_i' \ln(\mathbf{p}_i/\mathbf{q}_i) + \mathbf{w}_i' \ln(\mathbf{w}_i/\mathbf{u}_i) \tag{12.2.3}$$

subject to

$$\mathbf{y}_i = X_i Z_i \mathbf{p}_i + V_i \mathbf{w}_i \tag{12.2.2$'$}$$

$$\mathbf{1}_{K_i} = (I_{K_i} \otimes \mathbf{1}_M)\mathbf{p}_i \tag{12.2.4}$$

$$\mathbf{1}_T = (I_T \otimes \mathbf{1}_j)\mathbf{w}_i \tag{12.2.5}$$

where $\mathbf{q}_i$ and $\mathbf{u}_i$ are prior probability vectors for $\mathbf{p}_i$ and $\mathbf{w}_i$, (12.2.2′) is a constraint based on the observed data for $\mathbf{y}_i$, Y_i and E^*, and (12.2.4) and (12.2.5) are adding-up normalizing constraints. Results from Chapters 6–9 that deal with variants of the classical linear statistical model suggest that this formulation may lead to estimates of $\boldsymbol{\delta}_i$ that are slightly biased but have excellent precision and thus superior MSE's. Note, in this section and in the sections to come, we have used the GCE criterion. If uniform probabilities are used for $\mathbf{q}_i$ and $\mathbf{u}_i$, then the GME criterion $\max H(\mathbf{p}, \mathbf{w}) = -\mathbf{p}' \ln \mathbf{p} - \mathbf{w}' \ln \mathbf{w}$ results.

12.2.2 GCE FORMULATION 2

In the simultaneous equation literature it is customary, when attempting to estimate the unknown parameters in the ith equation of a SESM, to use information on all of the exogenous or predetermined variables from the complete system of equations. Consequently, another possible GCE formulation is to use the observed matrix of exogeneous variables E to transform the statistical model (12.2.2) to the moment form

$$E'\mathbf{y}_i = E'X_i Z_i \mathbf{p}_i + E'V\mathbf{w} \tag{12.2.6}$$

This moment condition can then be used as the consistency relation in the problem

$$\min I(\mathbf{p}_i, \mathbf{q}_i, \mathbf{w}_i, \mathbf{u}_i) = \mathbf{p}_i' \ln(\mathbf{p}_i/\mathbf{q}_i) + \mathbf{w}_i' \ln(\mathbf{w}_i/\mathbf{u}_i) \tag{12.2.7}$$

subject to the moment constraint (12.2.6) and the normalization constraints (12.2.4) and (12.2.5). If the ith equation is overidentified, the sampling performance of this formulation should be compared with that of the 2SLS–GMM estimator.

If the equation is just identified, then $E'X_i$ in (12.2.6) is a square non-singular matrix. If, in this case, the pure moment condition

$$E'\mathbf{y}_i = E'X_iZ_i\mathbf{p}_i \tag{12.2.8}$$

replaces (12.2.6) in the GME–GCE formulation, an interior solution provides the instrumental variable (IV) estimates. Results from earlier chapters suggest the use of the relaxed moment relation (12.2.6) should lead, in just identified or overidentified situations, to GCE estimates of $\boldsymbol{\delta}_i$ that are in small samples superior to estimates based on the pure moment condition (12.2.8) in terms of precision and bias.

12.2.3 GCE FORMULATION 3

Finally, in order to develop a GCE formulation that may be used to compare with GMM–2SLS estimation for an overidentified equation, let us make use of the idempotent matrix $E(E'E)^{-1}E'$ proposed by Basmann (1957) and rewrite the statistical model as

$$X_i'E(E'E)^{-1}E'\mathbf{y}_i = X_i'E(E'E)^{-1}E'X_iZ_i\mathbf{p}_i + X_i'E(E'E)^{-1}E'V_i\mathbf{w}_i. \tag{12.2.9}$$

Under this restatement of the statistical model, a GCE formulation may be stated as the problem

$$\min I(\mathbf{p}_i, \mathbf{q}_i, \mathbf{w}_i, \mathbf{u}_i) = \mathbf{p}_i' \ln(\mathbf{p}_i/\mathbf{q}_i) + \mathbf{w}_i' \ln(\mathbf{w}_i/\mathbf{u}_i) \tag{12.2.10}$$

subject to the moment condition (12.2.9) and adding-up normalization conditions (12.2.4) and (12.2.5). The pure moment condition

$$X_iE(E'E)^{-1}E'\mathbf{y}_i = X_iE(E'E)^{-1}E'X_iZ_i\mathbf{p}_i \tag{12.2.11}$$

is identical to the reparameterized first-order conditions for the 2SLS–GMM estimator. If (12.2.11) replaces the relaxed moment condition (12.2.9) as the consistency relation in the GCE formulation, then 2SLS–GMM estimates for $\boldsymbol{\delta}_i$ result. If the relaxed moment relation (12.2.9) is used in the GME–GCE formulation, and the bounded parameter space Z contains the true parameter vector $\boldsymbol{\delta}_i$, then the resulting estimates have under standard regularity conditions, the same large sample properties as the 2SLS–GMM estimators (see Judge *et al.*, 1988, pp. 641–3.) However, if the results from past chapters are any guide, the GME–GCE estimates involving (12.2.9) should, under a MSE measure, be superior in finite samples. The procedures used in Chapters 6 and 7 provide a basis for developing related analytical large sample results for these cases.

Within the context of a SESM and a simultaneous data generation mechanism, in the sections ahead we use the results of sampling experiments to illustrate and compare the sampling performance of the various GME formulations and traditional SESM estimation rules.

12.3 THE STATISTICAL MODEL AND EXPERIMENTAL DESIGN

To illustrate the performance of the GME for recovering information from a system of simultaneous equations, we report the results of two sampling experiments. Each sampling experiment consists of 500 replications of samples of 20 observations. The first experiment is similar to the one discussed in Judge *et al.* (1988, pp. 656–8). The data are generated from a system of three equations

$$\mathbf{y}_1 = -10\mathbf{y}_2 + 2.5\mathbf{y}_3 - 60\mathbf{h}_1 + \mathbf{e}_1 \qquad (12.3.1a)$$

$$\mathbf{y}_2 = 0.2\mathbf{y}_1 + 40\mathbf{h}_1 - 4\mathbf{h}_2 - 6\mathbf{h}_3 + 1.5\mathbf{h}_4 + \mathbf{e}_2 \qquad (12.3.1b)$$

$$\mathbf{y}_3 = 2\mathbf{y}_2 - 10\mathbf{h}_1 + 80\mathbf{h}_2 + 5\mathbf{h}_5 + \mathbf{e}_3 \qquad (12.3.1c)$$

where the y's represent endogenous variables, the h's represent exogenous variables and the $\mathbf{e}_i$ are normally distributed with null mean and covariance

$$\Sigma \otimes I_T = \begin{bmatrix} 227.55 & 8.91 & -56.89 \\ 8.91 & 0.66 & -1.88 \\ -56.89 & -1.88 & 15.76 \end{bmatrix} \otimes I_T \qquad (12.3.2)$$

Using traditional counting rules, equations (12.3.1a) and (12.3.1c) are over-identified and equation (12.3.1b) is just identified. The matrix of exogenous variables E that we used is taken from Table 15.1 of Judge *et al.* (1988). The parameter supports Z_i used for the unknown $\boldsymbol{\delta}_i$ are:

Equation 12.3.1a $\quad \mathbf{z}_1 = (-150, 0, 150)'$ for the intercept parameter,

$\quad \mathbf{z}_k = (-70, 0, 70)'$ for all the other parameters;

Equation 12.3.1b $\quad \mathbf{z}_k = (-120, 0, 120)'$ for all parameters;

Equation 12.3.1c $\quad \mathbf{z}_1 = (-200, 0, 200)'$ for the intercept parameter,

$\quad \mathbf{z}_k = (-120, 0, 120)'$ for all other parameters.

The error supports V_i are $\mathbf{v}_1 = (-55, 0, 55)'$; $\mathbf{v}_2 = (-3.5, 0, 3.5)'$ and $\mathbf{v}_3 = (-40, 0, 40)'$. The usual prior information normally available in practice was not included in the formulations. Consequently, uniform prior probability vectors $\mathbf{q}_i$ and $\mathbf{u}_i$ were used, along with the GME criterion $\max H(\mathbf{p}, \mathbf{w}) = -\mathbf{p}' \ln \mathbf{p} - \mathbf{w}' \ln \mathbf{w}$. Prior information, such as the signs of the parameters, would be easy to include and should improve estimator performance.

Table 12.3.1 Results of sampling experiments for equations (12.3.1a) and (12.3.1c) for 500 replications and $T = 20$

Estimator	Consistency relation	Equation (12.3.1a)		Equation (12.3.1c)	
		$\text{MSE}(\tilde{\boldsymbol{\delta}}_1)$	$\text{tr}(\text{Cov}(\tilde{\boldsymbol{\delta}}_1))$	$\text{MSE}(\tilde{\boldsymbol{\delta}}_3)$	$\text{tr}(\text{Cov}(\tilde{\boldsymbol{\delta}}_3))$
2SLS–GMM	(12.2.11)	384.73	348.26	903.01	848.95
GME–moment (2SLS)	(12.2.9)	256.11	231.71	357.47	348.83
GME–moment (E)	(12.2.6)	257.49	233.06	358.45	350.00
GME–data	(12.2.2)	124.49	74.84	279.27	121.80

12.3.1 EXPERIMENT 1

The empirical MSE results for the overidentified equations (12.3.1a) and (12.3.1c), using $T = 20$ observations and 500 replications, are reported in Table 12.3.1. For comparison we report the sampling results for the various estimators specified in Section 12.2. The preliminary nature of these sampling results should be kept in mind, and they should only be interpreted as suggestive of sampling performance when using one of the variants of the GME formulations.

These sampling results suggest that under a MSE measure, for the overidentified equations (12.3.1a) and (12.3.1c), the GME estimators are superior to the traditional 2SLS–GMM estimator that is normally used in practice. Of the GME formulations, the GME data formulation yields the best results for the two overidentified equations, with the GME moment and GME–2SLS relaxed moment estimators a distant second. Note for equation (12.3.1c) the large gain in MSE of the GME moment (2SLS) relative to the traditional 2SLS estimator. Also note the large precision gain in $\text{tr}(\text{Cov}(\tilde{\boldsymbol{\delta}}_1))$ of the GME estimators relative to the traditional 2SLS estimators. For this experiment, the differences in MSE, of the different estimators, for the just-identified equation (12.3.1b) were not significant.

12.3.2 EXPERIMENT 2

To demonstrate the qualities of the GME estimator with limited observations, we report the results of a second experiment consisting of 500 samples which uses the same experimental design as in Section 12.3.1 but with the exception that only 10 observations ($T = 10$) are used in each replication. These results are reported in Table 12.3.2. Again the GME estimators based on (12.2.9) and (12.2.2) are vastly superior under a MSE measure to the traditional 2SLS estimator. This result is important because in many cases only a limited number of observations are available when estimating the parameters of a simultaneous system of equations. This reduces the potential statistical consequences of

Table 12.3.2 Results of 500 sampling experiments for equation (12.3.1a) for $T = 10$

Estimator	$\text{MSE}(\tilde{\boldsymbol{\delta}}_1)$	$\text{tr}(\text{Cov}(\tilde{\boldsymbol{\delta}}_1))$
2SLS (12.2.11)	6250.10	1512.17
GME–2SLS (12.2.9)	425.55	213.98
GME–data (12.2.2)	411.59	227.45

having to work with a fixed coefficient model, when in fact the coefficients vary over time, space, individuals, etc. Although not reported, experiments with collinear exogenous variables were also carried through. In these cases, the MSE and precision gains for the GME estimators relative to the traditional 2SLS estimator were very significant and in line with the results of previous chapters.

12.4 ESTIMATING $\boldsymbol{\delta}$

Next consider estimating the unknown $\boldsymbol{\delta}$ coefficients for the complete system of equations (12.1.2) and (12.1.3). The statistical model is of the general form of the SUR model considered in Chapter 11. The exception is that the right-hand-side X_i variables in the SESM may contain one or more endogenous variables that are not uncorrelated with the equation noise $\mathbf{e}_i$.

In formulating a GME version of this model, we follow the multiple equation formulation of Chapter 11 and rewrite (12.1.2) as

$$\begin{bmatrix} \mathbf{y}_1 \\ \mathbf{y}_2 \\ \vdots \\ \mathbf{y}_N \end{bmatrix} = \begin{bmatrix} X_1 & & & \\ & X_2 & & \\ & & \ddots & \\ & & & X_N \end{bmatrix} \begin{bmatrix} Z_1\mathbf{p}_1 \\ Z_2\mathbf{p}_2 \\ \vdots \\ Z_N\mathbf{p}_N \end{bmatrix} + \begin{bmatrix} V_1\mathbf{w}_1 \\ V_2\mathbf{w}_2 \\ \vdots \\ V_N\mathbf{w}_N \end{bmatrix} \tag{12.4.1}$$

or

$$\mathbf{y} = X\boldsymbol{\delta} + \mathbf{e} = XZ\mathbf{p} + V\mathbf{w}. \tag{12.4.2}$$

The random vector $\mathbf{e}$ has mean $\mathbf{0}$ and

$$\text{Cov}(\mathbf{e}) = \Sigma \otimes I_T \tag{12.4.3}$$

and Σ is an unknown N-dimensional positive definite symmetric matrix. The unknown variance–covariance matrix Σ contains $(N(N+1)/2)$ unknown parameters σ_{ij} where, in line with Chapter 11, we represent the cross-equation error processes as the consistency relations

$$\frac{1}{T}\sum_t e_{ti}e_{tj} = \delta_{ij}\left[\left(\frac{1}{T}\sum e_{ti}e_{ti}\right)\left(\frac{1}{T}\sum e_{tj}e_{tj}\right)\right]^{1/2} \tag{12.4.4}$$

where $e_{ti} = \sum_j v_{ij}w_{tij}$. Given the statistical model (12.4.2) and (12.4.3), the problem is to recover from the data ($\mathbf{y}$, X) the unknown $\mathbf{p}$, $\mathbf{w}$ and $\boldsymbol{\delta}$.

One possible GME formulation involving the complete system of relations is

$$\max H(\mathbf{p}, \mathbf{w}) = -\mathbf{p}' \ln \mathbf{p} - \mathbf{w}' \ln \mathbf{w} \tag{12.4.5}$$

subject to

$$\mathbf{y} = XZ\mathbf{p} + V\mathbf{w} \tag{12.4.2$'$}$$

and the adding-up constraints (12.2.4), (12.2.5) and the covariance consistency relations (12.4.4). Alternatively, the three-stage least-squares (3SLS) estimator (see Judge *et al.*, 1988, pp. 646–7)

$$\boldsymbol{\delta}^* = \{X'[\hat{\Sigma}^{-1} \otimes E(E'E)^{-1}E']X\}^{-1}X'[\hat{\Sigma}^{-1} \otimes E(E'E)^{-1}E']\mathbf{y} \tag{12.4.6}$$

where $\hat{\Sigma}$ represents estimates of the unknown covariance matrix from 2SLS error estimates, or the full information ML method under the assumption of normal errors (see Judge *et al.*, 1988, pp. 652–4) are the estimators traditionally used with a complete system of equations.

12.4.1 SOME SAMPLING RESULTS

Using sample information generated from the sampling experiment discussed in Section 12.3, 500 replications and a sample size of 20 observations, the sampling performance of the GME estimator and the 3SLS estimator were compared, and the results are reported in Table 12.4.1.

As in the single equation MSE comparisons, the GME data formulation is, under squared error loss, superior to the traditional 3SLS estimator. In fact the MSE($\hat{\boldsymbol{\delta}}$) of the GME data formulation is superior to that of the 3SLS rule even under the unrealistic assumption that Σ is known. Note for this experiment

Table 12.4.1 Sampling results for the complete system of equations

Estimator	MSE($\boldsymbol{\delta}$)	Var($\hat{\boldsymbol{\delta}}$)
Feasible 3SLS	749.69	647.97
3SLS (known Σ)	709.01	609.40
GME-data (12.4.2)	404.72	197.25

that, in terms of the total empirical MSE for the GME data formulation, there is very little gain in considering the equations as a system rather than one at a time as we did in Section 12.3. The respective MSEs are 439.7 when estimating each equation separately and 404.7 on a system basis.

12.5 REMARKS

The GME approach to estimation in the simultaneous equation statistical model is a major departure from the traditional 2SLS, 3SLS and GMM estimation rules. Using relaxed moment conditions, such as (12.2.6) or (12.2.9), or the data relation (12.2.2) as consistency constraints, provide an information base that yields large gains in terms of smaller coefficient variances and MSEs. The results to date are suggestive of the improved performance of the GME formulations relative to traditional procedures. These preliminary results also suggest the possibility of recovering coefficient information and making inferences even in cases where, by traditional rules, an equation in a system of equations may be judged to be underidentified or the complete set of relations is imperfectly known. Also, it will be interesting in future research to investigate whether or not the model selection procedures discussed in Chapter 10 will be useful in locating extraneous endogenous and exogenous variables and sorting out the basic structure of the system. The formulations to be presented in Chapters 13 and 14 should provide a way of dealing with non-stationary and dynamic problems as it relates to an array of simultaneous equation statistical models.

REFERENCES

Basmann, R. L. (1957) A general classical method of linear estimation of coefficients in a structural equation. *Econometrica* **25**, 77–83.

Davidson, R. and MacKinnon, J. G. (1993) *Estimation and Inference in Econometrics*. Oxford University Press, New York.

Hansen, L. (1982) Large sample properties of generalized method of moments estimators. *Econometrica* **50**, 1029–54.

Judge, G., Hill, R. C., Griffiths, W. E., Lütkepohl, H. and Lee, T.-C. (1988) *Introduction to the Theory and Practice of Econometrics*, 2nd edn. John Wiley, New York.

PART V

Linear and non-linear dynamic systems

In Parts III and IV we studied fixed parameter formulations for single and multiple equations statistical models. If we allow the parameters to change or vary over time, the formulations of previous chapters have to be modified accordingly. Within this context, the objective of the chapters in this part is to develop an estimation procedure for linear or non-linear dynamic systems. In Chapter 13 the linear discrete-time dynamic system is investigated and a GME–GCE formulation is developed to simultaneously estimate the unknown parameters of the observation and state equations. In Chapter 14 the dynamic system is generalized to include control variables. After introducing the simpler linear control model, a generic non-linear control problem is introduced where the state variable, which is non-linearly related to other observables, is not observed. Finally, we analyse an inverse control problem, where one wishes to recover, simultaneously, the parameters of the quadratic, (utility), objective function, together with the unknown parameters of the observation and state equations. As this problem is an ill-posed and undetermined one, traditional methods may be employed only if a large set of assumptions are imposed on the system. The estimation procedures developed in Part V avoid these assumptions and are easy to implement and compute.

Larry Karp made a major contribution to the models developed in Chapter 14.

CHAPTER 13

Estimation and inference of dynamic linear inverse problems

13.1 INTRODUCTION

In much of the work in economics and econometrics it is traditional to work with a variant of the following finite, discrete-time, linear inverse problem

$$\mathbf{y} = X\boldsymbol{\beta} + \mathbf{e} \tag{13.1.1}$$

where $\mathbf{y}$ is a noisy T-dimensional vector of observables, $\boldsymbol{\beta}$ is a K-dimensional vector of unknown and unobservable coefficients, X is a linear operator that is a known $(T \times K)$ matrix and the model is closed with a noise vector $\mathbf{e} \sim \mathrm{N}(0, \sigma^2 I_T)$. Given information concerning only $\mathbf{y}$ and X, the objective is to recover the unknown K-dimensional vector $\boldsymbol{\beta}$ that cannot be measured directly. If this statistical model correctly describes the data generation process, it is natural to use some variant of the formulations in Chapters 6–9 to recover estimates of the unknown and unobservable $\boldsymbol{\beta}$ vector and the unknown error vector $\mathbf{e}$. However, many economic data sets are generated from relations that are dynamic, non-stationary and stochastic. If such data sets are modeled and estimated assuming a fixed-parameter stationary model, then the recovered parameters are inaccurate and often lead to poor forecasts and decisions.

In this chapter our interest is focused on linear dynamic systems. Our objective is to develop a formulation for recovering the parameters of a discrete-time linear stochastic relation, or system of relations, when faced with noisy economic data. We will show that this new formulation works well for both large and complete data sets, as well as for the more common case of limited and incomplete noisy data sets when standard regularity conditions may not be fulfilled. In terms of the statistical model (13.1.1), we are interested in the specification

$$y_t = \mathbf{x}_t'\boldsymbol{\beta}_t + e_t \tag{13.1.2}$$

where the K-dimensional vector $\boldsymbol{\beta}_t$ varies with $t = 1, 2, \ldots, T$. Therefore, the number of data points is typically smaller than the number of unknown parameters $\boldsymbol{\beta}_t$, for $t = 1, 2, \ldots, T$. Because of this, or due to other reasons such as a bad experimental design, *unless creative assumptions are made*, traditional estimation rules are not defined or may perform poorly. To cope with problems of partial-incomplete data in the case of time linear dynamic systems, we make use of the GME–GCE formalism developed in Chapters 6–7 to recover the unobservable $\boldsymbol{\beta}_t$ and e_t.

The format of the chapter is as follows. In Section 13.2 we review traditional time-linear dynamic system models. In Section 13.3 we specify a GME–GCE basis for recovering information in the case of a non-stationary inverse problem with noise. For simplicity in exposition, most equations of this chapter are presented in scalar notation. In Section 13.4 we present examples to reflect the reach and implications of the various formulations and solutions. In a concluding section we discuss the implications of our results for estimation and inference in dynamic linear models.

13.2 DYNAMIC LINEAR SYSTEMS

In the literature a typical dynamic system involves a set of directly *unobserved random variables* that reflect the *states* of the system and which follow a stochastic path over time. This path is usually represented by an equation that specifies the position (state) of the system as a function of the past positions and a random noise component. In addition, some noisy observations (outcomes), underlying the actual process, are available. Consequently, we have an inverse problem where estimation of the state of the system is not possible since:

- we do not have direct measurements of these random variables
- we do not know the exact initial values of the state variables.

The information recovery–estimation–inference problem is concerned with how to use the noisy *indirect* observations to obtain estimates of the states of the system and to predict future positions.

Given this general notion of a dynamic system, our interest is restricted to a discrete-time linear stochastic system. The observations (data), which are assumed to be linear combinations of the state vector, are collected at discrete points in time. Within this context a simple state-space representation of the system is provided by the following specification.

Let $\boldsymbol{\beta}_t$ represent the state of the system at time t and $\mathbf{y}_t$ represent noisy observations (outcomes of the system) at time t. Then, a state-space representation of the system is given by

$$\mathbf{y}_t = X_t \boldsymbol{\beta}_t + \mathbf{e}_t \qquad \text{(observation equation)} \qquad (13.2.1)$$

$$\boldsymbol{\beta}_t = A\boldsymbol{\beta}_{t-1} + \boldsymbol{\varepsilon}_t \qquad \text{(system-process equation)} \qquad (13.2.2)$$

where $\mathbf{y}_1, \mathbf{y}_2, \ldots, \mathbf{y}_T$ is a sequence of noisy $(P \times 1)$ observation vectors, X_t is a known $(P \times K)$ measurement-design matrix, $\mathbf{e}_t$ is a $(P \times 1)$ vector of observation errors, $\boldsymbol{\beta}_t$ is a $(K \times 1)$ state vector, A is a $(K \times K)$ known transition matrix and $\boldsymbol{\varepsilon}_t$ is a $(K \times 1)$ vector of state or system errors. Typically it is assumed that the random vectors $\mathbf{e}_t \sim \mathrm{N}_P(\mathbf{0}, \Sigma_t)$ and $\boldsymbol{\varepsilon}_t \sim \mathrm{N}_K(\mathbf{0}, \Psi_t)$, that Σ_t and Ψ_t are known and that $\mathbf{e}_t$ and $\boldsymbol{\varepsilon}_t$ are mutually independent. Further, prior information on the initial conditions $\boldsymbol{\beta}_0$ may exist. Given the above specification or a variant thereof, the objective is to recover $\boldsymbol{\beta}_t$, the state of the system at time t.

This general specification has led to the analysis of a large class of models in the literature, for example, the time varying coefficient model (Rosenberg, 1973; Swamy and Tinsley, 1980; Leybourne, 1993), the random coefficients model (Swamy, 1970), the Kalman filter (Kalman, 1960), and the Bayesian formulations (Maybeck, 1979; Broemeling, 1985; Normand and Tritchler, 1992).

Information recovery in general dynamic linear systems is complex and challenging since closed form solutions in many cases do not exist and/or estimation rules are undefined. Given this situation, which is a natural scenario for entropy-based formulations, in the sections to follow we modify the GME–GCE approach for estimation of these familiar problems.

13.3 A BASIC NON-STATIONARY INVERSE MODEL WITH NOISE

Consider a non-stationary statistical model in the form of a discrete-time linear observation equation

$$y_t = \mathbf{x}_t' \boldsymbol{\beta}_t + e_t, \qquad t = 1, 2, \ldots, T \qquad (13.3.1)$$

and the process or state (system) equation

$$\boldsymbol{\beta}_t = \mathbf{f}_t(\boldsymbol{\beta}_{t-1}) + \boldsymbol{\varepsilon}_t \qquad (13.3.2)$$

where the state equations are not restricted to be linear. Given information concerning the scalar y_t and the K-dimensional design vector $\mathbf{x}_t$, the objective is to recover estimates of the unknown and unobservable K-dimensional state vector $\boldsymbol{\beta}_t$, and the noise components ε_{tk} and e_t. In such a model, the number of parameters to be recovered is always greater than the number of data points and thus the model is ill-posed or underdetermined. As conventional procedures cannot handle this situation unless creative assumptions or restrictions are added, we introduce below a GME formulation for such problems. In formulating a basis for recovering these unknowns, we extend the stationary pure and noise inverse problem formulations of Chapters 3–12 and use a multiple entropy criterion function that involves the entropies of the unknowns $\boldsymbol{\beta}_t$, e_t and $\boldsymbol{\varepsilon}_t$.

13.3.1 THE GME–GCE FORMULATION AND SOLUTION

Within the framework of (13.3.1) and (13.3.2), and consistent with Chapter 6, we first reparameterize $\boldsymbol{\beta}_t$, e_t and $\boldsymbol{\varepsilon}_t$. The reparameterized unknown parameters are presented, in scalar form, in the following equations:

$$\sum_m z_{tkm} p_{tkm} = \beta_{tk}, \qquad \text{for } k = 1, 2, \ldots, K; \quad t = 1, 2, \ldots, T \tag{13.3.3}$$

$$\sum_j v_{tj}^e w_{tj}^e = e_t, \qquad \text{for } t = 1, 2, \ldots, T \tag{13.3.4}$$

$$\sum_i v_{tki}^\varepsilon w_{tki}^\varepsilon = \varepsilon_{tk}, \qquad \text{for } k = 1, 2, \ldots, K; \quad t = 1, 2, \ldots, T \tag{13.3.5}$$

where $\mathbf{z}$, $\mathbf{v}^e$ and $\mathbf{v}^\varepsilon$ are the support spaces with $M \geq 2$, $J \geq 2$ and $I \geq 2$ for $\boldsymbol{\beta}_t$, e_t and $\boldsymbol{\varepsilon}_t$ respectively.

Under this reparameterization, the observation equation (13.3.1) may be specified as

$$y_t = \mathbf{x}_t' Z_t \mathbf{p}_{tk} + \mathbf{v}_t^{e\prime} \mathbf{w}_t^e \tag{13.3.6}$$

and the state (system) equation (13.3.2) may be specified as

$$\boldsymbol{\beta}_t = f_{tk}(Z_{t-1} \mathbf{p}_{t-1,k}) + \mathbf{v}_t^{\varepsilon\prime} \mathbf{w}_{tk}^\varepsilon \tag{13.3.7a}$$

or in linear form as

$$\boldsymbol{\beta}_t = A Z_{t-1} \mathbf{p}_{t-1} + \mathbf{v}_t^{\varepsilon\prime} \mathbf{w}_{tk}^\varepsilon \tag{13.3.7b}$$

Given the reparameterized model (13.3.6) and (13.3.7) and a specific $\mathbf{f}$ the *non-stationary* GCE problem may be stated, using a criterion with three components, as

$$\min_{\{p_{tkm}\},\, \{w_{tj}^e\},\, \{w_{tki}^\varepsilon\}} I(\mathbf{p}, \mathbf{w}^e, \mathbf{w}^\varepsilon)$$

$$= \sum_t \sum_k \sum_m p_{tkm} \ln(p_{tkm}/q_{tkm}) + \sum_t \sum_j w_{tj}^e \ln(w_{tj}^e/u_{tj}^e) + \sum_t \sum_k \sum_i w_{tki}^\varepsilon \ln(w_{tki}^\varepsilon/u_{tki}^\varepsilon) \tag{13.3.8}$$

subject to the data

$$\sum_k \sum_m z_{tkm} p_{tkm} x_{kt} + \sum_j v^e_{tj} w^e_{tj} = y_t, \qquad \text{for } t = 1, 2, \ldots, T \qquad (13.3.9)$$

$$\beta_{tk} = f_{tk}\left(\sum_m z_{t-1,\,km} p_{t-1,\,km} \right) + \sum_i w^\varepsilon_{tki} z^\varepsilon_{tki},$$
$$\text{for } t = 2, 3, \ldots, T \quad \text{and} \quad k = 1, 2, \ldots, K \quad (13.3.10)$$

and the normalization–adding-up constraints

$$\sum_m p_{tkm} = 1, \qquad \text{for } k = 1, 2, \ldots, K \quad \text{and } t = 1, 2, \ldots, T \qquad (13.3.11)$$

$$\sum_j w^e_{tj} = 1, \qquad \text{for } t = 1, 2, \ldots, T \qquad (13.3.12)$$

$$\sum_i w^\varepsilon_{tki} = 1, \qquad \text{for } k = 1, 2, \ldots, K; \quad t = 2, 3, \ldots, T \qquad (13.3.13)$$

The prior information on the errors is, in the absence of other information, specified as $u^e_{tj} = 1/J$ for all $j = 1, 2, \ldots, J$ and for all t, and $u^\varepsilon_{tki} = 1/I$ for all $i = 1, 2, \ldots, I$ and for all t and k. The parameter spaces v^e_{tj} and v^ε_{tki} are specified to be uniformly *symmetric around zero.* The prior information on the β_{tk} is specified as q_{tkm}. If no prior information exists, we specify $q_{tkm} = 1/M$ for all t, k and m, where z_{tkm} is chosen such that it spans a sensible parameter state-space for each β_{tk}. If initial information such as non-negativity, non-positivity or an upper or lower bound exists for β_{tk}, this may be included specifying z_{tkm}.

Corresponding to the optimization problem (13.3.8)–(13.3.13), the Lagrangian function is

$$\begin{aligned} L = I(\mathbf{p}, \mathbf{w}^e, \mathbf{w}^e) &+ \sum_t \lambda_t \left[y_t - \sum_k \sum_m z_{tkm} p_{tkm} x_{kt} - \sum_j v^e_{tj} w^e_{tj} \right] \\ &+ \sum_t \sum_k \mu_{tk} \left[\sum_m z_{tkm} p_{tkm} - f_{tk}\left(\sum_m z_{t-1,\,km} p_{t-1,\,k,\,m} \right) - \sum_i v^\varepsilon_{tki} w^\varepsilon_{tki} \right] \\ &+ \sum_t \sum_k \delta_{tk} \left[1 - \sum_m p_{tkm} \right] + \sum_t \alpha_t \left[1 - \sum_j w^e_{tj} \right] \\ &+ \sum_t \sum_k \rho_{tk} \left[1 - \sum_i w^\varepsilon_{tki} \right] \end{aligned} \qquad (13.3.14)$$

with the optimal conditions

$$\frac{\partial L}{\partial p_{tkm}} = \ln(\tilde{p}_{tkm}/q_{tkm}) + 1 - \tilde{\lambda}_t z_{tkm} x_{kt} - \tilde{\delta}_{tk} + \tilde{\mu}_{tk} z_{tkm} - \tilde{\mu}_{t+1,k} f'_{t+1,k}(\cdot) = 0, \quad \text{for } k = 1, 2, \ldots, K, \quad m = 1, 2, \ldots, M, \quad t = 1, 2, \ldots, T \tag{13.3.15}$$

$$\frac{\partial L}{\partial w^e_{tj}} = \ln(\tilde{w}^e_{tj}/u^e_{tj}) + 1 - \tilde{\lambda}_t v^e_{tj} - \tilde{\alpha}_t = 0, \qquad \text{for } t = 1, 2, \ldots, T, \quad j = 1, 2, \ldots, J \tag{13.3.16}$$

$$\frac{\partial L}{\partial w^\varepsilon_{tki}} = \ln(\tilde{w}^\varepsilon_{tki}/u^\varepsilon_{tki}) + 1 - \tilde{\rho}_{tk} - \tilde{\mu}_{tk} v^\varepsilon_{tki} = 0, \quad \text{for } t = 2, 3, \ldots, T, \quad k = 1, 2, \ldots, K, \quad i = 1, 2, \ldots, I \tag{13.3.17}$$

$$\frac{\partial L}{\partial \lambda_t} = y_t - \sum_k \sum_m z_{tkm} \tilde{p}_{tkm} x_{kt} - \sum_j v^e_{tj} \tilde{w}^e_{tj} = 0, \qquad \text{for } t = 1, 2, \ldots, T \tag{13.3.18}$$

$$\frac{\partial L}{\partial \delta_{tk}} = 1 - \sum_m \tilde{p}_{tkm} = 0, \qquad \text{for } t = 1, 2, \ldots, T, \quad k = 1, 2, \ldots, K \tag{13.3.19}$$

$$\frac{\partial L}{\partial \alpha_t} = 1 - \sum_j \tilde{w}^e_{tj} = 0, \qquad \text{for } t = 1, 2, \ldots, T \tag{13.3.20}$$

$$\frac{\partial L}{\partial \rho_{tk}} = 1 - \sum_i \tilde{w}^\varepsilon_{tki} = 0, \qquad \text{for } t = 1, 2, \ldots, T, \quad k = 1, 2, \ldots, K \tag{13.3.21}$$

$$\frac{\partial L}{\partial \mu_{tk}} = \sum_m z_{tkm} \tilde{p}_{tkm} - f_{tk}(\cdot) - \sum_i v^\varepsilon_{tki} \tilde{w}^\varepsilon_{tki} = 0, \quad \text{for } t = 2, \ldots, T, \quad k = 1, 2, \ldots, K \tag{13.3.22}$$

where $f'_{tk}(\cdot) = \partial f(\cdot)/\partial p_{t-1,k,m}$.

Solving the system yields the solution

$$\tilde{p}_{tkm} = \frac{q_{tkm}}{\Omega^\beta_{tk}(\tilde{\lambda}_t, \tilde{\mu}_{t+1,k}, \tilde{\mu}_{tk})} \exp[\tilde{\lambda}_t z_{tkm} x_{kt} - \tilde{\mu}_{tk} z_{tkm} + \tilde{\mu}_{t+1,k} f'_{t+1,k}(\cdot)] \tag{13.3.23}$$

where

$$\Omega^\beta_{tk}(\tilde{\lambda}_t, \tilde{\mu}_{t+1,k}, \tilde{\mu}_{tk}) = \sum_m q_{tkm} \exp[\tilde{\lambda}_t z^\beta_{tkm} x_{kt} - \tilde{\mu}_{tk} z^\beta_{tkm} + \tilde{\mu}_{t+1,k} f'_{t+1,k}(\cdot)] \tag{13.3.24}$$

and

$$\tilde{w}^e_{tj} = \frac{u^e_{tj}}{\Psi^e_t(\tilde{\lambda}_t)} \exp[\tilde{\lambda}_t v^e_{tj}] \tag{13.3.25}$$

where

$$\Psi^e_t(\tilde{\lambda}_t) = \sum_j u^e_{tj} \exp[\tilde{\lambda}_t v^e_{tj}] \tag{13.3.26}$$

and

$$\tilde{w}^\varepsilon_{tki} = \frac{u^\varepsilon_{tki}}{\Psi^\varepsilon_{tk}(\tilde{\mu}_{tk})} \exp[\tilde{\mu}_{tk} v^\varepsilon_{tki}] \tag{13.3.27}$$

where

$$\Psi^\varepsilon_{tk}(\tilde{\mu}_{tk}) = \sum_i u^\varepsilon_{tki} \exp[\tilde{\mu}_{tk} v^\varepsilon_{tki}] \tag{13.3.28}$$

The solution in (13.3.23), (13.3.25) and (13.3.27) yields

$$\tilde{\beta}_{tk} = \sum_m z_{tkm} \tilde{p}_{tkm} \tag{13.3.29}$$

$$\tilde{e}_t = \sum_j v^e_{tj} \tilde{w}^e_{tj} \tag{13.3.30}$$

$$\tilde{\varepsilon}_{tk} = \sum_i v^\varepsilon_{tki} \tilde{w}^\varepsilon_{tki} \tag{13.3.31}$$

Note, in contrast to regularization procedures that were discussed in Chapter 8 and are traditionally used for ill-posed inverse problems (Titterington, 1985; O'Sullivan, 1986), this formulation of the non-stationary inverse model with noise does not contain a smoothing parameter. Further, and the unknowns in equations (13.3.23), (13.3.25) and (13.3.27), together with the unknowns in (13.3.29), (13.3.30) and (13.3.31), are recovered simultaneously and internally and without the usual assumptions regarding the distributions of the error terms. The $\tilde{p}_{tkm}$, $\tilde{w}^e_{tj}$ and $\tilde{w}^\varepsilon_{tki}$ provide, based on available information, a basis for estimation, inference and assessing the informational content of the model. Finally, the GCE model developed here applies for both linear and non-linear state equations, where in the non-linear case one has to specify f_{tk}. A non-linear example is provided in Chapter 14.

If no prior information exists, instead of using the generalized cross-entropy as is expressed in the objective function (13.3.8), we can use the GME formulation, which is just

$$\max_{\{p_{tkm}\}, \{w^e_{tj}\}, \{w^\varepsilon_{tki}\}} H(\mathbf{p}, \mathbf{w})$$

$$= -\sum_t \sum_k \sum_m p_{tkm} \ln(p_{tkm}) - \sum_t \sum_j w^e_{tj} \ln(w^e_{tj}) - \sum_t \sum_k \sum_i w^\varepsilon_{tki} \ln(w^\varepsilon_{tki}) \tag{13.3.32}$$

subject to (13.3.9)–(13.3.13).

This yields GME results that are equivalent to the GCE results when all the prior weights q_{tkm}, u^{ε}_{tki} and u^{e}_{tj} are uniform.

13.4 THEORETICAL AND EMPIRICAL ILLUSTRATIVE EXAMPLES

13.4.1 EXAMPLE 1

To reflect the operational nature of the formulation developed in Section 13.3, consider the problem of recovering the unknown parameters of a non-stationary aggregate linear demand relation

$$\begin{aligned} y_t &= x_{1t}\beta_1 + x_{2t}\beta_2 + x_{3t}\beta_3 + x_{4t}\beta_4 + e_t = \mathbf{x}_t'\boldsymbol{\beta}_t + e_t \\ &= \mathbf{x}_t' Z_t \mathbf{p}_{tk} + \mathbf{v}_t^{e\prime}\mathbf{w}_t^{e}, \qquad t = 1, 2, \ldots, T, \quad k = 1, 2, 3, 4 \end{aligned} \tag{13.4.1a}$$

$$\boldsymbol{\beta}_t = A\boldsymbol{\beta}_{t-1} + \boldsymbol{\varepsilon}_t = \boldsymbol{\alpha}' Z_t \mathbf{p}_{t-1,k} + \mathbf{v}_t^{\varepsilon\prime}\mathbf{w}_{tk}^{\varepsilon}, \qquad t = 2, 3, \ldots, T, \quad k = 1, 2, 3, 4 \tag{13.4.1b}$$

where y_t is consumption, x_{1t} is price, x_{2t} is the price of a substitute good, x_{3t} is income and x_{4t} is the price of a commodity that could either be a substitute or complement, e_t is a noise component associated with the observation equation, $\boldsymbol{\alpha}$ is a vector composed of the diagonal elements of A and ε_{kt} is a noise component associated with each β_{tk} for the system-process equation. Our objective is to recover the unknowns β_{tk} and α_k.

To provide a basis for gauging the performance of the GME estimator in a non-stationary, ill-posed setting, the following sampling experiment with 500 repetitions was designed. Using the price and income values for x_{tk} the outcomes y_t were generated using $\boldsymbol{\beta}_1 = (-0.6, 0.8, 1.5, 0.0)'$, $\boldsymbol{\alpha} = (0.5, 1.5, 1.0, 0.0)'$ and the noise components $e_t \sim \text{N}(0, 1)$ and $\varepsilon_{tk} \sim \text{N}(0, 0.25)$. In specifying the supports for $\boldsymbol{\beta}$ we incorporate our knowledge of the magnitude and signs of the parameters. That is, the parameter spaces for the $\mathbf{z}_k$ are $\mathbf{z}_{k=1} = (-0.8, -0.7, \ldots, 0)'$, $\mathbf{z}_{k=2} = (0, 2, \ldots, 16)'$, $\mathbf{z}_{k=3} = (1.1, 1.2, \ldots, 1.9)'$ and $\mathbf{z}_{k=4} = (-0.4, -0.3, \ldots, 0.4)'$. The errors supports $\mathbf{v}^e$ and $\mathbf{v}^{\varepsilon}$ are symmetric around zero.

Using the non-stationary GME formulation (13.3.32), subject to (13.4.1) and the adding-up constraints (13.3.11)–(13.3.13) as the basis for recovering $\boldsymbol{\beta}_1$ and $\boldsymbol{\alpha}$, we obtain the results given in Table 13.4.1 along with the corresponding mean squared errors of $\tilde{\boldsymbol{\beta}}_t$ and $\hat{\boldsymbol{\alpha}}$, are the averages of

$$\text{MSE}(\hat{\boldsymbol{\beta}}) \equiv \left[\sum_t \sum_k (\tilde{\beta}_{tk} - \beta_{tk})^2\right] \Big/ T, \qquad \text{MSE}(\tilde{\boldsymbol{\alpha}}) = \sum_k (\tilde{\alpha}_k - \alpha_k)^2.$$

Table 13.4.1 Estimates of $\hat{\beta}_{tk}$, $\hat{\alpha}_k$, MSE($\hat{\boldsymbol{\beta}}$) and MSE($\hat{\boldsymbol{\alpha}}$) for different levels of t where $e_t \sim N(0, 1)$ and $\varepsilon_{tk} \sim N(0, 0.25)$

$t = 2$		$t = 3$		$t = 4$		$t = 5$	
$\hat{\beta}_{1k}$	$\hat{\alpha}_k$	$\hat{\beta}_{1k}$	$\hat{\alpha}_k$	$\hat{\beta}_{1k}$	$\hat{\alpha}_k$	$\hat{\beta}_{1k}$	$\hat{\alpha}_k$
−0.47	0.53	−0.47	0.53	−0.47	0.52	−0.47	0.52
0.73	1.14	0.73	1.15	0.73	1.65	0.73	1.48
1.53	0.95	1.53	0.95	1.53	0.98	1.53	0.98
0.01	(0.00)	0.01	(0.00)	0.01	(0.00)	0.01	(0.00)
MSE($\hat{\boldsymbol{\beta}}$) = 0.0804		MSE($\hat{\boldsymbol{\beta}}$) = 0.2908		MSE($\hat{\boldsymbol{\beta}}$) = 0.2642		MSE($\hat{\boldsymbol{\beta}}$) = 0.3819	
MSE($\hat{\boldsymbol{\alpha}}$) = 0.1353		MSE($\hat{\boldsymbol{\alpha}}$) = 0.1272		MSE($\hat{\boldsymbol{\alpha}}$) = 0.0233		MSE($\hat{\boldsymbol{\alpha}}$) = 0.0013	

When the specified statistical model is consistent with the underlying non-stationary data generating process, the GME procedure for the underdetermined statistical model performs well for all T and as T increases the accuracy of the recovered parameters increases. Note, however, that the MSE($\hat{\boldsymbol{\beta}}$) measure reported is dependent on MSE($\tilde{\boldsymbol{\alpha}}$) since it measures the accuracy of the *whole* system for $t = 1, 2, \ldots, T$ and as MSE($\tilde{\boldsymbol{\alpha}}$) decreases MSE($\tilde{\boldsymbol{\beta}}_t$) decreases. The results of Table 13.4.1 are compared with two special cases of the same non-stationary model. Table 13.4.2 presents the case where $\boldsymbol{\varepsilon}_t = \mathbf{0}$, and the pure case where $e_t = 0$ and $\boldsymbol{\varepsilon}_t = \mathbf{0}$ is presented in Table 13.4.3. In the pure case for $T = 7$ the unknown parameters β_k and $\boldsymbol{\alpha}$ are exactly recovered and are consistent with that of mathematical inversion.

Note that $\boldsymbol{\alpha}$ is not reparameterized and the recovered $\hat{\boldsymbol{\alpha}}$ are point estimates. The reason for not reparameterizing $\boldsymbol{\alpha}$ is the following. Each $\boldsymbol{\beta}_k$ is changing over time according to α_k. Further, each $\boldsymbol{\beta}_k$ is represented as $\mathbf{z}'_{tk}\boldsymbol{\beta}_{tk}$, where the objective is to maximize the entropy of $\mathbf{p}_k$ for each k. As α_k just transforms the β_{tk} to the next state, $\beta_{t+1,k}$, there is no need to maximize the entropy of some distribution defined on the support for $\boldsymbol{\alpha}$ since this entropy is *already* maximized indirectly via $\mathbf{p}$.

Finally, it is interesting to note that if this model had been misspecified as a stationary one, where $\boldsymbol{\beta}_t = \boldsymbol{\beta}$, the entropy-based statistical model for recovering $\boldsymbol{\beta}$ would be

$$y_t = \mathbf{x}_t'\bar{\boldsymbol{\beta}} + e_t = \mathbf{x}_t'\mathbf{z}'\mathbf{p} + \mathbf{v}^e\mathbf{w}_t^e \tag{13.4.2}$$

In this case the recovered forecast errors *grow* over time, thereby suggesting that the stationary-fixed parameters model is *inconsistent* with the data analyzed.

13.4.2 EXAMPLE 2

To indicate the applicability of the model developed in Section 13.3, we follow Normand and Tritchler (1992) and analyze the observations on annual US

Table 13.4.2 Estimates of $\hat{\beta}_{tk}$ and $\hat{\alpha}_k$ for different levels of $t = 1, 2, \ldots, T$ where $e_t \sim N(0, 1)$, $\boldsymbol{\varepsilon}_t = \mathbf{0}$ and $\mathbf{v}^e = (-3, 0, 3)'$

$t = 2$		$t = 3$		$t = 4$		$t = 5$		$t = 6$		$t = 7$		$t = 8$	
$\hat{\beta}_{1k}$	$\hat{\alpha}_k$	$\hat{\beta}_{1k}$	$\hat{\alpha}_k$	$\hat{\beta}_{1k}$	$\hat{\alpha}_k$	$\hat{\beta}_{1k}$	$\hat{\alpha}_k$	$\hat{\beta}_{1k}$	$\hat{\alpha}_k$	$\hat{\beta}_{1k}$	$\hat{\alpha}_k$	$\hat{\beta}_{1k}$	$\hat{\alpha}_k$
−0.47	0.53	−0.48	0.51	−0.48	0.52	−0.48	0.51	−0.49	0.51	−0.51	0.50	−0.53	0.50
0.76	1.35	0.74	1.39	0.73	1.51	0.71	1.55	0.73	1.54	0.76	1.51	0.78	1.51
1.55	1.02	1.60	0.98	1.61	0.96	1.63	0.95	1.61	0.96	1.55	0.98	1.52	0.99
0.02	(3.99)	0.06	(0.96)	0.04	(0.51)	0.05	−0.08	0.06	(−0.15)	0.04	(−0.01)	0.03	(0.15)
$MSE(\hat{\boldsymbol{\beta}}) = 0.0327$		$MSE(\hat{\boldsymbol{\beta}}) = 0.0717$		$MSE(\hat{\boldsymbol{\beta}}) = 0.0309$		$MSE(\hat{\boldsymbol{\beta}}) = 0.0220$		$MSE(\hat{\boldsymbol{\beta}}) = 0.0210$		$MSE(\hat{\boldsymbol{\beta}}) = 0.0093$		$MSE(\hat{\boldsymbol{\beta}}) = 0.0077$	
$MSE(\hat{\boldsymbol{\alpha}}) = 0.0232$		$MSE(\hat{\boldsymbol{\alpha}}) = 0.0126$		$MSE(\hat{\boldsymbol{\alpha}}) = 0.0021$		$MSE(\hat{\boldsymbol{\alpha}}) = 0.0052$		$MSE(\hat{\boldsymbol{\alpha}}) = 0.0027$		$MSE(\hat{\boldsymbol{\alpha}}) = 0.0006$		$MSE(\hat{\boldsymbol{\alpha}}) = 0.0003$	

Table 13.4.3 Estimates of $\hat{\beta}_{tk}$ and $\hat{\alpha}_k$ for different levels of t where $e_t = 0$ and $\boldsymbol{\varepsilon}_t = \mathbf{0}$

$t=2$		$t=3$		$t=4$		$t=5$		$t=6$	
$\hat{\beta}_{1k}$	$\hat{\alpha}_k$	$\hat{\beta}_{1k}$	$\hat{\alpha}_k$	$\hat{\beta}_{1k}$	$\hat{\alpha}_k$	$\hat{\beta}_{1k}$	$\hat{\alpha}_k$	$\hat{\beta}_{1k}$	$\hat{\alpha}_k$
−0.47	0.53	−0.48	0.47	−0.47	0.52	−0.60	0.50	−0.62	0.49
0.76	1.37	0.75	1.50	0.73	1.56	0.80	1.50	0.80	1.50
1.56	1.02	1.58	0.97	1.62	0.95	1.50	1.00	1.50	1.00
0.02	(1.33)	0.03	(1.25)	0.04	(0)	0.06	(0)	−0.02	(0)
MSE($\hat{\boldsymbol{\beta}}$)=0.0317		MSE($\hat{\boldsymbol{\beta}}$)=0.020		MSE($\hat{\boldsymbol{\beta}}$)=0.0155		MSE($\hat{\boldsymbol{\beta}}$)=0.0008		MSE($\hat{\boldsymbol{\beta}}$)=0.0002	
MSE($\hat{\boldsymbol{\alpha}}$)=0.0180		MSE($\hat{\boldsymbol{\alpha}}$)=0.0018		MSE($\hat{\boldsymbol{\alpha}}$)=0.0061		MSE($\hat{\boldsymbol{\alpha}}$)=0.0000		MSE($\hat{\boldsymbol{\alpha}}$)=0.0001	

milk production, y_t, and the total number of cows, x_t, for the years 1970–82 that are presented in Figure 13.4.1. These data were analyzed by Normand and Tritchler (NT) with the objective of showing the use of an updating Bayesian network model in sorting out changing productivity over time. They used, in the context of (13.2.1) and (13.2.2), the linear growth model

$$y_t = \mathbf{x}_t'\boldsymbol{\theta}_t + e_t = [x_t \quad 0]\begin{bmatrix}\mu_t\\ \beta_t\end{bmatrix} + e_t = x_t\mu_t + e_t \tag{13.4.3}$$

and

$$\boldsymbol{\theta}_t = G\boldsymbol{\theta}_{t-1} + \boldsymbol{\varepsilon}_t = \begin{bmatrix}1 & 1\\ 0 & 1\end{bmatrix}\begin{bmatrix}\mu_{t-1}\\ \beta_{t-1}\end{bmatrix} + \begin{bmatrix}\varepsilon_{t1}\\ \varepsilon_{t2}\end{bmatrix} \tag{13.4.4}$$

where it is *assumed* that $e_t \sim N(0, 1)$ for all t and $\boldsymbol{\varepsilon}_t \sim N\left[\begin{pmatrix}0\\0\end{pmatrix}, \begin{pmatrix}0.15 & 0.1\\ 0.1 & 0.1\end{pmatrix}\right]$.

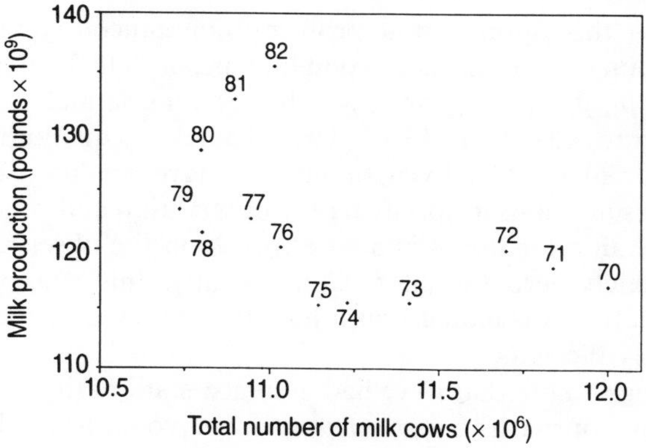

Figure 13.4.1 Annual milk production in the US, 1970–82

For $\boldsymbol{\theta}$, they used a vague prior $\boldsymbol{\theta}_0 = \begin{bmatrix} 10 \\ -1 \end{bmatrix}$ and for the covariance matrix, they used $S_0 = \begin{pmatrix} 100 & 0 \\ 0 & 10 \end{pmatrix}$. Thus, they take G as given and assuming $\boldsymbol{\theta}_0$, S_0, $\sigma^2_{y_t}$ and $\text{Cov}(\boldsymbol{\varepsilon}_t)$ are *known*, they use the data given in Figure 13.4.1 to estimate the level and growth components μ_t and β_t for $t = 1, 2, \ldots, 13$.

If we accept the structure of the Normand and Tritchler model (13.4.3) and (13.4.4) we may, consistent with the GME model of Section 3, reparameterize the statistical model as

$$y_t = x_t \mathbf{z}^{\mu'} \mathbf{p}_t^{\mu} + \mathbf{v}^{e'} \mathbf{w}_t^{e} \tag{13.4.5}$$

$$\mu_t = \mu_{t-1} + \beta_{t-1} + \mathbf{v}^{\varepsilon 1'} \mathbf{w}_t^{\varepsilon 1} \tag{13.4.6}$$

$$\beta_t = \beta_{t-1} + \mathbf{v}^{\varepsilon 2'} \mathbf{w}_t^{\varepsilon 2} \tag{13.4.7}$$

where, consistent with this problem,

$$\mathbf{z}^{\mu} = (8, 9, \ldots, 14)', \qquad \mathbf{v}^{e} = (-50{,}000,\ 0,\ 50{,}000) \quad \text{and} \quad \mathbf{v}^{\varepsilon} = (-1, 0, 1)'$$

is used as the relevant parameter spaces. Based on this specification we may within the context of Section 13.3, formulate the GME problem as

$$\max_{\{p^{\mu}_{tkm}\},\, \{w^{e}_{tj}\},\, \{w^{\varepsilon}_{tki}\}} H = -\sum_t \sum_m p^{\mu}_{tm} \ln(p^{\mu}_{tm}) - \sum_t \sum_j w^{e}_{tj} \ln(w^{e}_{tj}) - \sum_t \sum_k \sum_i w^{\varepsilon}_{tki} \ln(w^{\varepsilon}_{tki}) \tag{13.4.8}$$

subject to the stochastic consistency and process constraints (13.4.5)–(13.4.7), and the corresponding adding-up constraints on the probabilities, (13.3.11)–(13.3.13).

A solution to this optimization problem simultaneously yields estimates of the probabilities, and the corresponding means (13.3.29)–(13.3.31) yield estimates of μ_t, β_t, β_{t-1}, e_t, ε_{t1} and ε_{t2}. The resulting $\hat{\mu}_t$ and $\hat{\beta}_t = 0.2125 + \varepsilon_{t2}$ are given in Figures 13.4.2 and 13.4.3. These figures are qualitatively similar to the results reported by NT. Even though we have not used the traditional distributional assumptions in specifying the observation and process equations. The entropy solution for the estimated errors $\hat{e}_t$, in the observation equation, were approximately zero for all t. Consequently, this suggests that if the observation equation was modeled as a pure inverse relation, the results would be approximately the same.

It is interesting to note that if we had assumed stationarity ($\mu_t = \mu$) and had used the entropy approach to recover μ, then we would have obtained

$$y_t = x_t 10.902 + \hat{e}_t \tag{13.4.9}$$

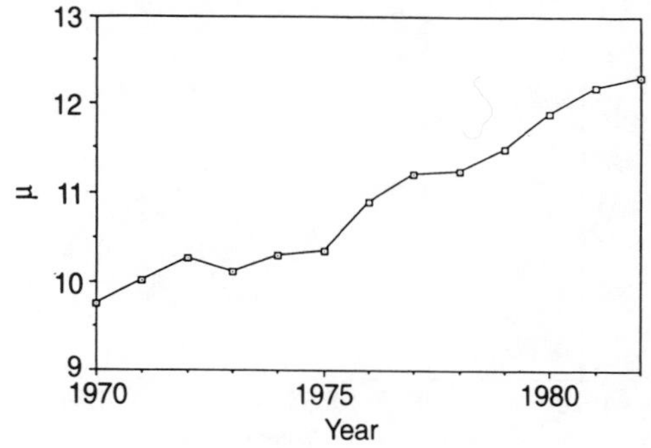

Figure 13.4.2 Estimated annual average productivity per year

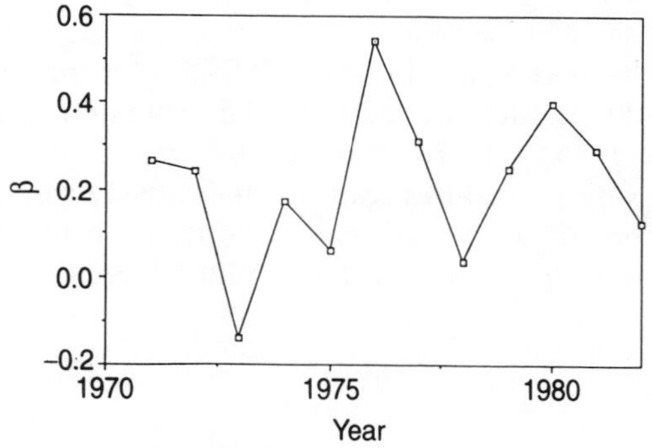

Figure 13.4.3 Estimated annual productivity growth

where

$$\hat{\mathbf{e}} = \mathbf{v}^{e\prime}\hat{\mathbf{w}}_t^e = (-13{,}818.3,\ -10{,}482.2,\ -7{,}529.7,\ -8{,}934.8,\ -6{,}844.7,\ -6{,}148.2,\ -92.1,\ 3{,}330.4,\ 3{,}685.5,\ 6{,}327,\ 10{,}674.1,\ 13{,}958.8,\ 15{,}461.9)' \tag{13.4.10}$$

Under this stationary specification the recovered errors are ordered over time and suggest that a fixed parameter model is not consistent with the data.

Alternatively, if knowledge of the system had suggested that a multiplicative adjustment equation was appropriate, a dynamic model of the following type might have been used:

$$y_t = x_t \mu_t + e_t \tag{13.4.11}$$

$$\mu_t = \alpha \mu_{t-1} + \varepsilon_t \tag{13.4.12}$$

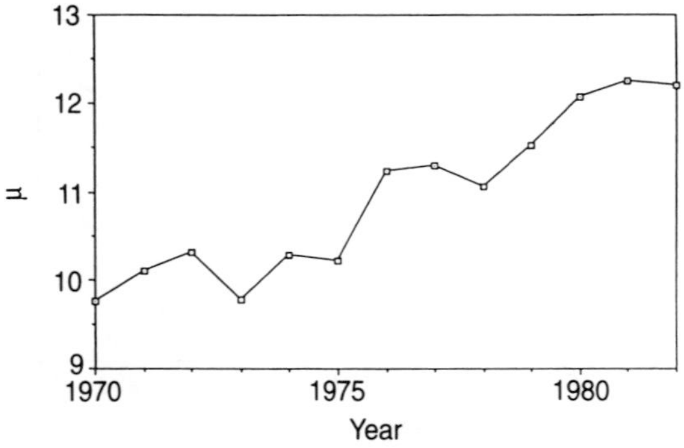

Figure 13.4.4 Estimated average annual productivity for the multiplicative case

where μ_t and α are the unknown parameters. If the GME approach to recovering information from this model is used then the estimated μ_t are presented in Figure 13.4.4, where $\hat{\alpha} = 1.0197$. Thus, the full set of dynamic models and information processing procedures lead to qualitatively similar estimates and conclusions. However, the statistical model specification requirements and the approaches to estimation and inference are quite different.

13.5 REMARKS

Most economic data are generated from a system of relations that are stochastic, dynamic and non-stationary. The dynamic and non-stationary characteristics mean that in many cases the number of unknown parameters is greater than the number of data points and thus the resulting economic-statistical model is ill-posed. For problems of this nature the entropy formalism provides an efficient basis for information recovery and inference based only on the information contained in the data and whatever non-sample-constraint information that is available. In order to obtain a solution traditional methods for handling ill-posed inverse problems with noise we must, in many cases, make use of a range of unsupported distributional and other assumptions that may have negative consequences for estimation and forecasting and are hard to implement. The methodology developed here is operational and a large number of efficient solution algorithms exist to handle a range of problems.

The model presented provides a general framework for recovering the parameters and forecasting for a large class of dynamic linear economic models and data sets. Some of the different special cases or variants of the model are:

- *A stationary model with noise or a pure non-stationary model.* In some cases the apparent noise in the observation equation (13.3.1) may be due to the non-stationarity of the parameters governing the system (see Chapter 5). Therefore, given a set of time-series observations, it may be possible to capture the data generation process as a pure non-stationary model instead of a stationary model with noise. In other words some stationary models with noise may actually be misspecified pure non-stationary models. Under this scenario the non-stationary GME model of Section 13.3 may be respecified without the errors e_t and ε_{tk}. Specifically, in the criterion H and in the constraints, arguments related to the errors are deleted. The resulting *pure* non-stationary model yields an exact mathematical solution for the well-posed pure non-stationary case.
- *A dynamic time series–cross-section model.* If we define $t = 1, 2, \ldots, T$ as the number of time periods and i as the number of cross section observations for each time period t, then we may define the data generation process for the observation equation (13.3.1) as $y_{it} = \beta_{1it} + \beta_{2it}x_{2it} + \beta_{3it}x_{3it} + \cdots + \beta_{Kit}x_{Kit} + e_{it}$ where y_{it} are the observed outcomes over $t = 1, 2, \ldots, T$, $i = 1, 2, \ldots, N$, the x_{Kit} are the known design variables and the e_{it} reflect the noise components for all i and t. This means that in this model the response parameters may vary over all i and t (see Chapter 9).
- *A non-stationary random coefficient model* with observation equation $y_t = x(\boldsymbol{\beta}_t + \boldsymbol{\delta}) + e_t$, where $\boldsymbol{\delta}$ is a random vector.
- *A control formulation of the linear dynamic system* (13.2.1) *and* (13.2.2). This problem is formulated in Chapter 14.

The GME–GCE methodology permits the modeling of a non-stationary process and offers efficient ways of including non-sample information and consistency relations. Consequently, this simple formulation contains the ingredients usually necessary for achieving forecasting precision.

REFERENCES

Broemeling, L. D. (1985) *Bayesian Analysis of Linear Models.* Marcel Dekker, New York.

Kalman, R. E. (1960) A new approach to linear filtering and prediction problems. *Transactions of the American Society of Mechanical Engineers, Series D., Journal of Basic Engineering* **82**, 34–45.

Leybourne, S. J. (1993) Estimation and testing of time-varying coefficient regression models in the presence of linear restrictions. *Journal of Forecasting* **12**, 49–62.

Maybeck, P. S. (1979) *Stochastic Models, Estimation and Control.* Academic Press, New York.

Normand, S. L. and Tritchler, D. (1992) Parameter updating in a Bayes network. *Journal of the American Statistical Association* **87**, 1109–15.

O'Sullivan, F. (1986) A statistical perspective on ill-posed inverse problems. *Statistical Science* **1**, 502–27.

Rosenberg, B. (1973) A survey of stochastic parameter regression. *Annals of Economic and Social Measurement* **2**, 381–97.

Swamy, P. A. V. B. (1970) Efficient inference in a random coefficient model. *Econometrica* **38**, 311–23.

Swamy, P. A. V. B. and Tinsley, P. A. (1980) Linear prediction and estimation methods for models with stationary stochastic coefficients. *Journal of Econometrics* **12**, 103–42.

Titterington, D. M. (1985) Common structures of smoothing techniques in statistics. *International Statistical Review* **53**, 141–70.

CHAPTER 14

Linear and non-linear dynamic systems with control

14.1 INTRODUCTION

In the previous chapter we developed a GME–GCE formulation for estimation of the unknown parameters of dynamic, discrete systems. In this chapter we generalize the study to linear and non-linear dynamic discrete-time models with control. This chapter is based on Golan, Judge and Karp (1996) and formulates three different, but related, dynamic models.

The first problem involves estimation of a dynamic linear system with control, where the observations on the state are noisy. This model is widely used in engineering, where the Kalman filter (Kalman, 1960) is usually employed, and in economics, where it is particularly useful analyzing the economics of natural resources (Mangel, 1985; Berck and Johns, 1991). For example in the natural resources area, we rarely observe the state variable. In such cases we have to use imperfect and indirect observations of other variables related to the state variable. Consequently, if we cannot observe the stock of fish, or some other renewable resource, but we do observe the cost of harvest, then we have to use these indirect observations in the estimation procedure. In this chapter we study the situation where it is necessary to estimate a set of parameters in the state equation in addition to the values of the state variable. In that case, there are likely to be a large number of unknowns relative to the number of observations, and classical estimation methods are inadequate. The GME approach provides an alternative in this seemingly indeterminate situation.

The second problem involves noisy state observations where the state equations and the observation equations are non-linear. The objective is to estimate the unknown parameters of the state and observation equations together with the unknown values of the state variables.

The third problem involves estimation of the parameters of the objective function, such as an agent's utility function, as well as estimation of the state equation in a linear-quadratic (LQ) control problem. This is known as the *inverse control problem.* Given any linear state equation and linear control rule, there exists a continuum of LQ objective functions for which the observed control rule constitutes the optimal solution to the LQ problem (Jameson and Kreindler, 1973). This means that the inverse problem is unidentified. More data can only improve estimates of parameters of the state equation and the control rule, but *cannot* overcome the identification problem.

The LQ control problem has been widely used as a basis for estimating dynamic econometric models (Sargent, 1978; Hansen and Sargent, 1980; Chow, 1981; Blanchard, 1983). In applications, zero-restrictions on parameter values are used to insure identification. In many cases these restrictions appear natural. However, when the LQ model is interpreted as a second order approximation to a general utility function which involves the state and control variables, the restrictions such as those used by Fulton and Karp (1989) may appear arbitrary. With the GME approach, it is not necessary to impose these restrictions.

The next section discusses the estimation problem of an imperfectly observed linear dynamic system with control, and provides an application of the procedure. Following sections deal with GME formulations and applications of the non-linear state equation and the inverse LQ problems where formulations, based on Chapters 9 and 11, of autocorrelations and SUR relations are included as well. A concluding section contains suggestions for further research.

14.2 A LINEAR, DYNAMIC SYSTEM WITH CONTROL PROBLEM

Consider a *traditional* dynamic linear discrete-time system (Maybeck, 1979; Broemeling, 1985) with observation equations

$$\mathbf{y}_t = X_t \boldsymbol{\beta}_t + \mathbf{e}_t \tag{14.2.1}$$

and system equations

$$\boldsymbol{\beta}_t = A\boldsymbol{\beta}_{t-1} + C\mathbf{u}_t + \boldsymbol{\varepsilon}_t \tag{14.2.2}$$

where $\mathbf{y}_1, \mathbf{y}_2, \ldots, \mathbf{y}_T$ is a sequence of T noisy $(S \times 1)$ observation vectors, X_t is a known $(S \times K)$ measurement-design matrix, $\mathbf{e}_t$ is a $(S \times 1)$ vector of observation errors, $\boldsymbol{\beta}_t$ is an unknown $(K \times 1)$ state vector, A is a $(K \times K)$ known transition-stationary adjustment process matrix, C is a $(K \times M)$ known matrix, $\mathbf{u}_t$ is a $(M \times 1)$ vector of control variables and $\boldsymbol{\varepsilon}_t$ is a $(K \times 1)$ vector of state or system errors. Typically it is assumed that the random vectors $\mathbf{e}_t \sim \mathrm{N}_S(\mathbf{0}, \Sigma_t)$ and $\boldsymbol{\varepsilon}_t \sim \mathrm{N}_K(\mathbf{0}, \Psi_t)$, that Σ_t and Ψ_t are known, and that $\mathbf{e}_t$ and $\boldsymbol{\varepsilon}_t$ are mutually independent. Given this specification interest centers on inferences for $\boldsymbol{\beta}_t$, the state of the system at time t.

In this section we consider a variant of the traditional formulation and assume that noisy observations $\mathbf{y}_1, \mathbf{y}_2, \ldots, \mathbf{y}_T$ are generated from an experiment of length T that cannot be repeated. To simplify the presentation, we formulate the model in terms of a single observation equation s, and omit the subscript s. Similarly, we can view it as $S = 1$. Consequently, (14.2.1) is specified as

$$y_t = \mathbf{x}_t'\boldsymbol{\beta}_t + e_t \tag{14.2.1'}$$

where the random error e_t has mean zero and scale parameter σ^2. Furthermore, *consistent with many problems normally found in practice, we assume in (14.2.1′) and (14.2.2) that the matrices A and C along with the covariance matrix Ψ_t and scale parameter σ^2 are unknown.* Given this specification the objective is to recover estimates of the unknown matrices A and C, the state vector $\boldsymbol{\beta}_t$ and the noise components ε_{tk} and e_t, when the data consists of time-series of both control and observation (state) vectors. Under this extended formulation the number of unknown parameters will usually exceed the number of data points and, if so, the statistical model is ill-posed, or underdetermined and cannot be solved by traditional estimation and inference procedures.

14.2.1 REPARAMETERIZATION

Consistent with earlier chapters, to convert the observation and process equations (14.2.1′) and (14.2.2) to a form that will permit a solution consistent with the generalized entropy principle developed in Chapter 6, we represent the unknowns probabilistically. For *each* β_{tk}, c_{km}, e_t and ε_{tk}, define a set of discrete support points $\mathbf{z}_{tk}^{\beta} = [z_{tk1}^{\beta}, z_{tk2}^{\beta}, \ldots, z_{tkD}^{\beta}]'$, $\mathbf{z}_{km}^{C} = [z_{km1}^{C}, z_{km2}^{C}, \ldots, z_{kmN}^{C}]'$, $\mathbf{v}_t^e = [v_{t1}^e, v_{t2}^e, \ldots, v_{tJ}^e]'$ and $\mathbf{v}_{tk}^{\varepsilon} = [v_{tk1}^{\varepsilon}, v_{tk2}^{\varepsilon}, \ldots, v_{tkI}^{\varepsilon}]'$, with corresponding weights $\mathbf{p}_{tk}^{\beta} = [p_{tk1}^{\beta}, p_{tk2}^{\beta}, \ldots, p_{tkD}^{\beta}]'$, $\mathbf{p}_{km}^{C} = [p_{km1}^{C}, p_{km2}^{C}, \ldots, p_{kmN}^{C}]'$, $\mathbf{w}_t^e = [w_{t1}^e, w_{t2}^e, \ldots, w_{tJ}^e]'$ and $\mathbf{w}_{tk}^{\varepsilon} = [w_{tk1}^{\varepsilon}, w_{tk2}^{\varepsilon}, \ldots, w_{tkI}^{\varepsilon}]'$. Consistent with this specification

$$\mathbf{z}_{tk}^{\beta\prime}\mathbf{p}_{tk}^{\beta} = \sum_d z_{tkd}^{\beta} p_{tkd}^{\beta} = \beta_{tk}, \qquad \text{for } k = 1, 2, \ldots, K, \quad t = 1, 2, \ldots, T \tag{14.2.3}$$

and

$$\mathbf{z}_{km}^{C\prime}\mathbf{p}_{km}^{C} = \sum_n z_{kmn}^{C} p_{kmn}^{C} = c_{km}, \qquad \text{for } k = 1, 2, \ldots, K \text{ and } m = 1, 2, \ldots, M \tag{14.2.4}$$

Having reparameterized both the unknown parameters and the error components we rewrite (14.2.1′) as

$$y_t = \mathbf{x}_t'\boldsymbol{\beta}_t + e_t = \mathbf{x}_t' Z_t^{\boldsymbol{\beta}}\mathbf{p}_t^{\boldsymbol{\beta}} + \mathbf{v}_t^{e\prime}\mathbf{w}_t^e \tag{14.2.5}$$

and the system-process equation (14.2.2) as

$$\boldsymbol{\beta}_t = A\boldsymbol{\beta}_{t-1} + C\mathbf{u}_t + \boldsymbol{\varepsilon}_t = A\boldsymbol{\beta}_{t-1} + Z^C\mathbf{p}^C\mathbf{u}_t + \mathbf{v}_{tk}^{\varepsilon\prime}\mathbf{w}_t^{\varepsilon} \tag{14.2.6}$$

where

$$Z^C\mathbf{p}^C = [Z_1^C\mathbf{p}_1^C \mid Z_2^C\mathbf{p}_2^C \cdots \mid Z_M^C\mathbf{p}_M^C] \tag{14.2.7}$$

and

$$Z_n^C\mathbf{p}_n^C = \begin{bmatrix} Z_{1n}^{C\prime} & & & \\ & Z_{2n}^{C\prime} & & \\ & & \ddots & \\ & & & Z_{nK}^{C\prime} \end{bmatrix} \begin{bmatrix} \mathbf{p}_{1n}^C \\ \mathbf{p}_{2n}^C \\ \vdots \\ \mathbf{p}_{K,n}^C \end{bmatrix} \tag{14.2.8}$$

Given this reparameterized system, the objective is to recover, without specifying any restrictive distributional assumptions, the unknown probabilities and the corresponding estimates of $\boldsymbol{\beta}_t$, A and C and the errors e_t and ε_{tk}.

Note that, as in the previous chapter and similar to the autocorrelation model of Chapter 9, in this formulation we have not reparameterized A. Therefore, instead of estimating probability distributions for the elements of A, we obtain only point estimates of those parameters. This means that in maximizing entropy, A appears in only the constraints of the optimization problem, and not directly in the criterion function (see equation 14.2.9). For expository purposes we assume that A is a diagonal matrix.

In some cases, given the support spaces, we may have some prior knowledge regarding particular characteristics of β_{tk}, C_{km}, e_t and ε_{tk}. If such information exists we follow the previous chapters and the GCE formulation and designate the prior information as $\mathbf{q}_{tk}^{\beta}$, $\mathbf{q}_{km}^{C}$, $\mathbf{q}_{tk}^{\varepsilon}$ and $\mathbf{q}_t^{e}$ defined on the sets $\mathbf{z}_{tk}^{\beta}$, $\mathbf{z}_{km}^{C}$, $\mathbf{v}_{tk}^{\varepsilon}$ and $\mathbf{v}_t^{e}$ respectively. We now turn to the GCE formulation of this problem.

14.2.2 REFORMULATION AND SOLUTION

Given the reparameterization, the generalized stochastic-control GCE problem may be stated, using a criterion with four non-negative probability components, presented for completeness in scalar-summation notation, as

$$\begin{aligned} \min_{\{a_{kk}\},\{p_{tkd}^{\beta}\},\{p_{kmn}^{C}\},\{w_{tj}^{e}\},\{w_{tki}^{\varepsilon}\}} \quad & I(\mathbf{p}^{\beta}, \mathbf{p}^{C}, \mathbf{w}^{e}, \mathbf{w}^{\varepsilon}) \\ = \sum_t \sum_k \sum_d p_{tkd}^{\beta} \ln(p_{tkd}^{\beta}/q_{tkd}^{\beta}) & + \sum_k \sum_m \sum_n p_{kmn}^{C} \ln(p_{kmn}^{C}/q_{kmn}^{C}) \\ + \sum_t \sum_j w_{tj}^{e} \ln(w_{tj}^{e}/q_{tj}^{e}) & + \sum_t \sum_k \sum_i w_{tki}^{\varepsilon} \ln(w_{tki}^{\varepsilon}/q_{tki}^{\varepsilon}) \end{aligned} \tag{14.2.9}$$

subject to the data-consistency relations

$$y_t = \sum_k \sum_d z^{\beta}_{tkd} p^{\beta}_{tkd} x_{kt} + \sum_j v^e_{tj} w^e_{tj}, \qquad \text{for } t = 1, 2, \ldots, T \tag{14.2.10}$$

$$\beta_{tk} = a_{kk} \sum_d z^{\beta}_{t-1kd} p^{\beta}_{t-1,kd} + \sum_m \sum_n z^C_{kmn} p^C_{kmn} u_{tkm} + \sum_i v^{\varepsilon}_{tki} w^{\varepsilon}_{tki}, \quad \text{for } t = 2, 3, \ldots, T; \quad k = 1, 2, \ldots, K \tag{14.2.11}$$

and the adding-up constraints

$$\sum_d p^{\beta}_{tkd} = 1, \qquad \text{for } k = 1, 2, \ldots, K; \quad t = 1, 2, \ldots, T \tag{14.2.12}$$

$$\sum_n p^C_{kmn} = 1, \qquad \text{for } k = 1, 2, \ldots, K; \quad m = 1, 2, \ldots, M \tag{14.2.13}$$

$$\sum_j w^e_{tj} = 1, \qquad \text{for } t = 1, 2, \ldots, T \tag{14.2.14}$$

$$\sum_i w^{\varepsilon}_{tki} = 1, \qquad \text{for } k = 1, 2, \ldots, K; \quad t = 2, 3, \ldots, T \tag{14.2.15}$$

where the unknown parameters are defined as

$$\sum_d z^{\beta}_{tkd} p^{\beta}_{tkd} = \beta_{tk}, \qquad \text{for } k = 1, 2, \ldots, K; \quad t = 1, 2, \ldots, T \tag{14.2.16}$$

$$\sum_n z^C_{kmn} p^C_{kmn} = c_{km}, \qquad \text{for } k = 1, 2, \ldots, K; \quad m = 1, 2, \ldots, M \tag{14.2.17}$$

$$\sum_j v^e_{tj} w^e_{tj} = e_t, \qquad \text{for } t = 1, 2, \ldots, T \tag{14.2.18}$$

$$\sum_i v^{\varepsilon}_{tki} w^{\varepsilon}_{tki} = \varepsilon_{tk}, \qquad \text{for } k = 1, 2, \ldots, K; \quad t = 2, 3, \ldots, T \tag{14.2.19}$$

and where a_{kk} is an element of the diagonal matrix A. The prior information on the errors, may in the absence of other information, be specified as $q^e_{tj} = 1/J$ for all $j = 1, 2, \ldots, J$ and for all t, and $q^{\varepsilon}_{tki} = 1/I$ for all $i = 1, 2, \ldots, I$ and for all t and k. The parameter spaces v^e_{tj} and v^{ε}_{tki} are specified to be *distributed uniformly around zero.* In the absence of any prior knowledge, the prior information on the β_{tk} and C_{km} is specified as $q^{\beta}_{tkd} = 1/D$, for all t, k and d, and $q^C_{kmn} = 1/N$, where z^{β}_{tkm} and z^C_{kmn} are chosen such that they span the possible admissible parameter state-spaces for each parameter. If initial information such as non-negativity, non-positivity or an upper or lower bound exists for each parameter, this may be included when specifying the supports.

Forming the Lagrangian and using the first-order conditions yields the solution

$$\tilde{p}^{\beta}_{tkd} = \frac{q^{\beta}_{tkd}}{\Omega^{\beta}_{tk}(\tilde{\lambda}_t, \tilde{\mu}_{t+1,k}, \tilde{\mu}_{tk})} \exp[\tilde{\lambda}_t z^{\beta}_{tkd} x_{kt} - \tilde{\mu}_{tk} z^{\beta}_{tkd} + \tilde{\mu}_{t+1,k} \tilde{a}_{kk} z^{\beta}_{tkd}] \tag{14.2.20}$$

where

$$\Omega^{\beta}_{tk}(\tilde{\lambda}_t, \tilde{\mu}_{t+1,k}, \tilde{\mu}_{tk}) = \sum_d q^{\beta}_{tkd} \exp[\tilde{\lambda}_t z^{\beta}_{tkd} x_{kt} - \tilde{\mu}_{tk} z^{\beta}_{tkd} + \tilde{\mu}_{t+1,k} \tilde{a}_{kk} z^{\beta}_{tkd}] \quad (14.2.21)$$

and

$$\tilde{p}^{C}_{kmn} = \frac{q^{C}_{kmn}}{\Omega^{C}_{km}(\tilde{\mu}_{tk})} \exp[\tilde{\mu}_{tk} z^{C}_{kmn} u_{tm}] \quad (14.2.22)$$

where

$$\Omega^{C}_{km}(\tilde{\mu}_{tk}) = \sum_n q^{C}_{kmn} \exp[\tilde{\mu}_{tk} z^{C}_{kmn} u_{tm}] \quad (14.2.23)$$

and

$$\tilde{w}^{e}_{tj} = \frac{q^{e}_{tj}}{\Omega^{e}_{t}(\tilde{\lambda}_t)} \exp[\tilde{\lambda}_t v^{e}_{j}] \quad (14.2.24)$$

where

$$\Omega^{e}_{t}(\tilde{\lambda}_t) = \sum_j q^{e}_{tj} \exp[\tilde{\lambda}_t v^{e}_{j}] \quad (14.2.25)$$

and

$$\tilde{w}^{\varepsilon}_{tki} = \frac{q^{\varepsilon}_{tki}}{\Omega^{\varepsilon}_{tk}(\tilde{\mu}_{tk})} \exp[\tilde{\mu}_{tk} v^{\varepsilon}_{ki}] \quad (14.2.26)$$

where

$$\Omega^{\varepsilon}_{tk}(\tilde{\mu}_{tk}) = \sum_i q^{\varepsilon}_{tki} \exp[\tilde{\mu}_{tk} v^{\varepsilon}_{ki}] \quad (14.2.27)$$

The solutions in (14.2.20), (14.2.22), (14.2.24) and (14.2.26) yield

$$\tilde{\beta}_{tk} = \sum_d z^{\beta}_{tkd} \tilde{p}^{\beta}_{tkd} \quad (14.2.28)$$

$$\tilde{C}_{km} = \sum_n z^{C}_{kmn} \tilde{p}^{C}_{kmn} \quad (14.2.29)$$

$$\tilde{e}_t = \sum_j v^{e}_{tj} \tilde{w}^{e}_{tj} \quad (14.2.30)$$

$$\tilde{\varepsilon}_{tk} = \sum_i v^{\varepsilon}_{tki} \tilde{w}^{\varepsilon}_{tki} \quad (14.2.31)$$

where λ_t and μ_{tk} are the Lagrange parameters associated with equations (14.2.10) and (14.2.11) respectively. Given (14.2.28), (14.2.29) and (14.2.31), the estimate of a_{kk} is determined by using equation (14.2.11). This formulation, designed to handle ill-posed cases, is a general non-linear inversion procedure for recovering both time-invariant and time-variant parameters A, C and $\boldsymbol{\beta}_t$. In line with Chapters 3–7, these estimates may be also used as a basis for defining measures of uncertainty and precision. Finally, we note that even though the objective function (14.2.9) has four components, it is basically just the dual criterion function, discussed in detail in Chapters 6 and 7, where the two components are, again, the signal ($\mathbf{p}^{\beta}$ and $\mathbf{p}^{C}$) and the noise ($\mathbf{w}^{e}$ and $\mathbf{w}^{\varepsilon}$).

14.2.3 RESULTS OF A SAMPLING EXPERIMENT

To reflect the operational nature of the information recovery method developed in this section, consider, within the context of (14.2.1′) and (14.2.2), the problem of recovering the unknown parameters of the following discrete dynamic linear system containing two control variables:

$$y_t = \mathbf{x}_t'\boldsymbol{\beta}_t + e_t = x_{1t}\beta_{1t} + x_{2t}\beta_{2t} + x_{3t}\beta_{3t} + e_t \quad \text{where} \quad \boldsymbol{\beta}_{t=1} = (2, -1.0, 1.0)' \tag{14.2.32}$$

and

$$\begin{bmatrix} \beta_{1t} \\ \beta_{2t} \\ \beta_{3t} \end{bmatrix} = \begin{bmatrix} a_{11} & 0 & 0 \\ 0 & a_{22} & 0 \\ 0 & 0 & a_{33} \end{bmatrix} \begin{bmatrix} \beta_{1,t-1} \\ \beta_{2,t-1} \\ \beta_{3,t-1} \end{bmatrix} + \begin{bmatrix} c_{11} & c_{12} \\ c_{21} & c_{22} \\ c_{31} & c_{32} \end{bmatrix} \begin{bmatrix} u_{1t} \\ u_{2t} \end{bmatrix} + \begin{bmatrix} \varepsilon_{1t} \\ \varepsilon_{2t} \\ \varepsilon_{3t} \end{bmatrix}$$
$$= \begin{bmatrix} 0.5 & 0 & 0 \\ 0 & 1.0 & 0 \\ 0 & 0 & 1.5 \end{bmatrix} \begin{bmatrix} \beta_{1,t-1} \\ \beta_{2,t-1} \\ \beta_{3,t-1} \end{bmatrix} + \begin{bmatrix} -0.5 & 0.5 \\ 0.3 & 0.4 \\ 0.6 & -0.3 \end{bmatrix} \begin{bmatrix} u_{1t} \\ u_{2t} \end{bmatrix} + \begin{bmatrix} \varepsilon_{1t} \\ \varepsilon_{2t} \\ \varepsilon_{3t} \end{bmatrix} \tag{14.2.33}$$

with noise components $e_t \sim N(0, 0.10)$ and $\varepsilon_{tk} \sim N(0, 0.10)$. Using values for $\mathbf{x}_t$ and $\mathbf{u}_t$ that are presented in Table 14.2.1, 100 samples (replications) of outcome values y_t were generated consistent with this model. The pure y_t, consistent with $e_t = \varepsilon_{tk} = 0$, were generated and are also presented in Table 14.2.1.

Table 14.2.1 The $\mathbf{x}_t$ and $\mathbf{u}_t$ used in the experiments reported in Tables 14.2.2 and 14.2.3, and the pure (without noise) $\mathbf{y}_t$

$\mathbf{x}_1$	$\mathbf{x}_2$	$\mathbf{x}_3$	$\mathbf{u}_1$	$\mathbf{u}_2$	$\mathbf{y}_t$ (pure)
1	0.693	0.693	0.693	1.386	2.000
1	1.733	0.693	1.733	0.693	1.744
1	0.693	1.386	1.733	1.386	6.383
1	1.733	1.386	0.693	1.792	12.096
1	0.693	1.792	2.340	0.693	19.826
1	2.340	0.693	1.733	1.792	20.193
1	1.733	1.792	2.340	1.386	53.135
1	2.340	1.386	2.340	1.792	68.020
1	2.340	1.792	1.733	1.386	121.500
1	0.693	0.693	0.693	0.693	65.840
1	0.693	1.792	1.733	0.693	241.227
1	1.733	1.792	0.693	1.792	370.680
1	2.340	1.792	2.340	0.693	556.813
1	0.693	0.693	2.340	1.386	316.857

The model was reparameterized in line with Section 14.2.1 where a symmetric around zero (uninformative) parameter support space was specified for the β_{tk}, c_{km}, e_t and ε_{tk}. The objective, given the data, is to recover the unknown β_{tk}, a_{kk}, c_{km} and the noise components e_t and ε_{tk}.

The GME recovered estimates of the unknown coefficients averaged over 100 replications, along with the corresponding mean squared errors MSE($\hat{\cdot}$), for samples of size $T = 5, 8, 12$, are given in Table 14.2.2. The MSEs reported in the table are sums of MSEs for collections of parameters; for example, the reported MSE for β_1 is the sum over k of the MSEs of β_{1k}.

The GME formulation appears to perform especially well over all T in the recovery of a_{kk}, and the estimates of a_{kk} reflected great stability from sample to sample. As we illustrated in a previous chapter, when information such as the signs of the parameters is specified, the accuracy of the recovered parameters improves significantly. Also, as T increases, sampling results indicate that the accuracy of the recovered parameters increases. Finally, using the $\mathbf{y}$ given in Table 14.2.1, the pure case where $e_t = v_{kt} = 0$ is presented in Table 14.2.3. Note that when $T = 12$, the number of data points is equal to the number of unknown parameters and the unknown parameters are exactly recovered. This result is consistent with the mathematical inversion solution.

Table 14.2.2 The recovered values of $\hat{\boldsymbol{\beta}}_1$, a_{kk} and $\hat{C}$ for $T = 5, 8, 12$ with $e_t \sim N(0, 0.10)$ and $\varepsilon_{tk} \sim N(0, 0.10)$ and the corresponding MSE($\hat{\cdot}$)

	$T = 5$				$T = 8$				$T = 12$			
	$\hat{\beta}_{1k}$	$\hat{a}_{kk}$	$\hat{C}$		$\hat{\beta}_{1k}$	$\hat{a}_{kk}$	$\hat{C}$		$\hat{\beta}_{1k}$	$\hat{a}_{kk}$	$\hat{C}$	
	1.77	0.55	−0.07	0.09	1.78	0.53	−0.02	0.06	1.90	0.46	−0.05	0.10
	−1.39	0.79	0.12	0.38	−1.38	1.00	0.30	0.40	−1.44	0.97	0.29	0.43
	1.65	1.56	−0.06	0.15	1.59	1.55	−0.01	0.12	1.39	1.50	0.10	0.26
MSE($\hat{\cdot}$)	0.389	0.051	0.178		0.453	0.019	0.171		0.386	0.017	0.161	

Table 14.2.3 The recovered values of $\hat{\boldsymbol{\beta}}_1$, a_{kk} and $\hat{C}$ for $T = 5, 8, 12$ with $e_t = \varepsilon_{tk} = 0$

	$T = 5$				$T = 8$				$T = 12$			
	$\hat{\beta}_{1k}$	$\hat{a}_{kk}$	$\hat{C}$		$\hat{\beta}_{1k}$	$\hat{a}_{kk}$	$\hat{C}$		$\hat{\beta}_{1k}$	$\hat{a}_{kk}$	$\hat{C}$	
	1.78	0.70	−0.15	0.11	2.35	0.52	−0.08	0.10	2.0	0.5	−0.5	0.5
	−1.31	0.96	0.18	0.51	−1.68	0.88	0.38	0.45	−1.0	1.0	0.3	0.4
	1.63	1.60	−0.16	0.18	1.16	1.54	0.14	0.16	1.0	1.5	0.6	−0.3
MSE($\hat{\cdot}$)	0.176	0.017	0.185		0.161	0.005	0.126		0	0	0	

14.3 A NON-LINEAR, DYNAMIC SYSTEM WITH CONTROL PROBLEM

In many cases the state equation is non-linear. To cope with this situation, consider a model that consists of two equations. The observation equation is

$$y_t = f(r_t, \mathbf{x}_{1t}, \varepsilon_{1t}; \boldsymbol{\beta}_1) \tag{14.3.1}$$

where the *unobserved* state variable (scalar) at time t is r_t; the scalar y_t and the vector of explanatory variables $\mathbf{x}_{1t}$ are observed; ε_{1t} is a random variable, and $\boldsymbol{\beta}_1$ is a vector of unknown parameters. The state equation that describes the evolution of r_t is

$$r_{t+1} - r_t = g(r_t, \mathbf{x}_{2t}, \varepsilon_{2t}; \boldsymbol{\beta}_2) \tag{14.3.2}$$

where the vector of observable variables $\mathbf{x}_{2t}$ may contain y_t and elements of $\mathbf{x}_{1t}$; ε_{2t} is a random variable, and $\boldsymbol{\beta}_2$ is a vector of unknown constant parameters. The problem is, given the observables y_t, $\mathbf{x}_{1t}$ and $\mathbf{x}_{2t}$, to estimate the unobserved values of the state variable, r_t, and the vector of parameters, $\boldsymbol{\beta} = (\boldsymbol{\beta}_1, \boldsymbol{\beta}_2)$.

This general model encompasses many special cases. One example, within the renewable resources literature, is where r_t is the biomass of fish, y_t is the harvest, and $\mathbf{x}_{1t}$ is the vector of fishing inputs. Another example is where y_t is the output of an agricultural good, r_t is a measure of environmental quality (e.g. nitrogen carryover, water or soil quality), $\mathbf{x}_{1t}$ are other productive inputs (e.g. labor, fertilizer), and $\mathbf{x}_{2t}$ are variables which affect the evolution of the environment (e.g. fertilizer, expenditures on drainage). As these two examples indicate, r_t may have a precise physical interpretation, such as biomass or nitrogen carryover, and in other applications it may be an index which summarizes many variables that we might not be able to list completely, let alone measure. In the latter case, the estimation of r_t produces a crop-specific index of environmental quality. The ability to estimate such an index, and to explain how it changes, may have great significance in environmental problems.

Other interpretations are also possible. For example, r_t may be an index of technical progress, which depends on R&D, or an index of capital stock, which depends on previous investment. We can also think of equation (14.3.1) as a random coefficients model. The random coefficients, r_t, change according to (14.3.2). In an entirely different setting, we can interpret r_t as expectational variables that evolve according to (14.3.2).

These examples are sufficient to illustrate the general importance of this model, which can be estimated in a number of ways. In the simplest case, the random variable ε_2 is absent, so that (14.3.2) is deterministic. Then we can use (14.3.2) to solve for r_t in terms of an initial condition r_0 and $\{\mathbf{x}_{21}, \mathbf{x}_{22}, \ldots, \mathbf{x}_{2,T-1}\}$. Substituting the result into (14.3.1) gives y_t as a function of r_0, $\{\mathbf{x}_{21}, \mathbf{x}_{22}, \ldots, \mathbf{x}_{2,T-1}\}$, $\mathbf{x}_{1t}$, $\boldsymbol{\beta}$ and ε_{1t} (see Spence, 1973; Stauber *et al.*, 1975, for natural resource applications). Even if ε_2 is present, we can use equation (14.3.2) to eliminate r_t. Upon substitution, however, we obtain a new vector of random variables in equation (14.3.1). The resulting covariance structure would be extremely complicated, involving among other things the unknown vector $\boldsymbol{\beta}$. At the very least, this would be a difficult numerical problem.

An alternative estimation strategy for this problem involves filters. For example, if (14.3.1) and (14.3.2) are linear, we can use the Kalman filter–maximum likelihood approach. With the Kalman filter, the prior on y_t (the estimate conditional on previous information) is determined as a function of the parameters $\boldsymbol{\beta}$ and r_0. Using these priors and our observations of y_t we can construct a likelihood function that is maximized with respect to $\boldsymbol{\beta}$ and r_0. Berck and Johns (1991) apply this method to a resource model. This method, despite its ingenuity, has a number of limitations. First, only information up to time t is used in writing the updating equation for the prior on y_{t+1}. Since the econometrician knows the entire sample, this represents an inefficient use of information. It might be possible to overcome this objection by running the Kalman filter forward and backward (resmoothing); at the very least, this would complicate the likelihood function, and make the numerical problem harder. Second, the linearity of the model is often a restrictive assumption when working with real data. For non-linear models, the extended Kalman filter could be used. Again, this increases the numerical complexity. Finally, the traditional assumption of normality may be unattractive, in which case some other filter should be used.

As this brief review illustrates, there are a number of estimation strategies that are available to estimate models such as (14.3.1) and (14.3.2), given sufficient data (and the maintained assumption of identification). However, these methods may be computationally infeasible, or at least very difficult, and are based on a range of distributional assumptions. Further, if there are fewer observations than unknowns, we are faced with an ill-posed problem.

14.3.1 MODEL FORMULATION

In order to illustrate the use of GME in estimating the model (4.3.1)–(4.3.2), we follow Golan *et al.* (1996) and specialize (14.3.1) and (14.3.2) to the following non-linear system:

$$y_t = r_t^{\beta_{11}} c_t^{\beta_{12}} l_t^{\beta_{13}} e^{\varepsilon_{1t}} \tag{14.3.3}$$

$$r_{t+1} - r_t = \beta_{21} r_t [\beta_{22} c_t^{\beta_{23}} - r_t] e^{\varepsilon_{2t}} \tag{14.3.4}$$

where y_t is agricultural output (per unit of land), which depends on environmental quality, r_t, labor, l_t, and chemical applications, c_t. Further, it makes sense to assume that all inputs have non-negative marginal products, so that β_{11}, β_{12} and β_{13} are non-negative. Equation (14.3.4) states that environmental quality follows a logistic growth equation, which is frequently used in resourse economics. The expression $\beta_{22}c_t^{\beta_{23}}$ is the 'carrying capacity' of environmental quality (the steady state). This expression is positive and decreasing in c_t, (i.e. chemicals degrade the environment), implying $\beta_{22} > 0$ and $\beta_{23} < 0$. Stability of equation (14.3.4) requires that $\beta_{21} > 0$.

Using the GME approach for our problem requires that we reparameterize the unknowns in (14.3.3) and (14.3.4) so they have the properties of probabilities. We now turn to this problem.

Reparameterization. To convert the observation and state equations (14.3.3) and (14.3.4) to a form that will permit a solution consistent with the entropy principle, we follow Section 14.2.1, and with each β_{1k}, β_{2k}, ε_{1t} and ε_{2t} we define a set of *two or more* discrete points $\mathbf{z}_k^{\beta_1} = [z_{k1}^{\beta_1}, z_{k2}^{\beta_2}, \ldots, z_{kD}^{\beta_1}]'$, $\mathbf{z}_h^{\beta_2} = [z_{h1}^{\beta_2}, z_{h2}^{\beta_2}, \ldots, z_{hM}^{\beta_2}]'$, $\mathbf{v}_t^{\varepsilon_1} = [v_{t1}^{\varepsilon_1}, v_{t2}^{\varepsilon_1}, \ldots, v_{tJ}^{\varepsilon_1}]'$ and $\mathbf{v}_t^{\varepsilon_2} = [v_{t1}^{\varepsilon_2}, v_{t2}^{\varepsilon_2}, \ldots, v_{tI}^{\varepsilon_2}]'$, with corresponding weights $\mathbf{p}_k^{\beta_1} = [p_{k1}^{\beta_1}, p_{k2}^{\beta_2}, \ldots, p_{kD}^{\beta_1}]'$, $\mathbf{p}_h^{\beta_2} = [p_{h1}^{\beta_2}, p_{h2}^{\beta_2}, \ldots, p_{hM}^{\beta_2}]'$, $\mathbf{w}_t^{\varepsilon_1} = [w_{t1}^{\varepsilon_1}, w_{t2}^{\varepsilon_1}, \ldots, w_{tJ}^{\varepsilon_1}]'$ and $\mathbf{w}_t^{\varepsilon_2} = [w_{t1}^{\varepsilon_2}, w_{t2}^{\varepsilon_2}, \ldots, w_{tI}^{\varepsilon_2}]'$.

Given the above reparameterization we can rewrite (14.3.3) and (14.3.4), in log form, as:

$$\ln(y_t) = \mathbf{z}_1^{\beta_1\prime}\mathbf{p}_1^{\beta_1}\ln(r_t) + \mathbf{z}_2^{\beta_1\prime}\mathbf{p}_2^{\beta_1}\ln(c_t) + \mathbf{z}_3^{\beta_1\prime}\mathbf{p}_3^{\beta_1}\ln(l_t) + \mathbf{v}_t^{\varepsilon_1\prime}\mathbf{w}_t^{\varepsilon_1} \tag{14.3.5}$$

$$\ln(r_{t+1}) = \ln(\mathbf{z}_1^{\beta_2\prime}\mathbf{p}_1^{\beta_2}) + \ln(r_t) + \ln(s_t) + \mathbf{v}_t^{\varepsilon_2\prime}\mathbf{w}_t^{\varepsilon_2} \tag{14.3.6}$$

where

$$\begin{aligned} s_t &\equiv \beta_{21}r_t\left[\frac{1}{\beta_{21}} + \beta_{22}c_t^{\beta_{23}} - r_t\right] \\ &= \mathbf{z}_1^{\beta_2\prime}\mathbf{p}_1^{\beta_2}r_t\left[\frac{1}{\mathbf{z}_1^{\beta_2\prime}\mathbf{p}_1^{\beta_2}} + \mathbf{z}_2^{\beta_2\prime}\mathbf{p}_2^{\beta_2}c_t^{\mathbf{z}_3^{\beta_2\prime}\mathbf{p}_3^{\beta_2}} - r_t\right] \end{aligned} \tag{14.3.7}$$

Given this system of equations, the objective is to estimate, without specifying the usual restrictive distributional assumptions, the unobservable r_t, the parameters $\boldsymbol{\beta}_1$, $\boldsymbol{\beta}_2$ and the errors $\boldsymbol{\varepsilon}_1$ and $\boldsymbol{\varepsilon}_2$.

Similar to the GME–autocorrelation formulation of Chapter 9 and the linear dynamics models of Chapter 13 and Section 14.2, we have not reparameterized r_t. Therefore, instead of estimating probability distributions for the unobserved r_t, we obtain only point estimates of those unknowns. This means that in maximizing entropy r_t appears in only the constraints of the optimization problem, and not directly in the criterion function.

Reformulation and solution. Given the reparameterization, the generalized stochastic non-linear GME problem may be stated in scalar-summation notation as

$$\max_{\{r_t\},\{\mathbf{p}_k^{\beta 1}\},\{\mathbf{p}_h^{\beta 2}\},\{\mathbf{w}_t^{\varepsilon 1}\},\{\mathbf{w}_t^{\varepsilon 2}\}} H(\mathbf{p}^{\beta_1}, \mathbf{p}^{\beta_2}, \mathbf{w}^{\varepsilon_1}, \mathbf{w}^{\varepsilon_2})$$
$$= -\sum_k \sum_d p_{kd}^{\beta_1} \ln p_{kd}^{\beta_1} - \sum_h \sum_m p_{hm}^{\beta_2} \ln p_{hm}^{\beta_2} - \sum_t \sum_j w_{tj}^{\varepsilon_1} \ln w_{tj}^{\varepsilon_1} - \sum_t \sum_i w_{ti}^{\varepsilon_2} \ln w_{ti}^{\varepsilon_2} \tag{14.3.8}$$

subject to the data-consistency relations (14.3.5) and (14.3.6), where s_t is defined according to (14.3.7), and the adding-up–normalization constraints

$$\sum_d p_{kd}^{\beta_1} = 1, \qquad \text{for } k = 1, 2, 3 \tag{14.3.9}$$

$$\sum_m p_{hm}^{\beta_2} = 1, \qquad \text{for } h = 1, 2, 3 \tag{14.3.10}$$

$$\sum_j w_{tj}^{\varepsilon_1} = 1, \qquad \text{for } t = 1, 2, \ldots, T \tag{14.3.11}$$

$$\sum_i w_{ti}^{\varepsilon_2} = 1, \qquad \text{for } t = 1, 2, \ldots, T-1 \tag{14.3.12}$$

Following Chapters 6 and 13, the optimal solution yields $\hat{p}_{kd}^{\beta_1}$, $\hat{p}_{hm}^{\beta_2}$, $\hat{w}_t^{\varepsilon_1}$, and $\hat{w}_t^{\varepsilon_2}$ which, by use of the reparameterization definitions yield the point estimates

$$\hat{\beta}_{1k} = \sum_d z_{kd}^{\beta_1} \hat{p}_{kd}^{\beta_1} \tag{14.3.13}$$

$$\hat{\beta}_{2h} = \sum_m z_{hm}^{\beta_2} \hat{p}_{hm}^{\beta_2} \tag{14.3.14}$$

$$\hat{\varepsilon}_{1t} = \sum_j v_{tj}^{\varepsilon_1} \hat{w}_{tj}^{\varepsilon_1} \tag{14.3.15}$$

$$\hat{\varepsilon}_{2t} = \sum_i v_{ti}^{\varepsilon_2} \hat{w}_{ti}^{\varepsilon_2} \tag{14.3.16}$$

Given (14.3.13)–(14.3.16), the estimates of r_t are determined by using (14.3.4).

14.3.2 RESULTS OF A SAMPLING EXPERIMENT

To reflect the operational nature of the GME method developed in this section, we constructed, within the context of (14.3.3)–(14.3.4), a sampling experiment where $\boldsymbol{\beta}_1' = (0.2, 0.3, 0.6)$, $\boldsymbol{\beta}_2' = (0.4, 5, -0.1)$ and noise components $\varepsilon_{1t} \sim$ N(0, 0.09) and $\varepsilon_{2t} \sim$ N(0, 0.09). Using values for c_t and l_t from Judge *et al.* (1988, p. 215), 100 samples of size $T = 6$, 10 and 20 were generated. If **r** is *known*, then for the samples of size $T = 6$ the number of unknown parameters exceeds the number of data points and the problem is ill-posed. However, since **r** is *unknown* the problem is ill-posed for any T. Our experiment illustrates that this

Table 14.3.1 The recovered average $\hat{\boldsymbol{\beta}}_{1k}$, $\hat{\boldsymbol{\beta}}_{2k}$, Var($\hat{\boldsymbol{\beta}}_1$), Var($\hat{\boldsymbol{\beta}}_2$), MSE($\hat{\boldsymbol{\beta}}_1$), MSE($\hat{\boldsymbol{\beta}}_2$) and the slope coefficient for $T = 6$, 10, 20 and 100 replications

	$T = 6$	$T = 10$	$T = 20$
$\bar{\hat{\boldsymbol{\beta}}}_{1k}$	0.42, 0.35, 0.52	0.35, 0.38, 0.49	0.28, 0.37, 0.54
Var($\hat{\boldsymbol{\beta}}_1$)	0.003, 0.004, 0.008	0.009, 0.005, 0.009	0.010, 0.004, 0.010
$\bar{\hat{\boldsymbol{\beta}}}_{2k}$	0.51, 4.92, −0.44	0.55, 5.43, −0.33	0.57, 5.53, −0.260
Var($\hat{\boldsymbol{\beta}}_2$)	0.007, 0.585, 0.016	0.010, 0.90, 0.020	0.014, 1.459, 0.024
MSE($\hat{\boldsymbol{\beta}}_1$)	0.023	0.021	0.013
MSE($\hat{\boldsymbol{\beta}}_2$)	0.247	0.398	0.604
MSE($\hat{\mathbf{r}}$)	5.587	3.220	2.467
Slope coefficient	0.52	0.63	0.71

estimation strategy can be used for a range of sample sizes. The model was reparameterized in line with Section 14.3.1 and consistent with the sign restrictions noted earlier. Specifically, the support spaces for all the production parameters, $\boldsymbol{\beta}_1$, are specified to be $\mathbf{z}_k^{\beta_1} = (0, 0.5, 1)'$ for all k, and the supports for $\boldsymbol{\beta}_2$ are $\mathbf{z}_1^{\beta_2} = (0, 0.5, 1)'$, $\mathbf{z}_2^{\beta_2} = (0, 5, 10)'$ and $\mathbf{z}_3^{\beta_2} = (0, -0.5, -1)'$. The errors' supports are specified to be symmetric around zero, with $\mathbf{v}^{\varepsilon_1} = \mathbf{v}^{\varepsilon_2} = (-0.9, 0, 0.9)'$ for all t.

The estimates of the unknown coefficients, averaged over 100 replications, along with MSE, the variances of $\boldsymbol{\beta}_1$ and $\boldsymbol{\beta}_2$ and the slope coefficient between the estimated $\hat{r}_t$ and the correct (unobserved) r_t, for sample sizes of $T = 6$, 10, and 20, are given in Table 14.3.1. The mean value of the unobserved r_t, over the 100 samples, is 4.74 for $T = 6$, 4.37 for $T = 10$ and 4.42 for $T = 20$. Note the satisfactory nature, over all T, of the estimates in terms of the location and the precision of the parameters. Even for the extreme case of $T = 6$, the estimates of $\boldsymbol{\beta}_1$ and $\boldsymbol{\beta}_2$ are consistent with those of $T = 10$ and 20 in terms of magnitudes and precision. As the number of observations increases, MSE($\hat{\boldsymbol{\beta}}_1$) and MSE($\hat{\mathbf{r}}$) decrease, while MSE($\hat{\boldsymbol{\beta}}_2$) increases. The reason for this increase is the additional compounded noise introduced by each additional observation. However, as expected, the overall MSE decreases with T. The accuracy of recovering r_t is reflected by the MSE($\hat{\mathbf{r}}$) and the slope coefficient.

To summarize, with minimal assumptions on the distribution and covariance structure, and despite the non-linearity of the problem, the GME formulation performs well in terms of precision and stability and is easy to compute.

14.4 AN INVERSE CONTROL PROBLEM

Given a solution for the dynamic linear and non-linear discrete time models of Sections 2 and 3, we now consider a general inverse control problem that contains an objective function along with the equations of motion. The discussion here follows the formulation of Golan *et al.* (1996). Consistent with much of the work in the literature we construct our formulation based on the following linear-quadratic control problem:

$$\min_{\mathbf{u}_t} W = \mathrm{E}\left\{\sum_{t=1}^{\infty} \delta^t(\boldsymbol{\theta}_t'\mathbf{x}_t - \mathbf{x}_t'B\mathbf{x}_t)\right\} \qquad \text{(objective function)} \qquad (14.4.1)$$

subject to

$$\mathbf{x}_t = A\mathbf{x}_{t-1} + C\mathbf{u}_t + \boldsymbol{\alpha}_t + \mathbf{e}_{1t} \qquad \text{(state equation or equation of motion)} \qquad (14.4.2)$$

where $\mathbf{x}_t$ is a K-dimensional vector of state variables (e.g., reserves, prices), B is an unknown $(K \times K)$ matrix, $\boldsymbol{\theta}_t$ is an unknown K-dimensional vector, $\mathbf{u}_t$ is an M-dimensional vector of control variables (e.g. production, resource search, investment), A is a $(K \times K)$ unknown matrix, C is an unknown $(K \times M)$ matrix with the same meaning as in (14.2.2), $\boldsymbol{\alpha}_t$ is a K-dimensional vector of intercepts, $\mathbf{e}_{1t}$ is a K-dimensional noise vector and δ is a discount factor. The solution, $\mathbf{u}_t^*$, to such a problem, is expressed as

$$\mathbf{u}_t^* = G\mathbf{x}_{t-1} + \mathbf{g}_t + \mathbf{e}_{2t} \qquad \text{(feedback rule)} \qquad (14.4.3)$$

where G is a $(M \times K)$ matrix of control parameters and $\mathbf{g}_t$ is an M-dimensional intercept vector for the feedback rule. For estimation we include in (14.4.3) an error $\mathbf{e}_{2t}$ to account for real world noisy observations. In this formulation the state of the system and the control variables $\mathbf{u}_t$ are observed. In terms of (14.2.1) and (14.2.2) this means we now observe $\boldsymbol{\beta}_t$. The focus is now on recovering the unknown matrices A and C and the vector $\boldsymbol{\alpha}_t$ along with $\boldsymbol{\theta}_t$ and B in the objective function and the parameters of the control feedback rule, $\mathbf{g}_t$ and G.

The recovery of the parameters in the objective function is referred to as an *inverse control problem.* The parameters of equations (14.4.2) and (14.4.3) are initially estimated and, using the necessary conditions that result from the optimization of (14.4.1), the objective function's parameters $\boldsymbol{\theta}_t$ and B are recovered. In a traditional context the control problem is ill-posed since there is an indeterminacy in recovering B and $\boldsymbol{\theta}_t$.

Given the time invariant matrices B, A, C and the vectors $\boldsymbol{\theta}_t$ and $\boldsymbol{\alpha}_t$, and following Chow (1975, 1983), the time invariant feedback rule G and the time variant intercept vector $\mathbf{g}_t$ can be calculated according to the following set of equations:

$$G = -(C'HC)^{-1}C'HA \qquad (14.4.4)$$

$$H = B + \delta(A + CG)'H(A + CG) \qquad (14.4.5)$$

$$\mathbf{g}_t = -(C'HC)^{-1}C'(H\boldsymbol{\alpha}_t - \mathbf{h}_t) \qquad (14.4.6)$$

$$\mathbf{h}_t = [I - \delta(A + CG)']^{-1}[-\boldsymbol{\theta}_t/2 + (A + CG)'H\boldsymbol{\alpha}_t] \qquad (14.4.7)$$

The set of equations (14.4.4)–(14.4.7) defines the parameters of the optimal control rule (14.4.3). As a result of bounded rationality, we include the possibility that agents make mistakes in solving their optimization problems. Consequently, in recovering the unknown parameters we use a system that includes a matrix of errors E in equation (14.4.4) with $\boldsymbol{\varepsilon}_1 = \text{vec}(E)$, and we add an error ε_{2t} to the right-hand side of (14.4.6).

Other procedures to recover the unknown parameters in (14.4.4)–(14.4.7) exist but they all are based on a large set of assumptions that are required to convert an ill-posed inverse problem into a well-posed one. For example, Chow (1983) suggests a two-stage least-squares method to estimate A, C, G, $\boldsymbol{\alpha}_t$ and $\mathbf{g}_t$ and then uses equations (14.4.4)–(14.4.7) to recover B and $\boldsymbol{\theta}_t$ while imposing a large set of zero restrictions.

14.4.1 REPARAMETERIZATION

Consistent with Sections 14.2 and 14.3, in this section we reformulate the GME method such that all the parameters of the system can be estimated simultaneously. Further, under the GME formulation we avoid the usual additional restrictions or assumptions, needed to estimate the parameters of such systems, while using only the available data comprised of the time-series observations on the state and control variables. Specifically, given the data points $\mathbf{x}_t$ and $\mathbf{u}_t$, we wish to recover simultaneously A, C, G, B, $\boldsymbol{\theta}_t$, $\boldsymbol{\alpha}_t$ and $\mathbf{g}_t$. Working toward this end, if we premultiply equation (14.4.6) by $C'HC$ and then substitute equation (14.4.7) into (14.4.6) we obtain

$$-C'[I - \delta R']^{-1}\boldsymbol{\theta}_t/2 = C'HC\mathbf{g}_t + C'[I - (I - \delta R')^{-1}R']H\boldsymbol{\alpha}_t \quad (14.4.8)$$

where $R = A + CG$.

Thus, with no assumptions on H, our objective is to recover B, H and $\boldsymbol{\theta}_t$, along with the other parameters, in a one step procedure. Reparameterizing the system-process equations in line with Section 4.3 yields the following observation equations:

$$\mathbf{x}_t = A\mathbf{x}_{t-1} + C\mathbf{u}_t + \boldsymbol{\alpha}_t + \mathbf{e}_{1t} = Z^A\mathbf{p}^A\mathbf{x}_{t-1} + Z^C\mathbf{p}^C\mathbf{u}_t + Z^\alpha\mathbf{p}_t^\alpha + \mathbf{v}^{1\prime}\mathbf{w}_t^1 \quad (14.4.9)$$

$$\mathbf{u}_t = G\mathbf{x}_{t-1} + \mathbf{g}_t + \mathbf{e}_{2t} = Z^G\mathbf{p}^G\mathbf{x}_{t-1} + Z^g\mathbf{p}_t^g + \mathbf{v}^{2\prime}\mathbf{w}_t^2 \quad (14.4.10)$$

The parameters recovered in (14.4.9) and (14.4.10) serve as the *data* for equations (14.4.4), (14.4.5) and (14.4.8). This is somewhat analogous to equation (14.2.2), where $\boldsymbol{\beta}_{t-1}$ serves as the data in the system-process equation, while $\boldsymbol{\beta}_t$ is the unknown parameter vector to be recovered based on $\mathbf{x}_t$ in the observation-consistency equation (14.2.1). In summary, the recovery of A, C and G permits recovery of H and B. These, together with estimate of $\mathbf{g}_t$, are then used to recover the vector of intercepts $\boldsymbol{\theta}_t$.

14.4.2 THE GME FORMULATION AND SOLUTION

Given the reparameterization (14.4.9) and (14.4.10) along with (14.4.4), (14.4.5) and (14.4.8), the GME problem may be stated, in vector form and using a multi-component criterion, as

$$\max_{\{\mathbf{p}^i\},\{\mathbf{w}^j\}} \quad H(\mathbf{p}^i, \mathbf{w}^j) = \sum_{i,j}\{-\mathbf{p}^{i\prime}\ln(\mathbf{p}^i) - \mathbf{w}^{j\prime}\ln \mathbf{w}^j\} \tag{14.4.11}$$

subject to

1. the data consistency relations

$$\mathbf{x}_t = Z^A\mathbf{p}^A\mathbf{x}_{t-1} + Z^C\mathbf{p}^C\mathbf{u}_t + Z^\alpha\mathbf{p}_t^\alpha + \mathbf{v}^{1\prime}\mathbf{w}_t^1 \tag{14.4.12}$$

$$\mathbf{u}_t = Z^G\mathbf{p}^G\mathbf{x}_{t-1} + Z^g\mathbf{p}_t^g + \mathbf{v}^{2\prime}\mathbf{w}_t^2 \tag{14.4.13}$$

2. the optimal control-consistency relations

$$A + CG = R \tag{14.4.14}$$

$$G = -(C'HC)^{-1}C'HA + E \tag{14.4.15}$$

$$B = H - \delta R'HR \tag{14.4.16}$$

$$-C'[I - \delta R']^{-1}\boldsymbol{\theta}_t/2 = C'HC\mathbf{g}_t + C'[I - (I - \delta R')^{-1}R']H\boldsymbol{\alpha} + \boldsymbol{\varepsilon}_{2t} \tag{14.4.17}$$

and

3. the adding-up constraints

$$(\mathbf{1}' \otimes I)\mathbf{p}_t^i = \mathbf{1}, \qquad \text{for } i = A, C, \boldsymbol{\alpha}, G, \mathbf{g}, \boldsymbol{\theta}, \mathbf{h} \tag{14.4.18}$$

$$(\mathbf{1}' \otimes I)\mathbf{w}_t^j = \mathbf{1}, \qquad \text{for } j = \mathbf{e}_1, \mathbf{e}_2, \boldsymbol{\varepsilon}_1, \boldsymbol{\varepsilon}_2 \tag{14.4.19}$$

where the reparameterization definitions are

$$Z^i\mathbf{p}^i = i, \qquad \text{for } i = A, C, \boldsymbol{\alpha}, G, \mathbf{g}, \boldsymbol{\theta}, \mathbf{h} \tag{14.4.20}$$

$$\mathbf{v}^{j\prime}\mathbf{w}^j = j, \qquad \text{for } j = \mathbf{e}_1, \mathbf{e}_2, \boldsymbol{\varepsilon}_1, \boldsymbol{\varepsilon}_2 \tag{14.4.21}$$

where $\mathbf{p}^i$ and $\mathbf{w}^j$ are the probabilities associated with the corresponding parameter spaces for i and j respectively. The error supports $\mathbf{v}^j$ are specified to be symmetric around zero. Note that we have specified four error components. The first two are associated with the data-consistency equations (14.4.12) and (14.4.13) and the other two are associated with the optimal control–consistency equations (14.4.15) and (14.4.17).

The solution to this optimization problem yields $\hat{\mathbf{p}}^i$ and $\hat{\mathbf{w}}^j$ which are used to recover point estimates of $\hat{A}$, $\hat{C}$, $\hat{G}$, $\hat{\mathbf{g}}_t$, $\hat{\mathbf{h}}_t$ and $\hat{\boldsymbol{\theta}}_t$. Finally, we may follow the discussion in Chapter 7 and introduce a weight factor $\gamma \in (0, 1)$ in the dual criterion function (14.4.11) in order to vary the tradeoff between precision and prediction.

14.4.3 RESULTS OF A SAMPLING EXPERIMENT

To indicate the operational nature of the formulation developed in this section, consider the problem of recovering the unknown parameters of the linear-quadratic control problem (14.4.1), (14.4.2) and (14.4.3) that involves a single state variable y_t and a single control variable u_t with $\boldsymbol{\theta}_t = \boldsymbol{\alpha}_t = \mathbf{0}$. These assumptions imply $\mathbf{g}_t = 0$. Thus, the specification for this problem is

$$\mathbf{x}_t \equiv \begin{pmatrix} y_t \\ u_t \end{pmatrix} = \begin{pmatrix} a & 0 \\ 0 & 0 \end{pmatrix}\begin{pmatrix} y_{t-1} \\ u_{t-1} \end{pmatrix} + \begin{pmatrix} c \\ 1 \end{pmatrix} u_t + \begin{pmatrix} e_{1t} \\ 0 \end{pmatrix} \tag{14.4.22}$$

or

$$\begin{aligned} \mathbf{x}_t &= A\mathbf{x}_{t-1} + C\mathbf{u}_t + \mathbf{e}_{1t} \\ &= Z^A\mathbf{p}^A\mathbf{x}_{t-1} + Z^C\mathbf{p}^C\mathbf{u}_t + V^1\mathbf{w}_t^1 \end{aligned} \tag{14.4.23}$$

with control feedback equation

$$\begin{aligned} u_t &= G\mathbf{x}_{t-1} + e_{2t} \\ &= Z^G\mathbf{p}^G\mathbf{x}_{t-1}\mathbf{V}^2\mathbf{w}_t^2 \end{aligned} \tag{14.4.24}$$

Given this specification along with the objective function

$$\min_{u_t} W = \mathrm{E}\left\{\sum_{t=1}^{\infty} \delta_t(-\mathbf{x}_t' B\mathbf{x}_t)\right\} \tag{14.4.25}$$

our objective is to recover the unknowns A, C, G and B using time series observations consisting of y_t and u_t and a discount factor of $\delta = 0.95$.

To generate data for y_t and u_t, in the sampling experiment equations (14.4.4) and (14.4.5) were used with

$$A = \begin{bmatrix} 1 & 0 \\ 0 & 0 \end{bmatrix}, \quad \mathbf{c} = \begin{bmatrix} 1 \\ 1 \end{bmatrix}, \quad B = \begin{bmatrix} -1 & -1 \\ -1 & -2 \end{bmatrix}$$

to yield the control parameters

$$G = \begin{bmatrix} -0.432 & 0 \\ 0 & 0 \end{bmatrix}$$

along with noise vectors e_{1t} and e_{2t}. In the experiment, all the support spaces Z^i and V^i are non-informative and symmetric-around-zero. The results are presented in Table 14.4.1 for 50 replications of samples of sizes $T = 2$, 6 and 10. The estimates reported in Table 14.4.1 are the averages of the estimates for the 50 replications.

Table 14.4.1 Estimates of A, **c**, G and B, from a sampling experiment of 50 replications, $T = 2, 6, 10$ and $\varepsilon_{1t} = \varepsilon_{2t} \sim \text{N}(0, 0.1)$

	$T = 2$	$T = 6$	$T = 10$
$\hat{A}$	$\begin{bmatrix} 0.38 & 0 \\ 0 & 0 \end{bmatrix}$	$\begin{bmatrix} 0.43 & 0 \\ 0 & 0 \end{bmatrix}$	$\begin{bmatrix} 0.49 & 0 \\ 0 & 0 \end{bmatrix}$
$\hat{\mathbf{c}}$	$\begin{bmatrix} -0.17 \\ 1.00 \end{bmatrix}$	$\begin{bmatrix} -0.19 \\ 1.00 \end{bmatrix}$	$\begin{bmatrix} -0.22 \\ 1.00 \end{bmatrix}$
$\hat{G}$	$\begin{bmatrix} -0.42 & 0 \\ 0 & 0 \end{bmatrix}$	$\begin{bmatrix} -0.44 & 0 \\ 0 & 0 \end{bmatrix}$	$\begin{bmatrix} -0.42 & 0 \\ 0 & 0 \end{bmatrix}$
$\hat{B}$	$\begin{bmatrix} -0.60 & -1.03 \\ -1.03 & -1.69 \end{bmatrix}$	$\begin{bmatrix} -0.60 & -1.03 \\ -1.03 & -1.71 \end{bmatrix}$	$\begin{bmatrix} -0.56 & -1.02 \\ -1.02 & -1.82 \end{bmatrix}$
MSE($\hat{A}$)	0.38	0.330	0.261
MSE($\hat{\mathbf{c}}$)	1.365	1.409	1.482
MSE($\hat{G}$)	0.003	0.005	0.008
MSE($\hat{B}$)	0.275	0.259	0.231
MSE(overall)	2.023	2.003	1.982

The unknown element in G is estimated quite accurately. Also, two of the unknown elements of B are recovered quite accurately for all T. However, the unknown element of **c**, c, is estimated with the wrong sign, and the (1, 1) element of B is off by approximately 40%. Even more serious is the fact that the estimate of B is not negative semi-definite, which implies that the control problem given by (14.4.1) and (14.4.2) is ill-posed (Chow, 1975).

The possibility that parameter estimates fail to satisfy various 'curvature properties' implied by theory arises with many estimation procedures, and the GME approach is no exception. In practice it is often very difficult to impose these restrictions in estimation. In our two-dimensional example, where the determinant has a simple form, it would be possible to impose negative semi-definiteness directly. However, this direct approach is unlikely to be practical where B has higher dimension. An alternative is to impose conditions that imply that B is negative semi-definite. For example, the dominant diagonal criterion (which requires that the absolute value of a diagonal element be larger than the sum of absolute values of off-diagonal elements in the same row), together with the requirement that diagonal elements be negative, guarantees definiteness. However, this restriction is stronger than the restriction on B implied by theory. In addition, the appearance of many absolute value operators in the constraints may cause numerical problems.

In view of this, we adopt a different remedy. The results in Table 14.4.1 indicate that we have attempted to infer too much from too little information. In practice, the econometrician will often have some information which we have

Table 14.4.2 Estimates of A, $\mathbf{c}$, G and B, from a sampling experiment of 50 replications, $T = 2, 6, 10$ and $\varepsilon_{1t} = \varepsilon_{2t} \sim \mathrm{N}(0, 0.1)$ and where Z^C is a non-negative parameter space

	$T = 2$	$T = 6$	$T = 10$
$\hat{A}$	$\begin{bmatrix} 0.92 & 0 \\ 0 & 0 \end{bmatrix}$	$\begin{bmatrix} 0.95 & 0 \\ 0 & 0 \end{bmatrix}$	$\begin{bmatrix} 0.99 & 0 \\ 0 & 0 \end{bmatrix}$
$\hat{\mathbf{c}}$	$\begin{bmatrix} 1.09 \\ 1.00 \end{bmatrix}$	$\begin{bmatrix} 1.05 \\ 1.00 \end{bmatrix}$	$\begin{bmatrix} 1.00 \\ 1.00 \end{bmatrix}$
$\hat{G}$	$\begin{bmatrix} -0.42 & 0 \\ 0 & 0 \end{bmatrix}$	$\begin{bmatrix} -0.44 & 0 \\ 0 & 0 \end{bmatrix}$	$\begin{bmatrix} -0.42 & 0 \\ 0 & 0 \end{bmatrix}$
$\hat{B}$	$\begin{bmatrix} -1.15 & -0.99 \\ -0.99 & -1.79 \end{bmatrix}$	$\begin{bmatrix} -1.08 & -1.00 \\ -1.00 & -1.79 \end{bmatrix}$	$\begin{bmatrix} -0.82 & -1.00 \\ -1.00 & -1.86 \end{bmatrix}$
MSE($\hat{A}$)	0.007	0.004	0.003
MSE($\hat{\mathbf{c}}$)	0.008	0.004	0.005
MSE($\hat{G}$)	0.004	0.005	0.008
MSE($\hat{B}$)	0.236	0.167	0.142
MSE(overall)	0.255	0.180	0.158

not used. For example, in many contexts, the sign of the impact of the control on the current state (i.e. the sign of c) may be known. To illustrate the effect of such information, we re-estimate the model under the restriction that the estimate of c is non-negative. This restriction is imposed by specifying the support of c as a non-negative interval $\mathbf{z}^C = (0, 1, 2, \ldots, 9)'$. Note that the non-negativity could be incorporated by using GCE.

Table 14.4.2 reports the results of this constrained estimation. It is not surprising that there is a considerable improvement in the estimate of c. However, it is noteworthy that the estimates of B also improve considerably. In particular, the estimated B is now negative definite. It is also interesting that the estimate of A_{11} is greatly improved. The estimate of G, which was already very good even without the additional information, is virtually unchanged. The estimates also become much more stable. The aggregate MSE is reduced by a factor of approximately 10. A large part of this reduction in instability is due to the fact that the estimate of c becomes much more stable. Further, the stability of A_{11} is also greatly increased.

This example illustrates that with a minimal amount of prior information, the GME approach provides good estimates for the non-linear inverse control problem. It also shows that in the absence of any prior information, the estimates may be unstable and may fail to satisfy curvature restrictions. This implies that the GME approach does not obviate the need for prior information in some circumstances. However, the striking result is that a minimal amount of such information, in the form of specifying the support Z^i

or in specifying some priors within the GCE formulation, leads to significant improvements.

In Tables 14.4.1 and 14.4.2 the variance of e_{it} is 0.1, which is a moderate amount of noise for this problem. Therefore, the experiment indicates that the degree of inaccuracy of the estimates in Table 14.4.1 is due almost entirely to the inherent lack of identification of the problem, rather than to the underlying randomness of the system. This conjecture is strengthened by the following result. Given that A, C and G are *known exactly*, we estimated B by using the GME formulation with (14.4.14)–(14.4.17) and the relevant adding-up constraints, and without the noise components. In this case,

$$\tilde{B} = \begin{bmatrix} -0.95 & -1.01 \\ -1.01 & -1.86 \end{bmatrix}$$

This estimate is only slightly closer to the true B than is the estimate obtained in Table 14.4.2 for $T = 10$. As the number of observations increases, or the measure of randomness decreases, our estimates of A, C and G should converge to the true values. However, since B is *underindentified*, there is no reason to expect that the estimates of that matrix should converge. This fact strengthens the significance of the numerical results we report above. We can not expect to recover the true value of B. We can only determine, by means of Monte Carlo exercises, how close on average we are likely to get.

14.5 COMPLEX COVARIANCE STRUCTURES OF THE DYNAMIC SYSTEM

In the analysis of the last three sections it was assumed that the errors are uncorrelated over time and across equations. As these assumptions are inconsistent with many data sets, we now extend the previous models to include a more general error-covariance structure. Following Chapter 9, we start with the dynamic system with autocorrelated errors and then proceed to the more general case, discussed in Chapter 11, where the errors are correlated across equations. To make notation easier, and with no loss of generality, we will formulate the following models within the framework of Section 14.2 and the GME–GCE model (14.2.9)–(14.2.15).

14.5.1 AUTOCORRELATED ERRORS

Following Section 9.2, if we assume that the errors of the single observation equation (14.2.1′) follow a first-order autoregressive process the linear dynamic model consists of the observation equations

$$y_t = \mathbf{x}_t'\boldsymbol{\beta}_t + e_t \tag{14.5.1}$$

the system equations

$$\boldsymbol{\beta}_t = A\boldsymbol{\beta}_{t-1} + C\mathbf{u}_t + \boldsymbol{\varepsilon}_t \tag{14.5.2}$$

and the first-order autocorrelation equations for (14.5.1)

$$e_t = \rho e_{t-1} + a_t \tag{14.5.3}$$

where $\mathbf{y}$, $\mathbf{x}_t$, $\boldsymbol{\beta}_t$, A, C, $\mathbf{u}_t$ and $\boldsymbol{\varepsilon}_t$ are defined in Section 14.2, and (14.5.3) is defined in equations (9.2.3)–(9.2.5). Having reparameterized the unknowns, the GME model is

$$\begin{aligned} \max_{\{a_{kk}\},\{p^{\beta}_{tkd}\},\{p^{C}_{kmn}\},\{w^{a}_{ij}\},\{w^{\varepsilon}_{tki}\},\rho} \quad & H(\mathbf{p}^{\beta}, \mathbf{p}^{C}, \mathbf{w}^{\varepsilon}, w^{a}) \\ = & -\sum_t \sum_k \sum_d p^{\beta}_{tkd} \ln(p^{\beta}_{tkd}) - \sum_k \sum_m \sum_n p^{C}_{kmn} \ln(p^{C}_{kmn}) \\ & - \sum_t \sum_j w^{a}_{tj} \ln(w^{a}_{tj}) - \sum_t \sum_k \sum_i w^{\varepsilon}_{tki} \ln(w^{\varepsilon}_{tki}) \end{aligned} \tag{14.5.4}$$

subject to the data-consistency relations

$$y_t = \sum_k \sum_d z^{\beta}_{tkd} p^{\beta}_{tkd} x_{kt} + e_t, \qquad \text{for } t = 1, 2, \ldots, T \tag{14.5.5}$$

$$\begin{aligned} \beta_{tk} = a_{kk} \sum_d z^{\beta}_{t-1kd} p^{\beta}_{t-1,kd} + \sum_m \sum_n z^{C}_{kmn} p^{C}_{kmn} u_{tkm} + \sum_i v^{\varepsilon}_{tki} w^{\varepsilon}_{tki}, \\ \text{for } t = 2, 3, \ldots, T; \quad k = 1, 2, \ldots, K \end{aligned} \tag{14.5.6}$$

the first-order autocorrelation relations

$$\begin{aligned} e_1 &= \sum_j v^{a}_{j} w^{a}_{1j} \qquad \text{for } t = 1 \\ e_t &= \rho e_{t-1} + \sum_j v^{a}_{j} w^{a}_{tj} \qquad \text{for } t > 1 \end{aligned} \tag{14.5.7}$$

and the adding-up constraints

$$\sum_d p^{\beta}_{tkd} = 1, \qquad \text{for } k = 1, 2, \ldots, K; \quad t = 1, 2, \ldots, T \tag{14.5.8}$$

$$\sum_n p^{C}_{kmn} = 1, \qquad \text{for } k = 1, 2, \ldots, K; \quad m = 1, 2, \ldots, M \tag{14.5.9}$$

$$\sum_j w^{a}_{tj} = 1, \qquad \text{for } t = 1, 2, \ldots, T \tag{14.5.10}$$

$$\sum_i w^{\varepsilon}_{tki} = 1, \qquad \text{for } k = 1, 2, \ldots, K; \quad t = 2, 3, \ldots, T \tag{14.5.11}$$

where the unknown parameters are defined as

$$\sum_d z^{\beta}_{tkd} p^{\beta}_{tkd} = \beta_{tk}, \qquad \text{for } k = 1, 2, \ldots, K; \quad t = 1, 2, \ldots, T \tag{14.5.12}$$

$$\sum_n z^{C}_{kmn} p^{C}_{kmn} = c_{km}, \qquad \text{for } k = 1, 2, \ldots, K; \quad m = 1, 2, \ldots, M \tag{14.5.13}$$

$$\sum_j v^{a}_{tj} w^{a}_{tj} = a_t, \qquad \text{for } t = 1, 2, \ldots, T \tag{14.5.14}$$

$$\sum_i v^{\varepsilon}_{tki} w^{\varepsilon}_{tki} = \varepsilon_{tk}, \qquad \text{for } k = 1, 2, \ldots, K; \quad t = 2, 3, \ldots, T \tag{14.5.15}$$

The optimal solution yields estimates of the signal and noise probability vectors, the point estimates of ρ, and the elements of the adjustment matrix A.

Using the same structure, the above adjustments are easy to include and compute and can be incorporated in any linear or non-linear dynamic model. Using the same approach and following Section 9.2.3, higher-order autocorrelation process of the errors can be incorporated as well. Finally, following this approach, and consistent with Section 9.3, if we have a reason to believe that the error structure is heteroskedastic, equation (9.3.9) may be added to the dynamic GME model.

14.5.2 ERROR CORRELATION ACROSS EQUATIONS

All the dynamic systems involve at least two sets of equations: a set of observation equations and a set of state equations. As these equations are related, it is expected that their random errors will be correlated. Within the framework of Chapter 11, which extends the single-equation GME model to the seemingly unrelated (SUR) set of equations, we generalize the model of Section 14.2 to accommodate for such a possibility.

In that case, within the GCE formulation, the model is similar to model (14.2.9)–(14.2.15) with the additional covariance–consistency relations (11.3.3):

$$\frac{1}{T}\sum_{t=1}^{T} e_{ts}e_{tl} = \delta_{sl}\left[\left(\frac{1}{T}\sum_{t=1}^{T} e_{ts}e_{ts}\right)\left(\frac{1}{T}\sum_{t=1}^{T} e_{tl}e_{tl}\right)\right]^{1/2}, \qquad \text{for } l \neq s \tag{14.5.16}$$

where there are $(S^2 - S)$ such relations for the observation equation (14.2.1′).

A *similar* set of equations describing the relationship between ε_{ts} and ε_{te} or between $\mathbf{e}_t$ and $\boldsymbol{\varepsilon}_t$, can be defined in an exact way. Having described the new set of covariance–consistency constraints, the GCE model consists of minimizing (14.2.9) subject to (14.2.10)–(14.2.15) and (14.5.16).

14.6 REMARKS

In this chapter we have extended the GME formulation to accommodate estimation of non-linear, dynamic systems. The first two problems involve recovering the parameters of a state equation and the values of a state variable when the state system is linear or non-linear and the state observation is noisy. Further, the case where the state variable is unobserved and is a complex stochastic function of other variables was also formulated. The third problem concentrated on recovering the parameters of the objective function and state equation for a linear-quadratic control problem. In each of these situations, traditional methods fail to yield a solution or demand restrictive assumptions.

There are several possible extensions to the applications presented here. It would be interesting to nest the two problems we studied and estimate the parameters, including those of the objective function, of a control problem where the state is imperfectly observed. This implies that controls are functions of noisy observations, rather than the state. For example, agents may employ the Kalman filter to make their inferences about the state. In this case, it would be necessary to estimate the parameters of the filtering equation. Another extension would be to use the GME formulation to estimate nonlinear dynamic models, using the Euler equations instead of closed form expressions such as the Ricatti equations. A third extension involves using GME to estimate market power in dynamic oligopoly models.

REFERENCES

Berck, P. and Johns, G. (1991) Estimating structural resource models when stock is uncertain: Theory and an application to Pacific halibut. In D. Lund and B. Oksendal (eds.), *Stochastic Models and Option Values*, pp. 243–66. North-Holland, Amsterdam.

Blanchard, O. (1983) The production and inventory behavior of the American automobile industry. *Journal of Political Economy* **91**, 365–400.

Broemeling, L. D. (1985) *Bayesian Analysis of Linear Models.* Marcel Dekker, New York.

Chow, G. (1975) *Analysis and Control of Dynamic Economic Systems.* John Wiley, New York.

Chow, G. (1981) *Econometric Analysis by Control Methods.* John Wiley, New York.

Chow, G. (1983) *Econometrics.* McGraw-Hill, New York.

Fulton, M. and Karp, L. (1989) Estimating the objectives of a public firm in a natural resource industry. *Journal of Environmental Economics and Management* **16**, 268–87.

Golan, A., Judge, G. and Karp, L. (1996) A maximum entropy approach to estimation and inference in dynamic models: Counting fish in the sea using maximum entropy. *Journal of Economic Dynamics and Control*, in press.

Hansen, L. and Sargent, T. (1980) Formulating and estimating dynamic linear rational expectations models. *Journal of Economic Dynamics and Control* **2**, 7–46.

Jameson, A. and Kreindler, E. (1973) Inverse problem of linear optimal control. *SIAM Journal of Control* **11**, 1–19.

Judge, G. G., Hill, R. C., Griffiths, W. E., Lütkepohl, H. and Lee, T.-C. (1988) *Introduction to the Theory and Practice of Econometrics*, 2nd edn. John Wiley, New York.

Kalman, R. E. (1960) A new approach to linear filtering and prediction problems. *Transactions of the American Society of Mechanical Engineers, Series D., Journal of Basic Engineering* **82**, 34–45.

Mangel, M. (1985) *Decision and Control in Uncertain Resource Systems.* Academic Press, New York.

Maybeck, P. S. (1979) *Stochastic Models, Estimation and Control.* Academic Press, New York.

Sargent, T. (1978) Estimation of dynamic labor demand schedules under rational expectations. *Journal of Political Economy* **86**, 1009–44.

Spence, A. M. (1973) Blue whales and applied control theory. Technical Report No. 108, Institute for Mathematical Studies in the Social Sciences, Stanford, California.

Stauber, M. S., Burt, O. and Linse, F. (1975) An economic evaluation of nitrogen fertilization of grasses when carry-over is significant. *American Journal of Agricultural Economics*, **57**, 463–71.

PART VI

Discrete choice-censored problems

In Parts III–V we have been concerned with statistical models with continuous left-hand-side outcome variables. We now extend the GME–GCE formulations for the special cases of discrete dependent variables and censored models. In Chapter 15, a GME formulation for the unordered multinomial response models is developed that includes ML–logit as a special case. In Chapter 16, the GME formulation of the censored (tobit) model is developed. This model is then generalized for estimation of the unknown parameters of ordered multinomial response data. For all the above GME models, sampling results are reported.

The models developed and presented in this Part are due to joint work with Jeffrey Perloff.

CHAPTER 15

Recovering information from multinomial response data

15.1 INTRODUCTION

In this chapter we propose a GME-GCE alternative to traditional maximum likelihood logit and probit formulations that provide a popular basis for estimating qualitative response models from unordered, multinomial, discrete choice data. The proposed model includes the ML estimator as a special case, is easy to compute and exhibits superior sampling performance relative to the ML estimator for any finite sample and for any number of unordered categories. The model and theory of this chapter are based on Golan, Judge and Perloff (1996).

In order to develop the statistical model that captures the basis of the data generation process, consider the following unordered multinomial discrete choice problem. Suppose, in an experiment consisting of N trials, that binary random variables $y_{1j}, y_{2j}, \ldots, y_{Nj}$ are observed, where y_{ij}, for $i = 1, 2, \ldots, N$, takes on one of J *unordered* categories for $j = 1, 2, \ldots, J$. Thus, on trial i, one of the J alternatives is observed in the form of a binary variable y_{ij}, that equals unity if alternative j is observed on trial i and zero otherwise. Let $p_{ij} = \Pr[y_{ij} = 1]$ and assume that p_{ij}, the probability of alternative j on trial i, are related to a set of explanatory variables through the model

$$p_{ij}(\boldsymbol{\beta}) \equiv \Pr(y_{ij} = 1 \mid \mathbf{x}_i, \boldsymbol{\beta}_j) = G(\mathbf{x}_i'\boldsymbol{\beta}_j),$$

$$\text{for } i = 1, 2, \ldots, N; \quad j = 1, 2, \ldots, J \qquad (15.1.1)$$

where $\boldsymbol{\beta}_j$ is a $(K \times 1)$ vector of unknown parameters, $\mathbf{x}_i' = (x_{i1}, x_{i2}, \ldots, x_{iK})$ is a $(1 \times K)$ vector of covariates, and $G(\cdot)$ is a function linking the probabilities

p_{ij} with the linear structure $\mathbf{x}_i'\boldsymbol{\beta}_j$. More generally, the covariates $\mathbf{x}_i$ could vary by category, but for convenience we focus on the basic case where the covariates do not change across categories.

If we use the traditional maximum likelihood approach, with log-likelihood function $L(G, \boldsymbol{\beta}_j) = \sum_i \sum_j y_{ij} \ln G(\mathbf{x}_i \boldsymbol{\beta}_j)$, the multinomial probit model and solution is obtained if $G(\cdot)$ in (15.1.1) is a standard Gaussian cumulative density function (c.d.f.). Alternatively, the multinomial logit model and solution is obtained in $G(\cdot)$ is a logistic c.d.f.

Although conventional maximum likelihood (ML) formulations (McFadden, 1974; Manski and McFadden, 1981; Maddala, 1983; Judge *et al.*, 1985; Greene, 1993) are widely used to model multinomial response data, some practical and conceptual problems remain. For example, in traditional parametric formulations a c.d.f. linking the multinomial probabilities and the covariates must be specified *a priori* to make the problem tractable. In terms of data, because of experimental design or non-experimental restrictions normally found in practice, the number of observations may be limited, the data may be partial or incomplete, or the covariates may be highly correlated and the design matrix ill-conditioned. In addition, traditional multinomial logit and probit formulations do not permit a simple way of introducing and evaluating the value of non-sample information on the unknown multinomial probabilities and response parameters. Finally, just as in the linear model of Chapters 6 and 7, the objectives of the researcher are dual and requires an estimation procedure that both predicts well and yields a high level of parameter precision. Traditional logit and probit formulations pursue only the single criterion of maximizing the likelihood. Recognizing the statistical consequences that follow from many of these difficulties, we propose a GME formulation and solution alternative that avoids many of the strong parametric assumptions or stability problems associated with the traditional ML approach to estimation and inference relative to qualitative choice problems.

In Section 15.2 the multinomial statistical model is reformulated and a pure maximum entropy (ME) solution for the multinomial probabilities and response (slope) parameters proposed by Denzau *et al.* (1989) and Soofi (1992) is reviewed and extended. We then compare the ME and the ML logit. In Section 15.3 a GME formulation is specified and a solution for the unknown parameters is given and asymptotic propectus and a convergence theorum are specified. A basis for including non-sample information in the formulation for the multinomial problem is presented in Section 15.4, and an extended GME formulation is specified in Section 15.5. In Sections 15.6 and 15.7 the information measures and a weighted dual loss function are specified. In Section 15.8 the results of limited sampling experiments, illustrating the GME and ML sampling performance, are reported. Conclusions and implications are presented in Section 15.8.

15.2 MODEL REFORMULATION AND A ME SOLUTION

15.2.1 MODEL TRANSFORMATION AND BACKGOUND

Generalizing (15.1.1) to include an additional noise component yields

$$y_{ij} = G(\mathbf{x}_i'\boldsymbol{\beta}_j) + e_{ij} = p_{ij} + e_{ij} \tag{15.2.1a}$$

where (15.1.2) may be written in vector notation as

$$\mathbf{y}_j = \mathbf{p}_j + \mathbf{e}_j \tag{15.2.1b}$$

or compactly over J as

$$\mathbf{y} = \mathbf{p} + \mathbf{e} \tag{15.2.1c}$$

where $\mathbf{y}_j$ and $\mathbf{x}_i$ are observed and $\mathbf{p}_j$ and $\mathbf{e}_j$ are unknown and unobserved.

Given this generalization, the objective is to recover both $\mathbf{p}$ and $\mathbf{e}$ simultaneously. If the *unknown and unobservable* $\mathbf{p}$ and $\mathbf{e}$ in (15.2.1c) are to be recovered, the indirect empirical measurements on the noisy observable $\mathbf{y}$ and the known covariates $\mathbf{x}_i$ must be used. In formulating the GME approach to the multinomial choice problem, we wish to introduce the information contained in the $(N \times K)$ matrix X of observable characteristics within the statistical model (15.2.1) that involves the NJ data ponts, y_{ij}. We do this by transforming the statistical model into the following linear (in $\mathbf{p}$), ill-posed inverse problem with noise:

$$(I_J \otimes X')\mathbf{y} = (I_J \otimes X')\mathbf{p} + (I_J \otimes X')\mathbf{e} \tag{15.2.1d}$$

The problem is ill-posed because there are KJ moment relations (data points) and NJ ($>KJ$) unknown multinomial parameters.

Three ways to solve the ill-posed problem (15.2.1d) are:

(i) to follow convention and impose parametric restrictions on the functional form linking the multinomial probabilities and the covariates (McFadden, 1974; Zellner and Rossi, 1984; Albert and Chib, 1993; Koop and Poirier, 1993)

(ii) to use a non-parametric or semi-parametric approach; or

(iii) to use a variant of the generalized maximum entropy formalism developed in Chapter 6.

Using method (i), if the parametric model is not correct, the costs of imposing the strong parametric restrictions required for estimation and testing are considerable. For method (ii), non-parametric or semiparametric smoothing methods (Ruud, 1993) that do not impose parametric restrictions on functional form face practical problems such as the curse of dimensionality and lack of finite sample results. For method (iii), the maximum entropy (ME) formalism of Chapter 3 and the GME formalism developed in Chapter 6, was designed to recover information from the data in the case of ill-posed, underdetermined pure and noise inverse problems. Consequently, to avoid the strong *a priori* restrictions of (i) and some of the potential problems of (ii), we use the GME procedure as the basis for analyzing the estimation and inference problem as it relates to multinomial response data.

15.2.2 A MAXIMUM ENTROPY (ME) FORMULATION

Following Denzau *et al.* (1989) and Soofi (1992), if in (15.2.1) we wish to assure that $\mathbf{p}$ preserves the observed sums of the attribute scores for each of the $k = 1, 2, \ldots, K$ covariates, then (15.2.1) is reduced to the pure inverse relation

$$(I_J \otimes X')\mathbf{y} = (I_J \otimes X')\mathbf{p} \tag{15.2.2}$$

Under this specification the multinomial probabilities $\mathbf{p}$ cannot be determined by direct inversion of (15.2.2). Thus, the data points may be equally consistent with a variety of different $\mathbf{p}$. Under the principle of maximum entropy, out of the possible multinomial probabilities *consistent* with the data, the maximally noncommittal choice is to select the $\mathbf{p}$ with minimum information content or equivalently, the maximum entropy. Thus, given the KJ constraints that force $\mathbf{p}$ to preserve the total values for each attribute, Denzau *et al.* (1989) and Soofi (1992) applied the pure inverse ME formulation as a basis for recovering the unknown $\mathbf{p}$. That is,

$$\max_{\mathbf{p}} H(\mathbf{p}) = \{-\mathbf{p}' \ln(\mathbf{p})\} \tag{15.2.3}$$

subject to the consistency relations

$$(I_J \otimes X')\mathbf{y} = (I_J \otimes X')\mathbf{p} \tag{15.2.4}$$

and the adding-up–normalization conditions

$$[I_{1J} \quad I_{2J} \quad \ldots. \quad I_{NJ}]\mathbf{p} = \mathbf{1} \tag{15.2.5}$$

The Lagrangian for the optimization problem (15.2.3)–(15.2.5) is

$$L = -\mathbf{p}' \ln(\mathbf{p}) + \boldsymbol{\beta}'[(I_J \otimes X')\mathbf{p} - (I_J \otimes X')\mathbf{y}] + \boldsymbol{\rho}'\{\mathbf{1} - [I_{1J}, I_{2J}, \ldots, I_{NJ}]\mathbf{p}\} \tag{15.2.6}$$

First-order conditions for the Lagrangian (15.2.6) form a basis for recovering the unknown $\mathbf{p}_j$ and the Lagrange parameters $\boldsymbol{\beta}_j$. Solving the optimization problem yields the solution

$$p_{ij}^* = \frac{\exp(-\mathbf{x}_i'\boldsymbol{\beta}_j^*)}{\Omega_i(\boldsymbol{\beta}^*)} = \frac{\exp(-\boldsymbol{\beta}_j^{*\prime}\mathbf{x}_i)}{1 + \sum_{j=2}^{J} \exp(-\boldsymbol{\beta}_j^{*\prime}\mathbf{x}_i)} \tag{15.2.7}$$

where

$$\Omega_i(\boldsymbol{\beta}^*) = \mathbf{1}' \exp(-\mathbf{x}_i'\boldsymbol{\beta}_j^*) = \sum_j \exp\left(\sum_k \boldsymbol{\beta}_{jk}^* x_{ij}\right) \tag{15.2.8}$$

The partition functions $\boldsymbol{\Omega}_i(\boldsymbol{\beta}_j^*)$ are normalization factors. The unknown $\boldsymbol{\beta}_j$ that link the p_{ij} to the $\mathbf{x}_i$ are the KJ Lagrange parameters that are determined so that the optimum solution p_{ij}^* satisfy the ME constraints (15.2.4) and (15.2.5) and, as common in the literature $\boldsymbol{\beta}_1 = 0$. The Hessian matrix is negative definite assuring a global solution. Specifically,

$$\frac{\partial^2 L}{\partial p_{ij} \partial p_{ij}} = -\frac{\mathbf{1}' \exp(-\mathbf{x}_i'\boldsymbol{\beta}_j)}{\exp(-\mathbf{x}_i'\boldsymbol{\beta}_j)} = -\frac{1}{p_{ij}} \tag{15.2.9}$$

where all the off-diagonal elements are zero. The consistency (pure inverse) relations (15.2.4), as noted by Soofi (1992), are just the log likelihood equations (first-order conditions) for estimating the multinomial probabilities under the traditional logit specification (Dykstra and Lemke, 1988). Consequently, the ME and ML multinomial logit solutions for p_{ij} are equivalent. Each p_{ij} is linked to the response coefficients β_{jk} through the Lagrange parameters for constraint (15.2.4). The ME linkage of the p_{ij} and $\mathbf{x}_i$ through the Lagrange parameters was noted by Denzau *et al.* (1989) and Soofi (1992). It is interesting to note that although the conceptual bases of the traditional multinomial logit and the ME formulation are different and under ME no particular functional form linking the p_{ij} and the $\mathbf{x}_i$ is specified, the solutions are equivalent. To show this, we follow Golan *et al.* (1996) and derive the information matrix for the ME formulation and then, as in Chapters 3 and 6, derive the dual ME formulation. Rearranging the Hessian (15.2.9) and summing over N yields

$$I(\mathbf{p}_j)_{\mathrm{ME}} = \sum_{i=1}^{N} \frac{\mathbf{1}' \exp(-\mathbf{x}_i'\boldsymbol{\beta}_j)}{\exp(-\mathbf{x}_i'\boldsymbol{\beta}_j)} \mathbf{1}\mathbf{1}' = \sum_i \frac{1}{p_{ik}} \mathbf{1}\mathbf{1}' \tag{15.2.10}$$

Finally, to compare (15.2.10) and the ML-logit information matrix, we convert (15.2.10) to the $\boldsymbol{\beta}_j$ space. Building on a result of Lehmann (1983, p. 118), we have

$$\begin{aligned} \left(\frac{\partial \mathbf{p}}{\partial \boldsymbol{\beta}_j}\right) I(\mathbf{p}_j)_{\mathrm{ME}} \left(\frac{\partial \mathbf{p}}{\partial \boldsymbol{\beta}_j}\right)' &= I(\boldsymbol{\beta}_j)_{\mathrm{ME}} = \sum_i \frac{\exp(-\mathbf{x}_i'\boldsymbol{\beta}_j)}{[\Omega_i(\boldsymbol{\beta}_j)]^2} \mathbf{x}_i\mathbf{x}_i' \\ &= \sum_i p_{ij} \frac{1}{\Omega_i(\boldsymbol{\beta}_j)} \mathbf{x}_i\mathbf{x}_i' = I(\boldsymbol{\beta}_j)_{\mathrm{ML}} \end{aligned} \tag{15.2.11}$$

where (15.2.11) is the jth diagonal block of J^2 blocks of dimension $(K \times K)$ and is identical to the ML information matrix.

Next, building on the Lagrangian and solution (15.2.7), we may rewrite, using the primal-dual result of Chapter 6, the ME problem (15.2.3)–(15.2.5) in an unconstrained dual form for the Lagrange multiples $\boldsymbol{\lambda}$

$$M(\boldsymbol{\lambda}_j) = \mathbf{y}'(I \otimes X')\boldsymbol{\lambda}_j + \sum_i \ln[\Omega_i(\boldsymbol{\lambda})] \tag{15.2.12}$$

It turns out that (15.2.12) is the same as the multinomial logit log likelihood function (Maddala, 1983, p. 36)

$$\begin{aligned}\ln L &= \sum_i \sum_j y_{ij} \ln p_{ij} = \sum_i \sum_j y_{ij} \ln\left(\frac{\exp(\mathbf{x}_i'\boldsymbol{\beta}_j)}{\sum_j \exp(\mathbf{x}_i'\boldsymbol{\beta}_j)}\right) \\ &= \sum_i \sum_j y_{ij}\mathbf{x}_{ik}\boldsymbol{\beta}_{jk} - \sum_j \ln[\Omega_i(\boldsymbol{\beta}_j)]\end{aligned} \tag{15.2.13}$$

where $\boldsymbol{\beta} = -\boldsymbol{\lambda}$. Consequently, the usual ML asymptotic properties follow. Having reviewed and extended the ME multinomial problem, we now discuss and formulate the GME multinomial problem developed by Golan *et al.* (1996).

15.3 GME FORMULATION

In developing the ME and ML solutions of Section 15.2.2, strong assumptions were needed to ensure that the consistency relations (15.2.4) hold. This is similar to the moment–GME formulation of Chapter 6 where the GME and ML–LS are equivalent when 'ignoring' the error terms. Consistent with the uncertainty about the statistical model that normally holds in practice, it would seem more realistic to avoid, in the ME approach, the strong requirement of (15.2.4) or, in the ML approach, the strong c.d.f. assumption, and to work with the more general noise inverse-consistency relations (15.2.1d). Further, by working with (15.2.1d) both $\mathbf{p}$ and $\mathbf{e}$ appear directly as unknown parameters in the inverse relation.

15.3.1 THE GME FORMULATION AND SOLUTION

As in all GME formulation, before specifying the model, we need to reparameterize the unknowns. As $\mathbf{p}$ is already in a probability form, we only need to reparameterize the elements of $\mathbf{e}$. In the multinomial case the outcomes for the random variable e_{ij} may range over the natural interval $[-1, 1]$ with corresponding probabilities in the interval $[0, 1]$. Following Chapter 6, we define over the interval $[-1, 1]$ a set of discrete points $\mathbf{v}_{ij} = [v_{ij1}, v_{ij2}, \ldots, v_{ijM}]'$ of dimension $M \geq 2$, with corresponding unknown probabilities $\mathbf{w}_{ij} = [w_{ij1}, w_{ij2}, \ldots, w_{ijM}]'$, and expected values $e_{ij} = \sum_m v_{ijm} w_{ijm}$, where $\sum_m w_{ijm} = 1$. Thus, under this reparameterization, we may rewrite the statistical model (15.2.1d) as

$$(I_J \otimes X')\mathbf{y} = (I_J \otimes X')\mathbf{p} + (I_J \otimes X')V\mathbf{w} \tag{15.3.1}$$

where both **p** and **w** are in the form of probabilities.

Given the reparameterized inverse relation (15.3.1) involving the unknown and unobservables **p** and **w**, the GME multinomial response problem may be stated as maximizing the dual objective function

$$\max_{\mathbf{p},\mathbf{w}} H(\mathbf{p}, \mathbf{w}) = \{-\mathbf{p}' \ln \mathbf{p} - \mathbf{w}' \ln \mathbf{w}\} \tag{15.3.2}$$

subject to the consistency conditions (data)

$$(I_J \otimes X')\mathbf{y} = (I_J \otimes X')\mathbf{p} + (I_J \otimes X')V\mathbf{w} \tag{15.3.3}$$

and the adding-up (normalization) constraints

$$[I_{1J} \quad I_{2J} \quad \ldots \quad I_{NJ}]\mathbf{p} = \mathbf{1}, \qquad \text{for } i = 1, 2, \ldots, N \tag{15.3.4}$$

$$\mathbf{1}'\mathbf{w}_{ij} = 1, \qquad \text{for } i = 1, 2, \ldots, N; \quad j = 1, 2, \ldots, J \tag{15.3.5}$$

The corresponding Lagrangian is

$$\begin{aligned} L = {} & -\mathbf{p}' \ln \mathbf{p} - \mathbf{w}' \ln \mathbf{w} + \boldsymbol{\beta}'[(I_J \otimes X')\mathbf{p} + (I_J \otimes X')V\mathbf{w} - (I_J \otimes X')\mathbf{y}] \\ & + \boldsymbol{\rho}'\{\mathbf{1} - [I_{1J}, I_{2J}, \ldots, I_{NJ}]\mathbf{p}\} + \boldsymbol{\delta}'(\mathbf{1} - \mathbf{1}'\mathbf{w}_{ij}) \end{aligned} \tag{15.3.6}$$

Solving the optimization problem yields the solution

$$\hat{p}_{ij} = \frac{\exp(-\mathbf{x}_i'\hat{\boldsymbol{\beta}}_j)}{\Omega_i(\hat{\boldsymbol{\beta}}_j)} \tag{15.3.7a}$$

where

$$\Omega_i(\hat{\boldsymbol{\beta}}_j) = \mathbf{1}' \exp(-\mathbf{x}_i'\hat{\boldsymbol{\beta}}_j) \tag{15.3.7b}$$

and

$$\hat{w}_{ijm} = \frac{\exp(-\mathbf{x}_i\hat{\boldsymbol{\beta}}_j V_j)}{\Psi_{ij}(\hat{\boldsymbol{\beta}}_j)} \tag{15.3.8a}$$

where

$$\Psi_{ij}(\hat{\boldsymbol{\beta}}_j) = \mathbf{1}' \exp(-\mathbf{x}_i'\hat{\boldsymbol{\beta}}_j V_j) \tag{15.3.8b}$$

Finally, from (15.3.1)

$$\hat{\mathbf{e}}_j = V_j \hat{\mathbf{w}}_j \tag{15.3.9}$$

The partition function $\Omega_i(\hat{\boldsymbol{\beta}}_j)$ and $\Psi_{ij}(\hat{\boldsymbol{\beta}}_j)$ are normalization factors. The unknown $\boldsymbol{\beta}_j$ that link the p_{ij} to the $\mathbf{x}_i$ are the KJ Lagrange parameters that are determined so that the optimum solution $\hat{p}_{ij}$ and $\hat{e}_{ij}$ satisfy the constraints (15.3.3)–(15.3.5). The solutions (15.3.7a) and (15.3.8a) are in exponential form and thus $\hat{\mathbf{p}}_j$ and $\hat{\mathbf{w}}_j$ are always positive. The normalization factors (15.3.7b) and (15.3.8) ensure that $\hat{\mathbf{p}}_j$ and $\hat{\mathbf{w}}_j$ have the properties of probabilities.

The recovered $\hat{p}_{ij}$ and $\hat{e}_{ij}$ are based only on the information in the consistency relations with no initial assumptions regarding the form of the function linking the p_{ij} and $\mathbf{x}_i'\boldsymbol{\beta}_j$. Because the $\hat{\boldsymbol{\beta}}_j$ are not unique, just as in (15.2.7) of the ME solution, a common normalization procedure $\boldsymbol{\beta}_1 = \mathbf{0}$ is imposed, where $\mathbf{0}$ is a $(K \times 1)$ zero vector.

In the GME formulations, the unknowns $\mathbf{p}$ and $\mathbf{w}$ are determined jointly so as to maximize (15.3.2) subject to constraints (15.3.3)–(15.3.5). Any prior knowledge concerning the multinomial probabilities p_{ij} can be added in a cross-entropy context as developed in the next section. The GME moment–consistency relations (15.3.3) are less restrictive than the ME and ML multinomial logit moment–consistency relations (15.2.4). By relaxing the ML–pure ME information–moment conditions (15.2.4) to the information–moment conditions (15.3.3), a larger set of solutions exist for the GME formulation that includes those consistent with (15.2.4). Consequently, the solution requirements for the $\mathbf{p}_j$ for GME are less binding. As a result it is possible for the recovered $\mathbf{p}_j$ to exhibit more uniformity than for the ML logit–pure ME solution.

In Section 15.2 we developed the relationship between the ME and ML approaches. In a similar way, we now demonstrate that the GME is related to a class of generalized logit formulations. Building on the Lagrangian (15.3.6), and using $\boldsymbol{\lambda}$ instead of $\boldsymbol{\beta}$, the dual unconstrained GME formulation is

$$\begin{aligned} M(\boldsymbol{\lambda}_j) &= -\mathbf{p}(\boldsymbol{\lambda})' \ln \mathbf{p}(\boldsymbol{\lambda}) - \mathbf{w}(\boldsymbol{\lambda})' \ln \mathbf{w}(\boldsymbol{\lambda}) + \boldsymbol{\lambda}'[(I_J \otimes X')\mathbf{y} - (I_J \otimes X')\mathbf{p} \\ &\quad - (I_J \otimes X')V\mathbf{w}] \\ &= -\mathbf{p}(\boldsymbol{\lambda})'[-\mathbf{x}_i'\boldsymbol{\lambda}_j - \ln \Omega_i] - \mathbf{w}(\boldsymbol{\lambda})'[-\mathbf{x}_i'\boldsymbol{\lambda}_j V_j - \ln \Psi_{ij}] \\ &\quad + \boldsymbol{\lambda}'[(I_j \otimes X')\mathbf{y} - (I_J \otimes X')\mathbf{p} - (I_J \otimes X')V\mathbf{w}] \\ &= \mathbf{y}'(I_j \otimes X')\boldsymbol{\lambda} + \sum_i \ln[\Omega_i(\boldsymbol{\lambda}_j)] + \sum_i \sum_j \ln[\Psi_i(\boldsymbol{\lambda}_i)] \end{aligned} \tag{15.3.10}$$

where $\boldsymbol{\lambda}$ are the Lagrange multipliers and $\boldsymbol{\beta}_j = -\boldsymbol{\lambda}_j$.

Keeping the relationship between $\boldsymbol{\lambda}_j$ and $\boldsymbol{\beta}_j$ in mind, it is obvious by looking at (15.3.10) that it is a generalized logit log likelihood function where the right-hand-side component of (15.3.10) corresponds to the noise component introduced in the GME formulation. Similar to the linear statistical model of Chapter 6, the gradient of (15.3.10) with respect to $\boldsymbol{\lambda}_j$ yields the moment consistency relations (15.3.3). Finally, as the sample size increases, the right-hand-side component approaches zero and (15.3.10) approaches (15.2.12). In other words, as the sample size becomes large, the GME solution approaches the ME, or ML, solution. This result, together with other analytic results, is discussed in the next section.

Before continuing to the next section, we emphasize, in line with Chapter 7, that even though for an optimal solution, $M = 2$ is a sufficient number of points in the error support V, a larger number of points yields superior results. See Golan *et al.* (1996) for sampling experiments and an empirical example.

15.3.2 INFERENCE

Given the Lagrangian (15.3.6), the distribution implied by (15.3.7) and (15.3.8) and the information-moment relations (15.3.3), the elements of the Hessian for the GME are

$$\frac{\partial^2 L}{\partial p_{ij}\partial p_{ij}} + \sum_m \frac{\partial^2 L}{\partial w_{ijm}\partial w_{ijm}} = -\frac{\mathbf{1}'\exp(\mathbf{x}_i'\boldsymbol{\beta}_j)}{\exp(\mathbf{x}_i'\boldsymbol{\beta}_j)} - \sum_m \frac{\mathbf{1}'\exp(-\mathbf{x}_i'\boldsymbol{\beta}_j V_j)}{\exp(-\mathbf{x}_i'\boldsymbol{\beta}_j V_j)} = -\frac{1}{p_{ij}} - \sum_m \frac{1}{w_{ijm}} \tag{15.3.11}$$

where all off-diagonal elements are zero. This leads to a negative definite Hessian matrix, ensuring a unique global solution for the p_{ij}'s. Given this result and the corresponding information matrices, we follow the analytical results developed and reported in Golan *et al.* (1996) to make an inferential comparison of the GME and ML logit-pure ME estimation rules.

Proposition 1. *At the limit,* $\hat{\mathbf{p}}$ *is a consistent estimator of* $\mathbf{p}$ *or* $\hat{\boldsymbol{\beta}}$ *is a consistent estimator of* $\boldsymbol{\beta}$, *the ME–ML logit solution vector is equivalent to the GME solution vector and the asymptotic* $\text{Var}(\hat{\boldsymbol{\beta}}_j)_{\text{GME}} =$ *asymptotic* $\text{Var}(\boldsymbol{\beta}_j^*)_{\text{ME–ML}}$.

Consequently, the usual asymptotic properties for the ML logit estimator follow for the GME estimator. As a consequence of this proposition, there exists an inverse relationship between the boundaries of V_j and N. A conservative choice for the boundaries of V_j are $\pm 1/\sqrt{N}$. For example, for $N = 100$ and $M = 3$, $\mathbf{v}_{ij} = (-0.1, 0, 0.1)'$.

Proposition 2. *For a given X and N, and for all* $0 < |\beta_{ij}| \ll \infty$ *the* $\text{Var}(\boldsymbol{\beta}_j)_{\text{GME}} \leq \text{Var}(\boldsymbol{\beta}_j)_{\text{ME}} = \text{Var}(\boldsymbol{\beta}_j)_{\text{ML logit}}$.

The following proposition identifies the different rates of convergence for GME and ME–ML logit estimates.

Proposition 3. *For a given* X, $0 < N < \infty$ *and* $M < \infty$, $I(\beta_{jk})_{\text{GME}} \geq (1 + J^2/M)I(\beta_{jk})_{\text{ME–ML logit}}$ *for all j, k or equivalently,* $(1 + J^2/M)\text{Var}(\beta_{jk})_{\text{GME}} \leq \text{Var}(\beta_{jk})_{\text{ME–ML logit}}$, *for all j, k where J is the number of categories and N is the number of observations.*

Proposition 3 shows that for any sample size N, the GME estimator converges at least $(1 + J^2/M)$ faster than the ME–ML logit estimator. As J increases, the difference in the rate of convergence increases by a factor of J^2/M. For example, in the case of orthonormal X's, $J = 3$ and $M = 2$, the variance of the GME estimator with $N = 30$, is at least as small as the ME–ML logit estimator with $N = 165$.

15.4 GCE FORMULATION

In some multinomial response problems we may have non-sample information from experience and/or theory, over and above that contained in the consistency and adding-up constraints. If such information exists for the p_{ij} in the form of q_{ij} it may be introduced through the cross-entropy (CE) formalism proposed by Kullback (1959) and Good (1963) and generalized in Chapter 6. Letting $\mathbf{q}$ and $\mathbf{u}$ be the prior probabilities for $\mathbf{p}$ and $\mathbf{w}$ respectively, the GCE formulation, in scalar notation, is

$$\min_{p_{ij},\, w_{ijm}} \quad I(\mathbf{p}, \mathbf{w}) = \left\{ \sum_i \sum_j p_{ij} \ln(p_{ij}/q_{ij}) + \sum_i \sum_j \sum_m w_{ijm} \ln(w_{ijm}/u_{ijm}) \right\} \tag{15.4.1}$$

subject to

$$\sum_i x_{ik} p_{ij} + \sum_i \sum_m x_{ik} v_{ijm} w_{ijm} = \sum_i x_{ik} y_{ij}, \qquad \text{for } k = 1, 2, \ldots, K; \quad j = 1, 2, \ldots, J \tag{15.4.2}$$

$$\sum_j p_{ij} = 1, \qquad \text{for } i = 1, 2, \ldots, N \tag{15.4.3}$$

$$\sum_m w_{ijm} = 1, \qquad \text{for } i = 1, 2, \ldots, N; \quad j = 1, 2, \ldots, J \tag{15.4.4}$$

with Lagrangian

$$\begin{aligned} L = {} & \sum_i \sum_j p_{ij} \ln(p_{ij}/q_{ij}) + \sum_t \sum_j \sum_m w_{ijm} \ln(w_{ijm}/u_{ijm}) \\ & + \sum_j \sum_k \beta_{jk} \left[\sum_i y_{ij} x_{ik} - \sum_i p_{ij} x_{ik} - \sum_i \sum_m v_{ijm} w_{ijm} x_{ik} \right] \\ & + \sum_i \sum_j \delta_{ij} \left[1 - \sum_m w_{ijm} \right] + \sum_i \rho_i \left[1 - \sum_j p_{ij} \right] \end{aligned} \tag{15.4.5}$$

and first-order conditions

$$\frac{\partial L}{\partial p_{ij}} = \ln(\tilde{p}_{ij}/q_{ij}) + 1 - \sum_k \tilde{\beta}_{jk} x_{ik} - \tilde{\rho}_i = 0, \quad \text{for } i = 1, 2, \ldots, N; \quad j = 1, 2, \ldots, J \tag{15.4.6}$$

$$\frac{\partial L}{\partial w_{ijm}} = \ln(\tilde{w}_{ijm}/u_{ijm}) + 1 - \sum_k \tilde{\beta}_{jk} v_{ijm} x_{ik} - \tilde{\delta}_{ij} = 0, \tag{15.4.7}$$

$$\text{for } i = 1, 2, \ldots, N; \quad j = 1, 2, \ldots, J; \quad m = 1, 2, \ldots, M$$

$$\frac{\partial L}{\partial \beta_{jk}} = \sum_i y_{ij} x_{ik} - \sum_i \tilde{p}_{ij} x_{ik} - \sum_i \sum_m v_{ijm} \tilde{w}_{ijm} x_{ik} = 0, \tag{15.4.8}$$

$$\text{for } j = 1, 2, \ldots, J; \quad k = 1, 2, \ldots, K$$

$$\frac{\partial L}{\partial \rho_i} = 1 - \sum_j \tilde{p}_{ij} = 0, \quad \text{for } i = 1, 2, \ldots, N \tag{15.4.9}$$

$$\frac{\partial L}{\partial \delta_{ij}} = 1 - \sum_m \tilde{w}_{ijm} = 0, \quad \text{for } i = 1, 2, \ldots, N; \quad j = 1, 2, \ldots, J \tag{15.4.10}$$

where $\tilde{\beta}_{jk}$, $\tilde{\rho}_i$, and $\tilde{\delta}_{ij}$ are the optimal Lagrange multipliers associated with each constraint. Consistent with the knowledge available for a particular problem, additional constraints may be added.

Solving the system of $(2NJ + JK + NJM + N)$ equations yields the optimal solutions

$$\tilde{p}_{ij} = \frac{q_{ij}}{\Omega_i(\tilde{\beta}_{jk})} \exp\left[\sum_k \tilde{\beta}_{jk} x_{ik}\right] \tag{15.4.11}$$

where

$$\Omega_i(\tilde{\beta}_{jk}) = \sum_j q_{ij} \exp\left[\sum_k \tilde{\beta}_{ik} x_{ik}\right] \tag{15.4.12}$$

and

$$\tilde{w}_{ijm} = \frac{u_{ijm}}{\Psi_{ij}(\tilde{\beta}_{jk})} \exp\left[\sum_k \tilde{\beta}_{jk} v_{ijm} x_{ik}\right] \tag{15.4.13}$$

where

$$\Psi_{ij}(\tilde{\beta}_{jk}) = \sum_m u_{ijm} \exp\left[\sum_k \tilde{\beta}_{jk} v_{ijm} x_{ik}\right] \tag{15.4.14}$$

The resulting solution for the Lagrangian β_{jk} may be used with the covariates x_{ik} for the categoric choice prediction and the recovered $\tilde{w}_{ijm}$ may be used with the error support $\mathbf{v}_j$ to recover the $\tilde{e}_{ij}$. The solution $\tilde{p}_{ij}$ in (15.4.11) is a function of prior information, the data and a normalization factor. If the q_{ij}

are specified such that each of the choices is equally likely to be selected (uniform distributions), the GCE result reduces to the GME result and (15.4.11) becomes

$$\tilde{p}_{ij} = \frac{\exp\left(\sum_k \tilde{\beta}_{jk} x_{ik}\right)}{\Omega_i(\tilde{\beta}_{jk})} = \hat{p}_{ij} \tag{15.4.15}$$

where

$$\Omega_i(\tilde{\beta}_{jk}) = \sum_j \exp\left(\sum_k \tilde{\beta}_{jk} x_{ik}\right) = \Omega_i(\hat{\beta}_{jk}) \tag{15.4.16}$$

15.5 AN EXTENDED GCE FORMULATION

In contrast to the GCE formulation of the previous section, perhaps more consistent with non-sample information normally found in practice, it may be more reasonable to permit a discrete probability distribution to be specified for each of the p_{ij}. Working toward this end we may specify for each p_{ij} and q_{ij}, a discrete probability distribution defined over the parameter space [0, 1] by a set of discrete points $\mathbf{z} = (z_1, z_2, \ldots, z_D)$ with corresponding probabilities π_{ijd} for $d = 1, 2, \ldots, D$, where $D \geq 2$. Thus, the natural probabilities p_{ij} are redefined as

$$p_{ij} = \sum_d \pi_{ijd} z_{ijd} \qquad \text{for all } i \text{ and } j \tag{15.5.1}$$

Similarly, the extended priors are defined as π^q_{ijd}. Under this formulation the extended GCE problem may be posed as follows:

$$\min_{\pi_{ijd},\, w_{ijm}} \quad I(\boldsymbol{\pi}, \mathbf{w}) = \sum_i \sum_j \sum_d \pi_{ijd} \ln(\pi_{ijd}/\pi^q_{ijd}) + \sum_i \sum_j \sum_m w_{ijm} \ln(w_{ijm}/u_{ijm}) \tag{15.5.2}$$

subject to (15.4.2), (15.4.4) and

$$\sum_j \sum_d \pi_{ijd} z_{ijd} = 1 \tag{15.5.3}$$

$$\sum_d \pi_{ijd} = 1, \qquad \text{for all } i, j \tag{15.5.4}$$

Under this formulation the π_{ijd} provide a probability measure over the D-dimensional parameter space for each p_{ij}. The optimization problem yields the solution $\tilde{\tilde{\pi}}_{ijd}$, and $\tilde{\tilde{w}}_{ijm}$. Finally, through the definitions (15.5.1) the $\tilde{\tilde{p}}_{ij}$ are recovered, and through the errors' definitions, the $\tilde{\tilde{e}}_{ij}$ are recovered. If all priors are uniform $\pi^q_{ijd} = 1/D$ then the extended GCE reduces to the extended GME.

As is shown throughout this monograph, the dual unconstrained formulation is computationally superior to the primal. Building on the Lagrangian, the dual extended GCE multinomial problem is

$$M(\boldsymbol{\lambda}_j) = y'(I_J \otimes X)\boldsymbol{\lambda} - \sum_i \sum_j \ln\left[\sum_d \pi^q_{ijd} \exp(\mathbf{x}_i'\boldsymbol{\lambda}_j Z_j)\right] - \sum_i \sum_j \ln\left[\sum_m u_{ijm} \exp(\mathbf{x}_i'\boldsymbol{\lambda}_j V_j)\right] \tag{15.5.5}$$

where $\boldsymbol{\beta}_j = \boldsymbol{\lambda}_j$, $v_{ijm} \in [-1, 1]$ and $z_{ijd} \in [0, 1]$. Maximizing $M(\boldsymbol{\lambda}_j)$ with respect to $\boldsymbol{\lambda}_j$ yields the optimal GCE solution.

15.6 INFORMATION AND DIAGNOSTIC MEASURES

In Chapters 3 and 7 we formulated the normalized entropy (information) measures for the pure inverse and the linear statistical model. We now extend it to the multinomial GME case. Because entropy is additive (Golan, 1988; Behara, 1990), we may, as Golan (1988, 1994) and Soofi (1992) have suggested, measure the importance of the contribution of each piece of data or constraint in the reduction of uncertainty concerning the unknown multinomial probabilities. As we have noted, the maximum possible entropy of the multinomial choice probabilities results when the data-consistency constraints (15.3.3) are not enforced and the distribution over each choice set is uniform. As we add each piece of effective data (consistency constraints), a departure from the uniform distributions results and a reduction in uncertainty occurs. The proportion of reduction in total uncertainty may be measured, in the case of multinomial probabilities, by the normalized entropy

$$S(\hat{\mathbf{p}}) = \left[-\sum_i \sum_j \hat{p}_{ij} \ln \hat{p}_{ij}\right] \Big/ (\ln(J) \cdot N) \tag{15.6.1}$$

where $S(\hat{\mathbf{p}}) \in [0, 1]$ or the *reduction in uncertainty information index* (Soofi, 1992) $I(\hat{\mathbf{p}}) = 1 - S(\hat{\mathbf{p}})$. The quantity $\ln(J) \cdot N$ represents maximum uncertainty and provides a basis for gauging the informational content. An $S(\hat{\mathbf{p}}) = 0$ implies no uncertainty whereas $S(\hat{\mathbf{p}}) = 1$, which means p_{ij} is uniform for all i and j, implies perfect uncertainty. Because $S(\hat{\mathbf{p}})$ is a relative measure of uncertainty it can be used to compare different cases or scenarios (see Chapter 10 for a detailed discussion). For example, an attribute (covariate) k can be eliminated and $S(K)$ can be compared to $S(K - 1)$. If both are equal, we can conclude, based on the data, that attribute k introduces no additional information and does not help in reducing the level of uncertainty concerning the unknown p_{ij}. A similar measure of normalized entropy for $\hat{\mathbf{w}}$ is

$$S(\hat{\mathbf{w}}) = -\hat{\mathbf{w}}' \ln \hat{\mathbf{w}} / (\ln(M) \cdot N \cdot J) \tag{15.6.2}$$

In line with Chapters 3 and 6, the normalized entropy for the GCE problem is

$$S(\tilde{\mathbf{p}}) = \left(-\sum_i \sum_j \tilde{p}_{ij} \ln \tilde{p}_{ij}\right) \Big/ \left(-\sum_i \sum_j q_{ij} \ln q_{ij}\right) \tag{15.6.3}$$

which reduces to (15.6.1) when $q_{ij} = 1/J$ for all i and j. In the same way $S(\hat{\mathbf{w}})$ can be extended to $S(\tilde{\mathbf{w}})$.

The normalized entropy measure for the extended GCE is

$$S(\tilde{\tilde{\mathbf{p}}}) = \left(-\sum_i \sum_j \sum_d \tilde{\tilde{\pi}}_{ijd} \ln \tilde{\tilde{\pi}}_{ijd}\right) \Big/ \left(-\sum_i \sum_j \sum_d \pi^q_{ijd} \ln \pi^q_{ijd}\right) \tag{15.6.4}$$

where the denominator reduces to $(\ln(D) \cdot N \cdot J)$ for the GME case. Finally, within the extended GME formulation, it is possible to define an information measure for each $\tilde{\tilde{p}}_{ij}$:

$$S(\tilde{\tilde{\mathbf{p}}}_{ij}) = \left(-\sum_d \tilde{\tilde{\pi}}_{ijd} \ln \tilde{\tilde{\pi}}_{ijd}\right) \Big/ \ln(D) \tag{15.6.5}$$

Given the information measures and the conclusions of Section 15.3.2, the following holds. As the constraints (15.2.4) are relaxed to be consistent with (15.3.3), $|\beta_{jk}|$ approaches zero while the optimal p_{ij} and w_{ijm} approach uniformity. Consequently, $S(\hat{\mathbf{p}})$ and $S(\hat{\mathbf{w}})$ approach 1. This implies that, always, $|\beta_{jk}|_{\text{GME}} \leq |\beta_{jk}|_{\text{ME–ML logit}}$ for all j, k, and, therefore, $S(\hat{\mathbf{p}})_{\text{GME}} \geq S(\hat{\mathbf{p}})_{\text{ME–ML logit}}$.

15.7 A DUAL CRITERION

Following the discussion in Chapter 7, we now briefly introduce a weight γ into the dual objective function. Incorporating $\gamma \in (0, 1)$ into the dual criterion (15.3.2) yields

$$H(\mathbf{p}, \mathbf{w}_j; \gamma) = -(1-\gamma)\mathbf{p}' \ln \mathbf{p} - \gamma \mathbf{w}' \ln \mathbf{w} \tag{15.7.1}$$

Maximizing (15.7.1) subject to constraints (15.3.3)–(15.3.5) yields the optimal (weighted) solution. Changing γ changes the prediction or estimation emphasis and the choice of γ determines this tradeoff. The recovered λ_{jk} are, under the dual objective (15.7.1), the recovered Lagrange parameters and for $\gamma \in (0, 1)$, $\hat{\beta}_{jk} = -\hat{\lambda}_{jk}(1/(1-\gamma))$. Similarly, the dual unconstrained GME problem is reformulated as

$$M(\boldsymbol{\lambda}_j; \gamma) = y'(I_j \otimes X)\boldsymbol{\lambda} + (1-\gamma) \sum_i \ln\left[\sum_j \exp\left(-\frac{1}{1-\gamma}\, \mathbf{x}_i' \boldsymbol{\lambda}_j\right)\right]$$
$$+ \gamma \sum_i \sum_j \ln\left[\sum_m \exp\left(-\frac{1}{\gamma}\, \mathbf{x}_i' \boldsymbol{\lambda}_j V_j\right)\right] \tag{15.7.2}$$

Given the conclusions of Section 15.3.2, the information measures and (15.7.2), we can make, using the results of Golan *et al.* (1996), the following statements relative to the impact of the choice of γ:

- $\text{Var}(\boldsymbol{\beta}_j)_{\text{GME}(\gamma)} \leq \text{Var}(\boldsymbol{\beta}_j)_{\text{ME, ML logit}}$, for all $\gamma \in (0, 1)$
- $S(\hat{\mathbf{p}})_{\text{GME}(\gamma)} \geq S(\hat{\mathbf{p}})_{\text{ME–ML logit}}$, for all $\gamma \in (0, 1)$
- As $\gamma \in (0, 1)$ increases, the information measure $S(\hat{\mathbf{p}})$ decreases and the information measure $S(\hat{\mathbf{w}})$ increases.
- For any sample of data, there is a unique $\gamma \in (0, 1)$ that corresponds simultaneously to

$$\min\left\{\sum_j \sum_k \text{Var}(\beta_{jk})\right\} \quad \text{and} \quad \max\{S = S(\hat{\mathbf{p}}) + S(\hat{\mathbf{w}})\}$$

To summarize the above results, for a given sample of data, if precision in the estimation of $\boldsymbol{\beta}_j$ is the objective, a data-based choice of γ is provided by $\max S(\gamma \in (0, 1))$.

15.8 A SAMPLING EXPERIMENT

The analytical results of Sections 15.3.2, provide conditions under which the GME–GCE estimators will be well behaved in large samples and give a basis for evaluating and comparing the performance of GME(γ) relative to ME–ML logit. In order to provide an empirical basis for comparing the small sample performance of the GME(γ) and ME, or traditional ML multinomial logit procedures, we present the results of Monte Carlo sampling experiments. Additional sampling experiments, and empirical analysis results based on a larger number of replications, are given in Golan *et al.* (1996).

15.8.1 DESIGN OF THE SAMPLING EXPERIMENT

Consider a multinomial response problem involving three choice categories $j = 0, 1, 2$ and four covariates x_{jk}, $k = 1, 2, 3, 4$. The choice response coefficients β_{jk} in the linkage function, $p_{ij} = G(\mathbf{x}_i'\boldsymbol{\beta}_j)$, are $\boldsymbol{\beta}_{1k} = (0, 0, 0, 0)'$, $\boldsymbol{\beta}_{2k} = (-1, 1, 2, -1)'$ and $\boldsymbol{\beta}_{3k} = (1, -1, -2, 1)'$. The x_{ik} were generated from a standard normal distribution.

Given the $\mathbf{x}_i$ and $\boldsymbol{\beta}_j$, and using (15.1.1), $p_{ij} = G(\mathbf{x}_i'\boldsymbol{\beta}_j)$ can be used to calculate the probability that $y_{ij} = 1$, for $i = 1, 2, \ldots, N$ and $j = 0, 1, 2$. The value of y_{ij} is determined, following Griffiths *et al.* (1987), by drawing a uniform random number on the unit interval to assign an observation to a category. For example, suppose the proportions $p_{i0} = 0.5$, $p_{i1} = 0.3$ and $p_{i2} = 0.2$. Then a random draw between [0, 0.5) is assigned to category zero, a random draw between [0.5, 0.8) is assigned to category one, and a random draw between [0.8, 1.0] is assigned to category 2.

Using this sample design 100 samples of size $N = 30$ and $N = 100$ were generated. Under a logistic c.d.f. specification, the traditional ML procedure (or the ME procedure) was used to recover the β_{jk} and to predict the choice outcomes. Alternatively, the more general GME(γ) procedure was used to recover the unknown p_{ij}, e_{ij} and β_{jk} and to predict the chosen category for each observation. Before presenting the sampling experiments, we present a detailed analysis of a single sample.

15.8.2 RESULTS OF A SINGLE SAMPLE

To illustrate the output from the GME(γ) procedure applied to multinomial response data consider the results of a single sample of $N = 100$ observations reported in Table 15.8.1. Keeping in mind this is only *one sample* that is being used for *illustration* purposes, some things to note are:

- relative to the GME(γ) formulation, the ML–ME formulation performed well in terms of prediction and reduction of uncertainty $S(\hat{\mathbf{p}})$ for the unknown multinomial probabilities, but poorly in terms of the mean squared error (MSE) of the β_{jk}
- relative to the ME and thus the traditional ML estimator, the GME (γ) estimator has, over all γ, significantly lower MSE for β_{jk}
- the GME ($\gamma = 0.5$) equally weighted estimator has the lowest MSE of β_{jk}
- ME ($\gamma = 0.8$ and 0.9) has, relative to the ME or ML estimator, the same number of category misses and about one-fourth or one-half the MSE of the β_{jk}
- the measure of uncertainty $S(\hat{\mathbf{p}})$ for GME(γ) monotonically decreases as γ increases.

To illustrate the impact, on the normalized entropy measure $S(\hat{\mathbf{p}})$ of not including one or more of the covariates (for more examples of the ME–ML case, see Soofi, 1992), we use a *single* sample, the GME($\gamma = 0.5$) estimator and a small sample size of $N = 30$. The first row of Table 15.8.2 shows the results for the unrestricted model. The next row shows the effect of excluding the x_4 covariate. Other rows show the effects of excluding one or more other covariates. Excluding x_3 or x_4 substantially increases the number of misses; however excluding x_2 only increases the number of misses by one. More importantly, dropping any covariate except x_2 substantially increases MSE($\hat{\boldsymbol{\beta}}$) and $S(\hat{\mathbf{p}})$. For example, dropping x_2 raises $S(\hat{\mathbf{p}})$ by only 0.012, whereas dropping

Table 15.8.1 GME (γ) and ME-ML estimator results for a single well-posed sample of $N = 100$

Estimator	Category misses	$\text{MSE} = \sum_j \sum_k \frac{(\hat{\beta}_{jk} - \beta_{jk})^2}{(J-1)K}$	$S(\hat{\mathbf{p}})$
GME ($\gamma = 0.1$)	22	0.414	0.675
GME ($\gamma = 0.2$)	22	0.258	0.624
GME ($\gamma = 0.3$)	22	0.162	0.588
GME ($\gamma = 0.4$)	23	0.108	0.561
GME ($\gamma = 0.5$)	23	0.096	0.539
GME ($\gamma = 0.6$)	23	0.131	0.520
GME ($\gamma = 0.7$)	23	0.228	0.502
GME ($\gamma = 0.8$)	21	0.432	0.484
GME ($\gamma = 0.9$)	21	0.837	0.465
ME–ML	21	1.751	0.442

Table 15.8.2 Impact on MSE of β_{jk} and uncertainty of p_{ij} of covariate choice, GME ($\gamma = 0.5$) and $N = 30$

Model	Misses	$\text{MSE}(\hat{\boldsymbol{\beta}})$	$S(\hat{\mathbf{p}})$	$\Delta S(\hat{\mathbf{p}})$
x_1, x_2, x_3, x_4	3	0.605	0.415	
x_1, x_2, x_3	7	0.860	0.509	0.094
x_1, x_2, x_4	7	1.560	0.568	0.153
x_1, x_3, x_4	4	0.608	0.427	0.012
x_1, x_2	7	2.426	0.655	0.240

x_3 raises it by 0.153. Thus, by these information measures, we have a basis for identifying how much each covariate contributes. Even with a limited number of observations, in the case of the GME($\gamma = 0.5$) estimator, there was no problem in obtaining a stable solution. Under the information measure $S(\hat{\mathbf{p}})$ the covariates x_3 and x_4 appear important in category prediction, MSE, and in reducing uncertainty concerning the multinomial probabilities. The covariate x_2 in *this sample* has an insignificant information value.

15.8.3 RESULTS OF A SAMPLING EXPERIMENT

The empirical $\text{MSE}(\boldsymbol{\beta}) = \sum_j \sum_k (\hat{\beta}_{jk} - \beta_{jk})^2/(J-1)K$, and the mean of the normalized entropy measures $S(\hat{\mathbf{p}})$ from 100 replications of a sampling experiment, using the design discussed in Section 15.8.1, $N = 100$ and $\mathbf{v}_{ij} = (-0.1, 0, 0.1)'$ are presented in Table 15.8.3. Consistent with the theoretical results of Section 15.3.2, and the single sample results of Section 15.8.2, the results from the

Table 15.8.3 Results of a sampling experiment, with 100 replications, $N = 100$

Estimator	Misses Min	Misses Average	Misses Max	MSE($\hat{\boldsymbol{\beta}}$)	$S(\hat{\mathbf{p}})$
ME–ML	11	21.1	32	0.870	0.451
GME ($\gamma = 0.1$)	10	21.6	32	0.702	0.745
GME ($\gamma = 0.5$)	11	21.4	30	0.269	0.527
GME ($\gamma = 0.9$)	11	21.1	32	0.342	0.479

sampling experiment reflect the superior performance characteristics of the GME(γ) estimator. Using the GME($\gamma = 0.5$) estimator puts equal weight on both the precision and prediction objectives. In this experiment under a balanced loss there is a very little loss in prediction (the average number of misses is virtually the same and the maximum number of misses is slightly lower) and a substantial gain in precision as illustrated by the reduced MSE($\hat{\boldsymbol{\beta}}$) relative to the ME–ML estimators. In Table 15.8.3, $S(\hat{\mathbf{p}})$ is the mean normalized entropy over the 100 replications.

In much applied work, the primary emphasis is on recovering and using estimates of the response coefficients β_{jk}. Consequently, the possibility of using the GME(γ) estimator to gain precision for the $\hat{\beta}_{jk}$, without sacrificing category prediction, is attractive. Other replicated sampling experiments, such as $N = 500$, which are not reported here, yielded essentially the same performance characteristics for the ME, ML logit and GME(γ) estimators as those reported in Table 15.8.3.

15.8.4 RESULTS WITH PARTIAL AND ILL-CONDITIONED DATA

Much of our experience with GME formulations suggests, in the case of ill-posed inverse problems, the superiority of the performance of the GME approach relative to traditional sampling theoretical methods. In the case of a small number of observations, a large number of covariates and/or an ill-conditioned covariate design matrix and using traditional estimation procedures, it is expected that the parameter estimates will be highly unstable, giving rise to high variance. Le Cessie and van Houwelingen (1992) discussed this problem in the case of multinomial response data and investigated the use of the ridge estimator. To explore this matter when GME(γ) procedures are used with multinomial response data, we use Monte Carlo procedures to evaluate the sampling consequences in finite samples of a small number of observations and/or an ill-conditioned covariate matrix.

Table 15.8.4 Results of a sampling experiment with 100 replications, $N = 30$

Estimator	Misses			$MSE(\hat{\boldsymbol{\beta}})$	$S(\hat{\mathbf{p}})$
	Min	Average	Max		
ME–ML	0	4.73	9	17100	0.331
GME ($\gamma = 0.5$)	1	5.76	9	0.317	0.547

Results for $N = 30$. Using the three category, four covariate problem and the data generation scheme of Section 15.8.1 to reflect the sampling consequences of a small number of observations, we report in Table 15.8.4 the results from 100 replications of a sampling experiment with samples of size $N = 30$. When $N = 30$ the $MSE(\boldsymbol{\beta}^*)$ for the ME–ML estimator reflects the computationally unstable nature of the solution. Alternatively, the $MSE(\hat{\boldsymbol{\beta}})$ for GME ($\gamma = 0.5$) was stable from sample to sample. The $MSE(\hat{\boldsymbol{\beta}})$ results for the GME estimator are also consistent with those of Table 15.8.3 for $N = 100$. A limited number of data points appear to have had (in the case of GME) a limited effect on sampling performance or conversely adding observations with this design did not add much information.

Results for an ill-conditioned design matrix. Using the three category and four covariate design of Section 15.8.1, to measure the degree of collinearity in design matrix we follow the experimental design of Chapter 8 and use a relatively high condition number $\kappa(X'X) = \lambda_L/\lambda_S$, which is the ratio of the largest and smallest characteristic roots (Belsley, 1991). As the degree of collinearity increases, $\lambda_S \to 0$ and $\kappa(X'X) \to \infty$. To reflect a design matrix consistent with significant collinearity and the nature of much economic data, we use the condition number $\kappa(X'X) = 90$. In this experiment $\boldsymbol{\beta}_{1K} = (0, 0, 0, 0)'$, $\boldsymbol{\beta}_{2K} = (-1, 1, 2, -1)'$ and $\boldsymbol{\beta}_{3K} = (-1.4, 1.5, 1, -1)'$. The results from 100 replications of samples of size $N = 100$ and GME($\gamma = 0.1, 0.5, 0.9$) are presented in Table 15.8.5. Despite

Table 15.8.5 Results of a sampling experiment with 100 replications, $N = 100$ and $\kappa(X'X) = 90$

Estimator	Misses			$MSE(\hat{\boldsymbol{\beta}})$	$S(\hat{\mathbf{p}})$
	Min	Average	Max		
GME ($\gamma = 0.1$)	48	56.85	65	1.660	0.999
GME ($\gamma = 0.5$)	47	56.72	66	4.797	0.997
GME ($\gamma = 0.9$)	47	55.65	64	37.700	0.979
ME–ML	47	56.69	67	95.671	0.956

Table 15.8.6 Results of a sampling experiment with 100 replications, $N = 30$ and $\kappa(X'X) = 90$

	Misses				
Estimator	Min	Average	Max	$\text{MSE}(\hat{\boldsymbol{\beta}})$	$S(\hat{\mathbf{p}})$
GME($\gamma = 0.1$)	9	14.49	20	1.656	0.999
GME($\gamma = 0.5$)	8	14.20	19	4.547	0.991
GME($\gamma = 0.9$)	8	13.87	20	41.514	0.932
ME–ML	8	13.76	21	163.18	0.849

the high degree of collinearity and an unfavorable signal–noise ratio, the GME estimator continued to perform well based on a squared error loss measure. In contrast, the traditional multinomial logit estimator was highly unstable and $\text{MSE}(\boldsymbol{\beta}^*)$ exceeded $\text{MSE}(\hat{\boldsymbol{\beta}})$ for GME ($\gamma = 0.1$) by a factor of 50 or, in the case of GME($\gamma = 0.5$), by a factor of 20.

Finally, we present in Table 15.8.6 the results of a sampling experiment involving a *small* number of data points, $N = 30$, and a design matrix with a condition number of $\kappa(X'X) = 90$.

In spite of an ill-conditioned design matrix and a small number of data points, the $\text{MSE}(\hat{\boldsymbol{\beta}})$ and prediction results for GME($\gamma = 0.5$) are virtually the same as for the $\kappa(X'X) = 90$ and $N = 100$ case. For multinomial response data from an ill-conditioned design, the GME($\gamma = 0.1$) estimator is a winner if the focus is on a squared error measure for the response coefficients. As might be expected, as the number of data points decreases the $\text{MSE}(\boldsymbol{\beta}^*)$ for the traditional multinomial logit estimator increases. However, as in the well-posed case, reducing the number of observations does not appear to significantly affect estimation performance.

We conclude this section with a short discussion of the extended GME formulation. The results reported here show the advantages of the GME(γ) formulation. As these results are quite good, using the extended GME formulation will not result in a better precision. However, the extended GME formulation is superior to the GME formulation in the case of a small number of observations. To demonstrate it, we compared the GME ($\gamma = 0.5$) with $\mathbf{v}_{ij} = (-0.2, 0, 0.2)'$ and $N = 30$ to the extended GME ($\gamma = 0.5$) with the same $\mathbf{v}_{ij}$ and $\mathbf{z}_{ij} = (0, 1)'$. Results of 100 samples show that the GME has $\text{MSE}(\hat{\boldsymbol{\beta}}) = 0.416$ while the extended GME has $\text{MSE}(\hat{\hat{\boldsymbol{\beta}}}) = 0.248$. In terms of misses, the GME has 5.51 misses while the extended GME has 5.65.

15.8.5 COMPARISON OF PROBIT AND GME

To test the robustness of the GME formulation, the GME estimator was compared with a *correctly specified* ML-probit estimator. Generating the data with the normal c.d.f. and as described in Section 15.8.1, the sampling experiment consisted of 100 samples of $N = 100$ and $J = 2$ categories and the coefficients $\boldsymbol{\beta}_0 = \mathbf{0}$ and $\boldsymbol{\beta}_1 = (1.5, -0.5, 1, -1)'$. Under this scenario, the percentage of y_{i0} is 22.6 and of y_{i1} is 77.4. The correctly specified ML–probit estimator yielded $\hat{\boldsymbol{\beta}}_{ML} = (1.74, -0.60, 1.20, -1.25)'$, with $\text{MSE}(\hat{\boldsymbol{\beta}}_{ML}) = 0.944$ and $\text{Var}(\hat{\boldsymbol{\beta}}_{ML}) = 0.783$. The estimates resulting from the GME estimator, with $\mathbf{v} = (-0.2, 0, -0.2)'$, are $\hat{\boldsymbol{\beta}} = (1.56, -0.49, 1.02, -1.03)$ with $\text{MSE}(\hat{\boldsymbol{\beta}}) = 0.163$ and $\text{Var}(\hat{\boldsymbol{\beta}}) = 0.158$.

The average number of *incorrectly predicted* (misses) categories are 11.12 for ML–probit and 10.88 for the GME. These precision and prediction results illustrate the robustness of the GME estimator with multinomial response data.

Additional experiments for different values of $\gamma \in (0, 1)$ yielded results consistent with previous tables. Finally, if incorrectly, the ML–logit estimator had been used with these data, $\text{MSE}(\hat{\boldsymbol{\beta}}^*) = 7.970$ results, and illustrates the statistical consequences of an incorrect choice between traditional ML estimators.

15.9 REMARKS

A GME formulation for the multinomial response problem is proposed. This formulation is a generalization of the ML estimator. Analytical and sampling results suggest the GME is superior to ML for any finite sample. Further, under traditional approaches to the multinomial response problem, a likelihood function and a c.d.f. linking the p_{ij} and $\mathbf{x}_i'\boldsymbol{\beta}_j$ are specified and KJ likelihood equations are used to obtain estimates of the $\boldsymbol{\beta}_j$ and thus the p_{ij} and e_{ij}. Because the NJ unknown p_{ij} exceed the KJ number of likelihood equations, only the assumption of a specific c.d.f. specification makes the maximum likelihood formulation a well-posed problem that can be solved for $\boldsymbol{\beta}_j$ and thus p_{ij}. The GME approach does not require such restrictive assumptions. We have also shown that under the dual unconstrained GME formulation, the GME solution can be viewed as a general class of logit models. In terms of complexity, the GME is as easy and fast to compute as ML.

The GME framework developed in Section 15.3 also forms the basis for specifying a GME formulation for the conditional logit problem (McFadden, 1974; Soofi, 1992), and a basis for recovering the K-dimensional $\boldsymbol{\beta}$ vector and the corresponding p_{ij} and e_{ij}. Finally, given the nature of the GME formulation, it appears to be robust to various data generation processes.

REFERENCES

Albert, J. H. and Chib, S. (1993) Bayesian analysis of binary and polychotomous response data. *Journal of the American Statistical Association* **88**, 669–79.

Behara, M. (1990) *Additive and Nonadditive Measures of Entropy*. John Wiley, New York.

Belsley, D. A. (1991) *Conditioning Diagnostics.* John Wiley, New York.

Denzau, A. T., Gibbons, P. C. and Greenberg, E. (1989) Bayesian estimation of proportions with a cross-entropy prior. *Communications in Statistics–Theory And Methods* **18,** 1843–61.

Dykstra, R. L. and Lemke, J. H. (1988) Duality of I projections and maximum likelihood estimation of log-linear models under cone constraints. *Journal of the American Statistical Association* **83,** 546–54.

Golan, A. (1988) *A Discrete Stochastic Model of Economic Production and a Model of Fluctuations in Production – Theory and Empirical Evidence.* Ph.D. Thesis, University of California, Berkeley.

Golan, A. (1994) A multi-variable stochastic theory of size distribution of firms with empirical evidence. *Advances in Econometrics* **10,** 1–46.

Golan, A., Judge, G. and Perloff, J. (1996) Recovering information from multinomial response data. *Journal of the American Statistical Association* **91.**

Good, I. J. (1963) Maximum entropy for hypothesis formulation, especially for multidimensional contingency tables. *Annals of Mathematical Statistics* **34,** 911–934.

Greene, W. H. (1993) *Econometric Analysis*, 2nd edn. Macmillan, New York.

Griffiths, W. E., Hill, R. C. and Pope, P. J. (1987) Small sample properties of probit model estimators. *Journal of the American Statistical Association* **82,** 929–37.

Judge, G. G., Griffiths, W. E., Hill, R. C., Lütkepohl, H. and Lee, T.-C. (1985) *The Theory and Practice of of Econometrics*, 2nd edn, John Wiley, New York.

Koop, G. and Poirier, D. J. (1993) Bayesian analysis of logit models using natural conjugate priors. *Journal of Econometrics* **56,** 323–40.

Kullback, J. (1959) *Information Theory and Statistics.* John Wiley, New York.

Le Cessie, S. and van Houwelingen, J. C. (1992) Ridge estimators in logistic regression. *Journal of Applied Statistics* **41,** 191–201.

Lehmann, E. (1983) *Theory of Point Estimation.* John Wiley, New York.

Maddala, G. S. (1983) *Limited Dependent and Qualitative Variables in Econometrics*, Cambridge: Cambridge University Press.

Manski, C. and McFadden, D. (Eds.) (1981) *Structural Analysis of Discrete Data with Econometric Applications.* MIT Press, Cambridge.

McFadden, D. (1974) Conditional logit analysis of qualitative choice behavior. In P. Zarembka (Ed.) *Frontiers of Econometrics*, pp. 105–42. Academic Press, New York.

Ruud, P. A. (1993) The semi-parametric maximum likelihood estimator of discrete dependent variable models. Unpublished paper, University of California, Berkeley.

Soofi, E. S. (1992) A generalizable formulation of conditional logit with diagnostics. *Journal of the American Statistical Association* **87,** 812–16.

Zellner, A. and Rossi, P. E. (1984) Bayesian analysis of dichotomous quantal response models. *Journal of Econometrics* **25,** 365–93.

CHAPTER 16

Recovering information from censored response data

16.1 INTRODUCTION

In this chapter we are concerned with a variant of the linear statistical models where observations on the dependent variable are partial or incomplete. In particular, we focus on the censored statistical model and use, instead of traditional maximum likelihood (ML) procedures, a GME formulation to recover the unknown and unobservable parameters. A generalization of the GME formulation for recovering the unknown parameters of ordered multinomial problems is presented as well. This chapter is based on Golan, Judge and Perloff (1995).

To reflect the censored case, assume the linear statistical model

$$y_t^* = \mathbf{x}_t'\boldsymbol{\beta} + e_t \tag{16.1.1}$$

where y_t^* can take on values over the real line; $\mathbf{x}_t$ is a K-dimensional vector of measurable attributes or factors; $\boldsymbol{\beta}$ is a K-dimensional unknown parameter vector; and e_t is a random error. No moment restrictions or distributional assumptions are imposed on the noise component $\mathbf{e}$. If y_t^* is observed, (16.1.1) takes the form of the traditional linear statistical model. In contrast to the traditional statistical model, suppose we observe a new censored random variable y_t that is a transformation of the original y_t^* defined by

$$y_t = y_t^*, \qquad \text{if } y_t^* > 0 \tag{16.1.2a}$$

$$y_t = 0 \qquad \text{if } y_t^* \leq 0 \tag{16.1.2b}$$

Under conventional error assumptions this sample selection transformation (16.1.2) is a censored regression or tobit model (Tobin, 1958; Amemiya, 1984). The correct likelihood is specified, the maximum likelihood estimator (MLE) is consistent and asymptotically efficient for $\boldsymbol{\beta}$. However, models with parametric distributions may be subject to distributional misspecifications which may lead to inconsistent estimates. Further, if there are missing observations, or the error distribution is other than the normal or logistic, the likelihood function may be complicated and the task of maximizing the likelihood function burdensome. In addition, the distribution underlying the likelihood function may be unknown, replication of the sample is unnatural if not impossible, and/or the statistical model may be ill-posed. Consequently, to mitigate some of these statistical consequences, we relax many of the traditional parametric assumptions and use, for the Tobit problem, a generalization of the maximum entropy (GME) estimation method to recover the unknown and unobservable parameters.

The chapter is organized as follows. In Section 16.2, the statistical model is reparameterized, so that the unobservables are in the form of probabilities. In Section 16.3 the censored data problem is reformulated in a GME–GCE context. In Section 16.4, sampling results are presented. In Section 16.5, the ordered multinomial problem is formulated as a direct extension of the censored formulation. Section 16.6 contains some concluding remarks. A discussion of a simple formulation to handle missing observations on one of the X variables is given in the Appendix.

16.2 MODEL TRANSFORMATION AND REPARAMETERIZATION

Given the GME–GCE formulations developed in Chapter 6, we focus on the censored regression-inverse problem with noise

$$\mathbf{y}^* = X\boldsymbol{\beta} + \mathbf{e} \tag{16.2.1}$$

where the objective, given $\mathbf{y}^*$ and X, is to recover estimates of the unknown and unobservable $\boldsymbol{\beta}$ and $\mathbf{e}$ vectors. No specific restrictions are imposed on e_t, and each β_k and e_t may take on values over the real line. Following Chapter 6, in order to make use of the GME dual criterion in formulating a basis for recovering these unknowns, the elements of both the unknown $\boldsymbol{\beta}$ and $\mathbf{e}$ vectors are reparameterized so the unknowns have the properties of probabilities.

In terms of $\boldsymbol{\beta}$, as in Chapter 6, we transform the possible outcomes for β_k by defining a set of $M \geq 2$ discrete points $\mathbf{z}_k = [z_{k1}, z_{k2}, \ldots, z_{kM}]'$, where $z_{k1} \leq \beta_k \leq z_{kM}$, and a vector of corresponding unknown weights $\mathbf{p}_k = [p_{k1}, p_{k2}, \ldots, p_{kM}]'$, such that $\beta_k = \mathbf{z}_k'\mathbf{p}_k$ and $\sum_m p_{km} = 1$.

Also, as in Chapter 6, we transform the possible outcomes for e_t to a (0, 1) space by defining a set of $J \geq 2$ discrete points $\mathbf{v}_t = [v_{t1}, v_{t2}, \ldots, v_{tJ}]'$, where $v_{t1} \leq e_t \leq v_{tJ}$, and a vector of corresponding unknown weights that have the properties of probabilities $\mathbf{w}_t = [w_{t1}, w_{t2}, \ldots, w_{tJ}]'$, such that $e_t = \mathbf{v}_t'\mathbf{w}_t$ and $\sum_j w_{tj} = 1$. In the reparameterization the support spaces $[v_{t1}, v_{t2}, \ldots, v_{tJ}]$ and $[z_{k1}, z_{k2}, \ldots, z_{kM}]$ are chosen to span the relevant parameter spaces for each

$\{\beta_k\}$ and $\{e_t\}$. Under this reparameterization the model (16.2.1) may be specified as

$$\mathbf{y}^* = XZ\mathbf{p} + V\mathbf{w} \tag{16.2.2}$$

If for a particular problem it is natural to have the β_k constrained to be non-negative or non-positive and contained in a particular part of the parameter space, z_{km} can be so defined. Alternatively, uninformative (symmetric around zero) supports may be used in **z** and **v**, and informative supports, which may be negated by the data, may be introduced through cross-entropy. In the next section we review traditional tobit and develop a GME formulation for the traditional tobit problem.

16.3 GME–GCE CENSORED DATA FORMULATIONS

16.3.1 THE TRADITIONAL TOBIT MODEL

Under the GME variant of statistical model (16.2.1), assume the true underlying data are $(y_t^*, \mathbf{x}_t)$ and that we observe data $(y_t, \mathbf{x}_t)$, where the y_t^* are scalars and the $\mathbf{x}_t$ are K-dimensional vectors of certain measurable attributes or factors. Some of the y_t^* are censored and we use the value $\{y_t = 0\}$ for the missing observation. Otherwise $y_t > 0$. Thus the y_t are generated by the mechanism

$$y_t = \max\{0, \mathbf{x}_t'\boldsymbol{\beta} + e_t\}, \qquad \text{for } t = 1, 2, \ldots, T \tag{16.3.1}$$

where the e_t are unobservable errors and $\boldsymbol{\beta}$ is a K-dimensional unknown parameter vector. In terms of this formulation, we find it convenient to order the observations and write the statistical model (16.1.2) as

$$\mathbf{y} = X\boldsymbol{\beta} + \mathbf{e} = \begin{bmatrix} \mathbf{y}_1 \\ \mathbf{y}_2 = \mathbf{0} \end{bmatrix} = \begin{bmatrix} X_1 \\ X_2 \end{bmatrix}\boldsymbol{\beta} + \begin{bmatrix} \mathbf{e}_1 \\ \mathbf{e}_2 \end{bmatrix} \tag{16.3.2}$$

where $\mathbf{y}_1$ is observed and $\mathbf{y}_2$ is unobserved and X_1 and X_2 are the corresponding attribute-design matrices. Models (16.3.1) or (16.3.2) provide more information than the model with discrete choice equations in that both the sign and the values of $\mathbf{y}_1^*$ can be observed.

Given this statistical model, various sampling theory and Bayes' estimation procedures have been proposed (Tobin, 1958; Amemiya, 1973, 1978, 1981; Heckman, 1979; Greene, 1981, 1983, 1993; Powell, 1984, 1986; Chib, 1992). Most of these methods are motivated by asymptotic and/or computational ease.

16.3.2 THE GME–TOBIT FORMULATION

Combining (16.2.2) and (16.3.2) yields the reparameterized model

$$\begin{bmatrix} \mathbf{y}_1 \\ \mathbf{y}_2 = \mathbf{0} \end{bmatrix} = \begin{bmatrix} X_1 \\ X_2 \end{bmatrix} Z\mathbf{p} + \begin{bmatrix} V_1\mathbf{w}_1 \\ V_2\mathbf{w}_2 \end{bmatrix} \tag{16.3.3}$$

Under this reparameterization, the GME formulation is

$$\max_{\mathbf{p},\, \mathbf{w}_1,\, \mathbf{w}_2} \quad H(\mathbf{p}, \mathbf{w}_1, \mathbf{w}_2) = \{-\mathbf{p}' \ln \mathbf{p} - \mathbf{w}_1' \ln \mathbf{w}_1 - \mathbf{w}_2' \ln \mathbf{w}_2\} \tag{16.3.4}$$

subject to the data

$$\mathbf{y}_1 = X_1 Z\mathbf{p} + V_1\mathbf{w}_1 \tag{16.3.5}$$

$$\mathbf{0} \geq X_2 Z\mathbf{p} + V_2\mathbf{w}_2 \tag{16.3.6}$$

and the adding-up constraints

$$(I_K \otimes \mathbf{1}_M')\mathbf{p} = \mathbf{1}_K \tag{16.3.7}$$

$$(I_{T_1} \otimes \mathbf{1}_J')\mathbf{w}_1 = \mathbf{1}_{T_1}, \qquad \text{for } t = 1, 2, \ldots, T_1 \tag{16.3.8}$$

$$(I_{T_2} \otimes \mathbf{1}_J')\mathbf{w}_2 = \mathbf{1}_{T_2}, \qquad \text{for } t = 1, 2, \ldots, T_2; \quad T_1 + T_2 = T \tag{16.3.9}$$

Unless prior information dictates otherwise, the Z, V_1 and V_2 are typically specified as symmetric around zero. As before, the GME criterion function (16.3.4) has *two main* components: the noise and the signal. As such, there is a balance between prediction and precision, where now $\mathbf{w}_1$ and $\mathbf{w}_2$ together compose the $\mathbf{w}$ vector of the linear model of Chapter 6.

Forming the Lagrangian and proceeding as in previous chapters, the results for this formulation yield the following estimates $\hat{\mathbf{p}}$, $\hat{\mathbf{w}}_1$ and $\hat{\mathbf{w}}_2$:

$$\hat{p}_{km} = \frac{\exp(-Z_{km}' X_k' \hat{\boldsymbol{\lambda}})}{\Omega_k(\hat{\boldsymbol{\lambda}})} \tag{16.3.10}$$

where

$$\Omega_k = \sum_h \exp(-Z_{km}' X_k' \hat{\boldsymbol{\lambda}}) \tag{16.3.11}$$

and

$$\hat{w}_{tj}^i = \frac{\exp(-V_{ij}\hat{\boldsymbol{\lambda}})}{\Psi_t^i(\hat{\boldsymbol{\lambda}})}, \qquad \text{for } i = 1, 2 \tag{16.3.12}$$

where

$$\Psi_t^i = \sum_j \exp(-V_{tj}\hat{\boldsymbol{\lambda}}) \tag{16.3.13}$$

Based on these, the point estimates are

$$\hat{\boldsymbol{\beta}} = Z\hat{\mathbf{p}} \tag{16.3.14}$$

$$\hat{\mathbf{e}}_1 = V_1\hat{\mathbf{w}}_1 \tag{16.3.15}$$

$$\hat{\mathbf{e}}_2 = V_2\hat{\mathbf{w}}_2 \tag{16.3.16}$$

Given estimates of $\boldsymbol{\beta}$ and $\mathbf{e}_2$, we can obtain the following estimates of the unobserved $\mathbf{y}_2^*$:

$$\hat{\mathbf{y}}_2^* = X_2Z\hat{\mathbf{p}} + V_2\hat{\mathbf{w}}_2 = X_2\hat{\boldsymbol{\beta}} + \hat{\mathbf{e}}_2 \tag{16.3.17}$$

Under assumptions normally fulfilled in practice $\text{plim}(\hat{\boldsymbol{\beta}}) = \boldsymbol{\beta}$ for the normed moment censored model. For the basis of this and other large sample results see Golan *et al.* (1995).

16.3.3 AN ITERATIVE GME ESTIMATOR

Given estimates of the unobserved $\mathbf{y}_2^*$ in (16.3.17), one possibility is to follow Brieman *et al.* (1993) and use these estimates in a multistage GME formulation. Under this scenario, the first stage estimates $\hat{\mathbf{y}}_2^*$ in (16.3.17) replaces the unobserved (missing) $\mathbf{y}_2^*$ in (16.3.6) and the new (second stage) consistency relation is rewritten as

$$X_2Z\hat{\mathbf{p}} + V_2\hat{\mathbf{w}}_2 = \hat{\mathbf{y}}_2^* \geq X_2Z\mathbf{p} + V_2\mathbf{w}_2 \tag{16.3.18}$$

Using the observable $\mathbf{y}_1$ and the estimated $\hat{\mathbf{y}}_2^*$ values, the GME procedure is repeated to obtain estimates of $\boldsymbol{\beta}$ and $\mathbf{e}$ over two iterations.

16.3.4 GENERALIZED CROSS-ENTROPY

In some problems we may have information, from experience and/or theory, over and above that contained in the consistency and adding-up constraints (16.3.5)–(16.3.9). If such prior information for the $\boldsymbol{\beta}$ or $\mathbf{e}$ vectors exists, it may be introduced through the GCE formulation introduced in Chapter 6 and based on Kullback (1959) and Good (1963).

To develop a generalized cross-entropy formulation, within the reparameterization of Section 16.2, let $\mathbf{q}_k = [q_{k1}, q_{k2}, \ldots, q_{km}]'$ be prior probabilities defined on the support $\mathbf{z}_k = [z_{k1}, z_{k2}, \ldots, z_{km}]'$ such that $q^{\boldsymbol{\beta}} = \mathbf{z}_k'\mathbf{q}_k$. Also, consistent with the set of discrete points $\mathbf{v}_t$ define the corresponding *prior* probabilites $\mathbf{u}_t^i = [u_{t1}^i, u_{t2}^i, \ldots, u_{tJ}^i]'$ for $i = 1, 2$. Using these definitions, the GCE formulation may be stated, in scalar form, as

$$\min_{\{p_{km}\},\{w_{t1j}\},\{w_{t2j}\}} I(\mathbf{p}, \mathbf{w}_1, \mathbf{w}_2)$$
$$= \sum_k \sum_m p_{km} \ln(p_{km}/q_{km}) + \sum_j \sum_{t_1} w_{t_1j}^1 \ln(w_{t_1j}^1/u_{t_1j}^1) + \sum_j \sum_{t_2} w_{t_2j}^2 \ln(w_{t_2j}^2/u_{t_2j}^2) \tag{16.3.19}$$

subject to constraints (16.3.5)–(16.3.9). This optimization yields the GCE solution $\tilde{\boldsymbol{\beta}}$, $\tilde{\mathbf{e}}_1$ and $\tilde{\mathbf{e}}_2$ along with the predicted $\tilde{\mathbf{y}}_2^*$. As before, if all prior probabilities are uniform, GCE reduces to GME solution.

16.3.5 RANDOM CENSORING

To this point we have considered fixed-censoring models. For completeness, in this subsection we briefly discuss the case where the left-hand variable y_t is generated by a random censorship. Thus one observes (y_t, d_t, x_t) with

$$y_t = \max(y_t^* = X_t\boldsymbol{\beta} + e_t, \mu_t), \qquad d_t = I_{[y_t < \mu_t]}, \qquad t = 1, 2, \ldots, T \quad (16.3.20)$$

where the μ_t are independent random variables that are usually assumed independent of $\mathbf{x}_t$ and e_t in (16.3.1) and $I_{[\cdot]}$ is a zero–one indicator function. Estimators by Miller (1976), Buckley and James (1979), Koul *et al.* (1981) and Honoré and Powell (1994) have been proposed to accommodate random censoring. An alternative random censoring model has been proposed by Cheng and Wu (1994) where $\mu_t = g(\mathbf{x}_t, \varepsilon_t)$ and ε_t is a random error. In each of these random censoring models the modification of the fixed censoring GME formulation to accommodate random censoring is direct. For example, when $\mu_t = g(\mathbf{x}_t, \varepsilon_t)$ the fixed censoring model (16.3.1) becomes

$$y_t = \max(\mathbf{x}_t\boldsymbol{\beta} + e_t, \mu_t = g(\mathbf{x}_t, \varepsilon_t)) \quad (16.3.21)$$

where in the GME model (16.3.4)–(16.3.9) the inequality constraint (16.3.6) is replaced by

$$\mu_t = g(\mathbf{x}_t, \varepsilon_t) \geq X_2Z\mathbf{p} + V_2\mathbf{w}_2 \quad (16.3.22)$$

and the new model is (16.3.4), (16.3.5), (16.3.22) with normalization constraints (16.3.7)–(16.3.9). Alternatively, when μ_t is independent of $\mathbf{x}_t$ and e_t, the inequality data constraints (16.3.6) are reformulated as

$$\mu_t \geq X_2Z\mathbf{p} + V_2\mathbf{w}_2 \quad (16.3.23)$$

The new model is (16.3.4), (16.3.5), (16.3.23) and (16.3.7)–(16.3.9).

16.4 SAMPLING EXPERIMENTS

In order to illustrate the small sample performance of the GME–tobit formulation relative to the least squares (LS) and maximum likelihood (ML) counterparts, we present the results of limited sampling experiments. Although the GME estimator does not have a sampling theory basis, the sampling results permit a basis for comparing performance in a repeated sample context. More experiments are reported in Golan *et al.* (1995).

16.4.1 EXPERIMENTAL DESIGN 1

For this sampling experiment, consider the traditional tobit problem (16.3.2) where the design matrix X is of order $(T \times 3)$, and $\mathbf{y}$ is a $(T \times 1)$ vector consisting of T_1 observed values and $T_2 = T - T_1$ censored observations, $\boldsymbol{\beta}$ is a $(K \times 1)$ vector of unknown parameters and $\mathbf{e}$ is a $(T \times 1)$ vector of i.i.d. random variables with mean zero and unit variance. In terms of error distributions, the normal, Student-t with three degrees of freedom and chi-square with four degrees of freedom were analyzed. (See Chapter 8 for more results of non-normal error distributions within the linear statistical model.) Two alternative levels of censoring (35% and 55%) and sample sizes ($T = 20, 30$) were considered. Two design matrices, X, were used. One design matrix involved an ascending variable (to control the degree of censoring) and the other variables were generated from a standard normal random variable. For the other design matrix the X's were generated from standard normals. In each case the design matrices were identical over all replications. In general, the experiments follow those of Paarsch (1981) and Tessema (1993).

First consider results from 100 replications using the experimental design involving $T = 20$ observations, approximately 35% censoring, an X matrix made up of one ascending variable and drawings from two standard normal random variables, $\boldsymbol{\beta} = (-0.75, 1, 1)'$ and normal, $t_{(3)}$ and $\chi^2_{(4)}$ random errors. To reflect, under the $t_{(3)}$ error distribution, the incidence of fat tails, error supports of $\mathbf{v} = (-16, 0, 16)$ were used. The information from this experiment is reported in Table 16.4.1. For each of the GME, LS and ML estimators the mean square error of $\text{MSE}(\hat{\boldsymbol{\beta}}) = \|\boldsymbol{\beta} - \hat{\boldsymbol{\beta}}\|^2/100$, the $\text{Var}(\hat{\boldsymbol{\beta}})$, the average of the replicated values of $\beta_1, \beta_2, \beta_3$, and the percent censored is reported. As expected the LS estimates miss the β values quite badly, and have, relative to the GME and ML estimators, a large $\text{MSE}(\hat{\boldsymbol{\beta}})$. Under each distribution the $\text{MSE}(\hat{\boldsymbol{\beta}})$ for the GME estimator is approximately constant and smaller than that of the ML estimator that is based on a normal error assumption. Over all distributions $\text{Var}(\hat{\boldsymbol{\beta}})$ for the GME estimator is superior by a factor of 2 or more relative to the ML estimator. The worst sampling performance of the ML estimator as measured by $\text{MSE}(\hat{\boldsymbol{\beta}})$ is under the $\chi^2_{(4)}$ error distribution. The average of the estimated β's for the ML estimator is pretty much on target for all the error distributions and superior to GME.

In applied work, to reflect ignorance regarding the scale parameter and the underlying distribution, one may use the (sample) three-sigma rule where sigma is approximated in the following way. Given the observed upper bound of $\mathbf{y}$ and the percent of censored observations in each sample, the lower bound of the unobserved $\mathbf{y}$, $\mathbf{y}^*$, may be calculated by assuming it is distributed uniformly. Use then made of $\hat{\boldsymbol{\sigma}}_y$ to determine the bounds of $\mathbf{v}$ where

$$\hat{\boldsymbol{\sigma}}_y = \sqrt{\frac{(y_{\max} - \hat{y}_{\min})^2}{12}}.$$

Table 16.4.1 Results of a sampling experiment with 100 replications of the tobit model: Comparison of GME, ML and LS for normal (0, 1), $\chi^2_{(4)}$ and $t_{(3)}$ error distributions, 35% censured data, $T = 20$, $\boldsymbol{\beta} = (-0.75, 1, 1)$, $z_k = (-10, 0, 10)$ for all k, $v = (-8, 0, 8)$ for normal (0, 1) and $\chi^2_{(4)}$ error distributions, and $v = (-16, 0, 16)$ for $t_{(3)}$

	Normal (0, 1) distribution				$t_{(3)}$ distribution			$\chi^2_{(4)}$ distribution		
	$\boldsymbol{\beta}$	GME	LS	ML	GME	LS	ML	GME	LS	ML
MSE($\hat{\boldsymbol{\beta}}$)		0.33	0.72	0.42	0.32	0.68	0.40	0.36	0.70	0.54
Var($\hat{\boldsymbol{\beta}}$)		0.26	0.17	0.42	0.19	0.22	0.39	0.29	0.21	0.49
Mean of $\hat{\beta}_1$	−0.75	−0.69	−0.55	−0.80	−0.60	−0.54	−0.82	−0.63	−0.49	−0.78
Mean of $\hat{\beta}_2$	1.0	1.22	1.66	0.98	0.74	1.58	0.92	1.16	1.58	0.77
Mean of $\hat{\beta}_3$	1.0	0.84	0.72	0.99	0.79	0.73	1.01	0.81	0.70	1.02

A detailed discussion of the choice of $\mathbf{v}$ and the *insensitivity* to the choice of Z is given in Golan, Judge and Perloff (1995), where it is shown that using $\boldsymbol{\sigma}_y$ as a basis for the three-sigma rule performs well in *all* sampling experiments.

16.4.2 EXPERIMENTAL DESIGN 2

Next, consider an experiment involving 100 replications of samples of size $T = 30$, approximately 55% censoring, an X matrix made up of drawing from standard normal random variables, $\boldsymbol{\beta} = (2, 1, -3, 2)'$, normal and $\chi^2_{(4)}$ random errors and GME, GCE, LS and ML estimators. In addition, a two-stage GME estimator that uses estimates $X_2\hat{\boldsymbol{\beta}}$ from the first stage, in the second stage, is included in the experiment. This experiment was also designed to provide information regarding estimator performance under collinearity or poor experimental design. As before we measure the degree of collinearity or poor design (data), with the condition number $\kappa(X'X) = \lambda_L/\lambda_S$. To reflect minimal collinearity we use $\kappa(X'X) = 10$. To reflect moderately high collinearity that may be consistent with much economic data, we use $\kappa(X'X) = 90$. To introduce information concerning correct sign for the β_k, we use the GCE formulation. The results for this experiment are reported in Table 16.4.2.

Under a condition number of $\kappa(X'X) = 10$ and normal errors, the results for the GME and ML estimators are qualitatively the same as those reported

Table 16.4.2 Results of a sampling experiment of 100 replications, $T = 30$, $\kappa(X'X) = 10, 90$, $\boldsymbol{\beta} = (2, 1, -3, 2)$, $\mathbf{z}_k = (-10, 0, 10)$, $\mathbf{v} = (-5, 0, 5)'$ and normal (0, 1) and $\chi^2_{(4)}$ error distributions

	GME	2-Stage GME	GCE	ML
Normal (0, 1), $\kappa(X'X) = 10$				
MSE($\tilde{\boldsymbol{\beta}}$)	9.24	8.25	1.90	13.94
Var($\tilde{\boldsymbol{\beta}}$)	2.15	2.21	0.59	13.90
Average misses	2.63	–	2.48	4.21
% censored	55	55	55	55
Normal (0, 1), $\kappa(X'X) = 90$				
MSE($\tilde{\boldsymbol{\beta}}$)	10.10	8.91	1.75	81.85
Var($\tilde{\boldsymbol{\beta}}$)	1.73	1.94	0.52	81.80
Average misses	2.42	–	2.39	4.35
% censored	54	54	54	54
$\chi^2_{(4)}$, $\kappa(X'X) = 90$				
MSE($\tilde{\boldsymbol{\beta}}$)	12.44	10.37	2.08	124.28
Var($\tilde{\boldsymbol{\beta}}$)	2.56	2.60	0.91	123.34
Average misses	3.06	–	2.9	4.91
% censored	60	60	60	60

for the experiment in Table 16.4.1. Note for the two-stage GME estimator there is approximately a 10% gain over the one-stage GME estimator relative to $\text{MSE}(\hat{\boldsymbol{\beta}})$ and $\text{Var}(\hat{\boldsymbol{\beta}})$. When correct sign information is introduced relative to the β_k the GCE estimator is much superior by a factor of 5 or more relative to the GME and ML estimators.

Under a condition number of $\kappa(X'X) = 90$ and normal errors the results for the GME, and two-stage GME and GCE are approximately the same as for $\kappa(X'X) = 10$. However, under collinear X's, the ML estimator results for $\text{MSE}(\hat{\boldsymbol{\beta}})$ and $\text{Var}(\hat{\boldsymbol{\beta}})$ increase quite dramatically. Unlike the GME estimator that performs well for both ill-posed and well-posed problems, the high level of sampling variability for the ML estimator is consistent with performance results encountered in earlier chapters with a range of statistical models. While the sampling performance of the GME estimator is not affected by a condition number of $\kappa(X'X) = 90$ and $\chi^2_{(4)}$ errors, the $\text{MSE}(\hat{\boldsymbol{\beta}})$ for the ML estimator was greater than that for the GME estimator by a factor of 10. Similar experiments in which the number of samples is much larger (Golan *et al.*, 1995) yield the same basic results.

16.5 EXTENSIONS

In closing we note that in multinomial-response problems when the multinomial-choice variables are ordered, traditional logit and probit formulations (McFadden, 1974, 1984) fail to account for the ordinal nature of the left-hand-side outcome variables and other estimation and inference procedures are necessary. Fortunately, it is possible to specify the ordered-multinomial-response problem as a general censored statistical model and use, as an alternative to traditional ordered ML procedures, the GME basis for recovering information about the unknowns. Again, unlike traditional ordered multinomial formulations that make use of maximum likelihood (ML) procedures, in the GME formulation weak error specifications are imposed.

In this context consider the latent regression problem is

$$\mathbf{y}^* = X\boldsymbol{\beta} + \mathbf{e} = XZ\mathbf{p} + V\mathbf{w} \tag{16.5.1}$$

where $\mathbf{y}^*$ is unobserved, and the following is observed:

$$\mathbf{y} = 0, \qquad \text{if } \mathbf{y}^* \le \mu_1 \tag{16.5.2}$$

$$\mathbf{y} = 1 \qquad \text{if } \mu_1 \le \mathbf{y}^* \le \mu_2 \tag{16.5.3}$$

$$\mathbf{y} = 2 \qquad \text{if } \mu_2 \le \mathbf{y}^* \le \mu_3 \tag{16.5.4}$$

$$\vdots$$

$$\mathbf{y} = J - 1 \qquad \text{if } \mu_{J-1} < \mathbf{y}^* \tag{16.5.5}$$

where the μ_j are category boundaries. For convenience we let $\mu_1 = 0$. Under this formulation the boundary specifications μ_j may be either known or unknown.

We now present a GME formulation for the ordered multinomial problem, where the μ's, along with $\boldsymbol{\beta}$ and $\mathbf{e}$, are unknown. Having reparameterized $\boldsymbol{\beta}$ and $\mathbf{e}$ as before, we have to reparameterize $\boldsymbol{\mu}$. Toward this end, define a parameter space $\mathbf{c}_j$ for μ_j where $\mathbf{c}_j'\mathbf{m}_j = \mu_j$ and $\mathbf{m}_j$ is the corresponding vector of probabilities to be recovered from the data. With this addition, the GME formulation with unknown μ's is as follows:

$$\max_{\mathbf{p},\, \mathbf{m}_j,\, \mathbf{w}_j} \; H(\mathbf{p}, \mathbf{m}, \mathbf{w}) = -\mathbf{p}' \ln \mathbf{p} - \mathbf{m}_j' \ln \mathbf{m}_j - \mathbf{w}_j' \ln \mathbf{w}_j \qquad (16.5.6)$$

subject to the data consistency

$$X_1'\boldsymbol{\beta} + \mathbf{e}_1 = X_1'Z\mathbf{p} + V_1\mathbf{w}_1 \le \mathbf{c}_1'\mathbf{m}_1, \qquad \text{for } y = 0 \qquad (16.5.7a)$$

$$\mathbf{c}_{j-1}'\mathbf{m}_{j-1} < X_j'\boldsymbol{\beta} + \mathbf{e}_j = X_j'Z\mathbf{p} + V_j\mathbf{w}_j \le \mathbf{c}_j'\mathbf{m}_j \qquad \text{for } y = 1, 2, \ldots, J-1 \qquad (16.5.7b)$$

$$\mathbf{c}_{J-1}'\mathbf{m}_{J-1} < X_J'\boldsymbol{\beta} + \mathbf{e}_J = X_J'Z\mathbf{p} + V_J\mathbf{w}_J \qquad \text{for } y = J-1 \qquad (16.5.7c)$$

and the adding-up constraints.

The optimal solution yields $\hat{\mathbf{p}}_k$, $\hat{\mathbf{w}}_j$ and $\hat{\mathbf{m}}$, which in turn yield $\tilde{\boldsymbol{\beta}}$, $\hat{\mathbf{e}}_j$ and $\tilde{\boldsymbol{\mu}}$. The Hessian is negative definite and the solution is globally unique. In this context the tobit formulation is a special case of the ordered multinomial problem. For a development of the GME formulation for the ordered problem, the corresponding analytic results, small sample properties and the dual GME formulation, see Golan *et al.* (1995). As in the censored case, the ordered multinomial GME estimator performs well over a range of error distributions.

16.6 REMARKS

The GME approach is a feasible alternative to traditional ML procedures for recovering estimates of unknown parameters from censored response data. As in the preceding chapters, the GME approach offers several desirable advantages over conventional ML approaches: it can recover information in the case of small samples, large number of covariates or when the covariates are highly correlated and yields a solution when other methods may fail. Further, the GME formulation does not require restrictive assumptions on the error distribution and appears to be robust over a large class of distributions. The GME approach is also a feasible way to achieve the estimation objective in ordered multinomial problems. A discussion of a simple formulation to handle missing observations on one or more of the X variables is given in the Appendix.

REFERENCES

Amemiya, T. (1973) Regression analysis when the dependent variable is truncated normal. *Econometrica* **41**, 997–1016.

Amemiya, T. (1978) The estimation of a simultaneous equation generalized probit model. *Econometrica* **46**, 1193–205.

Amemiya, T. (1981) Qualitative response models: a survey *Journal of Economic Literature* **19**, 1483–536.

Amemiya, T. (1984) Tobit models: a survey. *Journal of Econometrics* **24**, 3–61.

Brieman, L., Tsur, Y. and Zemel, A. (1993) On a simple estimation procedure for censored regression models. *Annals of Statistics* **21**, 1711–20.

Buckley, J. and James, I. (1979) Linear regression with censored data. *Biometrika* **66**, 429–36.

Cheng, K. F. and Wu, J. W. (1994) Adjusted least squares estimates for the scaled regression coefficients with censored data. *Journal of the American Statistical Association* **89**, 1483–91.

Chib, S. (1992) Bayes inference in the tobit censored regression model. *Journal of Econometrics* **51**, 79–99.

Golan, A., Judge, G. and Perloff, J. (1995) Recovering information from censored and ordered multinomial response data under a nonparametric error specification. Unpublished paper, University of California, Berkeley.

Good, I. J. (1963) Maximum entropy for hypothesis formulation, especially for multidimensional contingency tables. *Annals of Mathematical Statistics* **34**, 911–34.

Greene, W. H. (1981) On the asymptotic bias of the ordinary least squares estimator of the tobit model. *Econometrica* **49**, 505–13.

Greene, W. H. (1983) Estimation of limited dependent variable models and the method of moments. *Journal of Econometrics* **21**, 195–212.

Greene, W. H. (1993) *Econometric Analysis*, 2nd edn. Macmillan, New York.

Heckman, J. J. (1979) Sample selection bias as a specification error. *Econometrica* **47**, 153–61.

Honoré, B. and Powell, J. L. (1994) Quantile regression under random censoring. Unpublished paper, University of California, Berkeley.

Koul, H., Susarla, V. and Van Ryzin, J. (1981) Regression analysis with randomly right-censored data. *Annals of Statistics* **9**, 1276–88.

Kullback, J. (1959) *Information Theory and Statistics.* John Wiley, New York.

Little, R. T. A. and Rubin, D. B. (1987) *Statistical Analysis with Missing Data.* Wiley, New York.

McFadden, D. (1974) Conditional logit analysis of qualitative choice behavior. In P. Zarembka (ed.), *Frontiers of Econometrics*, pp. 105–42. Academic Press, New York.

McFadden, D. (1984) Econometric analysis of qualitative response models. In

Z. Griliches and M. Intriligator (eds.), *Handbook of Econometrics*. North-Holland, Amsterdam.
Miller, R. G. (1976) Least squares regression with censored data. *Biometrika* **63**, 449–64.
Paarsch, H. J. (1981) A Monte Carlo comparison of estimators for censored regression models. *Journal of Econometrics* **24**, 197–213.
Powell, J. L. (1984) Least absolute deviations estimation for the censored regression model. *Journal of Econometrics* **25**, 303–25.
Powell, J. L. (1986) Symmetrically trimmed least squares estimation for tobit models. *Econometrica* **54**, 1435–60.
Tessema, G. A. (1993) A Monte Carlo analysis of alternative estimators of the tobit model. Unpublished paper, University of New England.
Tobin, J. (1958) Estimation of relationships for limited dependent variables. *Econometrica* **26**, 24–36.

APPENDIX

MISSING OBSERVATIONS

In practice, researchers often find that certain observations from the design matrix, as in the censored model, are missing from the data set. The problem is especially common in the social sciences and other fields that employ non-experimental data. Given that the GME–GCE formulations are designed to make use of whatever information that is *available*, one possibility is to adapt the consistency constraints to account for the missing data.

To see this, consider an example in which the data set for the GLM consists of T observations and K explanatory variables. Further, suppose that the first T_1 observations on the K covariates are missing. Given enough observations, researchers may simply estimate the unknown model parameters, $\boldsymbol{\beta}$, without the first T_1 observations, although this is clearly an inefficient approach. Alternatively, the missing values may be imputed (Little and Rubin, 1987) so that traditional estimation tools can be applied to the augmented data set.

Within the generalized entropy framework, consider a revised set of GCE-data consistency constraints that account for the missing observations for $\mathbf{x}_1$

$$y_t = \sum_{k=1}^{K-1} \sum_m x_{tk} z_{km} p_{km} + \sum_j v_{tj} w_{tj}, \qquad \text{for } t = 1, \ldots, T_1 \tag{16.A.1}$$

$$y_t = \sum_{k=1}^{K} \sum_m x_{tk} z_{km} p_{km} + \sum_j v_{tj} w_{tj} \qquad \text{for } t = T_1 + 1, \ldots, T \tag{16.A.2}$$

It is important to note that the error supports for the first T_1 observations must be adjusted to account for the missing terms, which are implicitly handled as part of the associated disturbances. Otherwise, the point estimates of the parameters will be affected or there may not even be a feasible solution to the GME–GCE problem. However, using the empirical three standard deviations rule for each sample ensures a feasible solution.

If we have some information about the sign or magnitude of the missing observations, they can be treated like another set of unknowns in the censored inverse problem of Section 16.3. That is, we can specify a finite and discrete support for each of the missing values of $\mathbf{x}_k$ and recover a probability distribution on this support. The resulting generalized entropy problem selects distributions on the unknown explanatory variables, parameters and errors so that the observed information is satisfied.

PART VII

Computational notes

In this part, we provide some partial notes on the computational aspects of the GME–GCE estimators. In particular, we provide the background for:

- solving the dual, unconstrained GME–GCE models
- solving the primal problem with constraints (which can be non-linear or in the form of inequalities)

  and

- discuss software availability.

CHAPTER 17

Computing GME–GCE solutions

17.1 INTRODUCTION

As noted in the preceding chapters, most (non-trivial) generalized entropy problems do not have closed-form solutions. Hence, researchers wishing to apply the GME–GCE techniques must bear some computational burdens. The purpose of this chapter is to assure the reader that these burdens are modest. First, we discuss feasible computing environments for the primal and dual problems and compare the numerical characteristics of each approach. Then, we provide a series of examples based on two familiar problems, Jaynes' dice problem (Chapter 2) and the bounded mean problem (Chapter 7). For each case, we include computer code to solve the primal (GAMS) and dual (SHAZAM) problems. We conclude the chapter with an example that is more similar to problems encountered in practice, a linear model of beer demand. A GAMS program for the primal version of the problem is included, and we introduce a new set of GME–GCE commands for the SHAZAM computing environment.

17.2 COMPUTING ENVIRONMENTS

To complete the exercises presented in the preceding chapters, we have used a variety of computing tools. For most primal problems, we found GAMS (Brooke *et al.*, 1992) to be an easy and robust computing environment. To reduce the computing time for primal-form Monte Carlo exercises, we also used C programs to call constrained optimization and other numerical routines from the NAG (Numerical Algorithms Group) library. Although we have limited experience with other constrained optimization packages, we do know that GAUSS and Matlab are feasible alternatives.

GAMS programs and NAG routines may also be used to solve dual GME–GCE problems, but the range of unconstrained optimization tools is rather broad. For convenience, we also used SHAZAM (White *et al.*, 1990), a popular programming environment designed to solve econometric problems, including unconstrained optimization. Given the strict concavity of the dual GCE objective function, SHAZAM users may solve GME–GCE problems with the same set of tools employed in maximum likelihood problems. Further, the dual problems are typically well-behaved, and users may employ less sophisticated methods if GAMS or SHAZAM is unavailable. For example, we solved a range of problems with C programs based on Newton's method and the Newton–Raphson algorithm. Although these techniques were generally less efficient than the more refined optimization routines, they achieved identical solutions (Miller, 1994).

Although the dual approach is attractive for many reasons, some problems do not satisfy the saddlepoint property (Proposition 6.1) and may not be expressed in an unconstrained form. For example, any of the problems that employ dynamic (Chapters 13–14), non-linear (Chapters 9 and 14), or inequality (Chapter 16) consistency constraints are not conformable to the dual approach. However, these problems may be expressed in primal form and solved with constrained optimization tools.

It is important to note that the dual approach may encounter numerical difficulties in some problems. The most likely of these rare cases is exponential overflow in one or more of the partition functions. That is, the arguments to $\exp(\cdot)$ may become too large for reasonable values of $\boldsymbol{\lambda}$, which causes a floating point error. Of course, exponential overflow may arise in a variety of other settings, including maximum likelihood problems in the exponential family. The tolerance for numerical exceptions depends on the particular computing package and machine, but it is often in the neighborhood of exp(700). If exponential overflow (or another numerical exception) occurs at an intermediate stage, the computing algorithm may be unable to solve the problem, even if an interior solution exists. Although programmers may be able to avoid difficulties by using alternate starting values or different step-sizes, some problems may not be *numerically* conformable to the dual approach. In such cases, the primal approach is less likely to encounter numerical exceptions and may be used to solve the GME–GCE problem.

17.3 JAYNES' DICE PROBLEM

To demonstrate the computational ease of solving GME–GCE problems, we begin with a simple example, Jaynes' dice problem. The problem is a good starting point because it does not involve parameter supports or disturbances. Recall that we know the mean (y) of the multinomial distribution supported on $\{1, \ldots, 6\}$, and we must recover estimates of the unknown probabilities. The primal form of the problem is expressed in the GAMS programming language, and the dual problem is written in SHAZAM code.

17.3.1 GAMS CODE FOR THE PRIMAL PROBLEM

The following GAMS code is a simplified version of the program we used to solve the dice problem. Experienced GAMS users will notice that many common options have been omitted for the sake of clarity.

```
SET I INDEX /1*6/;
PARAMETER
    X(I) Support /1 1
                  2 2
                  3 3
                  4 4
                  5 5
                  6 6/;
POSITIVE VARIABLE P(I) Probabilities;
VARIABLE OBJ Objective;
EQUATIONS
    OBJECTIVE   Entropy Objective
    ADD         Additivity Constraint
    CONSIST     Consistency Constraint;
OBJECTIVE. . OBJ =E= -SUM(I, P(I)*LOG(1. e-9+P(I)));
ADD. . SUM(I, P(I)) =E= 1;
CONSIST. . SUM(I, X(I)*P(I)) =E= 4;                  (17.3.1)
Model DICE /ALL/;
Solve DICE Maximizing OBJ Using NLP;
DISPLAY P. L;
DISPLAY OBJ. L;
```

For demonstration purposes, the observed mean of the die is taken to be 4 (see equation 17.3.1), and the corresponding solution is provided in Chapter 2. By changing the mean, users should be able to replicate the table accompanying the discussion of the dice problem. Although each `P(I)` is defined to be a positive variable in the GAMS program, we have included a small positive constant (`1.e-9`), which should be larger than machine epsilon, to avoid numerical exceptions in the `LOG()` terms. In some cases, near-boundary solutions may cause numerical problems, and users may need to set explicit upper and lower bounds on the probabilities to avoid difficulties.

17.3.2 SHAZAM CODE FOR THE DUAL PROBLEM

The dual version of the dice problem may be solved using the '`NL`' command in SHAZAM. Assuming the observed mean is 4, an example program for the dice problem is

```
DO #=1,6
GEN1 X# = #
ENDO
GEN1 Y = 4
NL 1 / NCOEF=1 MINFUNC COEF=LHAT
EQ Y*L+LOG(EXP(-X1*L)+EXP(-X2*L)+EXP(-X3*L)
    +EXP(-X4*L)+EXP(-X5*L)+EXP(-X6*L))
COEF L 0
END
GEN1 OMEGA = 0
DO #=1,6
GEN1 OMEGA = OMEGA + EXP(-X#*LHAT)
ENDO
GEN1 H = 0
DO $=1,6
GENR P$ = EXP(-X$*LHAT)/OMEGA                    (17.3.2)
GENR H = H - P$*LOG(P$)
PRINT P$
ENDO
PRINT H
STOP
```

As in the preceding section, experienced SHAZAM users will note that some common options are omitted for clarity.

After forming the support for the die, {X1, . . . , X6}, and the mean, Y = 4, the 'NL' command is used to set up the problem for SHAZAM. The dual objective function is specified in the 'EQ' statement, and the starting value for the search is set at L = 0. SHAZAM uses numerical gradients to the search for the optimal Lagrange multiplier, so the gradient is not included in the code. If it were required, the gradient is simply

```
Y - P1*X1 - . . . - P6*X6
```

where the probabilities, {P1, . . . , P6}, are formed as in Equation (17.3.2). After computing the optimal Lagrange multiplier, it is saved to LHAT and used to form the ME probabilities. As well, the entropy of this distribution is computed and saved in H. In traditional ME problems like the dice example, the dual objective function derived in Chapter 6 reduces to the efficient algorithm developed by Agmon *et al.* (1979).

If a non-uniform prior distribution, {Q1, . . . , Q6}, is available, the dual CE problem may be solved by modifying the 'NL' statement as follows:

```
NL 1 / NCOEF=1 MAXFUNC COEF=LHAT
EQ Y*L-LOG(Q1*EXP(X1*L)+Q2*EXP(X2*L)+Q3*EXP(X3*L)
     +Q4*EXP(X4*L)+Q5*EXP(X5*L)+Q6*EXP(X6*L))        (17.3.3)
COEF L 0
END
```

We now *maximize* the objective function over L, and the function is only altered by the change of signs in the EXP( ) terms and in equation (17.3.3). Also, the prior probabilities must be used to form OMEGA and the posterior probabilities.

17.3.3 REFINING THE DUAL APPROACH

For simple problems like the dice example, note that the computational burden may be further reduced by embedding the first term in the objective function in the second term. That is, we can rewrite the first term in equation (17.3.3) as

$$y\lambda = \ln(\exp(y\lambda))$$

By combining the differences of the logarithmic terms, the objective function may be rewritten as

$$\ln(\exp((y - x_1)\lambda) + \cdots + \exp((y - x_6)\lambda))$$

The ln() function is strictly monotonic, so the problem may be solved by choosing λ to maximize

$$\exp((y - x_1)\lambda) + \cdots + \exp((y - x_6)\lambda)$$

Although this simplification is only applicable in dice-like problems, it may provide significant gains in computing efficiency if a problem must be solved repeatedly (e.g. exponential tilting of bootstrap distributions (Efron and Tibshirani, 1993, p. 353)).

17.4 THE BOUNDED MEAN PROBLEM

Our next task is to show that the computing burden is not much greater in GME–GCE problems with noise and parameter supports. For the bounded mean problem (Chapter 7), recall that we observe a singleton, y, from a normal distribution with unknown mean, β, and unit variance. Given prior knowledge that $\beta \in [-c, c]$, we want to recover β from the sample and non-sample information. The problem satisfies the saddlepoint property and may be expressed in primal or dual form. As before, we provide a GAMS program to solve the primal problem and a SHAZAM program for the dual problem.

17.4.1 GAMS CODE FOR THE PRIMAL PROBLEM

The GAMS program used to solve the primal version of the bounded mean problem is slightly more complex than the preceding GAMS code for the dice problem. In this case, we add the parameter and error supports, Z and V, as well as the corresponding probability distributions and constraints.

```
SET M INDEX /1*2/
    J INDEX /1*2/;
PARAMETER
    Z(M) Parameter Support /1 -1
                            2  1/
    V(J) Error Support /1 -1
                        2  1/;
SCALAR GME Point Estimate;
POSITIVE VARIABLE P(M) Parameter Probs;
POSITIVE VARIABLE W(J) Error Probs;
```

```
VARIABLE OBJ Objective;
EQUATIONS
    OBJECTIVE Entropy Objective
    ADD1      Parameter Additivity Constraint
    ADD2      Error Additivity Constraint
    CONSIST   Consistency Constraint;
OBJECTIVE.. OBJ =E= -SUM(M, P(M)*LOG(P(M)))
                    -SUM(J, W(J)*LOG(W(J)));
ADD1.. SUM(M, P(M)) =E= 1;
ADD2.. SUM(J, W(J)) =E= 1;
CONSIST.. SUM(M, Z(M)*P(M)) + SUM(J, V(J)*W(J)) =E= 0.5;
Model MEAN /ALL/;
Solve MEAN Maximizing OBJ Using NLP;
GME = SUM(M, Z(M)*P.L(M));
DISPLAY GME;
```

As in Chapter 7, the parameter supports are based on $c = 1$. For demonstration purposes, the observation is taken to be 0.5, and the error supports are set at $v = \pm 1$. After GAMS computes the GME distributions, the point estimate of β is recovered as the posterior mean of the parameter distribution. In this case, the point estimate is GME = 0.250.

17.4.2 SHAZAM CODE FOR THE DUAL PROBLEM

Using the same information employed in the GAMS program, an example SHAZAM program for the dual version of the bounded mean problem is

```
SAMPLE 1 1
GEN1 Y = 0.5
GEN1 BAYES = (EXP(Y)-EXP(-Y))/(EXP(Y)+EXP(-Y))
GEN1 C = 1
GEN1 V = 1
NL 1 / NCOEFF=1 MINFUNC COEF=LHAT
```

```
EQ Y*L+LOG(EXP(-C*L)+EXP(C*L))+LOG(EXP(-V*L)+EXP(V*L))
COEF L 0
END
GENR OMEGA = EXP(-C*LHAT)+EXP(C*LHAT)
GENR PSI = EXP(-V*LHAT)+EXP(V*LHAT)
GENR H = 0
GEN1 P1 = EXP(C*LHAT)/OMEGA
GEN1 P2 = 1 - P1
GEN1 W1 = EXP(V*LHAT)/PSI
GEN1 W2 = 1 - W1
GEN1 GME = -C*P1 + C*P2
GEN1 H = -P1*LOG(P1)-P2*LOG(P2)-W1*LOG(W1)-W2*LOG(W2)
PRINT P1 P2 W1 W2 H
PRINT GME BAYES
STOP
```

As before, the observation is set at `Y = 0.5`, and the parameter and error bounds are set at `C = V = 1`. Using the observation, the Bayes posterior mean is calculated and named `BAYES`. The dual objective function is expressed in the '`EQ`' statement, which is minimized over `L`. The optimal Lagrange multiplier is stored in `LHAT` and is used to form the GME probabilities for the unknown parameters and errors. Finally, the GME point estimate, `GME`, is computed as the posterior mean of the parameter distribution. For comparison purposes, the Bayesian posterior mean is 0.462, and the GME point estimate is 0.250. As well, the optimal Lagrange multiplier for the dual GME problem is $\hat{\lambda} = -0.255$, and the joint entropy of the parameter and error distributions is 1.323.

In simple problems like the dice and bounded mean examples, it is easy to check for feasible solutions before computing the optimal solution. That is, the observed mean in the dice problem must lie strictly between 1 and 6, and the observation in the bounded mean problem must satisfy $Y \in (-C - V,\ C + V)$. In more complex problems, users may be unable to readily verify that the primal constraint set is non-empty. Although the strict concavity or convexity of the dual objective function may be determined by a grid search, users may find it easier to write the problem in primal form and allow the computing package (e.g. GAMS) to check for feasible solutions. As previously noted, the primal form may also be used to avoid certain numerical difficulties that can arise in the dual case.

17.5 A LINEAR MODEL OF BEER DEMAND

The dice and bounded mean problems are useful examples for demonstrating the ease of computing GME–GCE solutions, but the problems encountered in practice are typically much larger. We conclude the computing examples with a more realistic case, a linear model of beer demand with 30 observations and 5 unknown parameters. The linear model is expressed in logarithmic form

$$\ln(\mathbf{Q}) = \beta_1 + \beta_2 \ln(\mathbf{P}_B) + \beta_3 \ln(\mathbf{P}_L) + \beta_4 \ln(\mathbf{P}_R) + \beta_5 \ln(\mathrm{M}) + \mathbf{e} \quad (17.5.1)$$

where $\mathbf{Q}$ is the quantity of beer demanded, $\mathbf{P}_B$ is the price of beer, $\mathbf{P}_L$ is the price of other liquor, $\mathbf{P}_R$ is the price of remaining goods and services, and M is income. The data are taken from Table 11.1 in Griffiths *et al.* (1993, p. 372). As before, we present a GAMS program to solve the primal problem, and then introduce a set of commands that may appear in a future version of SHAZAM.

17.5.1 GAMS CODE FOR THE PRIMAL PROBLEM

The GAMS commands required to solve a GLM-based problem are not much more extensive than used in the preceding examples. In this case, the beer demand data are arranged in a table, `DATA`, in the data file `beer.dat`. GAMS opens the file with the '`$INCLUDE`' statement, and the components of `DATA` are used to form the dependent variable, `Y`, and the design matrix, `X`.

The remainder of the code is similar to the earlier primal programs, and the batch file of GAMS commands may be written as

```
SET T INDEX /1*30/
    K INDEX /1*5/
    M INDEX /1*5/
    J INDEX /1*3/
    N INDEX /1*5/;
$INCLUDE "beer.dat"
PARAMETERS
   Z(M) Parameter Support /1 -5.0
                           2 -2.5
                           3  0.0
                           4  2.5
                           5  5.0/
```

```
    V(J) Error Support /1 -1.0
                        2  0.0
                        3  1.0/
    BHAT(K) Parameter Estimates
    X(T,K)  Explanatory Variables
    Y(T)    Dependent Variable;
POSITIVE VARIABLES
    P(K,M) Parameter Probabilities
    W(T,J) Error Probabilities;
VARIABLE OBJ Objective;
Y(T) = LOG(DATA(T,"1"));
X(T,"1") = 1;
X(T,"2") = LOG(DATA(T,"2"));
X(T,"3") = LOG(DATA(T,"3"));
X(T,"4") = LOG(DATA(T,"4"));
X(T,"5") = LOG(DATA(T,"5"));
EQUATIONS
    OBJECTIVE Objective Function
    ADD1(K)   Parameter Additivity Constraints
    ADD2(T)   Error Additivity Constraints
    CON(T)    Consistency Contraints;
OBJECTIVE.. OBJ =E= -SUM(K,SUM(M,P(K,M)*LOG(P(K,M))))
                    -SUM(T,SUM(J,W(T,J)*LOG(W(T,J))));
ADD1(K).. SUM(M, P(K,M)) =E= 1;
ADD2(T).. SUM(J, W(T,J)) =E= 1;
CON(T).. SUM(K, X(T,K)*SUM(M, P(K,M)*Z(M)))
          +SUM(J, W(T,J)*V(J)) =E= Y(T);
Model BEER /ALL/;
Solve BEER Maximizing OBJ Using NLP;
BHAT(K) = SUM(M, P.L(K,M)*Z(M));
DISPLAY BHAT;
```

From GAMS, the GME solution is $\hat{\boldsymbol{\beta}} = [0.082, -0.840, -0.194, 0.158, 0.505]'$, and the joint entropy of the parameter and error distributions is 40.89. The LS estimate cited by Griffiths *et al.* (1993) is $\hat{\boldsymbol{\beta}}_{LS} = [-3.243, -1.020, -0.583, 0.210, 0.923]'$.

17.5.2 NEW SHAZAM COMMANDS FOR THE DUAL PROBLEM

Although the '`EQ`' statement in the '`NL`' command structure is very flexible, the objective function must be written in scalar form. Consequently, the dual objective function will be very difficult to express if the number of components is very large (i.e. T, K, M, or J). To allow users to solve large GME–GCE problems, a '`GME`' command will be included in future versions of SHAZAM.

The structure of the '`GME`' command will be similar to the '`OLS`' command, which is familiar to SHAZAM users. For the beer demand model, the dual GME problem may be solved with the following code:

```
SAMPLE 1 30
FILE 4 beer.dat
READ(4) Q PB PL PR M
GENR Y = LOG(Q)
GENR X1 = 1
GENR X2 = LOG(PB)
GENR X3 = LOG(PL)
GENR X4 = LOG(PR)
GENR X5 = LOG(M)
DIM Z 5 5 V 30 3
GENR Z:1 = -5
GENR Z:2 = -2.5
GENR Z:3 = 0
GENR Z:4 = 2.5
GENR Z:5 = 5
GENR V:1 = -1
GENR V:2 = 0
```

```
GENR V: 3 = 1

GME Y X1 - X5 / NOCON ZENTROPY=Z VENTROPY=V

STOP
```

After the observations are retrieved and converted to logarithmic form, the parameter and error support matrices, Z and V, are established. In the background, SHAZAM uses the provided information to form the dual objective function, allowing users to avoid programming lengthy 'EQ' statements. After solving the problem, SHAZAM returns the optimal Lagrange multipliers, GME probability distributions, normalized entropy measures, point estimates of $\boldsymbol{\beta}$ and $\mathbf{e}$, and approximate standard errors of $\hat{\boldsymbol{\beta}}$.

Aside from the formation of the support matrices, Z and V, the required set of instructions is very similar to other SHAZAM commands. Informative prior distributions may be employed under the dual GCE framework, as in each of the preceding examples. Further, the new 'GME' command will be able to solve a range of linear inverse problems based on the GLM, including classical ME–CE problems. A set of related commands to recover Markov transition probabilities and to solve qualitative choice problems may also be included in forthcoming versions of SHAZAM.

17.6 REMARKS

The purpose of this chapter is to familiarize potential users of GME–GCE methods with some basic computing issues. Although we noted a few prominent computing packages used in our work, the range of available resources is growing with time. By presenting a few simple programs, we believe GAMS and SHAZAM users can easily solve these and other GME–GCE problems. Further, the GAMS and SHAZAM command structures are relatively user-friendly, and readers who are familiar with other computing environments should be able to translate the provided code.

REFERENCES

Agmon, N., Alhassid, Y. and Levine, R. D. (1979) An algorithm for finding the distribution of maximal entropy. *Journal of Computational Physics* **30**, 250–8.

Brooke, A., Kendrick, D. and Meeraus, A. (1992) *GAMS: A User's Guide, Release 2.25*. Scientific Press, South San Francisco, CA.

Efron, B. and Tibshirani, R. J. (1993) *An Introduction to the Bootstrap*. Chapman & Hall, New York.

Griffiths, W. E., Hill, R. C. and Judge, G. G. (1993) *Learning and Practicing Econometrics*. John Wiley, New York.

Miller, D. (1994) Solving generalized maximum entropy problems with unconstrained numerical techniques. University of California, Berkeley.

White, K. J., Wong, S. D., Whistler, D. and Haun, S. A. (1990) *SHAZAM User's Reference Manual Version 6.2*, McGraw-Hill, New York.

PART VIII

Epilogue

In the trek that started with Chapters 1 and 2, we stated the following problems and pitfalls in attempting to recover information from data:

- The economic data that we use to reflect economic processes and institutions are generated by economic relations that are stochastic, dynamic, non-stationary and simultaneous; and are, in general, partial-incomplete and non-experimentally or passively generated.
- The economic-statistical models that are used to describe economic processes and institutions are incompletely or incorrectly known.
- Under traditional approaches to estimation and inference, these model-data characteristics lead in many cases to ill-posed, underdetermined economic-statistical models.
- In order to achieve tractability using traditional procedures, there is, in many cases, a significant divergence between the actual and the creatively assumed economic-statistical model.
- While the objective of working with tractable, well-posed mathematical and statistical problems has had some successes in the discovery of new knowledge, it has led in many cases to erroneous interpretations and conclusions.
- Traditional estimation and inference procedures are in many cases ill-suited to deal with situations when replications of the data are unnatural, if not impossible. Furthermore, if not enough is known about the underlying data generation process to specify a form for the likelihood function, then no bias for proceeding is provided. In the face of these problems we recognise that.
- If traditionally, in describing data generation processes, economic-statistical models are ill-posed, then in information recovery and the development of information processing rules, it is important to seek a basis for reasoning in these logically indeterminate situations.
- It is important to develop information processing and recovery procedures that work effectively with both ill-posed and well-posed problems and that lets analysts avoid having to make assumptions that they do not wish to make.

- Within the estimation and inference world described above, the maximum entropy formalism may provide an efficient basis for information recovery and the development of information processing rules.

Now, 15 chapters later, it seems appropriate to review the problem setting these propositions and the basis for information recovery that we have developed, and to summarize some of the advantages of GME and GCE relative to conventional estimation and inference procedures. In this respect, relative to GME–GCE, the following items appear to us to be important:

- The formulations do not require the use of the usual restrictive parametric assumptions.
- The formulations provide a basis for recovering, with a degree of precision, information in the case of small samples, a large number of unknowns, a large number of covariates and/or covariates that are highly correlated.
- The GCE formulation provides a simple basis for introducing non-sample information, the natural magnitude or range of unknown parameters, and evaluating the value of this information.
- Unlike most traditional estimators, the GME–GCE formulations make use of a *dual* criterion function that permits, by the use of weights, a choice between estimation precision and prediction objectives.
- The formulations contain, in some cases, traditional estimation rules as special cases.
- The formulations and the corresponding information processing rules yield, relative to traditional procedures, more precise estimates in finite samples, and have conventional asymptotic performance.
- The formulations provide useful diagnostic and information measures.
- The resulting solution satisfies the logical and the consistency (data) constraints of the problem.
- The formulation structure is especially useful in eliciting and using information that is available for analysis purposes or in identifying information that is available but has been left out.
- The formulations make it easy to work with models consistent with data generation processes that are non-linear, dynamic, non-stationary and stochastic and thus possibly involve a large number of unknown parameters.
- The formulations offer a new way to recover information when the data are generated by processes that are stochastic and *simultaneous.*
- Solution algorithms for solving these non-linear inversion problems are easy to implement in any nonlinear optimization software such as GAMS or Matlab and will soon be in software packages such as SHAZAM.

The research underlying the formulations and results presented in this monograph started about five years ago. As often happens, when you start thinking about things in a different way, many new problems are suggested. Thus, in many ways the work has just begun and much remains to be done. However, at this point we feel a need to stop and have the formulations, methods and conclusions reviewed, evaluated and – most of all – applied.

SELECTED READINGS

The following is an incomplete list of readings in the area of maximum entropy that supplements the references given at the end of each chapter.

Behara, M. (1990) *Additive and Nonadditive Measures of Entropy*. John Wiley, New York.

Bevensee, R. M. (1993) *Maximum Entropy Solutions to Scientific Problems*. Prentice-Hall, Englewood Cliffs, NJ.

Buck, B. and Macaulay, V. A. (1991) *Maximum Entropy in Action: A Collection of Expository Essays*. Oxford University Press.

Csiszár, I. (1991) Why least squares and maximum entropy? An axiomatic approach to inference for linear inverse problems. *The Annals of Statistics* **19**, 2032–66.

Davis, H. T. (1941) *The Theory of Econometrics*. Principia Press, Bloomington, IN.

Erickson, G. J. and Smith, C. R. (1988) *Maximum-Entropy and Bayesian Methods in Science and Engineering*. Kluwer, Dordrecht.

Fougere, P. F. (1990) *Maximum Entropy and Bayesian Methods*. Kluwer, Dordrecht.

Friedman, K. and Shimony, A. (1971) Jaynes' maximum entropy prescription and probability theory. *Journal of Statistical Physics* **3**, 381–4.

Gelman, A. (1989) Constrained maximum entropy methods in an image reconstruction problem. In J. Skilling (ed.) *Maximum Entropy and Bayesian Methods*, pp. 429–35. Kluwer, Dordrecht.

Gokhale, D. V. and Kullback, S. (1978) *The Information in Contingency Tables*. Marcel Dekker, New York.

Good, I. J. (1963) Maximum entropy for hypothesis formulation, especially for multidimensional contingency tables. *Annals of Mathematical Statistics* **34**, 911–34.

Grandy, W. T. (1985) Incomplete information and generalized inverse problems. In C. R. Smith and W. T. Grandy (eds.), *Maximum-Entropy and Bayesian Methods in Inverse Problems*. D. Reidel, Boston.

Grandy, W. T. and Schick, L. H. (eds.) (1991) *Maximum Entropy and Bayesian Methods, Laramie, Wyoming, 1990*. Kluwer, Dordrecht.

Gray, R. M. (1991) *Entropy and Information Theory*. Springer-Verlag, New York.

Gull, S. F. and Daniel, D. J. (1978) Image reconstruction from incomplete and noisy data. *Nature* **272**, 686–90.

Gull, S. F. and Skilling, J. (1983) The maximum entropy method. In J. A. Roberts (ed.) *Direct Imaging*, pp. 267–80. Cambridge University Press.

Jaynes, E. T. (1985) Where do we go from here. In C. R. Smith and W. T. Grandy (eds.) *Maximum Entropy and Bayesian Methods in Inverse Problems.* D. Reidel, Boston.

Jeffreys, H. (1967) *Theory of Probability*, 3rd edn. Oxford University Press.

Jones, L. K. (1989) Approximation-theoretic derivation of logarithmic entropy principles for inverse problems and unique extension of the maximum-entropy method to incorporate prior knowledge. *SIAM Journal on Applied Mathematics* **49**, 650–61.

Justice, J. H. (ed.) (1986) *Maximum Entropy and Bayesian Methods in Applied Statistics: Proceedings of the Fourth Maximum Entropy Workshop, University of Calgary, 1984.* Cambridge University Press.

Kapur, J. N. (1989) *Maximum Entropy Models in Science and Engineering.* John Wiley, New York.

Kapur, J. N. and Kesavan, H. K. (1993) *Entropy Optimization Principles with Applications.* Academic Press, New York.

Kullback, J. (1959) *Information Theory and Statistics.* John Wiley, New York.

Sengupta, J. (1990) Maximum entropy in applied econometric research. University of California, Santa Barbara, Dept. of Economics.

Sengupta, J. K. (1993) *Econometrics of Information and Efficiency.* Kluwer, Dordrecht.

Shore, J. E. and Johnson, R. W. (1980) Axiomatic derivation of the principle of maximum entropy and the principle of minimum cross entropy. *IEEE Transations on Information Theory* **26**, 26–37.

Skilling, J. (1989a) The axioms of maximum entropy. In J. Skilling (ed.) *Maximum Entropy and Bayesian Methods in Science and Engineering*, pp. 173–187. Kluwer, Dordrecht.

Skilling, J. (ed.) (1989b) *Maximum Entropy and Bayesian Methods, Cambridge, England, 1988.* Kluwer, Dordrecht.

Smith, C. R. and Erickson, G. J. (eds.) (1987) *Maximum-Entropy and Bayesian Spectral Analysis and Estimation Problems: Proceedings of the Third Workshop on Maximum Entropy and Bayesian Methods in Applied Statistics, Wyoming, USA, August 1–4, 1983.* Kluwer, Dordrecht.

Smith, C. R., Erickson, G. J. and Neudorfer, P. O. (eds.) (1992) *Maximum Entropy and Bayesian Methods: Proceedings of the Eleventh International Workshop on Maximum Entropy and Bayesian Methods of Statistical Analysis, Seattle, 1991.* Kluwer, Dordrecht.

Smith, C. R. and Grandy, W. T. (1985) *Maximum-Entropy and Bayesian Methods in Inverse Problems.* Kluwer, Dordrecht.

Theil, H. (1967) *Economics and Information Theory*. North-Holland, Amsterdam.
Theil, H. and Fiebig, D. G. (1984) *Exploiting Continuity: Maximum Entropy Estimation of Continuous Distributions*. Ballinger, Cambridge, MA.
Thompson, A. M. (1989) On the use of quadratic regularization with maximum entropy image restoration. In J. Skilling (ed.), *Maximum Entropy and Bayesian Methods*, pp. 497–504. Kluwer, Dordrecht.
Tikochinsky, Y., Tishly, N. Z. and Levine, R. D. (1984) Consistent inference of probabilities for reproducible experiments. *Physical Review Letters* **52**, 1357–60.
Zellner, A. (1988) Optimal information processing and Bayes theorem, *American Statistician* **42**, 279–84.
Zellner, A. (1990) Bayesian methods and entropy in economics and econometrics. In W. T. Grandy and L. H. Shick (eds.), *Maximum Entropy and Bayesian Methods*, pp. 17–31. Kluwer, Dordrecht.
Zellner, A. and Highfield, R. A. (1988) Calculation of maximum entropy distributions and approximation of marginal posterior distributions. *Journal of Econometrics* **37**, 195–209.

Index